The Secret Life
of Movies

The Secret Life of Movies

Schizophrenic and Shamanic Journeys in American Cinema

JASON HORSLEY

McFarland & Company, Inc., Publishers
Jefferson, North Carolina, and London

LIBRARY OF CONGRESS CATALOGUING-IN-PUBLICATION DATA

Horsley, Jason, 1967–
 The secret life of movies : schizophrenic and shamanic journeys in American cinema / Jason Horsley.
   p.   cm.
 Includes bibliographical references and index.

 ISBN 978-0-7864-4423-6
 softcover : 50# alkaline paper

 1. Schizophrenia in motion pictures. 2. Mental illness in motion pictures. 3. Motion pictures — Social aspects. 4. Motion pictures — United States — History — 20th century. I. Title.
 PN1995.9.S247H67   2009
 791.43'6561—dc 22   2009019306

British Library cataloguing data are available

©2009 Jason Horsley. All rights reserved

No part of this book may be reproduced or transmitted in any form or by any means, electronic or mechanical, including photocopying or recording, or by any information storage and retrieval system, without permission in writing from the publisher.

On the cover: Bruce Willis as James Cole in *Twelve Monkeys*, 1995 (Universal Pictures/Photofest)

Manufactured in the United States of America

McFarland & Company, Inc., Publishers
 Box 611, Jefferson, North Carolina 28640
 www.mcfarlandpub.com

To Ashley,
for the companionship of those early days,
and the all-night movie sessions;
and to the brother, my incorrigible Other —
and to friendship in opposition.

Contents

Preface 1
Introduction: From Thesis to Diagnosis 5

PART I. CHRONIC SYMPTOMS AND RECURRING THEMES

1. The Occult Text: *The Good, the Bad, and the Ugly* and the Alchemy of Individuation 15
2. Courting the Other: Quests for Completion 33
3. Scars: The Hero as Psychopath 57
4. Weeping Alone: The Counterculture Fails to Communicate . . . 80
5. The Revolting Male: Jack Nicholson and the Schizophrenic Journey 93
6. Into the Wild: John Boorman's Explicit Myths 108
7. A Glass Darkly: Brando and Bertolucci's *Last Tango* 121
8. The Man Behind the Mask: Roman Polanski's Dementia Tales 130
9. Beautiful Freaks: Tim Burton's Celebrations of Specialness . . 143
10. The Great American Psychopath 158

PART II. SCRYING THE CULTURE

11. Stealing Candy/Healing Laughter: The Evolution of the Schizo Comedy 175
12. Advocating Satan 191
13. God's Channel 202

14. Paranoia: A Conspiracy by Any Other Name 211
15. Where Is My Mind? Notes on Purity of Impulse
    in *Fight Club* 227
16. Aliens "R" Us: Race Intimations of *Metamorphosis* 242
17. Behind Closed Doors: Antithesis and Antidote 253

Epilogue: Rounding Up the Usual Suspects 278
Chapter Notes 281
Bibliography 283
Index 285

Preface

The Secret Life of Movies was written as a follow-up to *The Blood Poets,* which was about savagery and violence in American movies. The reason I wrote about violence was simple: I wanted a thesis that would include all my favorite movies, and I soon realized that the common thread running through them was violence, destruction. As I set about writing the book, I found out a lot about why I liked certain movies, and about the basic appeal of vicariously experiencing, via movies, things we would otherwise be careful to avoid in real life. If you narrowed it down to one thing, it would be "intensity." Movies provide the kind of intensity which we would only experience in real life if we were in crisis, when such experiences tend to be traumatic; but in movies, as in Greek tragedy, they are potentially cathartic. During the process of writing *The Blood Poets*, I discovered a great deal about the movies I liked and why I liked them, and therefore about my own psyche. These were movies I had seen many times, and in the process of writing about them, looking for ways to develop my thesis, it opened up a Pandora's Box. I found out that, by writing about movies, I was able to go into realms of the psyche and of society normally closed to me. This gave me a clue: movies were like windows onto the collective psyche. The things I liked about movies at a conscious level were much less revealing than what appealed to me at an unconscious level.

That gave me the idea of the occult text. Many movies *seem* to be about fictional scenarios, but actually they are archetypal. Like myths, they allow us to uncover and map areas of the psyche that otherwise hidden from us. If we scratch the surface of a sci-fi movie or a horror movie, for example, we find that they are using the same archetypes as ancient myths, and that they serve as a kind of psychological blueprint. But movies are unlike myths, in the sense that they are superficially much more sophisticated, more "realistic." Even sci-fi or horror movies are more realistic than ancient myths, which often aren't populated by human beings at all, and which are full of impossible possibilities. (Even fantasy movies attempt to be realistic, and when they aren't they are either considered to be kids' movies or just bad ones.) The realism of popular entertainment means that the mythic function of movies is more hidden; it gets suppressed through the process of conceiving and making the movie, to the point that even the filmmakers usually aren't aware of it. Mythmakers were generally aware of what they were doing, of giving coded information in the form of a narrative so that the average person could enjoy the story, while "initiates" could read it in a more abstract way, as a mythic blueprint. But movies are different.

Movies are like myths at a different stage in our society, a stage when we are more ego-developed beings, when we have a more rigid sense of identity, and so our sense of reality is also more rigid. This means we require our myths to be more realistic as well. Because we have disconnected from our subconscious, movies have to be more covert in their mythic unfolding. It was only by analyzing movies for *The Blood Poets* that I found out about this occult text. It intrigued me, because it was like movies themselves had an unconscious. The filmmakers obviously had an unconscious, but unlike mythmakers they were not working from it—to some extent, perhaps, but not entirely. They might be aware of the subtext or they might not, but even if they were aware of it, there would be a still *deeper* subtext, and that was where the real "juice" was. Essentially, I was drawn then to look at movies not only that had hidden texts (all movies do), but that dealt with the unconscious in an overt fashion, and with the conflict between the conscious and unconscious mind of the protagonist. That drew me naturally to the idea of madness, and specifically schizophrenia: the idea that there could be a conflict between one's perception of self and one's reality, between what one consciously believed was real and what one unconsciously felt was true. Schizophrenia is to do with a splitting of the self from the environment, so that the self doesn't feel a part of the environment. You could even say that the more the ego develops, the deeper schizophrenia becomes; in which case, those diagnosed as schizophrenics, and who experience a loss of identity, are in a sense *less* schizophrenic than the rest of us—because they are more acutely aware of their condition. As I looked more deeply into the subject, or rather as I was writing about it, I realized that this state paralleled the act of watching a movie itself: a disconnection from the reality we are seeing (on the screen), as well as from our immediate environment (the theater or living room). That's the pleasure of movies—to be emotionally involved in a surrogate reality without having to take part in it. So the pleasure of movies—and the reason violent or tragic movies are often cathartic—relates to the schizophrenic nature of watching movies, the possibility of observing our environment without being a part of it. This is the schizophrenic experience: through the act of watching movies, one ceases to exist as a self.

There is a mystic tradition similar to this idea—that of dissociating from objective experience to view one's life from the outside, i.e. "as a movie." That was also what I was looking for, the shamanic dimension of movies, their shaping of our perceptions, and the parallels between schizophrenia and experiences of other realities. Here we return to ancient myths. The violence in a sense related to the symptoms: in *Blood Poets*, I analyzed the symptoms and followed them to the conditions, which led me to a diagnosis of schizophrenia: the cut-off of the mind/identity from the physical world. Having described the symptoms, I wanted to describe the condition itself, and even if possible to find a cure. That became *The Secret Life of Movies*. It was an attempt to use movies more deliberately as a way to diagnose a culture. Movies are made by a collective of individuals to meet the demands of a whole population, so what we see is not informed by an individual's unconscious but by the collective unconscious. Movies are shaped by collective dreams through the plastic medium of film: shamanic tools used unconsciously. At times the tool is used consciously: films like *The Matrix* or *Fight Club* actually *become* shamanic experiences because the unconscious and conscious minds of the filmmakers work together, so text and subtext are intertwined rather than at odds. In writing this book, I allowed movies their occult function as collective dreams that, if analyzed, provide information in symbolic form on the condition of society and of the species. It's rather like taking a blood sample, a psychic blood sample from the collective unconscious. By looking at movies, we can judge the state of health of the system — our culture and society.

Although *The Secret Life of Movies* does not directly draw on the work of Carl Jung, it is informed by it. Jung was a psychologist as a shaman, or vice versa. He entered the field of psychology realizing that it was actually the same field that shamans had worked in for thousands of years. Psychology is a science in that it follows and maps principals, conditions, that to a certain extent are empirical or universal. The shadow, the anima and animus, these are principals that apply to absolutely everyone on the planet, so far as we know at least. Psychology is a science and can be used like one, but as the study of the psyche, it's not a hard science but a soft one. It requires imagination and creativity, both to understand and to apply it.

While the basic idea of this book can be compared to psychology and dream analysis, these are really just ways to update it into terms the modern, rational person can understand. A more primitive or "superstitious" mindset could understand this book's premise more easily, since the "superstitious" mindset is also more open to the realities of the psyche; for example, to the idea that our whole culture could be a sort of collective dream, "the imagination of God," say, or the perspective of an animistic universe, a living conscious system. These ideas are acceptable to a primitive understanding without resorting to psychological terms. Within that frame of reference, then, what I'm doing predates psychology: it's a form of scrying, based on the understanding that nothing in nature is random. Whether goat entrails, tea leaves floating in a cup, or an egg in a glass of water, the patterns these things create is a coded language that can be deciphered by the shaman for a variety of purposes. This is the nature of myth, except that myths are consciously designed by sorcerers or shamans to be recognized by others of their kind.

Movies are both less and more pure than that. Being shaped by the unconscious makes them more pure, but they are also shaped by the conscious agendas of commerce, propaganda, popular taste, etc., agendas which overlay the work, rather like a person who edits his dreams to make them more "wholesome" or entertaining. Movies have been heavily edited and filtered, but the basic components still come from the unconscious. As long as you can sift through the noise and get to the signal, you can still use them to diagnose; even the noise can be diagnosed because it emphasizes the ways in which we block out our unconscious. These questions inspire this book.

Introduction:
From Thesis to Diagnosis

"Movies have stolen our dreams. Of all betrayals, this is the worst."
— *F. Scott Fitzgerald*

As all good scholars know (though they may not admit it), a thesis is only as good as the argument which backs it. The flip-side of this is that all theses can be proven so long as the "scholar" is sufficiently ingenious. The quantum physicist will find particles when looking for particles and waves when in need of a wave, and likewise, an adept scholar can find all the evidence he needs to uphold his thesis, simply by looking hard enough. Where there is a text, there will always be a subtext, a sub-subtext, and so on, ad infinitum. Life is an onion — it comes in layers. Yet beneath each of the layers is only more onion.

If the art of the academic is to invent a thesis and then prove it (and so justify another paper), it follows that the primary challenge, his task, is to come up with a thesis which can be justified without bending the texts *too* severely out of shape. The better the thesis, the easier it is to prove. Any "subtext" should not be buried too deeply below the surface of the text; it should not be too many layers down, and should have at least *some* relation to the popular, accepted reading of the text itself. Otherwise, "hidden" simply becomes obscure. If we are going to be felling trees and describing sounds, best to be sure there is at least *someone* in the forest with us. Academia can be a lonely place.

The recent but rapidly growing movement known as "synchromysticism" is anything but an academic discipline. Rather than emerging from the hallowed halls of academia, synchromysticism was born on the Internet, a new, more "upbeat" development in the paranoid community (i.e., among occultists and conspiracy theorists) that attempts to see beyond the darker aspects of society, politics, and popular culture, to a cosmic design. A form of postmodern animism, as the name suggests, synchromysticism combines Jung's notion of meaningful coincidences with the quest for the divine, or self-actualization through experience of the divine. Not the first thing most of us associate with movies, and yet nor is it the last. Martin Scorsese was surely not alone in comparing the experience of sitting in a movie theater with attending church.

Synchromysticism (and this present work) underlines a common theme beneath three apparently disparate areas: that of the religious quest for meaning or "signs," the shamanic/animistic relationship with Nature, and the schizophrenic's inability to distinguish between reality and fantasy. All three of these areas can be seen to converge in the experience of both watching and making (and of "reading") movies. Movies are a means for people who are alienated from all three areas of experience—from the religious, the shamanistic, and the schizophrenic—to pursue a meaningful relationship with their unconscious, while remaining a functional part of society. They act as modern, popular myths, not so much to live by as *to escape into*.

This fact—that we now use our myths to escape from reality rather than reach a deeper understanding of it—relates to the first part of my thesis: that "society"—as what comes between us and our deeper reality—is itself *a form of schizophrenia*. Human beings are becoming progressively more and more schizoid due to the imposition of a false structure which we know as society. Hence schizophrenia is not an isolated phenomenon of which certain unfortunate individuals can be said to suffer but a collective condition that pertains to all of us, to varying degrees. Since our collective schizophrenia has been covered up and denied—by the very social forms that have caused it in the first place—the proof of our condition can only surface, indirectly, through cultural artifacts such as movies. Hence, popular movies become a means to diagnose (though also exacerbate) this condition. The second part of my thesis—that of the secret life of movies—is the flip side of the first.

As a member of society I have no choice but to include myself in this diagnosis (as schizophrenic). It would be presumptuous to write about a subject without having a personal acquaintance with it, and I am fully aware that to believe movies have a covert function or hidden text (beyond the apparent meanings given to them by their various makers) by which to communicate with us *is itself a symptom of schizophrenia*.

The nature of existence is similar to a hall of mirrors, mirrors within mirrors, onions beneath onions. In matters of psychoanalysis I am layman; I do not subscribe to the idea of schizophrenia as a disease. It seems to me that the problem of schizophrenia, if such it is, must go far deeper than either physical or mental causes, into a sickness of the soul. I highly doubt that schizophrenia, as has been suggested, is evidence that "the brain is badly in need of repair,"[1] nor can I imagine any way to mend such a hypothetical split, crack, or leakage. The assumption in diagnosing schizophrenia is that there are schizophrenics, and then there are the rest of us. We assume that schizophrenia is a deviation from a desirable state of health and normality to which the schizophrenic must be returned, and so "repaired."

But what if R.D. Laing and Heath Ledger's Joker are correct, and schizophrenics are actually *ahead of the curve* in their delusions of an "unreal" world, and their all too real perceptions of it? What if it is (in part) our own incapacity to comprehend their experiences that condemns them to the suffering of the "insane"? In an aboriginal culture, a little boy saying he is going to grow up to be a blue grasshopper might be taken as evidence of the boy's potential to be a shaman. In our own society, it is the first symptoms of schizophrenia, or, at best, an overactive imagination best treated with Ritalin. Such a mind, though it may well be "unbalanced," may also require a different kind of balancing to that of other, more "normal" minds. In Western society, however, there are no such concessions given as to the possible, intrinsic differences between minds. All minds are assumed to belong to a common, consensus "reality," and any deviance from this consensus is seen as sickness, psychosis, revolt.

Having said all that, here are some fundamental "facts" about schizophrenia. The word comes from the Greek *Schizo*, split, and *Phrenia*, mind. According to MaryEllen Walsh in *Schizophrenia*, what Eugen Bleuler (the psychiatrist who coined the term in 1911) "was trying to convey was the split between perception and reality." This all-too-subtle (and profound) diagnosis has, in the collective understanding, been supplanted by a more profane (and largely erroneous) definition of schizophrenia as "split-personality." Walsh goes on to state, "Schizophrenia is one of the most misunderstood diseases on the planet.... [It] is a collective wastebasket."

Schizophrenia (which in the UK is often termed "manic depression") is indeed more common than most of us realize. In 1985, the statistics said that one in every hundred people suffered from an acute form, and up to one in eight from "a milder form of the disorder." In Ireland, however (according to Walsh), the number is as high as one in twenty-five (acute cases, that is; one may presume substantially more people suffer from the "milder forms"). Statistics, of course, only include diagnosed schizophrenics, and it seems fair (in the interests of our thesis) to double this number to include all those cases who, for whatever reason, fail to make it into the statistics. In which case, we may have as many as one in six people throughout the world suffering from at least a mild form of schizophrenia.*

Among the most extreme symptoms of schizophrenia are auditory hallu-

---

*In Ireland, it would be closer to two thirds! Walsh suggests the solanine in potatoes may be responsible for this. To this day, the poetic Irish retain a healthy respect for myths and a charming, atavistic belief in fairies. This itself is cause enough for a diagnosis of schizophrenia these days.

cinations, voices that come from inside or outside of the subject's head, often as comments about that person's behavior (as in those pesky angels and devils of folklore). At times, the person's own thoughts may become audible. What is known as "blunted affect" Walsh defines as "acting like a zombie ... loss of ego boundaries ... a vagueness about the sense of self, who one is and where one is going." Walsh cites a lack of interest in the world and one's own course in it. Regarding "relationship to the external world": "Often there isn't any. Withdrawn and preoccupied ... indifferent to human contact.... Friends may be avoided, work neglected, showers not taken. All add up to the person's 'not being the same.'"* Walsh goes on to name "one of the saddest hallmarks of schizophrenia: the loss of pleasure. *Anhedonia* is the official word for it.... It means that joy, affection, desire, pride, humor are all drained away. What makes life worth living disappears slowly, relentlessly, until nothing seems to be left of the schizophrenic but a shell, a staring robot ... the lights go out one by one. It is the death of the spirit." Does this sound familiar?

As Walsh notes, most mental cases are not especially violent; in fact they are less violent, statistically speaking, than supposedly sane people. "Ninety-five percent of the murders committed every year in the United States are committed by people who are sane ... many schizophrenics are exactly the opposite of the aggressive madmen of the myth — that is, they are timid, afraid of being further hurt in their vulnerable state." Violence and schizophrenia, then, are "quite independent of each other." Even so, there *is* a relation, and it is this: both violence and schizophrenia are the results of — or at the very least inextricably bound up with — repression. Both can be seen as consequences of a social environment that is severely restrictive and that denies a free, healthy expression of emotions and, above all, sexuality. Violence is the externalization of this frustration, schizophrenia its internalization, but both can be seen as symptoms of a common "disease" — society. I might qualify such a statement, or make it somewhat less apocalyptic, by saying that both violence and insanity are the inevitable price we pay for living in a civilization that depends — in order to be civilized — on repressing our emotional-sexual natures.

This is the devil (and the Joker) in the pack, the hidden thread that runs through so many popular movies today. Like a virus through the bloodstream, it moves freely from savagery to schizophrenia, twin horns of the beast that, if not interchangeable, are certainly complementary.

As already stated, the thesis of this work — fittingly enough — is two-fold.

---

*Walsh (a mother whose child was diagnosed schizophrenic, the afore-mentioned "blue grasshopper" boy) asks, "How would you feel if you heard voices that seemed to come from an invisible source, thought that the TV set was out to get you, lost your job because of lack of motivation, lost your friends because you couldn't 'relate,' and alienated your family so that they disowned you.... [If] *you couldn't tell where you left off and the world began.* What's amazing is that people with schizophrenia function at all with these handicaps."

It revolves not only around the schizophrenic basis of society (and of consensus reality), but, as a secondary argument upon which this primary argument depends, the idea of a "hidden text." As synchromysticism contends, this occult under layer can be found not just in popular movies but in *everything*. If we live in a schizophrenic society, it follows that not only we ourselves but all our various creations have hidden personalities — secret lives — just waiting to be discovered. Even as we live our "conscious" lives oblivious to the deeper, unconscious urges and desires playing out below the surface, so movies — as living artifacts and products of this same unconscious — are possessed of both right and left hemispheres, text and subtext. Naturally, these two theses (like the two hemispheres of the brain, thesis and antithesis) are really one thesis: synthesis.

The whole subject of schizophrenic cinema has so many intertwining layers that one could go on forever. Perhaps at the heart of it all lies the common appeal that simulations of reality have for us, our desire to lose ourselves in a projection of reality. This is what movies are all about: the pleasure of experiencing "life" in a passive manner, and so disassociating from it, being immune to the consequences. Movies have helped accelerate the process whereby humans have become witnesses to their own lives. At the same time, and by the same token, movies have the potential (only rarely met) to offer us a solution for this split by showing us that reality itself is a projection, and on the other side of schizophrenia (through the looking glass) is "shamanic" reality, namely, the ability to be in two places at once. When we watch a movie, we are both in our bodies and outside of them. And for body, also read "world."

It is at base a schizophrenic desire to get lost in a false (movie) reality, yet this desire is also a reflection, an imitation (or debasement), of the collective, "religious" desire to reconnect to a higher reality. Neal Gabler, in *Life: the Movie, How Entertainment Conquered Reality*, cites Harvard psychology professor Hugo Munsterberg on "the almost mesmerizing effect" of movies; Munsterberg reports how "'sensory hallucinations and illusions have crept in; neurasthenic persons are especially inclined to experience touch or temperature or smell or sound impressions from what they see on the screen. The associations become so vivid as realities, because the mind is so completely given up to the moving pictures.'" [Gabler continues:] "What made the movies seem even more real, and what made them even more powerful in their effect, was how the audience mentally processed them. As Munsterberg noted, the movies played in our heads seemed to replicate our own consciousness. Conspiring with the dark, they cast a spell that lulled one from his own reality into theirs *until the two merged....* [M]ovies seemed to *cross the line that separated reality from imagination.*"[2]

Schizophrenia and movies — and religious and shamanic consciousness — both stem from an ability to blur the lines between perception and reality, to merge dreams and waking, to step outside ourselves and experience a heightening of our senses, be it of paranoia, art, or vision. The allure of all these things (and even madness has its allure) relates to a common desire: the desire to go *beyond*. It might be said that it is the profoundly "decadent," gloom-ridden state of today's world that accounts for this yearning. It might also be argued that it's precisely this mystical yearning to go beyond — to seek satisfaction elsewhere than in the nitty-gritty — that has accelerated the decay of our environment and turned our reality into the dismal soul-trap it is today. Both points of view can be argued until kingdom come; neither will get us very far.

The desire to go beyond — whether in sex, drugs, madness, mysticism, or movies — is plainly a sublimated desire for death. What is beyond life but death? The destructive (irresponsible) nature of this yearning is plain; and yet such desire is also the source of all creative endeavors, all bids for change, illumination, transformation. There appears to be no other way of creating a better vision than by first destroying the old one that has enslaved us; but if we are enslaved to a vision of a world that offers nothing but pain and misery, the question is, where did this vision first spring from, if not our own minds?

Movies take us outside ourselves. They allow us to be in two places at once: outside, looking in, and inside, looking around. We can enjoy all manner of destruction and mayhem knowing we are safe inside a movie theater, that it is all illusion. As Gabler writes, "This dual consciousness was integral to the pleasure we felt. We could be frightened without being threatened, feel romance without the pangs, mourn without an actual loss."[3] Beyond this passive and profane pleasure, there is a deeper one: that of extending the possibilities of perception itself. Through movies we can experience, second-hand but also at will (while retaining control of the experience), what the schizophrenic is overwhelmed by and what the shaman must work a lifetime to come to grips with: the ability to merge our perceptions with the world at large. To put it another way, we get to experience our perceptions as shaping the world that we (temporarily) inhabit, simply because we are — like Morpheus and the gang in *The Matrix*— able to enter in and out of the "reality" (i.e., the movie) at will. As such, we are interacting with "reality" while at the same time remaining separate from it. We are both outside and above it.

Movies may actually exacerbate schizophrenia, however, by encouraging us to be passive witnesses, to live our lives vicariously through images with which (save through our perceptions) we have no organic relation. Certainly this opportunity to enjoy life without any of the messy entanglements or embarrassments that life is made up of— to see without being seen — is perhaps the primary appeal of movies, and maybe also of mysticism too? As Pauline Kael once noted, it comes down to the anonymity and impersonality of sitting in a theater, just enjoying ourselves, not having to be responsible, not having to be "good." Maybe you just want to look at people on the screen and know they're not looking back at you, that they're not going to turn on you and criticize you. [One can hardly help thinking of Woody Allen's *The Purple Rose of Cairo* at this juncture.] Perhaps the single most intense pleasure of moviegoing is this non-aesthetic one of escaping from the responsibilities of having the proper responses required of us in our official (school) culture ... in the darkness at the movies where nothing is asked of us and we are left alone, the liberation from duty and constraint allows us to develop our own aesthetic responses.... Irresponsibility is part of the pleasure of all art.[4]

As Kael makes plain, the pleasure of passive enjoyment is both a snare and an opportunity: a snare because it allows us to succumb to a solipsist stupor in which we don't need to think, much less act, for ourselves; an opportunity in that, within such a vacuum, we are free to summon our own imaginative capabilities, our "aesthetic responses," and, potentially, to reenter the real world with a new perspective. Movies may well engender schizophrenia in people—and synchromysticism may be a glorified and self-satisfied symptom of this schizophrenia. But they may also be helping us to adapt to an already schizophrenic world, giving us the opportunity to deal with it in an indirect but no less instructional fashion, to transform our perceptions of it. Both movies and synchromysticism answer "a subtle desire to remodel the world by projecting onto it, cinematically, the doubles of our imagination."[5] Perhaps, by being illusions within the illusory arena of the world, movies are windows onto a greater reality? To many of us (I include myself here), a movie like *The Matrix* may be considerably closer to our own experience of reality than a supposedly "real-life" news program will ever be. It strips away the artifice and the comfortable hypocrisy of the mundane veil, a veil which we have conspired to place between our naked psyches and the universe at large.

If we are divided—split—by the act of perceiving, caught in a funk of uncertainty about what is real and what merely appears to be, perhaps this split is more than merely a "disorder of the brain" and is actually *good* for something? A chink in the armor of reason through which the power of the imagination rushes in, flooding our senses with the glories of the irrational? Perhaps, as synchromysticism has it, the gods themselves consider these light-shows we enjoy so innocently to be fitting forms by which to infiltrate our psyches? Haven't we all at one time or another felt the TV to be talking directly to us, then laughed it off as our crazy imagination? Don't we often sense that apparently innocuous artifacts are really laden with hidden meanings and coded messages? Haven't we all felt like the whole world was hard-wired to our psyches? Is that really an affliction, a curse? Or is it the first, disorienting experience of being in direct communication with the universe?

If (as Jean Baudrillard once quipped) Disneyland was invented to disguise the fact that the United States is just one great, big amusement ride built to distract us from the true state of our lives—what about movies?⁶ Are they God's way of telling us what is really going on? If everything is an image of an image, a copy of a replica of a clone of a simulacra, why *not* seek reality down this tunnel of mirrors, on the other side of a movie screen?

PART I.
CHRONIC SYMPTOMS AND RECURRING THEMES

1

The Occult Text:
The Good, the Bad, and the Ugly and the Alchemy of Individuation

The whole subject of schizophrenia is, for obvious reasons, one that has for the most part only been addressed *indirectly* by American movies. Schizophrenia is a subject that modern science and psychotherapy has yet to come to grips with, much less the culture of mass entertainment. Above all I believe this relates to our insistence on designating it as something *outside* the average person's experience, something that is by definition abnormal and so beyond the understanding of most moviegoers. This is an error. Fragmentation of self, disassociation from reality, loss of identity, are all symptoms of the modern age. As such, they form the inevitable subtext of popular modern movies, at least the most interesting or progressive (though not necessarily best) of them. As I shall presently argue, these hidden themes or occult texts often come into being — aptly enough — quite *unconsciously*, as it were in spite of the filmmakers' conscious intentions. This is evident in the case of genre movies (horror and sci-fi, for example) that on the one hand deal with quite foreign (even alien) external characters and events, while on the other — thematically speaking — address all-too familiar, *internal* conditions common to us all.

The whole notion of an occult text in popular movies is one that (again for obvious reasons) is lost upon the majority of moviegoers. It is a concept that remains largely academic, and for this reason one that even many filmmakers (at least those of the Hawks/Ford, no-nonsense school) have little time for. In tracing what I might (for the purpose of the thesis) call "the hidden personality" of popular movies, I have of necessity had to look at these movies with something other than your average (casual) moviegoer's eye. Instead of merely seeking to be entertained by the stories, I have taken to reading between the lines in order to analyze these stories (and the protagonists that move them forward) for hidden meanings that, quite possibly, the original storytellers never intended. This is not so different from the psychoanalyst's approach to his patient. Obviously, the therapist is not seeking amusement or distraction by listening to his patient; rather he is seeking for some *clue* by which to unravel the secret workings of the patient's unconscious mind. At this juncture, the argument might well be raised that a popular movie is not a human being but merely an artifact created by human beings, and as such vastly more limited. One could argue that a movie, like any other artifact, is only and precisely what it appears to be, that it *has* no unconscious to speak of, and that any meanings that are hidden at all are only so because of being consciously *put there* by the filmmakers. Such an argument is naïve, and I sincerely doubt that anyone inclined to raise it will have made it this far; so let us move on.

So just how is it that certain artifacts may be found to contain so many hidden layers of meaning? How is it that something that might once reasonably have been assumed to be no more than an exciting shoot-'em-up Western is now being touted as a profound and intricate study of the secret workings of the schizophrenic mind? Surely not merely by the conceit of the author? I contend that *the dual nature of every enterprise relates to the dual nature of Nature (the psyche) itself.*

For example, as regards movies, the eternal question is: art, or entertainment? And then, following this, what exactly is the difference, and can the two not happily co-exist? As Pauline Kael once noted, while all art must, ipso facto, be entertainment, not all entertainment is necessarily art. So where does the distinction lie, and how can the two functions (if such they be) be found to complement and enhance one another? Here I am indebted to Neal Gabler and his insightful work, *Life: The Movie; How Entertainment Conquered Reality*. Gabler traces the word "entertainment" to Latin roots *inter* (among) and *tenere* (to hold) and writes how entertainment "sinks its talons into us and pulls us in, holding us captive, taking us both deeper into the work and into ourselves, or at least into our own emotions and senses, before releasing us." He goes on to state that "Art was said to provide *ekstasis*, which in Greek means 'letting us stand outside ourselves,' presumably to lend us perspective."[1] As such, he posits art and entertainment as, if not mutually exclusive, at the very least *diametrically opposed*. And yet, since Gabler is (quite correctly) talking of the *effects* of the two modalities and not their intrinsic natures, the fact remains that whether an artifact be art or mere entertainment *depends to a certain extent on the response of the viewer*. In the case of art, the relationship between the artifact and the observer is indeed a one-on-one affair, much like a dialogue between a teacher and a pupil. In the case of entertainment, the relationship is profoundly, if subtly, different; it is a relationship between a collective body and its chosen distraction, and is not a dialogue so much as a diatribe. If art appeals to the individual in us, entertainment reduces us to one more ass on the seat, another unit in the mass, the collective. Art awakens, while entertainment relaxes, stupefies, or puts us to sleep — it is the difference between a psychedelic effect and a narcotic one. The question then arises: how exactly can art also serve the secondary, apparently counteractive purpose of entertaining us: how can it take us outside ourselves to give us new perspective while at the same time taking us deeper into ourselves, so denying us such a perspective? Herein enters the essentially divided nature of movies, the most entertainment-based of art forms, and consequently the most schizophrenic medium ever conceived.

A movie such as *The Good, the Bad, and the Ugly* does indeed serve two apparently opposed functions; it exists in two seemingly separate forms, if you will, and is possessed of a dual personality. On the one hand, we have a rousing, seemingly mindless action cowboy movie for boys, full of sadistic violence, crude humor, and bombastic set pieces. On the other hand, there is a graceful, operatic, and fairly obscure (though also profound) meditation on the pitfalls of mercenary behavior and the dynamic interactions between the ego and the Id. On the one hand, we are swept away by the sheer sensation of the spectacle, entirely oblivious to the film's deeper meanings (even perhaps gaining impressions quite contrary to them). On the other hand, so far as we are sensitive to the hidden personality or occult text of the movie, we are allowed to step outside ourselves (along with the other characters in the movie) and perceive the absurdity, pathos, and mythic beauty of it all. Plainly, it is possible to enjoy the movie at both levels, as both profane entertainment and sublime (or mythic) art, just as it is possible to be inside oneself and outside at the same time, to experience enthrallment and ecstasy simultaneously. And this, I would wager, is the true art of the motion picture (natural heir to the stagecraft of Shakespeare), and the final, transcendent (shamanic) meaning and function of the schizophrenic experience.

Now that our premise has been addressed, let us move on. In most cases in this present work my approach has been to analyze the characters and their specific actions within a movie's narrative, not merely as *if* they were real, but *as* real (just as a psychotherapist would analyze his patient's actions in relation to the greater unfolding of his psyche, with all the complexity and ambiguity this implies). This is a conceit, but a necessary one, just as it is necessary for a therapist to attribute wisdom and depth to his patient that the patient may not necessarily be aware of himself: in order to tap this potential. Obviously, for this to pay off at all, the movies (and patients) in question must possess (however "unconsciously") a sufficient degree of creative insight, philosophical depth, emotional maturity, and so forth, *themselves*. Otherwise we will be seeking in vain for pearls in pig food.

It is my contention — because it is my experience — that there is *invariably* an under layer of meaning, an occult text, to the actions and events of everyday life. This under layer (the mythic dimension of life) is what serves to instruct us as to the nature not only of ourselves and those involved with us but of reality itself. In a nutshell, I believe that there is always (though with varying degrees of clarity or significance) a *metaphorical* quality to events which allows us to grow and learn *from* them, and not merely succumb *to* them. As Jung and Campbell approached ancient myths — as psychological blueprints that map an evolutionary design — so I approach movies, that is to say, *schizophrenically*.

It follows that, the closer movies approximate or emulate such ancient myths (not in content, necessarily, but in style), the better they will justify and vindicate this approach. The proof will ever be in the pudding, in any case. My idea is that, through such an approach, these movies (like the ancient myths we are now deprived of) will provide us with *information* about our current state of development as human beings. With few exceptions, the movies that most deserve the term "great," those that have become enduring classics beloved by many, are not the movies that realistically depict life as it "is" but rather those that successfully reveal life's mythic qualities to us. However, if life itself is a myth — a blueprint — by which we may some day access a greater Reality, there *are* cases of movies that so effectively depict realistic scenarios that they do achieve mythic dimensions (greatness) without ever actively aspiring to them. (*Taxi Driver* is a leading example; also *The Godfather Part Two*, which to a large part renounced the mythic underpinnings of the first film but did not diminish its power for that.) But for the most part, those movies that are dear to my heart, and those that (to me) successfully encapsulate some facet of our nature and predicament, are often as not those that are most unabashedly mythical in design.*

The Good, the Bad, and the Ugly is a film I saw perhaps a dozen times before its "occult text" ever occurred to me. It is entirely unnecessary to observe the film's "deeper" (i.e., buried) meanings to appreciate its beauty and grandeur (its greatness) *as a movie*. There is even something rather simple-minded about Leone and Eastwood's final Western together, the last and most ambitious of their "Dollar" trilogy. Certainly, if one takes it at face value as a simple action adventure comedy, it's pretty basic. It is rather as an absurdist character study and an epic piece of surrealist/revisionist history that the film stands out from other Westerns. Yet what gives this movie its resonance and endurance as a work of art must finally be measured by its relevance to our times; and this in turn depends on just how well it holds up as a mythic artifact, a mirror through which we may glimpse, in part, the condition of our collective psyche, in all its fragmented and bloody intricacy.

---

*To give a few examples of American movies that qualify (not all great ones but certainly beloved, and hence enduring): *Frankenstein, King Kong, It's a Wonderful Life, The Wizard of Oz, Harvey, The Searchers, Vertigo, Bonnie and Clyde, The Wild Bunch, McCabe and Mrs. Miller, Jaws, The Empire Strikes Back, Brazil, Blue Velvet, The Matrix, Fight Club, The Lord of the Rings*.

1. The Occult Text: *The Good, the Bad, and the Ugly*

I am fully aware of the arbitrary, game-like nature of the following analysis, and of the fact that, with sufficient passion, diligence, and prejudice, *any* movie at all can be made to render up a subtext to fit the scholar's thesis. (This is not to say it is easy, only that it is *possible*.) Umberto Eco, in his groundbreaking conspiracy novel *Foucault's Pendulum*, included just such a chapter that demonstrated how the parts of an ordinary car engine might be found to correspond with the various Keys of the Kabbala. Eco (besides proving his intellectual gamesmanship) was here demonstrating the universality of the Kabbala and not the hidden order of car engines; but of course, the two facts are inseparable. Just so is it here. Aleister Crowley performed a similar exercise in his *Book 4*, when he analyzed children's nursery rhymes for their "occult" content and found them to yield quite solid esoteric meanings. I feel that I am in sufficiently reputable company, then, and upholding a not overly frivolous tradition, by subjecting Sergio Leone's greatest Western to the same treatment. Those readers who are anything less than (at least mildly devoted) aficionados of the movie, however, might want to skip to the next chapter.

The Good, the Bad, and the Ugly is a schizophrenic journey. As briefly as we can, then, let us map this schizophrenic journey. First off, it is interesting to note that Leone poses not dual but *triple* consciousness, a three-way split by which the psyche is torn, not between good and bad, but between bad and ugly (a double negative, ugly being only partially redeemed evil). It is the friction between the two "evils" that potentially allows the psyche to attain the "third state," a state of grace beyond duality, that of "the good." In such an arrangement, goodness depends not on opposing badness but on transcending such oppositions entirely, pitting "bad" against "ugly," and so weaseling between the two.

The ugly is Tuco (Eli Wallach), also known as "the Rat." A crude, mercenary opportunist bent on personal advantage at any cost, Tuco also happens to be a "devout" Catholic who crosses himself whenever he kills someone. Tuco is pure survival instinct: wits, cunning, deviance, persistence, and durability. What he lacks in finesse or intelligence, he makes up for in guile and adaptability. "Ugly" refers to his brutish nature, his uncouthness and physical slovenliness, his lack of *grace*. Although crude, Tuco is anything but incompetent, however. He is a skilled gunfighter, an accomplished tracker, and a professional thief and bandit.

The bad is Angel Eyes (Lee Van Cleef), cold, cruel, calculating, a killer with a vicious bent and a perverse mercenary's code of "honor."* Even more

---

*In his first scene Angel Eyes arrives at a large family home (where he first hears about the cache of gold that is the plot's ostensible motor), and accepts the food he is offered by his prey. The man, knowing why Angel Eyes is there, offers him double his money if he'll leave him alive and kill the man who hired him instead (Baker). Angel Eyes laments that, "I always see the job through," shoots the man, and kills his son when he comes to the rescue. He than Tuco, Angel Eyes is in it wholly for the money. Seeking a cache of gold stolen by infantryman Bob Carson, Angel Eyes is a precisely tuned machine programmed for one thing only; the only human emotion he betrays is a sadistic relish in the heinousness of his actions. Tuco may be an unprincipled scoundrel, but Angel Eyes is completely devoid of conscience. He is every bit as cunning and deviant as Tuco (and far more intelligent and ambitious), but he lacks imagination, spontaneity, initiative. He is never seen to be alone but is always affiliated in one way or another, always working for or with someone else. A "freelance" killer, he is nonetheless a slave to his own mercenary nature. When we first meet him, he is working for Baker, a sick old man confined to his bed (Leone frequently associates evil with sickness in his films). Hence Angel Eyes is affiliated from the start with disease and decay. Of course, Angel Eyes soon kills Baker (on assignment from the man he just killed *for* Baker), and so he is seen as perennially masterless: a ronin who murders his own master.

The good, Blondy (Clint Eastwood), is a far more enigmatic character. Stealthy, silent, and graceful, Blondy remains curiously aloof most of the time, as if enjoying his own private game; it is this detachment, or irony, that separates him from the others. Though apparently motivated by the same base needs and material desires, this is (as we shall see) an illusion, a ruse. Blondy is driven by altogether different needs. He is — unbeknownst to himself and maybe even to Leone (ah, but *we* know better!) — on a schizophrenic journey for self-knowledge. Blondy is the only character of the three who undergoes profound changes through the course of the movie. His nature as "the good" is anything but a given; Blondy only *becomes* good — heroic — by overcoming the respective "bad" and "ugly" sides of his nature. He confronts, overcomes, integrates, assimilates, rejects, and destroys the various facets of personality that impede him on his quest. This quest is ostensibly for buried treasure, but again — we know better. In terms of our occult text, the buried treasure is code for the hidden self, the alchemical gold.

When we first meet Blondy* he is saving Tuco from three bounty hunters

---

(continued) then returns to collect the rest of his payment from his employer Baker, a sick, bed-ridden old man. Angel Eyes informs Baker that before he killed him, his victim gave him money. "I think his idea was that I kill you." The two men laugh over the absurdity of this; Angel Eyes' smile fades and his eyes grow hard. "Only trouble is," he says, "when I get paid, I always see the job through." Whereupon he kills his employer.

*Of all the three dollar movies, *The Good, the Bad, and the Ugly* comes the closest to ever officially naming the Clint Eastwood character; and yet, conversely, it is only in this film that he can really be said to be nameless. In *A Fistful of Dollars* his name is revealed at the very end as "Joe." In *For a Few Dollars More*, he is briefly identified as "Monco." But in *The Good, the Bad, and the Ugly* it is only Tuco's labeling him after his most obvious attribute (his golden hair) that effectively names him. After all, if Blondy has an actual name beyond this, why would he put up with Tuco's epithet? It stands to reason that Tuco only uses this label because he lacks any other name by which to address him.

1. The Occult Text: *The Good, the Bad, and the Ugly*

eager to collect the reward money. Blondy kills the three men with his usual aplomb, then turns Tuco in himself. When Tuco is about to hang, Blondy, from a safe distance, shoots the rope and so rescues him a second time, thus forming a profit-based partnership in which Tuco is the perennial fall-guy and Blondy his betrayer and savior, both in one. Here is the essential nature of Blondy's dilemma, his conflict. His line of work (his choice of profit) dictates that he be in constant duplicity — he is divided. When Tuco tries to haggle for a larger slice of their profits, insisting that the risk is his, Blondy tells Tuco, "You may run the risks, my friend, but I do the cutting. If we cut down on my percentage, it's liable to interfere with my aim."

The next time we see this uneasy alliance at work, Blondy's aim — his focus — has indeed been thrown off, not by a cut in his profits but by the intrusion of *a third element*: the bad. Angel Eyes just "happens" to be at the scene of Tuco's most recent hanging; somehow he intuitively *knows* that "not all men with a rope around their neck get to hang." Leone here unambiguously suggests a telepathic link between the three men, specifically between Blondy and Angel Eyes. Otherwise how could Angel Eyes know that "even a filthy beggar like that has got a protecting angel: a golden-haired angel watches over him"?* Somehow, by spotting this arrangement between Tuco and Blondy, Angel Eyes throws it off balance and upsets Blondy's normally impeccable aim. This — according to our esoteric reading — is the moment at which "the bad" infiltrates the psyche of "the good" and so unbalances it (cuts its "percentage"), causing it to falter. It is also Blondy's first temptation.

His missing of the mark (he has to shoot a second time and Tuco almost hangs as a result) gives Tuco understandable misgivings about their deal, and he harangues Blondy until Blondy loses all patience and "unties" their partnership. Tuco snaps, "When you feel that rope around your neck, you can feel the devil bite your ass!" Blondy thinks this over. "You're right," he says, pulling Tuco off the horse by the rope. "It's getting tougher." His "protection" is no longer "good." Blondy can feel Tuco like the devil at *his* ass and wants to be rid of him; without further ado he leaves him in the desert. Ironically, it is with this callous act (prompted by mercenary greed, his "percentage") that Leone chooses to introduce Blondy to us, as "the good." No protecting angel he, "the good" has just failed the first temptation. Nothing we have seen so far can justify such a designation.

---

*It's an unwritten tradition in genre movies that certain characters — in certain circumstances — are possessed of all-but-supernatural powers of intuition. This sixth sense is what makes them the protagonists, after all — they are "the best" at what they do, be it good or be it evil — and it serves to up the ante of the melodrama by making its players all-but superhuman in their skills. But in *The Good, the Bad, and the Ugly* it is less a generic device and more a genuine indicator of Leone's subtext — that of schizophrenia. The characters' uncanny intuition allows them to be aware of one another's movements and makes them appear to be eerily connected, like different sides of a single psyche.

Having experienced a "glitch" in his own performance (by which self-doubt has entered into his psyche), Blondy reacts defensively and attempts to extricate himself from the partnership with perhaps excessive zeal. Blondy senses something is amiss, but fails to correctly identify the cause of his misgivings (which is not Tuco but Angel Eyes). At a simple level, Blondy is sick and tired of this uncouth, "sawed-off runt" whom he feels is cramping his style, and who "will never be worth more than $3000." At a deeper, unconscious level, however, Blondy is pushing him away because Tuco — the trickster figure who tests and undermines (by mocking) the hero's integrity — is exacerbating his own flagging confidence. Blondy feels that if he gets rid of Tuco — his own distorted reflection — he can effectively deny the very weaknesses that got him tangled up with him in the first place (above all, his mercenary qualities and his duplicitous nature). This is the reason Blondy's treatment of Tuco is so unnecessarily brutal, when he abandons him in the desert (his hands still tied) to die.

When Blondy tells Tuco, "Back to town is only a hundred miles or so. If you save your breath I feel a man like you can manage it," he is clearly putting Tuco's capabilities to the test. This is part of their (unconscious) understanding as "partners," as different sides of a single psyche vying for power. But above all, Blondy is trying to free himself of his "ape," and this of course he cannot do, at least not so easily or so callously. Blondy's "fall from grace" sets off a chain reaction. The next scene after this is of Angel Eyes viscously beating Bob Carson's Mexican girlfriend so as to discover Carson's whereabouts. The woman is introduced as the local soldiers' whore, and seen cursing them as they leave her in the dirt: "You filthy rats!" she shouts. Tuco, the "filthy beggar," "known as the rat," has been sentenced, among other things, as a rapist. When Angel Eyes beats the woman (this being his own preferred brand of kicks, apparently), the association of words seems to make Tuco complicit in the beating, and by extension Blondy also, whose own "fall from grace" can be seen as not only precipitated by but also "unleashing" Angel Eyes, the bad (that damn percentage again!). The ego is now running amok.

Tuco survives Blondy's "test," and proceeds to hunt him down for revenge, becoming Blondy's shadow, the monkey on his back. He tracks Blondy first of all to a hotel room in town, then pays three gunmen to distract Blondy by coming through the door (Blondy is ready for them of course: the canon fire eases off at a critical moment and Blondy hears their spurs), while Tuco comes in by the window. (There is a variation of their recurring dialogue: "There are two kinds of spurs in this world, my friend. Those who come in by the door, and those who come in by the window.") Tuco arranges Blondy's ceremonial execution by hanging: a symmetrical and theatrical justice by which he unconsciously buys Blondy the time he needs to escape. In fact, Blondy is saved by divine intervention (a canon ball hits the hotel), thus proving his angelic properties to be anything but figurative.

Not one to give up so easily, Tuco trails Blondy a second time. This time he literally "apes" him; rooting out the remains of Blondy's campfires, each time getting closer and closer to his prey, until he finally finds a cigar butt still smoldering; he puffs triumphantly on the discarded cheroot, knowing his prey is close. Tuco finds Blondy up to his old tricks with a new partner (Shorty), preparing to shoot the rope. Still caught in the same line of work, Blondy is plainly in need of "guidance" from his trickster-shadow partner Tuco. At Tuco's decree, Shorty hangs, and Blondy is led at gunpoint into the desert. "Where we going?" he asks. "Where *I'm* going," Tuco corrects him. Riding his mule, obscenely content with his own sunshade and water supply, he shoots a hole in Blondy's gourd, then shoots his hat off for good measure. "Like that you won't have to carry so much!" He explains how they are going to cross a desert that even the army is afraid to venture into. "No one will set foot in this hell, except you and me." "Only a hundred miles through this desert," he mocks Blondy. "If you save your breath I feel a man like you can manage it. And if you don't manage it, you'll die."

Blondy is getting his comeuppance, and there is nothing here in Leone's staging to suggest that Tuco is acting out of excess vindictiveness. Blondy has to prove he can take as good as he gives; this — the walk through the wilderness — is his trial by fire. In psychological terms it signifies what Aleister Crowley referred to as a period of "dryness," in which the soul thirsts for fulfillment but is unable to find satisfaction or relief, being a barren wasteland unto itself. The desert signifies the id — the unconscious — through which the ego must journey in order to be purged. In occult terms, it is "the crossing of the abyss."

What is Blondy's downfall is also Tuco the trickster's finest hour. The roles are reversed: the ego (hero) has been overthrown by the crude usurper. Yet, as a result, a new balance is struck between the two men, between the "good" and the "ugly." No longer superhuman, Blondy cannot endure his trial and must again be saved by divine intervention. At the precise moment Tuco is about to put Blondy out of his misery, again comes the sound of distant thunder. This time it is not canon fire but a runaway stagecoach, thundering riderless through the desert and arriving with a Morricone choir of trumpets. Tuco reins it in and (forgetting all about Blondy) finds a dying soldier among the other dead bodies. Tuco is about to finish the soldier off when the man, in a desperate bid for life, promises Tuco the secret of buried gold. He begs for water but Tuco only wants to hear about the gold; the man — who gives his name as Bob Carson — tells Tuco the name of the cemetery where the gold is buried, but before he can give Tuco the name on the grave, still pleading for a drink, Carson loses consciousness. Tuco goes off furiously to find water, telling him "Don't die till I get back!" While Tuco is gone, Blondy, supernaturally inspired, crawls over to Carson and gets the name on the grave; moments later Carson dies.

Tuco in a rage threatens to kill Blondy, who gasps, "If you do that you'll always be poor, just like the greasy rat that you are." "Don't die like that pig!" wails Tuco. The two men are now allied by circumstance. Their new partnership is still founded on mercenary greed, but the stakes, and the rewards, are considerably higher. Blondy, for his part, has passed the second temptation. He has faced the Adversary and heard the voice of God: a dying man who gives him the name of a dead man, a name that is the key not only to his continued survival (against all the odds) but to his future wealth and empowerment. The trip to the abyss has not been a total loss. Tuco — now Blondy's best friend — takes him to a nearby monastery to recuperate, and there confronts his own brother. This is the emotional centerpiece of the film, and the funniest and most touching scenes are here. Tuco, hovering about, asking the monks if Blondy has spoken yet ("He's like a brother to me!"), uses all his wiles — and his considerable acting ability — to try and trick the name out of Blondy (he tells him he is dying, so he may as well unburden himself); but even delirious, Blondy is too shrewd to fall for Tuco's tricks. He gasps out: "I'll sleep better ... knowing ... I have my *good* friend ... to protect and ... watch over me." With these words, their uneasy alliance is cemented.

Tuco not only lies to the monks about Blondy being "like a brother," he also lies to Blondy that he has no family, that he is, like Blondy, "all alone. I have you, you have me." In actual fact, Tuco only *thinks* he is lying. In the following scene, when he confronts his brother, he discovers that he is indeed without family. His brother stands in pious judgment on Tuco ("Outside of evil what else have you managed to do?"), telling him bitterly that their mother has been dead for years, while their father died just a few days ago, asking for Tuco on his deathbed. Tuco accuses his brother of being a coward, claiming that he became a priest because he was too afraid to choose Tuco's path ("the hard way"). The priest loses his saintly cool and slaps Tuco, who punches him and knocks him to the ground. Tuco helps him up and leaves, rejecting his brother's belated attempt at reconciliation. He has severed all family ties now, replacing his blood brother with a spirit brother, Blondy. By "killing" his own family, Tuco has aligned himself with the self-determining path of the warrior (or bandit). As such, Blondy is Tuco's only remaining link to humanity, but also to "the divine."

Family of course is central to Leone's vision, and a large part of how he *identifies* his characters (and their "virtues"). Angel Eyes is literally a family killer: he is the negation of all life, pure self-preservation and mercenary instinct. He is decay. Tuco is only figuratively a family killer (though he may be a real rapist). We learn that he did indeed have a family (despite denying it) but that he has now lost it, partly by choice; and Leone conveys the sorrow of his aloneness more acutely than anything else in the film. Tuco's confrontation with his brother may soften him up some, but in any case he forms a new kinship, or at least affiliation, with Blondy, his surrogate brother. From here, they embark on their quest together. Blondy's past is never disclosed, nor is he ever associated with family in any way. He is an immaculate conception, and from this comes his impeccable "aim," his detachment, his ironic grace, and his "goodness."

Once Blondy has recovered sufficiently, the two men ride off in search of the cemetery (since he knows the destination, Tuco, the ape, is leading); before they get far, however, they are intercepted by a wagonload of soldiers. Tuco's function in the movie, by and large, is to put his foot in it; on this occasion, seeing the soldiers from a distance, he assumes them to be grays and shouts out "God is on our side!" Realizing (when it is already too late) that they are in fact dust-covered blues, Blondy quips, "God is not on our side cuz he hates idiots," whereupon they are taken as prisoners. They arrive at a concentration camp run by a dying captain unable to keep his second-in-command, Angel Eyes, from taking over. When Tuco answers to the name of Carson (since it is at Blondy's own prompting that Tuco does so, Blondy is perhaps unconsciously trying to rid himself of Tuco), Angel Eyes twigs that the two men are on the trail of Carson's gold, and takes Tuco off to be tortured. While Tuco is being viciously beaten by Wallace, the prisoners' band plays a melancholy dirge, knowing full well that the music is expressly to cover the sounds of torture.[2] Tuco finally succumbs at the point where he is about to lose his eyes, and gives up the name of the cemetery.

Angel Eyes then takes Blondy into the torture chamber, not to torture him ("Not that you're any tougher than Tuco, but you're smart enough to know that talking won't save you"), but to offer him a partnership. Blondy, with his options severely limited, agrees. Tuco meanwhile (now of no use to Angel Eyes) is taken off by Wallace to be executed. Blondy is finally free of his "ape"—but at a price. He must form a new alliance with the dark side of his psyche—"the bad"—and so undergo the third temptation. If Blondy is the angel, Angel Eyes at this point becomes his means for *seeing* the truth. And the truth is that he — Blondy — is little different from his enemy. Blondy's third temptation is to temporarily *align* himself with "the bad," in order to eradicate it once and for all. Only so can he discover the buried gold (the higher self of alchemy) and be free of his ape, Tuco. Free to become, finally and forever, a force of "good."

A pause here to consider what I have (perhaps fancifully) cited as Blondy's "three temptations." To clarify this idea, I will borrow some terms from Carlos Castaneda and his hidden personality, don Juan Matus (the greatest double act in 20th century literature[3]). Don Juan cites four enemies of the man of knowledge: fear, clarity, power, and finally, old age. We are concerned only with the first three here, however, and how they appear to synchronize with the three temptations of Christ in the desert.

The first enemy (temptation) is fear. Blondy misses his shot. The ego recoils from its negative aspects (Angel Eyes), pushing them away into "unconsciousness," repressing them (Blondy dumps Tuco in the desert). Like Christ tempted to turn stones into bread, Blondy abuses his power through fear of his own weakness: he's thinking only of mercenary things (i.e., hunger for bread) and this is his weakness, his ugly side. Unlike Christ, Blondy fails the first temptation, succumbing to fear of the unknown, which is but his own reflection (his ape), and turns Tuco into "Shorty." But the battle is still on. The ape, Tuco, persists and eventually confronts Blondy, enabling the ego to conquer its fear of the unknown by forcing it to confront the barren waste of reason (what Morpheus in *The Matrix* calls "the desert of the real").

The second enemy of the man of knowledge is clarity. By thinking he could see everything clearly and dumping Tuco (repressing his "ugly" nature, as if it were that simple), Blondy has wound up dying of thirst in the empty desert of his own solipsism. He succumbs to despair, but is saved at the last minute by divine intervention. For Christ, the second temptation was to cast himself down so the angels would lift him up. Blondy in the desert gives in, surrenders to death, and forces the angels to intervene (the chariot of the dead arrives). Blondy is giving in to his own virtue, his "goodness" or passivity, too early. He's no angel yet, and in his "clarity" he has seriously overestimated his infallibility. Blondy thought if he was rid of Tuco, his percentage would go up and his aim would improve. But his aim didn't improve because he couldn't get rid of his "ape" (shadow) that easily. His falling back on his "goodness" (his sense of professionalism, rather than real virtue) was the equivalent of jumping into the abyss: his clarity let him down, he just wasn't that *good*. So he dies in order to be reborn, meaning that the ego is both parched and *flooded* by exposure to the desert sun (the Self). In this state, Blondy's consciousness is such that he can retain only a single idea: the name of a dead man (which, as it turns out, is "unknown"!). The ego's greatest fear is thus confronted: it is reduced to nothing.

The third enemy (temptation) of the man of knowledge is power. When Blondy aligns himself with Angel Eyes, he has a sweet deal. He is rid of his ape Tuco, he has his split of the money, and an easy, swift passage with Angel Eyes and the "bad men" at his side. But Blondy forgoes this power for, one presumes, the more attractive (and reliable) option of hanging out with Tuco, his "ugly" side. (Compared to Angel Eyes, Tuco doesn't look so bad.) Blondy has power enough now with Tuco by his side. (Tuco helps Blondy dispose of Angel Eyes' flunkies, those faceless demons, and is then disarmed, or retired, when it comes time to dispatch Angel Eyes himself.) Blondy's actual turn-around, we might note, coincides with his one and only tender moment until now, when he is seen stroking a kitten in an abandoned building, so acknowledging his capacity for *kindness*. The kitten as it were awakens Blondy's conscience as to the destructive dangers of power, the need to apply tenderness to keep a balance. He foregoes mere mercenary (ego) convenience for the chance of a little camaraderie with Tuco. Hence he finds his true power. For Christ, the third temptation was when Lucifer offered him the world if he would only bow down to him. This is the test of power. If Blondy gives in to his mercenary nature (once his goodness has failed him), though he will gain power, it will corrupt him. This trap Blondy falls into only momentarily — strategically — before the kitten and Tuco's gunshot awaken his conscience.

To return to our narrative: through ingenuity and ruthlessness, Tuco escapes the clutches of Wallace and so evades execution one more time. He makes his own way towards their shared destination, while Blondy suffers a little longer the company of Angel Eyes and his men, maintaining the illusion of being one of them. (It is only by acting as the bad man that he can discover how against his nature it is.) Significantly, the only time we see Blondy as part of the group is when he is holding the kitten, thus demonstrating (to us, though not to Angel Eyes) just how *unlike* the other men he is. Blondy hears a gunshot and recognizes it at once as Tuco's. (Actually this is impossible, since Tuco is an escaped prisoner and must just as surely have been separated from his guns while in the POW camp. But it only further confirms the existence of a telepathic link between the two men.) "Perfect timing," Blondy says, speaking to the kitten (to which he has even given a name).

Tuco is taking a bath on the other side of town and is ambushed by an old enemy he mistakenly left alive; Tuco — rather improbably — shoots the man with a gun submerged in bath water, concealed by the bubbles. Blondy wanders casually off to find his real partner, coldly shooting down the man Angel Eyes sends after him, thereby unequivocally terminating their partnership. Since he knows that Tuco is close, he now feels confident enough to take on Angel Eyes and his men. Blondy finds Tuco by following his inner antennae, and together they wipe out Angel Eyes' band. Angel Eyes escapes, leaving a note for them, a note which Tuco vainly attempts to read. "See you later, id-, idi —" Blondy takes the note. "Idiots," he reads, handing it back to Tuco. "It's for you." Blondy is now putting his ape (and his id!) in its place.

Back on the trail, Tuco is boasting of his prowess and assuring Blondy he will get them to their destination when, as if on cue, they are intercepted and taken as prisoners, once again by the Blues. At the camp — and once again with rash impetuosity — Tuco improvises by stating that they are there to volunteer. The following scenes, in which Leone shows us the folly and futility of mass-destruction, also give us Blondy's first indisputably heroic deed, when he blows up the bridge the soldiers are fighting over. As a result, he not only gives the dying captain a last moment of happiness (destroying the bridge was the Captain's fondest wish), but possibly saves many of the men's lives, too (since they now have nothing to be fighting over). Blondy blows up the bridge primarily for his own convenience (so "these idiots will go somewhere else to fight," as Tuco puts it); but even so, we begin to see Blondy in a new light after this. It's clear that he is equally motivated by a desire to bring an end to the senseless slaughter (Blondy laments that he's "never seen so many men wasted so badly").* He also earns a new, begrudging respect from Tuco (who certainly only goes along with Blondy's plan because it facilitates his own desires), to the point that Tuco (while they are rigging the bridge with dynamite) suggests they trade secrets and so bring a level of trust into their alliance. Blondy complies but, all-too-familiar with Tuco's deviant nature, insists that Tuco give up his end of the secret first. This moment signifies a truce, an agreement, between the two sides of the psyche: an end to duplicity and mistrust, and a new level of co-operation. This done, the bridge is blown, the captain dies with a smile on his face, and the battle (if not the war) is ended. Tuco and Blondy are now officially partners in crime. Having crossed the Abyss together, they have blown up the bridge and brought an end to a senseless conflict, in the process opening their own path to the buried gold. The exploding bridge is the only orgasm — in the absence of any women in the film (besides Carson's floozy and the fainting, widowed mother at the movie's opening) — that the two men can enjoy. Blowing up the bridge "consummates" their own coupling. Soon after — Tuco having gotten Blondy to "put out" his half of the secret — Tuco runs out on Blondy.

Before this, on the other side of the river, Blondy comes across another dying man, a wounded soldier to whom he offers a last toke on his cheroot. This is, following immediately after his official graduation to heroic status, Blondy's first show of goodness; by the standards Leone has set up for Blondy until now, it borders on saintliness. The dying man's taking his last breath from Blondy's cheroot signifies a kind of transference — an empathy — passing between the two men. Blondy establishes himself finally in our eyes as capable of compassion; in a word, the solar hero. By showing tenderness towards a dying man in his last moments, he proves that he has learnt to value life, and

---

*It's indicative of the anarchic spirit of Leone's vision that the one overtly heroic act in his movie is an act of outright destruction. Leone plainly sympathizes even less than his characters do with the insane bids for power and progress of government that leads to such senseless slaughter. The bridge facilitates crossing over between territories, hence is a power point that both sides struggle for and will make almost any sacrifice to attain. By destroying the basis of the struggle — the man-made artifact — the location returns to its original, natural state as a simple river, and so becomes irrelevant to the political machinations. Of course, Tuco and Blondy can still cross the river, but *under their own power* (they have to wade). Leone is advocating a return to individual action, or responsibility, over governmental. Hence his vision is basically anarchist.

to understand the need for "goodness." By bringing a measure of peace to a dying man's soul, he attains a certain grace himself. The direct result of this is Blondy's "transformation" into the Man with No Name. In exchange for his own coat (with which he covers the dying man), he takes the dead man's poncho; and since it is the same poncho already familiar to us from the first two movies, the effect is something like that of Clark Kent putting on his red-and-blues at last. By the act of donning his magical cloak, by going from "Blondy" to "No Name," the protagonist attains — or regains — his mythical, otherworldly status and becomes once again an angel, albeit (inevitably) an Angel of Death.*

At this point, Tuco steals the dead soldier's horse and gallops off in search of the goal, abandoning Blondy. Blondy, unruffled by the inevitable betrayal, coolly lights the fuse on a handy canon (using the same cheroot he shared with a dead man) and (his "aim" now preterhumanly precise) blows Tuco off his horse. Tuco staggers about in the clouds of dust while Blondy lights another canon. The next blast sends Tuco crashing into a gravestone, whereupon he realizes that he has arrived, finally, at the promised land: Xibalba, the Land of the Dead. The following scene is the movie's highpoint, as Tuco rushes headlong through the cemetery, surrounded by seemingly endless rows of tombstones, to Morricone's soaring orchestral strains, in search of a single grave. Death is of course the central motif of *The Good, the Bad, and the Ugly*, as befits not only all good Westerns but all self-respecting schizophrenic texts. The quest for self amounts to no less than the knowledge of good and evil, which is, after all (mythically speaking), knowledge of death. Blondy allows Tuco to run free through the maze in order to save himself the trouble of having to look for the grave. Now that his "ape" has been properly trained, it can be unleashed in order to perform its duties. The fact that Leone has already established Tuco's illiteracy does not seem to bother him here; apparently Tuco can read exactly as well as circumstances demand. He finds the designated grave, that of "Arch Stanton," and begins digging. Once he is almost done, Blondy arrives and tosses him a shovel, telling him to finish the job.

Why he does this when he knows that it is the wrong grave is anyone's guess. Apparently it is another case of his supernatural intuition at work, since Angel Eyes arrives at this point and, getting the draw on both of them, finds to his chagrin that there is nothing in the grave but Arch Stanton's mortal remains. For No Name, now on the very brink of full integration, divine intervention has merged with supernatural foresight and impeccable strategy. Having regained his advantage (he never really lost it), he proposes a contest. He

---

*Curiously, it is only at this point that Clint Eastwood's performance comes to life. For most of the film, his presence is all-but obliterated by Eli Wallach's scene-stealing Tuco (probably Wallach's finest hour as a performer). In the last few scenes, however, Eastwood has a chance to shine. Maybe he feels lost without his poncho?

will write down the *true name* of the grave (where the treasure is) on a stone, place the stone in the middle of the flagstone *corrida*, and the three men will shoot it out. The survivor will then turn the stone and claim the treasure. "It's a lot of money," says No Name. "We're gonna have to earn it."

Since No Name has already taken the bullets out of Tuco's gun (unbeknownst to Tuco), the contest is finally between him and Angel Eyes alone: the good and the bad, with the ugly as a passive (anything but mute) witness. No Name kills Angel Eyes, who falls neatly into an open grave, whereupon No Name shoots his hat and gun in after him. Evil has been gracefully erased, leaving no traces. Now only the ugly remains. Blondy points out the correct grave. Tuco, stammering over the word "Unknown," finally twigs: "There's no name on it!" "There's no name on the stone, either," replies No Name, wryly, showing Tuco the blank stone. His game was rigged, evidently; and although the other two might easily have deduced, given the time, that the treasure was buried in the *unmarked* grave next to that of Arch Stanton, No Name was never in any doubt about who would live to claim it. The unknown soldier is the keeper of the hidden gold. Of *course* death has no name — and who would know better the true nature of the unknown than (avenging angel of death) the man *with* no name? (Leone's foresight here is pretty supernatural itself; since *A Fistful of Dollars* wasn't released in the U.S. until 1967, a year after he made *The Good, the Bad, and the Ugly*, the epithet "Man with No Name" hadn't even been invented yet. Yet his games with names, and the lack thereof, already uncannily anticipated this mythos.)

The unarmed Tuco digs up the treasure and wallows obscenely in it, like a hog in slime. At which point, he looks up and sees No Name, holding a noose with his name on it. This is Blondy's last act of "betrayal," only now he is assuming Tuco's role as trickster. Since he never actually intends to let Tuco hang, but only wants him to *believe* that he is leaving him to die, No Name is simply playing a particularly cruel game at this point. He puts the noose around Tuco's neck and has him stand on a flimsy wooden cross for support, leaving Tuco's share of the gold at his feet, tantalizingly out of reach. Then, with a wry smile, he rides off. Poor Tuco, taken in all the way — the trickster tricked, the ape "aped" — is left whimpering helplessly on the brink of nonexistence. He is now hanging over his own abyss, an abyss he'll never cross, plainly (the ugly doesn't have it in him to be that "good"), but one that he now gets to gaze into.

No Name is playing out his role as merciless avenger for the last time, but ironically, all for show. He is no longer driven by the old revenger urges, or by genre conventions, but is only enjoying a last laugh at Tuco's expense, giving him a taste of his own medicine. When No Name/Blondy reappears on the horizon, Tuco's relief is rapidly curtailed by his realization that Blondy intends to make the shot (and so sever the rope around Tuco's neck) from an

1. The Occult Text: *The Good, the Bad, and the Ugly*

The three aspects of the psyche vie for supremacy: Tuco (Eli Wallach), Angel Eyes (Lee Van Cleef) and Blondy (Clint Eastwood) face-off in *The Good, the Bad and the Ugly* (1966, United Artists).

impossible distance. Tuco realizes that his salvation might just as likely be his end. No Name makes the shot, of course: his aim is once again impeccable, more so than ever in fact, since all traces of "doubt" (split perception, or schizophrenia) have been removed along with Angel Eyes and he can now see clearly. He leaves Tuco (his hands still tied) howling obscenities, rich at last but still unsatisfied, forever ugly, while "the bad" rests eternal in an unmarked grave, unrecognized, assimilated, forgotten. And the good — now triumphantly, gloriously, *ironically* so — rides into the sun, having snatched wisdom (gold) from the jaws of death (the grave), and regained his natural, solitary state as a wandering star.

The occult text reveals itself. Picture this: a stone circle (*corrida*) at the heart of Hades; at the center of this circle is a stone *with no name on it*. (And it is by placing the stone in the center of the circular *corrida* that No Name, the solar hero, completes the astrological glyph for the Sun: ☉) Three characters, or "virtues," situate themselves on the circumference of the circle (making a grand trine), each one vying for the philosopher's stone. By this method — or strategy — the three-fold ego approaches enlightenment (rather like three spermatozoa competing for the ovum). The good eradicates the bad, and tames and suppresses the ugly, putting it to its own uses (whereupon it leaves it hanging), riding out of Hell with the alchemist's gold under his saddle. Jung's process of individuation is complete. The controlling intelligence (ego) confronts its dual nature (the bad and the ugly) in the labyrinth of the unconscious (Sad Hill). It disposes of evil altogether, thereby canceling the previous duality. "Ugly" is thus reigned into the ego's service (disarmed but still useful), facilitating the ego's business in the unconscious realm (having got him to locate the grave, Blondy has Tuco dig up the gold). Once the ugly has served its purpose, it is left behind. "Ugly" is the final mask which the ego wears in order to navigate the underworld. As a functioning personality (and all personalities are by definition at best ugly, at worst plain bad), it has outlived its usefulness and must be "hung up" long enough for the good to get free of its influence, once and for all. Blondy of course shoots Tuco down from a safe distance, and even gives him his share of the gold (though he may never have the stone), leaving him in hell (consigned to the unconscious). Thus unburdened of its shadow, the ego, now free of all attachments, identity, or name, rides off into Infinity. Enlightenment: that's what it is. Duality has been overcome; the third point—which takes off from (but has no part of) the other two—has been attained. The schizo is a shaman. Hallelujah.

The Good, the Bad, and the Ugly is a crude but poetic mythological text. It is a mischievous, ironic, largely unwitting but nonetheless elaborate blueprint for the passage from conflict, fragmentation, and suffering (schizophrenia) to harmony, integration, self-determination and individuation — shamanic or solar consciousness. It's also a rousing, stylized, free-form epic Western with all the necessary ingredients of first-class "mindless" (visceral, blissful) entertainment, and it's this very dual nature that makes it a work of art. How many people who see the movie will receive even the faintest whiff of such an "occult text"? One in a thousand, at best; it took me twenty years and countless viewings before I did. But once you spot it, it changes everything, and that's the beauty of it. That's what makes the text "occult," after all, and that's why the treasure is buried: so only those with sufficient ingenuity and determination will ever get to ride off with the gold.

2

Courting the Other: Quests for Completion

> Schizophrenia: a psychotic disorder characterized by loss of contact with the environment and by disintegration of personality.
> — Webster's definition

R.D. Laing was one of the first to point out the basic parallels between the schizophrenic and the mystical experience. In the simplest terms, he remarked that the schizophrenic is one who is drowning in the ocean of his experience while the shaman has learned to swim through it. I use the term "shaman," as differentiated from "mystic," since the latter tends to imply passivity, all-too common to the schizophrenic. In fact, passivity is a primary characteristic of the schizophrenic in all his dealings with the world, and so schizophrenia is perhaps an all-too-natural state for the cinemagoer, one he can easily relate to (even if he does not actually succumb to it). *Movies tend to cater to, if not actively encourage, schizophrenia, at a collective rather than an individual level.*

Besides passivity, another leading characteristic of schizophrenia is that of fragmentation. Though commonly thought of as "split personalities," schizophrenics in fact suffer from a general fragmentation of the psyche. It is not a dual identity they suffer from, but a lack of identity altogether. They do not have the luxury of continuity of self, something the rest of us take for granted. They also lack the capacity to draw a clear line between reality and fantasy, inner and outer, objective and subjective. It may quickly be seen how this latter, while the curse of the schizophrenic, is the very *sine qua none* of movies — suspension of disbelief. Movies are designed expressly to blur this line, if not by their actual content then certainly by their technique. It should come as no surprise, then, to note how movies seem to be more and more drawn towards depicting the schizophrenic experience, in various (often covert) ways. From *The Cabinet of Dr. Caligari* onwards, movies have naturally gravitated towards depictions of the inner workings of the human psyche. Since they tend towards sensationalism, and to invoking strong emotional responses, movies naturally lean more towards madness than sanity (just as they are predisposed towards depictions of chaos and violence rather than of peace and order). On the one hand, this can be seen as addressing an already existing condition in society and helping us come to terms with it; on the other, it can be seen as deliberately — albeit ingenuously — aggravating this condition, serving not only to exploit it but to *engender* it in society. This is a chicken and egg question: Is our growing fascination with and addiction to movies the result or the *cause* of our growing dissociation from "reality?" Probably it is a little of both; mostly, I think, it is something else altogether.

Movies, especially American movies, have always both inspired and been inspired by a sense of paranoia. At least since the 1940s, with *film noir*, the sense of something being amiss in American society, of a secret, hidden center of corruption, of dementia, has been increasingly evident in both our more serious and our more frivolous cultural artifacts. Movies — being primarily an entertainment medium and not a philosophical one — have been free to exaggerate and embellish upon this basic sense of unease. As such, in a strange, largely unacknowledged fashion, they have anticipated it.

Paranoia — the meaning of which is "out of mind" (in the same way that paranormal means "beyond the normal") — has a tendency, like all fears, to be self-fulfilling. There are two ways we can interpret paranoia: as what is beyond the mind, in the sense of having no actual reality outside of it; or what is "outside mind," in the sense of being greater *than* the mind, transcending it, taking consciousness to the next plateau. These meanings are opposed: one states that the paranoid's impressions are less than real, the other that they are *more* than real. Paranoia has generally been understood in the former sense — as something not founded in reality, that originates in the mind even as it unhinges it (in the same way, paranormal activity has been delegated to the realm of science fiction, unfit for serious research). Yet the secondary meaning has remained with us, slowly gaining in credibility in recent years. Paranoia, in this alternate sense, is something that is justified, based in actual experience, though still outside the accepted view of things. "Just because you are paranoid doesn't mean they're not out to get you" is a phrase that became popular in the 1960s, when current events (and disclosure of past ones) were beginning to make our worst fantasies seem tame by comparison. Today, in our blasé, post-millennial acceptance of the most outlandish possibilities, there is a certain irresistible logic to this.

Schizophrenia, which in many ways goes hand in hand (in the profane perspective) with paranoia, can be seen similarly. Are we beginning to view society, humanity — reality itself— as basically fragmented and irrational and chaotic *because* we are becoming schizophrenic? Or are we becoming schizophrenic as a necessary *response* to the evidence that reality is intrinsically duplicitous, that

2. Courting the Other: Quests for Completion

it was even set up to be this way? It is all in our point of view, and the question of chicken or egg becomes irrelevant, finally, when one begins to realize (like quantum physicists, and like Neo in *The Matrix*) that, if our perceptions are true, there *is* no chicken and there is no egg. There is only perception.

Movies are the most popular medium of our day. They are the modern-day equivalent of myths, our collective dreams and nightmares. As such, they have a function beyond that of mere entertainment. It might be thought of as a secondary function, so far as the conscious intent and appeal of movies goes at least; but, so far as their significance in the greater scheme of things— regarding the development of the human race, and so forth — this "secondary" function is considerably more intriguing. What it comes down to is the gradual disclosure of the unconscious, of certain truths about ourselves and our society, generally those of a more deranging, unsettling, and unpleasant nature (since these are the truths we are reluctant to look at directly). These truths (not historical truths but psychological ones), being repressed, are forced to find more devious, "disreputable" outlets; individually, this occurs through dreams and nightmares, while at a collective level, they emerge through the various forms of entertainment with which we distract ourselves. It is a characteristic irony of the unconscious that the very media we use to avoid these unpleasant truths serve to bring them back to us in a disguised form. This is how the unconscious *works*. What cannot come through the front door comes by the back.

The more we repress something in our day-to-day lives, the more it is obliged to seek alternate channels. The more certain unpalatable ideas are denied ordinary expression, the more they will emerge through the various art forms (since art, like dreams, is sourced in the unconscious). The nature of this subterfuge is to allow such repressed truths to surface without our having to take them seriously (just we refuse to take our dreams seriously). Hence the more disreputable or popular the medium, the more suitable it is for this subterfuge. What medium is more disreputable than movies? It seems fair to add that it is not so much movies being popular that makes them disreputable, but their being disreputable that makes them popular. If so, this is one more subterfuge of the id — nothing if not cunning — to assure its message, however concealed and obscure, reaches the maximum number of psyches in the shortest possible time.

What follows is a brief history of schizophrenic cinema. The lurking unease of the *film noir* in the 1940s (following the grisly revelations of Nazism and the atom bomb) quickly gave way to the all-out paranoia of the sci-fi movie in the 1950s. It's instructive to note how the 1950s were, by all accounts (despite Hiroshima and Nagasaki), an idyllic time in the U.S. in which all was for the best in the best of all possible worlds. TV had been introduced into the home and the great nation was secure in righteousness and supremacy (the

You can run but you can't hide. Kevin McCarthy and Dana Wynter fleeing the Other in *Invasion of the Body Snatchers* (1956, Allied Artists).

atom bomb the ultimate demonstration of "Might Is Right"). And yet, despite (or because of?) this apparent security and serenity in both society and the home, paranoia had come into its own as popular entertainment. This was most famously embodied in "The Twilight Zone" TV series, and in such films as *Invasion of the Body Snatchers, Invasion from Mars, Quatermass*, and a whole host of "infiltration from within" movies that practically became a genre unto themselves during this period. The standard interpretation of this subgenre phenomenon is that it was all an expression of a very real paranoia, one concerning Communist infiltration by the Soviet Union.

Ignoring if we may (for now) the question of actual flying saucer sightings, this was still a gross simplification. The truth was something deeper, more universal, and more timeless than any fleeting historical phenomenon (whether UFOs or Communism), for the whole "Red Menace" phenomenon was itself an expression, a symptom, of the paranoia growing with every passing year in the American people. It was nothing less than the early signs of a collective schizophrenia which was to become, by the turn of the millennium, a runaway condition to which no one was immune. Kevin McCarthy's hysterical plea (in *Invasion of the Body Snatchers*), "They're everywhere!" has indeed proved prescient.

Above all, the sci-fi movie paranoia is an example of how the further from actual, conscious acknowledgement of the "disease" society was (in the beatific 1950s), the more outlandish and far-fetched (and disreputable) the diagnoses were, the further our "alienness" (schizophrenia) had to be projected onto a proverbial "Other." No one at the time could possibly have cited the plethora of paranoid sci-fi movies and *The Twilight Zone* TV shows as evidence of America's instability as a nation. That would have been absurd.

In the 1960s, however, the counterculture emerged and the Other came home to roost. Paranoia came to be seen as — far more than the concoction of unbalanced minds — having actual, historical foundation. This shift-over from unfounded to founded paranoia began with the Cuban missile crisis and the John Kennedy assassination, and rapidly gained momentum with the various other assassinations, the Vietnam war, the Manson murders, and so forth. The Beatles and garage bands soon decided that rock 'n' roll was about more than holding hands, and groups such as The Doors, The Jimi Hendrix Experience, and The Velvet Underground brought the dark side of the American dream to the mainstream, via the hungry youth with their dissatisfied minds. Movies were not far behind. Towards the end of the decade — in existentialist rebellion movies such as *Blow Up, Cool Hand Luke, The Graduate, Easy Rider,* and *Midnight Cowboy*— the seamy underside of American society and the alienated state of its youth was beginning to reveal itself, and the cracks were beginning to show. *Five Easy Pieces, The Passenger, Last Tango in Paris, The Last Detail, Chinatown,* even apparently gentle nostalgia pieces like *The Last Picture Show,* were all consolidating this sense of unease and forging a cinematic renaissance from it. (The influence of European and especially French "New Wave" cinema cannot be underestimated in this renaissance. Paranoia and its partner in crime, cynicism, were for obvious reasons far more firmly established in Europe than in America.)

It was during this period that not only paranoia but movies themselves began to gain a credibility they had previously lacked. In fact, the two (movies and paranoia) could be seen as working hand-in-hand at infiltrating the collective American psyche. On the one hand, the new realism, despair, cynicism, and wised-up political paranoia was giving movies a new maturity. On the other hand, movies —first and foremost a populist medium — were bringing previously unpalatable ideas to the mass psyche, thereby making them, if not more respectable, certainly more familiar. By the 1980s, paranoia and cynicism would (in the movies) have become familiar to the point of contempt.

This was all quite inevitable, as inevitable as the encroachment of a cancer that goes untreated. What need for alien invasions or demonic possession when all-too-real political conspiracies and assassinations were making our imaginary fears seem frivolous by comparison? Truth or fiction, historical or supernatural, such disclosures were all serving the same purpose: that of making it plain that something was rotten in Denmark. Most of these movies so simplified the situation, however, that they weren't diagnosing the actual problem much better than the sci-fi movies of the 1950s had. In the sci-fi movie, the situation was reduced to "human race vs. aliens." In the counterculture movie, it was reduced to youths vs. grown-ups, individual vs. establishment, artist or dropout vs. "the system." It was the same "us and them" dichotomy done over, by which all ills could be laid at the door of "the Other." This led to endless revolt, and ever-augmenting schizophrenia, since both sides believed in their own righteousness to the bitter end. The aliens believed they were entitled by their superiority to take over the Earth. The humans believed they were obliged to fight the aliens in the name of human freedom. The youths believed they were the chosen ones, enlightened and destined to inherit the Earth from the corrupt (who had proved themselves unworthy). The establishment, the ruling classes and the older generations, believed they were duty-bound to fight the licentious tide of youth in the name of the old values that had served them so well until now. Each "side" made of its opponent an "Other." It demonized it and so precluded any possibility of reconciliation—or even understanding—between the two. The battle raged, and the schism grew.

In a sense, it was preferable to direct paranoia against *the aliens*, since this at least united humans as a race (a white race, at least). Once the 1960s took off, not only the black and yellow man but people's own children became the enemy, and the option of a truce began to seem ever more distant. (This was foreshadowed in the sci-fi genre by *The Village of the Damned*, 1960, in which children *are* the aliens. When Jim Morrison sang—in "The End"—"All the children are *insane*," parents everywhere nodded their heads dourly in agreement.) Nonetheless, the redirection of paranoia from aliens to communists to our own children was essentially a *positive* movement from fantasy to reality, and it signified the slow but steady (and painful) acceptance of the veracity and the urgency of paranoia. It showed that people's unconscious fears—by becoming more firmly based in an everyday acceptance of "the real"—were beginning to surface into consciousness. Movies about corrupt adults and alienated youths were obviously taken more seriously than movies about flying saucers and alien pods, just as were the fears themselves. To this extent, they represented progress, albeit a progress of the symptoms as much as the diagnosis.

In *Five Easy Pieces*, the hero is a hostile, alienated loner whose lack of respect or compassion for others is easily excused as a simple "failure to communicate." This "failure to communicate" had by now become a buzz phrase of the decade, coined by Strother Martin's sleazy prison guard in the rebel-martyr fantasy, *Cool Hand Luke*. The American crisis was not yet a spiritual

2. Courting the Other: Quests for Completion

"Don't kid yourself they belong to you, they're the start of the coming race." Aryan alien uberkids take over a small community in *The Village of the Damned* (1960, MGM).

crisis (it wasn't until the 1990s that American movies would begin to address this possibility), but it was certainly an existential one. The lines of communication were down. The fundamentals of language, our basis for understanding, were breaking apart. Older generations were especially susceptible, despairing of ever understanding the youth with their "groovy"s and their drug-soaked eulogies and their paranoid denunciations of authority. At this time, the idea of a right brain/left brain split was not part of common parlance, but with hindsight that is how it begins to look today. The establishment, or older generations, represented the fixed, unchanging, restrictive laws of the left brain; the psychedelic youth, with their love of creative expression, sexual freedom, and pagan ritual, stood for the imaginative possibilities of the right brain. Since language — polarity based, rational thought — was the strict province of the left brain, the "Old World," it made sense that the new antihero was essentially non-communicative and that he took refuge in surly, sulky silence. What he was experiencing at an inner level, there were no words to communicate without reducing to meaningless absurdity. Words were the tool of the enemy, the Other, and any attempt at communication would only be playing into its hands. Best simply to play a concerto on the back of truck, eat 50 eggs and knock the heads off parking meters, or move to Alaska. Communications had broken down because there was no sense in communicating anymore. It was not failure, it was refusal to *try*. The rift was too great.

Beyond any doubt, Jack Nicholson was the leading "spokesman" for the new youth in this period. He embodied inarticulation, alienation, revolt. His cynicism was inseparable from his cool, his hostility proof of his integrity. He rechanneled machismo into angry young man-ism and made it legit again. His Bobby in *Five Easy Pieces* (the first in a series of portrayals that continued through *Carnal Knowledge, King of Marvin Gardens, The Passenger, The Last Detail, Chinatown,* and finally *One Flew Over the Cuckoo's Nest*) is the fullest prototype of the schizophrenic hero at that time, a hero who would find his apotheosis (in 1999) with Brad Pitt/Edward Norton's Tyler Durden of *Fight Club*.

It was during this period (the late 1960s early 1970s, and with Nicholson in full swing) that the once conventional hero became, in effect (potentially), a psychopath. In fact, the transition (from all-too-sane to borderline demented) began a decade earlier, with Ford's groundbreaking *The Searchers*, consolidated two years later by Hitchcock's *Vertigo* (and, to a lesser degree, *Psycho*). In these two movies, the once dependable hero began to show the wear and tear of the times and to develop distinctly psychotic tendencies. When seen through today's "enlightened" prejudices, he becomes what he always was: an obsessed, controlling, and finally destructive personality driven by demons. (In both cases sexual demons — but then, are there any other kind?) What made these two movies so remarkable at the time had become quite commonplace by the 1970s, the decade in which "the anti-hero" came into his own. Increasing evidence of living in a psychotic society allowed for, even demanded, a complete reevaluation of our role models.

The fact that popular movie heroes were becoming steadily more unstable, obsessive, and paranoid, indicated a similar process of "unhinging" in the collective psyche. There was a growing realization that what was driving humans was something other than previously assumed. Moral values such as honor, compassion, the pursuit of truth and justice, the upholding of the law, were no more motivations for Scottie McFerguson or Ethan Edwards than they were for Norman Bates. Rather, these men (heroes only so far as they were protagonists, portrayed by leading men with a record for heroic roles) were driven by personal obsessions that had little or nothing to do with the selfless values once vouchsafed the hero. They were motivated by private demons and acted not heroically but pathologically. As a result, they were denied the hero's victory and the Hollywood happy ending, and were seen to be isolated, broken men, condemned to a sense of loneliness and failure. This is just as true of Ethan Edwards, left to wander the desert endlessly, as it is of Scottie and Norman, who are abandoned to rot anonymously in lunatic asylums or rest homes (assuming Scottie doesn't hurl himself to his death right after Maddy does, which remains a distinct possibility). Yet the differences between these demon-possessed schizophrenics and the standard Western or thriller hero were subtle at best, and both *Vertigo* and *The Searchers,* with but a few minor changes (a happy ending for *Vertigo* and a couple of excisions from *The Searchers*), could arguably have passed for standard genre works.

By the 1970s, however, no such doubts remained. There was no question of taking the characters portrayed by Nicholson or Dustin Hoffman as anything but deeply disturbed individuals. This did not mean they were not perceived as heroes; they remained people for audiences to look up to and root for. They were still essentially role models to the youth, not in spite of but *because of* their more disturbed (and disturbing) qualities: their apparent instability and tendency towards neurosis, even schizophrenia. Paranoia, both collective and individual, was gradually moving from a delusional thing to something fully justified by (and finally inadequate to) the times. In a weird way, schizophrenia (or at least mysticism) was coming to be seen as the only sane response to the times. Certainly Laing, among others in the 1960s, helped romanticize insanity, offering the dubious luxury of calling it enlightenment. Leary, Kesey, Castaneda, Burroughs, the Beats, all were proponents of a new, "suprarational," right-brain approach to existence. With the self-induced dementia of psychedelic drug use, they were arguing for the schizophrenic experience as a necessary step towards overcoming the limits imposed by left-brain, patriarchal programs. Kesey's *One Flew Over the Cuckoo's Nest* was in many ways the head cornerstone of this new edifice of anti-rationality or controlled schizophrenia (a classic oxymoron for the times), and it is certainly no coincidence that the lead role of MacMurphy went to the youth's unofficial spokesperson, Jack Nicholson. The character of the Chief who feigns deaf-muteness in order not to be sullied by the lies and follies of an irredeemable society was the embodiment of the futility of communication. It was the apotheosis of the (red) wise man who keeps his silence in the land of babblers. Only so, by remaining uncontaminated, was his final bid for freedom successful. Yet it was the doomed babbler MacMurphy who had planted the seed.

Cuckoo's Nest (the movie) was in many ways the death song of the counterculture. The establishment quickly did away with the romantic loser-rebel martyr myth, which lasted roughly from *The Graduate* through to MacMurphy (about the same duration that the Hollywood movie renaissance lasted, as it happens). During this period, Hollywood wasted no time concocting a reactionary solution with its brutal cop movies (from *Dirty Harry* and *Walking Tall* onwards) and its sentimental nostalgia pieces (*The Way We Were, The Sting,* etc.). On the other hand, for a few brief years, artists like Coppola, Fosse, Peckinpah, Boorman, Altman, Polanski, Scorsese, De Palma, and Bertolucci were making unprecedentedly audacious steps towards diagnosing the problem. For a brief time, with the great (and not-so great) American 1970 movies (*The Godfather, Cabaret, A Clockwork Orange, Straw Dogs, McCabe and Mrs. Miller, Harold and Maude, Deliverance, Last Tango in Paris, Mean Streets, The*

Last Detail, Phantom of the Paradise, Badlands, Pat Garrett and Billy the Kid, The Conversation, The Long Goodbye, Chinatown, The Texas Chainsaw Massacre, The Godfather Part Two, Bring Me the Head of Alfredo Garcia, Nashville, Taxi Driver, Carrie), the art form seemed to have a direct line to the divided psyche of the nation, and did not flinch from the schizophrenic experience.

These movies came as close as movies had ever come to looking squarely into the face of the dilemma; not only did they admit that there *was* a problem (without dressing it up in latex or bearskins or feathers), but they began to suggest a reason behind it. What all these movies had in common was a profound sense of alienation, not only from society, but from humanity itself, or from the values and assumptions that it adhered to. They did not offer any kind of solution, however; not, at any rate, besides senseless acts of violence. When *Taxi Driver* came along in 1976, part of the enormity of its impact was due to the fact that it summed up all the rage, frustration, pain, and alienation of the preceding years, the groping and fumbling of the artists and movies of this time; it expressed (albeit in a most primitive fashion) what they had *all* been struggling to express. Travis Bickle, himself a sort of weird synthesis of Ethan Edwards, Scottie McFerguson, and Norman Bates, was beyond doubt an archetype for our times, and as a result the movie—more than any other of the period expect perhaps *The Godfather*—found a central place in modern pop culture. Travis was paranoia incarnate.

The bloodbath that ended *Taxi Driver*—the schizophrenic's orgasm, his sole means of connecting to a world he could perceive only darkly, in pieces— also signaled an end to the creative renaissance in Hollywood, curtailing (for a while at least) the serious investigations into schizophrenia that had begun less than a decade earlier. On the one hand, *Cuckoo's Nest* smothered the schizo in his bed: a silent death, a mercy killing. On the other, *Taxi Driver* showed the terrible consequences of allowing the paranoid full expression (the paranoid here being Scorsese as much as Travis). A few years later, John Hinckley's attempted assassination of Reagan would confirm the truth of such fears, as would Bernard Goetz's Bickle-esque display on the New York subway. The bottom line was that, if such artistic investigations and creative expressions were leading to this, it was better to shut down that train of thought altogether, and pursue a different line. The following year, *Star Wars* arrived.

Star Wars was retrogressive cinema; it harked back to more "innocent" times when good could fight evil in the traditional colors of black and white. The triumphant ceremonials at the end of the film were a bold-faced evocation of the Nazi propaganda film, *Triumph of the Will*, yet few considered the implications of this. This was only sci-fi, after all; we were back on safe ground. It's amusing to note the parallels between this "solution" and the ending of *Taxi Driver*, in which Travis is temporarily pacified and placated by his outburst (above all, perhaps, for being embraced as hero by a society even more schizoid than him). We leave him knowing that the next explosion is only a matter of time: the situation has been momentarily relieved, but what drove Travis to madness has not been addressed. As a result, the next outburst is not only inevitable but will inevitably be worse and more catastrophic than the last. A parallel might be drawn with the reemergence of the old heroic values propagated by *Star Wars*, with its quasi-Nazi happy ending, all of which depended on ignoring the fact that these values had already been destroyed — by Scorsese and others — and, as such, were no more than a sop for the masses: a pacifier to keep them happy while the next storm gathered.

To the schizophrenic (shamanic) understanding, life doesn't imitate art: it imitates lousy science fiction. It's not that we consciously fulfill the hokey prophecies of sci-fi, but that our unconscious knowledge (the unconscious being essentially timeless) of things to come surfaces through the more suprarational media, those of sci-fi, fantasy, and, to a lesser extent, supernatural horror. (Horror movies tap into atavistic rather than futuristic consciousness.) The paranoid mind perceives certain agendas at work in society, agendas of (let us say) "mind control" that employ both popular television and mainstream movies to work their influence. The essence of these (perhaps imaginary but nonetheless clearly defined) agendas is to quash any and all "psychedelic"* changes that may be occurring in the collective psyche, employing the most banal and retrogressive fantasies to do so. The point stands: *Star Wars* was lousy science fiction with a sound mythical base, but it was far from progressive in its intentions, and far from "psychedelic" in its effects. It was not prophecy so much as nostalgia. Its childish schemata were meant to reassure, to lull, rather than challenge or disturb. Otherwise, it could never have been the success that it was, nor would it have had such an enormous, incalculable, influence on American movies.

Star Wars did not resuscitate the sci-fi genre; that would have allowed movies to address the schizophrenic experience all over again with a new audacity, in fresh and adventurous ways (something that wouldn't happen for another twenty

---

*I use the term "psychedelic," in the absence of any other convenient one, to convey the idea of a right-brain perspective seeping through into left-brain perceptions, without necessarily resulting in outright schizophrenia. Obviously, the association is with chemical or plant substances that alter consciousness without apparently causing any serious damage. It may well be that many of these substances are so rigidly controlled and suppressed in our society not because of their innate harmfulness but precisely because of their potential, in the jargon of that time, for cleansing the doors of perception and revealing an infinite new world of possibilities to us. In a word, it is the psychedelic not the narcotic which is perceived as a threat to the social order: its positive potential for change, rather than its negative potential for harm, is what is most severely resisted by the status quo. As such, "psychedelic" may refer to any agent that helps us wake up to our latent shamanic possibilities, narcotic to anything that helps numb us to it.

years*). *Star Wars* was a success not because of its ideas but because of its sentiments. It was not its originality but its familiarity that allowed it to take hold of the American youth and give birth to a new infatuation. And adults could get hooked on it too, since it took them back to their childhood, the days of Flash Gordon, Dan Dare, and Buck Rogers. It was as if "The Twilight Zone" had never happened. *Star Wars* was embraced by the mainstream (by the public and by Hollywood itself) above all for strengthening an illusion that was on the point of being destroyed forever. It effectively threw not only movies but audiences themselves back into a peaceful, untroubled slumber. This was escapism of the purest, most infantile kind, and it confirmed for studio heads and moviegoers alike that what was wanted of movies—what would really *sell*—was forgetting, not remembering. It was at this point that the action-fantasy blockbuster was born, and the primary function of movies was "discovered" (decided): an opiate for the masses. If the only alternatives for dealing with the schizophrenic experience involved either apocalypse or euthanasia (*Taxi Driver* and *Cuckoo's Nest*, respectively), then heavy drugging became the most viable option.

In many ways, the 1980s and 1990s were the worst period for American movies to date, and it is plainly no coincidence that they were also the time of heaviest denial. While the 1970s saw an artistic peak for American movies, it also boasted a wealth of thought-provoking, subversive and genuinely disturbing (though not necessarily *good*) horror and sci-fi movies, from *Night of the Living Dead* and *Rosemary's Baby*, through *The Texas Chainsaw Massacre* and *Shivers, Dark Star, God Told Me To, Carrie, Martin, Dawn of the Dead*, all the way up to *Alien* (which was the first, fatal step towards the mainstream). But in the 1980s, there was an endless dirge of vapid, sadistic slasher flicks, most of which were sequels or spin-offs to *Halloween* and *Friday the 13th* (two enormously popular horror movies that came out at the end of the 1970s). So far as expressing the schizophrenic experience, these movies came about as close as *Porky's* comes to communicating the joys of sex. A genuinely scary movie is, by its very nature, as much a threat to the drugged out, narcoleptic slumber of audiences as an intellectually provoking work (albeit in very different ways). Horror and sci-fi, at their best (or even at their worst, so long as they are uninhibited expressions of their makers' unconscious), tend to serve both these functions at once, scaring us viscerally while provoking us intellectually. In order to combat this all-too "psychedelic" effect, without doing away with the genres altogether (which would have been next to impossible), it was

---

*By the late 1990s, things had changed considerably, and what is most remarkable about *The Matrix*—which was briefly the *Star Wars* for its time, until the sequels sunk the franchise—was that it was the first sci-fi movie since Lang's *Metropolis* to mix progressive prophecies and subversive commentaries with a thrilling storyline and kick-ass FX. It was the first sci-fi movie in an age to do full justice to its ideas, and to be true to its populist roots without compromising the integrity of its philosophical vision.

necessary to reduce them to their most primitive, uninspired forms. Audiences went along with this, being essentially complicit with studio heads in desiring an undisturbed slumber party from movies. Since it was unthinkable to render the horror movie totally harmless without stripping it of its *raison d'être*, the genre was reduced to family rollercoaster rides (*The Amityville Horror, Poltergeist, Fright Night*, etc.) and plotless exercises in sadistic brutality (*Prom Night, My Bloody Valentine*, etc.). Beyond this, and beyond the works of a few die-hard mavericks such as David Cronenberg, Wes Craven, and John Carpenter (and briefly Brian De Palma), most horror movies of the period were derived from Stephen King stories.

The sci-fi movie, on the other hand, could more easily be domesticated and rendered harmless: declawed and defanged, without entirely relinquishing its pedigree. By merging it not only with those fairy tales of old but with budding New Age philosophies (with all their carefully contrived vacuity), it was possible to create a sci-fi movie that the masses could sleep happily through and come out refreshed and placated to their banal, oh-so sane lives. This was all part of the cinema of forgetting, and went directly against (was a deliberate foil to) the cinema of paranoia which sci-fi had originally served so well. Writing about the "recuperative cinema" of the 1980s — the movie trends that serve to keep certain realities at bay — Robin Wood (in *Hollywood: From Vietnam to Reagan*) wastes no time pointing out a host of political and social (and sexual) realities that can be cited as threats to audiences' peace of mind and the maintenance of its illusion. All these various factors can be reduced to a single, hideous and undeniable truth that encompasses them all. The name of the bogeyman that was being kept at bay was schizophrenia.

If we see movies as a psychological tool, it follows that they would be most useful in suppressing (if not addressing, it has to be one or the other) a psychological condition, and this condition is schizophrenia. A drugged patient is protected (not merely by the drugs but also by his environment) from overstimulating influences that might aggravate his psychosis. It is in this sense that the recuperative cinema — what Wood terms "papering the cracks" — was deemed necessary. Unpleasant realities use disreputable mediums in order to express themselves; for suppression of these same realities, more "reputable" means are required. By the 1980s, the violence and insanity of American society had become such a staple part of everyday lives (and TV shows) that horror and sci-fi movies had a rapidly diminishing role to play in the scheme of things. What took over was something more insidious, relating not to disclosure of the truth but to its suppression and gradual perversion. This way, schizophrenia and psychosis — and its most obvious offshoot, irrational violence — could be assimilated into the mainstream and turned into a commodity. Thus the action movie was born, as a central factor in the continued debasement of both American movies and their audiences.

Traditionally, horror movies threatened primarily by showing audiences sides of life, of their own psyche, that normally we didn't have to look at save in nightmares (which by and large were consigned to childhood). Such movies served to reveal, however hokily, possible realities besides our own, to allow perceptions of the world that were not only more frightening, but also more wondrous, more awe-ful. The fact that in the 1980s horror movies were almost totally stripped of their staple characters, their supernatural under layers — the vampires and werewolves and monsters which had hitherto characterized the genre — illustrated a denial of this wondrous aspect of the id. In place of Dracula and Frankenstein, audiences were given the schizo with the kitchen knife, axe, screwdriver, whatever. The horror movie was not merely defanged, it was exorcised; in effect, it was castrated. It's especially ironic — in light of our present argument — that the replacement of the supernatural monster with the mundane psycho was itself part of the means for keeping at bay the truth of our own schizophrenia! Had the "schizos" in these movies been treated with anything resembling artistry or empathy (as in *Taxi Driver*, or at least to the extent of *Psycho* or *Texas Chainsaw Massacre*), then things would have been quite different. As it was, between them, Michael Myers and Jason did away with just about any sympathy we had left for the devil.

During this period, and barring the work of De Palma — which is really *sui generis* — *The Stepfather* was about the only exception; in all other cases the "schizo" was actually far less human than the vampires and werewolves and monsters of old Universal, RKO, and Hammer horror movies had been. On the other hand, the preponderance of special effects, and the tendency of the horror film (as with all the other genres) to emulate the action movie (the Holy Grail of entrepreneurial Hollywood), meant that even those few supernatural horror movies that did sneak by involved dehumanized monsters with little more personality than Godzilla. (Godzilla, it might be noted, was a cold-blooded Japanese imitation of King Kong, the original all-too-human monster.) All in all, and with a few exceptions (the werewolf did OK for a while with *The Howling* and *An American Werewolf in London*), the supernatural side of movies — always the most healthy and accommodating of outlets for the schizophrenic experience — had been thoroughly denigrated by the mid 1980s.

There is no need to suggest an actual conspiracy at work here when the cynicism of marketing will suffice. An insane populace does not go shopping. Some of these "recuperation" movies are actually among the best of the period, and certainly a leading filmmaker, Steven Spielberg (even more than George Lucas), was their prime instigator. And although most if not all of the by-products of his work (children both bastard and legit) ranged from saccharine to contemptible, films like *Close Encounters* and *ET* (and especially Irvin Kershner's *The Empire Strikes Back*), are, for all their infantilism and soporific qualities, highlights of the period. This is due above all to Lucas and Spielberg's successfully tapping into a genuine *mythic reserve*, a fount of unconscious longing and desire, and giving it true voice. In a way, these films were truly recuperative. They were balm for our condition. Unfortunately, they are also lacking in balance, both in themselves and within the greater spectrum of Hollywood movies. Balm is all very well provided it is accompanied by a full diagnosis, and precedes at least an attempt at a cure. Not only did these movies fail to diagnose (much less treat) the schizophrenic experience, in the end they failed to serve as a decent balm, and became only an irritant.

Cocoon and its ilk are among the most nauseating of Hollywood artifacts, of this or any period. To the suffering schizophrenic soul they are the equivalent of a senile old uncle who patronizes us with platitudes, driving us to despair (and maybe even murder). The impossibility of communication. It was here that the sci-fi movie crossed over into inspirational fantasy, New Age sermon, creeping closer in spirit to the likes of *Field of Dreams* and *Forrest Gump*. These movies (the quasi-spiritual trend that began with *Ghost* and *Field of Dreams* and continued with drippy dreck like *City of Angels, What Dreams May Come,* and so forth) are among the most dishonest popular movies in history; it is perhaps fair to say that they were popular in exact proportion to their dishonesty. At this point, the cinema of recuperation becomes the cinema of disinformation. Here was the flip side of paranoia: the religious impulse in its most debased form.

There was however a kind of underground outlet, a leak if you will, through which the (ever escalating) schizophrenic experience could continue to flow. We are back, as if having traveled through time, to the same basic situation as seen in the 1950s, only now the drive-in and B-movie have gone the way of the dinosaur and been replaced by the video market. For anyone who cares to seek it, there is in fact a plethora of provocatively plotted sci-fi (and even horror) movies that were made in the 1980s and 1990s. He would have to seek high and low and far and wide, however, since most of these movies have disappeared "straight to video"; he would also have to endure, beyond most film critics' levels of endurance, movies quite unwatchably awful (I say with authority, having watched many of them myself).*

These movies dealt with darker, more challenging truths, but once again — in the Reagan/Bush years of retroactive jargon and perfected newspeak — they were forced into the most disreputable outlets. The existence of movies like Carpenter's *The Thing, Escape from New York* and *They Live,* of *The Terminator, Blade Runner, Jacob's Ladder,* Cronenberg's *The Brood* and *The Fly,* as well as a whole host of lousy movies with great plots (most of which were total flops)

---

*New Line Cinema was one of the few (if not the) major producers of such fare, and in fact Wes Craven's *Freddy Krueger* is probably the single notable supernatural horror movie creation of the 1980s. But even these films are little more than inspired dreck.

proved, if nothing else, that the total suppression of certain ideas (once psychedelic, now merely deranged) was all but impossible. It was only a matter of time before the cracks began to appear again and such ideas gained the respectability (and the outlet) that they needed.

Paranoia about the past (horror) and the future (sci-fi) thus taken care of, that only left paranoia for the present. Political conspiracy movies had died the death with De Palma's *Blow Out*; and yet, since public awareness of the reality *behind* the movies remained, it was clearly not possible to suppress the subject altogether. In consequence, certain paranoid perspectives became an intrinsic part of the Hollywood Weltanschauung in general, most specifically (and here was the rub) that of the comedy-fantasy genre. Madness and paranoia were to become strictly a laughing matter, as once again the truth was forced to debase itself in order to get out. As a result, the whole "black helicopter/government's-out-to-get-you" paradigm became incorporated liberally into glib action fantasies and sci-fi comedies, from *Starman, Splash, War Games, Blue Thunder*, all the way through to *Men in Black*. In the process, once pressing fears were reduced to more peripheral (lunatic fringe) concerns, to be forgotten by all but undiscerning folk, the "believe anything" crowd. In a word, kids, paranoids, and geriatrics. (And since society does not respect its young any more than it does its ancients, its sick, or its demented, their opinion didn't really count anyway.) When helicopters chase Tom Hanks and his mermaid, or Karen Allen and her starman, across fields and valleys, we are never for a minute asked to condemn our government for such evils. We are allowed to accept this as a simple generic device, and if we are also led to accept it as "the way things are" (or *would* be, if mermaids and starmen existed), it does not trouble us overly. We are too blissed out by the romantic comedy aspects, the Hollywood sheen, for a few black helicopters (or a glimpse of schizophrenia) to spoil the fun.

Not just nihilism but out-and-out derangement became an accepted subtext of mainstream comedy, however, though once again the generic familiarity softened any harder edges. This is how Hollywood gets its messages across: it *sells* them to us, above by making them seem non-threatening, "user-friendly," *familiar*. Once we begin to recognize the conventions of the genre, we can sit back and relax, and the subconscious meanings can begin to filter through. One such arena for schizoid notions to frolic in was what I have called the "Deconstructing the Yuppie" subgenre — the comedy of anxiety. From early still-borns such as *King of Comedy* to first, limping prototypes like *Desperately Seeking Susan, National Lampoon's Vacation*, and *Planes, Trains and Automobiles*, to the quasi-Surrealist genre-definer *After Hours* and genuine oddities like *Something Wild*, the master text for the schizophrenic comedy was indubitably *Blue Velvet*, a genre unto itself. By the time of Polanski's *Frantic*, a subgenre had come (quietly and surreptitiously) into existence, and audiences could hardly be sure anymore if they were watching a comedy, a thriller, or some uneasy hybrid of the two. Upwardly mobile anxiety was just a newfangled treatment of Hitchcock's beloved "ordinary man in extraordinary circumstances" shtick: the cinema of peril. And from the days of heroines tied to the tracks (and audiences running from the movie train), cinema has been about nothing so much as *peril*.

This "Chapel Perilous" relates to the passivity of audiences (whether forced or voluntary), which in turn is linked to schizophrenia. It is the schizophrenic's sense of wild panic that paralyses him and renders him passive. The hero (or heroine) must *always* be in peril of some kind, be it of not getting the girl or not saving the world. Even the 1930s screwball comedies, with their vampish females and henpecked men (something like an American comedy of manners, except of course that Americans *have* no manners), can be seen clearly through the lens of the schizophrenic experience. From *noir* (where hazardous dames were still coming on strong), to sci-fi flying saucers and soul eaters, to horror goblins (zombies, vampires, and the whole slithering crew), to the Establishment, to hoodlums and terrorists and the CIA, all-too-briefly into the tormented psyche of our own isolation and dissociation, then quickly back to sharks and storm troopers, random psychopaths and bogeymen, and finally back to screwball dames (though by *After Hours* and *Fatal Instinct* they had become homicidally so), the Other has continued to shift and mutate. By this point, if the everyday urban existence that makes up our meat and potatoes had itself become a source of peril to us, it was certainly no laughing matter. Precisely for this reason (laugh that ye not weep being a Hollywood mandate), the line between fear and hysteria had become so blurred that it was often hard to tell whether any of this was meant to be taken seriously or not.

Woody Allen's *Zelig* and *The Purple Rose of Cairo* remain the most fully realized and enchanting expressions of the comedy of schizophrenia to date. In many ways they are the culmination of a decade of comic neuroses-investigations from which Allen forged his reputation. (In *Zelig*, Allen was coming clean, admitting once and for all that the world's greatest comedy filmmaker was a nobody at heart.) By the time of Mike Nichol's *Regarding Henry* (and soon *Forrest Gump*), it was no longer necessary to qualify the idea that goodheartedness and simple-mindedness were one and the same: it was a given. On the other side of things, reality without the luxury of serendipitous lobotomy was beginning to look a lot like Terry Gilliam's *Brazil*, a bittersweet ode to schizophrenia. Dementia was now amok, on film sets (*The Stunt Man*), in high schools (*Heathers*), and at Las Vegas bachelor parties (*Very Bad Things*); comedy had become so nihilistic, so demented, that it was no longer anything to laugh at. (The crossover between comedy and horror served the horror film far more favorably than it did the comedy. *American Werewolf in London, Evil Dead* (with is endless imitators), and *Scream* were both scary and amusing, as well as refreshing in their irreverence. Comedies like *Very Bad Things* were just plain horrible.)

Comically sanctioned chaos allowed madness a way into the family home, whether merely dysfunctional (*Home Movies*), or wholly fragmented (*Where the Heart Is*, in which tribal rearrangements allow the creative side of schizophrenia to blossom). The madness provided (potentially) the family with the means for renewal, or at least relief. So far as society went, however, these upheavals spelt anarchy, and gave rise to the totalitarian impulse (repression at its most desperate). Terry Gilliam's *Brazil* is probably the most epic, heartfelt rendering of the schizophrenic experience of the period, and Gilliam himself has demonstrated more empathy for the demented than perhaps any other major American director in recent years (with Tim Burton a close runner up). For the individual as much as for society, the encroachment of chaos could only spell disaster: at best it was a purging by fire, at worst a meaningless and traumatic ordeal (as in *After Hours*, *Frantic*, etc.).

But in all these films, schizophrenia was something that came from *without*; it was externalized and rendered circumstantial, rather than integral. Be the circumstances those of financial ruin, domestic turmoil, kidnapping, irate lynch mobs, or full-fledged social breakdown, all of these characters were strangers to the schizophrenic experience. They were innocent bystanders at their own apocalypse. Schizophrenia is such a touchy subject in Hollywood precisely because audiences are so hard-pressed to retain their sympathy for the schizoid; and audience sympathy is practically the *sine qua none* of the "hit" movie. The unwillingness of audiences to sympathize with runaway schizophrenics was at least partially responsible for the failure of movies like *Straight Time* and *The King of Comedy*, despite their being films of unusual subtlety and interest, boasting some of the actors' very best work (Hoffman especially reached a nasty peak in this film). What made these movies so refreshing was at the same time what made them unpalatable to the public: they were unflinching depictions of sociopathic personalities. Hollywood wanted its schizos to be huggable, charismatic, a little closer to Richard Gere in *Breathless*, perhaps (and his manic depressive of *Mr. Jones*), in which the nihilistic thug of Belmondo was transformed into a devil-may-care charmer with occasionally homicidal urges.

Even Harrison Ford made an excursion into this terrain with *Mosquito Coast*, and suffered his first real financial flop as a result. Leading man-as-schizophrenic was plainly an idea whose time had not yet come. More palatable by far was Ford's harmless kook (lobotomized by a random bullet) of *Regarding Henry*, which itself was little more than a "sophisticated" variation on the hugely popular subgenre of the time, the child-in-man's-body movie. Starting with *Big*, *Like Father Like Son*, *Vice Versa*, etc., these movies were an infantile expression (and repression) of the schizophrenic desire to relinquish control of our actions and take refuge in the passive wonder (and irresponsibility) of the child. The whole "finding the child within" theme, so central to the sentimental ethos of this period, was in fact no less than a sublimated symptom of the schizophrenic experience: grown-ups in denial.

Allen's *Zelig* was a more honest and inspired portrait of this child-man in a state of total isolation from his environment and from his own psyche — the nebbish who wishes only to belong, the everyman who becomes a nobody in order to get along. This was palpably a time of identity crisis for Americans, and Leonard Zelig, as much as any modern movie hero of this period, was a man of his time. Once again this idea was being sentimentalized and rendered "sympathetic" for digestion by the masses, however (in *Rain Man*, the anguished autist, desperately seeking a sense of reality — some connection to world of chimera — was taken to Las Vegas). Finally, with the sheer stupefaction of *Forrest Gump*, the schizo got to be a war hero. By this point, the dynamic schizophrenics of *Straight Time* and *Breathless* had been successfully lobotomized and put to work; the celebration of specialness had turned into a ticker tape parade to conformity.

While Tom Hanks was reducing autism to eccentricity, a new kind of actor — most fully exemplified by Johnny Depp — was making a career out of playing lovable (though often dangerous) freaks of a darker variety. Depp's most unsettling quality was his androgynous nature, and in melancholy kitsch like *Crybaby, Edward Scissorhands,* and *Benny and Joon*, he was the pin-up boy for the maladjusted. By the time of *What's Eating Gilbert Grape*, he had become the actor of his generation, above all perhaps for bringing a fresh new dose of empathic conviction to the portrayal of the outcast. He seemed just naturally drawn to schizophrenic parts, and even his more conventional roles (the lackluster *Nick of Time* or *Secret Window*, and his masterly *Donnie Brasco*) retained a certain desperate quality to them: these were men on the brink, and the basic schizophrenic idea — that of a crossover between fantasy and reality — was here incorporated into the traditional storylines (where it became instead the blurring of the line between right and wrong). *Fear and Loathing* was a natural choice on Depp's exploratory path — willful dementia of drug-use being an almost obligatory experience for the aspiring schizo. Schizophrenia is the split between right and left hemispheres of the brain seen as individual fragmentation of the psyche, as internal conflict; it is the war of the sexes, of anima and animus, as it rages eternal in the human soul. All this made Johnny Depp — Hollywood's very own black sheep, an actor of shifty, uncertain sexual identity — the natural spokesman in the 1990s (following Nicholson's 1970s neurotic), for a kinder, gentler schizophrenic experience.

Meantime, in the social stratosphere, the war between the hemispheres was manifest in confusion and hostility between the sexes. If sentimentalizing the male required a corresponding vilification of the female, what resulted was emasculation in place of emancipation. Romanticizing the feminine-male and demonizing the masculine-female brought the sexes not closer together but further apart. The schizophrenic male was seen to be incorrigible but lovable, possibly dangerous, certainly irresponsible, and if not suicidal then still marked for disaster. Whether the volatile lover of *Breathless* or the simpering moron of *Forrest Gump*, these males were not fit to survive in a world they never made. On the other (female) hand, the psychotic bitch of *Fatal Attraction* or *The Hand That Rocks the Cradle* became the scheming harpy of *Basic Instinct*, the icy siren of *The Last Seduction*, the supercool assassins of *The Long Kiss Goodnight, Nikita*, etc., and finally, happily, the sassy sorceresses of *Bound* (a less felicitous alternative being the suicidal floozies of *Thelma and Louise*). All these sexual role games were as it were the dynamic between the sexes, the dueling of the divided psyche, as it struggled to find some balance between opposing points of view.

Hollywood flirted with the vagrant's life while spinning capitalist success stories wholesale, only occasionally striking up some sort of uneasy balance — in the yuppie morality tales for example, in which total destitution was seen as only a phase, a step on the path towards personal integrity, not the end but the means of redemption. How many times have we seen the ambitious young sharpshooter get ahead in his company, through ruthlessness and cunning unassuaged by ethical considerations, only to find out just how little it profit a man ... etc., etc. The old themes are the best ones, and morality plays never had quite such a solid case for condemning the soullessness of our times as they do today. If there was no refuge in madness, no safety in sex, no future in (dis)honest labor, and no solace in the home, what did that leave? The very environment was turning against us (*Blue Sky, Safe*); suburbia was seen to be just a flimsy façade for the most grotesque aberrations (*Happiness, American Beauty*). Repression was beginning to take its toll, temptation was fast becoming irresistible, and transgression starting to seem the only attractive option — the only remaining pleasures being those still forbidden to us. As the libido surged forth in all its evil splendor, as the sterile veneer was torn asunder, the Id burst out its plastic bag, the walls of Jericho crumbled, the American Dream became a farce, the American Home a bloodbath. There was no longer a reason to be civilized if civilization was breaking down in tandem with our own crumbling psyches. The uninhibited Id doesn't mean to be destructive. It is only natural, however, that it strike out first of all at everything that has kept it caged, starting with the genteel lie of civilization. Where once quitting one's job had been enough, now only the most cardinal acts of revolt would suffice.

In 1968, with *Night of the Living Dead*, the domestic apocalypse needed flesh-eating zombies to convince us. By 1999, with *Happiness* and *American Beauty*, people were all zombies anyway; and for daddy to drug and sodomize young boys, or for mommy to come home and find daddy's brains on the carpet, none of this was really a big deal anymore (and certainly it required no *supernatural* explanation). By the time of Kubrick's *Eyes Wide Shut*, the American family had become so removed from anything identifiably human that there seemed to be nothing left to salvage. The schizophrenic family lived, happily ever after, in total isolation from the world and from each other, lost in pot-soaked sexual fantasies, a nightmare of jealousy and impotent desire. The dementia was so deeply buried that there seemed no cure that wouldn't be terminal. These humans had denied their natural urges so long they were like corpses already, and nothing short of a violent death was likely to redeem them. (Admittedly in the case of *Eyes Wide Shut* this was the fault of the filmmakers, and hardly intended.) By portraying the modern American family as empty and loveless (and in need of a little "loosening up"), these films gutlessly sidestepped the fact that the modern American family was patently insane. Kubrick's *The Shining*, twenty years earlier, though barely less creaking and inept a work than *Eyes Wide Shut*, came light years closer to depicting the truth of the matter (Kubrick got more and more removed from human experience as the years rolled by). If Home was a living Hell, it was because Hell was where the heart *used* to be. It's perhaps telling that the most persuasive solution to the dysfunctional nuclear family came from David Cronenberg—the man responsible for *The Brood*—and entailed a return to the atavistic tradition of blood sacrifice. In *A History of Violence*, the answer to the problems of society and family both is delivered as plainly as a flint hatchet to the skull: it's back to the primal or bust. The ancestors know best.

While dysfunctional couples were slaying and betraying one another and marriage was fast going out of style, the perfect couple seemed to consist of at least one dead member. *Ghost*, Spielberg's grisly *Always* (more like a threat than a promise), *Field of Dreams* (in which the hero was merely brain-dead), *City of Angels*, *What Dreams May Come*, were all movies that worked hard, in their sap-headed manner, at offering a sentimental solution to the schizophrenic dread of the times. Death, lo and behold, was just another obstacle on the rocky road of romantic love. These movies played shamelessly on the most paltry and simple-minded fantasies of mass audiences, once again sidestepping the real issue (romantic love is just another distraction on the greased slide to death). They took the schizophrenic experience (that of separation and anguish first of all, then more precisely that of hearing voices, believing in spirit worlds, and so forth), and reduced it to a rosy, cozy, bedtime story about the afterlife. Fortunately, there were movies that at least tried to balance out this sentimental misinformation with a little honest psychology, thereby giving more thoughtful and convincing depictions of the schizophrenic experience: movies like *Stir of Echoes*, *The Sixth Sense*, *Bringing Out the Dead*, and *Fallen* reflected (no more than adequately, but still) a genuine concern, a pressing need to address the question of death. This in turn forced audiences to look at possibilities beyond the mundane drudgery of their daily routines, and represented a reaching out to the unknown, a dipping of the toe, maybe even a whole foot, into the murky waters of the spirit world. Beyond death, possibly, but most certainly beyond consensus reality or rational cognition.

In *A Prisoner of Sex*, Norman Mailer wrote that paranoia was nothing less than belief in the devil. If so, then Religion, as collectively embraced by the masses, is faith that God is better, bigger, and stronger than the devil. It functions as a sop and a comfort for our ever-encroaching terror and despair in the face of the world, a tonic for that sinking feeling that the devil has gotten the upper hand. Seen in this light, movies serve a dual purpose. They may disclose unpalatable truths to us indirectly and thereby allow our unconscious necessary expression. But they may also cover up these truths, placating us with skillfully fabricated lies designed to create the very opposite impression: that everything is fine, that nothing has really changed, that all this madness is just a passing phase and love will conquer in the end. (It ought to be noted that the *conclusion* of these saccharine movies need not be false, only the means by which they arrive at it.) The sap-headed affirmations of these old, long-outmoded values (of sentimental Hollywood of the 1980s and 1990s), as well as the cynical brutalism of action movies, served to suppress and divert the growing sense of paranoia and schizophrenia in society. The fact that 90 percent of these movies are not only dubious vehicles for propaganda but thoroughly lousy movies only confirms this suspicion.

Since the schizophrenic experience has always been, now more than ever, the closest equivalent to the artistic one — that of the creative individual in an increasingly machine-like world — it follows that interesting and challenging movies are invariably also subversive ones, ones that address, and effectively partake of (with the awareness of the artist), the madness in which we live. This doesn't mean they can't have a religious or life-affirming dimension; one of the best of these recent movies (*The Matrix*) owes much of its appeal precisely to such a dimension. But as a general rule, the schizophrenic movie, like the schizophrenic individual, is driven into a corner by the overwhelming nature of its impressions, and takes refuge in societal rules based, above all, on a denial of soul. What better way for the schizo to *protect* his soul than to deny he has one, that such an idea even exists? The schizophrenic is tormented only secondarily by the world in which he lives; what torments him first and foremost is his own psyche. By rejecting the one — the world — he effectively is left with the other — his soul. Finding this to be the true source of his torment, he naturally rejects this also. As a result, the religion of our time — a schizophrenic time in which few values can be seen to have value — is nihilism. This is the chosen belief system of the younger generation: to reject all beliefs whatsoever. It is the ultimate expression of the postmodern, fragmented, schizophrenic experience, of paranoia beyond paranoia: to deny everything as not only worthless and meaningless, but as *unreal*. With movies like *The Matrix* and *Fight Club*, the schizophrenic experience has come into its own.

If 1999 was the watershed year for schizo cinema (*Being John Malkovich, Bringing Out the Dead, Matrix, Fight Club, American Beauty, Eyes Wide Shut, Magnolia, The Insider, Ghost Dog, The Sixth Sense, Sleepy Hollow, Run Lola Run, Boys Don't Cry, Man on the Moon*), the years since have also afforded a surprising wealth of movies that describe, to varying degrees of success, the schizophrenic experience. *Memento, Requiem for a Dream, Gladiator, Waking Life, Mulholland Drive, The Pledge, Prozac Nation, Julian Donkeyboy, A Beautiful Mind, Insomnia, Adaptation, In America, Confessions of a Dangerous Mind, Punch-Drunk Love, 21 Grams, The Mothman Prophecies, The Others, Matchstick Men, Mystic River, United States of Leland, The Corporation, The Singing Detective, Around the Bend, Eternal Sunshine of the Spotless Mind, The Aviator, I Heart Huckabees, Closer, Sin City, The Libertine, Matador, Mirrormask, Down in the Valley, Harsh Times, The Exorcism of Emily Rose, Edmund, V for Vendetta, Capote, A Scanner Darkly, Alpha Dog, The Fountain, Stranger Than Fiction, The Departed, The Hoax, Inland Empire, Michael Clayton, You Kill Me, Reign Over Me, Lars and the Real Girl, There Will Be Blood, The Assassination of Jesse James by the Coward Robert Ford, Synecdoche New York, The Changeling, Choke, The Curious Case of Benjamin Button*, even silly dreck like *Mr. Brooks* and *Awake* or mainstream pulp like *X2, Dark Knight*, and *Watchmen*, are all doing their best to represent the ever-deepening split in the collective psyche between haves and have-nots, sane and insane, disempowered mass and super-powered elite, young and old, believer and non-believer, ignorant and informed, deluded and disillusioned, paranoid and complacent. They may not be offering up a cure, but they are doing an excellent job of deepening the diagnosis.

If, as Freud taught us, Civilization = Repression, there are three questions we may wish to ask.

First: Repression of What? Second: Repression How? Third: What Price Civilization? The first consideration is crucial, since there are inarguably things that *need* to be repressed, if only for the time being (while other, more pressing things are acknowledged), and at least if civilization is to continue existing at all (a question which will be addressed subsequently). Ergo, some repression is worse than others. The urge to kill our fellow men when they annoy us, it might be argued, is something that needs to be repressed. Which brings us to the second question: How?

This is precisely where (and why) the arts come in, be they fine or base, blessed vision or damned advertising. The arts, and the various bastard media technologies they have spawned (devil's tools all, from the printing press to virtual reality), possess an authority in our lives that we rarely, if ever, become aware of (they work best when they work surreptitiously). In the beginning was the word, and the word was a command (though today it is more of a subliminal suggestion). Thou shalt not kill, for starters. In movies, it's clearly a different affair; in movies, killing is not only acceptable, it's the best way to get ahead. This is not a million miles away from the Law of the Jungle: "kill or be killed."

If movies "help" us to repress our (now outmoded) killing instinct, they do so at a price. No instinct can be repressed without being rechanneled. There is always a safety valve, and in the last forty years, movies have served as a safety valve for the violence in civilized man's soul probably more than any other single factor save sports. What is *really* being suppressed is not the killing but the sexual impulse, however. That is really all there *is*—in animal man—to be suppressed. Presumably this accounts for why our violent fantasies have become so twisted, our sexual fantasies so violent. Schizophrenia is the price of cutting ourselves off from our life force. By such a reckoning, civilization comes to be seen as the primary blight upon the schizophrenic (would-be shamanic) mind. Which brings us to the third question.

The product of repressing humans' (animal) sexual nature was civilization. The price of civilization, for the animal man, is schizophrenia: a splitting off from the reality of our sexuality. The only sane conclusion for the schizophrenic, at this point, is that civilization itself is unreal. As in *The Matrix* and *Fight Club*, such a realization banishes all inhibitions, for better or for worse, for sorcery or savagery. The schizo is released from bondage, to become One, in the precise moment that civilization collapses around him. That is the solution, but it is also the price. Where we go from here is anyone's guess.

3

Scars: The Hero as Psychopath

> It's not easy to like something you know nothing about.
> — The Man with No Name, on "peace," *A Fistful of Dollars*

The Western movie hero has generally been the American male's idealized view of himself, and even to some extent the female's idealized view of maleness. John Ford's *The Searchers* (1956) was a rude reminder for terminally adolescent males of the implications of this fantasy ideal. Commonly viewed as the most influential — if not the greatest — Western ever made, the film exposes the Western hero as at best deeply troubled, at worst plain psychotic. Forty years before *Unforgiven*, John Wayne's Ethan Edwards revealed the gunslinger as a lonely, embittered man, driven to do "what a man's got to do" not by duty but by compulsion — by private demons of rage, jealousy, and regret. Ethan Edwards is your classic split personality (even his name suggests this: the two Es implying twin egos). He is a man of the plains, a hunter, a warrior, a wanderer, a loner isolated by his chosen lifestyle and by his predilection for violence, who nonetheless yearns (against his better judgment) to *belong*.

Ethan has rejected the solace and companionship of family, while his brother Aaron has married and reared several children. At the start of the movie, Ethan arrives at Aaron's ranch after three years of wandering. Ethan, we soon realize, is in love with Aaron's wife, Martha, and we are given to understand (through Ford's delicate and assured directorial touches) that Martha loves and desires Ethan. We can only presume that it is Ethan's commitment to solitude, his refusal to be "reigned in," that made Ethan and Martha (or Ethan and *any* woman) an impossible match, and that consequently drove Martha into the arms of Aaron, the family man. As a result of this, perhaps, Ethan secretly smolders with jealousy and resentment for his brother Aaron, possibly even harboring an unconscious desire to see him dead so that he might claim Martha for his own. If so, Aaron (Abel to Ethan's Cain) is the first suggestion of Ethan's dual-personality, the split in his psyche.

Aaron embodies (both symbolically and literally) the conflict between Ethan's desire and (what he presumably sees as) his duty, a duty not only to his brother, but also to his true nature, that of solitary man. His jealousy reveals that Ethan is divided against himself, having denied his sexual (procreative) instincts. Perhaps he believes he does this out of loyalty to his brother, from a desire not to come between Aaron and Martha, but it seems doubtful if family duty alone would be enough to repress Ethan's powerful desire for Martha. Aaron represents all that Ethan has denied in himself, and as such is a threat to his peace of mind as much as a comfort for his soul (by being with him he can experience Martha vicariously, as her brother-in-law). At the same time, by refusing to admit his jealousy and hostility for Aaron, even to himself, and by doing the decent thing and repressing his desire for Martha (remaining passive), his soul is oppressed by longing. Just being around the happy family is a source of anguish to him, as evidenced by what follows.

At a subtextual level, the Comanche slaughter of the family is the result of Ethan's repressed id exploding and tearing apart the marital idyll which torments him. If Ethan had acted dishonorably (whether to start a fresh life with Martha or merely for the sake of momentary sensual pleasure), he would have broken up the happy home, perhaps; but it would at least have been an honest expression of his desire. Instead, Ethan's id, denied the natural outlet of adultery, manifests a more radical solution, and Aaron's family is brutally wiped out.

Ethan's shadow nature is represented by the sneaky, bloodthirsty hordes of Comanches (for whom Ethan has a pathological hatred from the start), as they descend upon the happy home and reduce it to singed rubble and carcasses. Through clever subterfuge, the Comanche lure Ethan and the other men (sans Aaron) away from the ranch, and the moment the ranch is unprotected, they move in. The Comanches rape and kill Martha, murder Aaron and his son Ben, mutilate the bodies, and make off with the two daughters, Lucy and Debbie (Lucy is later found raped and murdered also). Discovering the desecrated bodies, Ethan is both horrified and vindicated by the hideous turn of events. Both his conscious fear and his secret desire have been realized. Above all, perhaps, it is his awareness of having secretly *willed* the slaughter that appalls Ethan, and which compels him to spend the next five years of his life on the Comanche trail, seeking revenge. Thus begins the search (did ever a Western have a more perfect title?)—the quest of the fragmented soul for reunion with its denied and forsaken other half. The schizophrenic journey.

At this point, Ethan is split three ways. Aaron, his slain brother, has now become Scar, Ethan's *Doppelgänger*, the face of the Other that he must find and erase to know peace again. The violated Martha has become the innocent Debbie, Martha's prepubescent daughter, abducted by Scar and his band of savages, to be raised as a mate (or, from Ethan's self-lacerating perspective, to be violated and debased as a sex slave). Debbie, like her mother Martha, represents Ethan's unsullied, unattainable *anima*. She is the pure feminine that he can only love from afar (Martha because she belonged to Aaron, Debbie because she was still a child). The thought of this image of perfect feminine grace and beauty being debased and destroyed by the subhuman Scar is intolerable to Ethan. The reason it is intolerable is that Scar, the Other, is a stand-in for Ethan's own repressed desire to do the same. Not only must he seek and destroy Scar to avenge Martha and the others, he must do the same to Debbie, since he knows that by the time he finds her she will have been contaminated by Scar's "unnatural" lusts.

Ethan rationalizes (at least we imagine he does; he never openly discusses his reasons for wanting to destroy Debbie) that this is a mercy killing, that Debbie, having been stripped of her humanity, is better off dead than living as an Comanche. But his reasons are personal, selfish, and irrational. Ethan's lack of heroic motives, his submission to private, neurotic drives, are what make him a true prototype for the schizophrenic hero. While still appearing to act as the Western hero is *supposed* to act, he is in fact the first completely schizoid protagonist in American movies. It's especially fitting that the character of Ethan should be played by John Wayne, who more than any other actor in movie history embodied the strong, silent nobility of the lone frontiersman. With *The Searchers*, the American hero became a psychopath, and yet — what was most intriguing of all — nothing had really changed.

If Wayne himself claimed the role of Ethan to be his personal favorite, presumably this was above all because it afforded him with a rare opportunity to *act*. But, besides being a fair bit more brooding, moody, and obsessive than his other roles, Ethan is to all intents and appearances the same Wayne persona that audiences had come to know so well. For years, *The Searchers* was taken by the majority of viewers as little more than a particularly dark entry in the ever-growing Wayne-Ford Western canon. It *is* possible (or at least once was) to watch the film with only a cursory, peripheral awareness of the lead character's psychotic tendencies, and to see Ethan as merely a more ruthless and unsympathetic version of the standard John Wayne figure. For this what he is. But *The Searchers* reveals the isolation, fragmentation, and self-loathing at the heart of the Western hero as created (primarily) by Wayne and Ford (though also Wayne and Hawks, Stewart and Mann, and so forth). In short, it reveals the schizophrenic nature of the whole American experience, of the national character. "How the West was won" might be rephrased "How the Other was kept at bay"— both being achieved by the same means, the systematic destruction of the Native American peoples.

As Ethan's shadow, his *Doppelgänger*, Scar acts out his repressed nature. This is overtly suggested in the movie by details such as both men speaking the other's language, and by matching shots of Ethan and Scar (at different times) standing over a submissive Debbie. Both men wish to "take her in," both wish to possess her physically, even though Scar acts where Ethan forbears. It is significant that, unlike what the standard revenge format would normally demand, it is not Ethan himself who kills Scar, but Debbie's half brother (and half-Indian at that), Marty. In fact, Ethan is not even present to witness it. There is no suggestion that Ethan is denied the pleasure of revenge, either. He seems primarily preoccupied with Debbie, and apparently it is enough that Scar die. Ethan does not need the satisfaction of killing him.*

Ethan's hatred of Scar is leavened by an awareness of their essential affinity, their sameness. Ethan does not hate Scar so much as what he stands for and, above all, what he has done. It is his acts that he reviles, above all because they reflect Ethan's own secret desires. Ethan's hatred of Scar for destroying what he held most sacred is mixed up with envy for not having done it himself, for not having had the *freedom* to do so. If Scar is wanton sexuality and unbridled savagery (absence of repression), Ethan is restrained desire. He is self-disciplined, but the fetters of civilization weigh heavy upon him. As such, neither man can exist without the other: without repression there can be no civilization, and without savagery (pure instinct), there is nothing to civilize, nothing to repress. As complementary forces, Ethan and Scar are equals on equal ground, and recognize one another as essentially complicit. They are both warriors, hunters, men of proud individuality. The key difference between them, besides the manner in which they treat dogs (Ethan is seen patting a dog and Scar throwing a stone at one), is that Scar (like Aaron) is a family man, ironically enough the one thing Ethan can never be. And what a bitter irony it is for Ethan to see that, for all the savagery of his soul, Scar has attained what he can only dream of: a sense of belonging.†

There can be little doubt with all this in mind that Ethan feels a deep and tormenting (because inadmissible to his conscience) envy for Scar and his lifestyle, especially since he can never knuckle down to being a house-husband

---

*Perhaps it is more to the point to say that Ford does not engender this need in the audience. Imagine in *The Patriot* if Mel Gibson's son had killed off the bad guy (as for one refreshing moment it seemed had happened), thereby denying the hero and villain their inevitable, hate-filled, blood-soaked standoff. The audience, likewise denied the visceral satisfaction of the blood thriller pay-off, would have been bewildered (and incensed) by such a letdown. The thirst for blood has by now become so deeply inculcated into modern audiences that they actively need to have it quenched.

†In fact, Scar has not one but multiple wives, hence families; not only does he have his squaws but he also has the abducted white woman — Ethan's secret desire — Debbie. The pagan implications of this are horrifying to Ethan's Christian conscience. Yet Ethan himself shows an affinity, or at least sympathy, for pagan rituals when he shoots out the Comanche warrior's eyes to curse his soul to wander the earth forever, never to enter into Comanche paradise. Obviously this is not the act of a Christian, and by putting stock in pagan belief (albeit for the sake of revenge), Ethan shows inherent respect for the Comanche culture (just as he does by learning their language). In the process, he reveals his own pagan soul.

himself (like his brother Aaron). The polygamous arrangements of Scar, in which the husband has many (non-clinging) wives who raise his many kids while he gets to hunt and fight the white man, must be painfully appealing to Ethan. Such an arrangement could only seem like the perfect solution, if only he were not blinded by social conditioning and crippled by repression. This is the essence of the schizophrenic experience: the battle between reason and atavism, between repression and instinct, civilization and savagery. What is remarkable about *The Searchers* is that it parallels the external, dramatic conflict (that of cowboys and Indians) with an internal, psychological conflict at the heart of its protagonist: Ethan's tormented psyche is seen to reflect, not just vaguely but *precisely*, the genocidal chaos taking place in the nation.

It is perhaps Ethan's begrudging, fiercely repressed envy of Scar, and of the uninhibited lifestyle he represents, that curbs his hatred and makes a classic stand-off between the two men unnecessary for the film's dramatic (as well as thematic) closure. At the last moment, Ethan turns away from his shadow, dimly aware that he cannot destroy it without becoming it (a step he is not prepared to make). This gentle note of redemption, or at the very least ambiguity, is what makes *The Searchers* such a profoundly responsible work, both for the genre and in its director's oeuvre. By doing away for the first (and practically last) time in action cinema with the convention of the hero-villain stand-off, by exposing and at least partially diagnosing the pathology of revenge — the confusion and torment behind acts of violence — *The Searchers* is a unique work of pathos and sobriety. It is also one of a half dozen key works that kick-started the American cinema of schizophrenia.

When the hero kills the villain in mythic fables, it is Cain killing Abel, Horus and Set, William Wilson and his double, Luke and Darth Vader, matter meeting anti-matter. What is suggested is an act not of destruction but of reconciliation. It is only at the point the Hero confronts, overcomes, and assimilates all that is "Other" within himself that he becomes whole; only so can he be healed. This is as far a cry from the action movie denouement (be it Western, war, crime, or whatever) — in which the gunslinger seeks revenge under the cloak of justice — as Ethan is from Rambo. The difference is that *The Searchers*, aware of this difference, points to the inadequacy of revenge as a surrogate for redemption. Ford's film is fully open about the fact that its hero is a schizoid in search of wholeness, and that killing his enemy will do nothing but increase his sense of fragmentation, by confirming and intensifying the difference between them. The murder act in myths is symbolic, not literal; its healing power depends on the hero's realization that the enemy to be slain is within himself. At the point he realizes his complicity with the villain, he is freed from the pressure of denial, the crippling burden of repression that is the true source of his anguish. There is no longer any *need* to kill the villain (though his death may still be required), since his power to torment the hero is cancelled by this realization. In a sense, they go from enemies to brothers, even (at an alchemical pinch) to *lovers*.

By the end of *The Searchers* (once he learns that Scar is dead, and chooses to embrace Debbie rather than kill her), Ethan does achieve some small degree of grace. This grace is what gives *The Searchers* whatever greatness it has as a movie. Ethan has learned enough to relinquish his hatred and his jealousy, to take Debbie in his arms (chastely) to protect her, and be the loving father that he always had it in him to be (if only for a moment). He has come to accept Debbie's existence outside his own selfish desire for her, his twisted, idealized image of her. By forsaking his anima-fixation and realizing that, however contaminated Debbie may be by her ordeal, he still loves her, Ethan is able to heal a terrible wound in his soul. But he knows it will take more than this to change his basic nature. Regardless of whether Scar is dead, the Other is alive and well, still out there, and will never let him rest. More dimly perhaps, he knows that the Other lives deep inside his cold and lonely heart, at the root of all his torments, that he will carry it with him wherever he goes, and that those he loves must be protected — not *by* him, but *from* him. For should he be foolish or weak enough to remain (as his heart longs for), it will only be a matter of time before his raging, unquenchable id will bring disaster upon them again.

The final, famous shot of the film has Ethan framed in the doorway of the family home, seen from the inside, the open desert behind him. He pauses for a moment, as if deliberating, then turns and slopes off into the desert; the

The wandering Hero. Ethan Edwards (John Wayne) disappears into the wasteland in *The Searchers* (1956, Warner Bros.).

3. Scars: The Hero as Psychopath

door closes and he is swallowed up in darkness. The image is one of the most poignant and eloquent in the history of movies, and sums up all the loneliness and longing of the Western hero. A man of violence cannot opt for peace, any more than a wild cat can live on daisies — without denying his very nature. He can respect it, admire it even, and fight to defend and uphold it. But he can never enjoy it.

Vertigo's Scottie Ferguson (James Stewart) is a man who has lost all heart. He is not merely the impotent male as hero but a closet schizophrenic and a failed suicide to boot. At the commencement of *Vertigo* (1958) — following the psychedelic nightmare spirals of the opening credits — Scottie is seen to be quite literally losing his grip. Following a brief rooftop chase, he is left hanging by his fingertips over a precipice, with neither the strength to pull himself to safety nor the abandon (the courage?) to let go.

The rooftop chase sequence (which *The Matrix* tellingly quoted for its opening sequence) ensures that *Vertigo* begins in motion, a motion (the swirling trance of vertigo) it sustains to the end. *Vertigo is* motion, be it that of pursuit or that of plummeting. The only stasis is unequivocally connected to stagnation or death (when the hero winds up catatonic, and the heroine splayed out on stone), and only at the end of the movie do movement and inertia meet, when the hero is paused on the edge of the abyss once more, swaying gently between madness and death. The way that motion is central to *Vertigo* is perhaps what makes it one of the most powerful and beloved motion pictures of all time. And yet, for all the hero's movements, he is only ever going in circles: spiraling to the center like a fly caught in the web of his own compulsion. This compulsion is poor, schizophrenic Scottie's will to death.

It's maybe superfluous to point out that vertigo is less a fear of heights than the fear of falling and, beyond even that, fear of *landing*. One cannot separate the stages (the one who jumps can't anyway), but I think it's safe to say that if man had wings, his fear of heights would quickly become a thing of the past. At the same time, not only birds and insects but also cats, and probably most animals, don't suffer from a fear of heights *except* when falling. Instincts being what they are, it is perhaps only through *fear itself* that an animal can fall, at least short of unforeseen accidents or divine intervention. We have all walked a narrow path over an abyss and noted how our balance is severely jeopardized by the act of looking down. We all suffer from vertigo, but if it is not part of our instinctive programming, it follows that it is only *conscious* awareness of painful death (that damn landing!) which causes this fear. And this, I believe, is linked to the suicidal impulse. It is our own fear and folly that precipitates us into the abyss.

Vertigo leaves Scottie Ferguson hanging over this abyss, looking down. It never bothers to save him, however, and we never see his deliverance (the only man seen to try, a policeman like Scottie, falls to his death while Scottie watches in guilt-racked horror). To all appearances, then Scottie is hanging for the rest of the film, making one possible interpretation of the narrative that it is Scottie's *unlived* life, flashing before his eyes as his fingers give way and the fall begins. Certainly Hitchcock's approach to the material would support this reading (a reading which is irrelevant, beyond its charm, to any further readings). Either way, Scottie never for a moment ceases to hang by his fingernails: the abyss is beneath him for the entirety of the film until the very end, by which time we have come full circle, and once again Scottie is teetering, now like a diver over a waterfall, working up the courage to dive. By this time, Scottie's final precipitation is inevitable: it is the nature of his compulsion to return to the edge, and in the end, gazing is not enough. If he has taken all this time to work his way to the abyss, then it is expressly in order to jump.

What precipitates Scottie into madness (as for so many) is the love of an unobtainable woman. A war rages within him between his fear and his desire for this obscure object. This war opens a split in his psyche (familiar to us all), through which demons enter. Scottie's self-hatred works secretly away at eroding all the finer promises of true love. He lives in a state of anxiety over the fact that he is a coward. His own weakness caused another man's death and the trauma has rendered him impotent. He cannot even climb a stepladder without reliving the terrible moment — terrible not because it led to the man's death but because it revealed Scottie's impotence, his inadequacy as a man. Like the cowardly lion, Scottie is basically a good sort who lacks courage. But though he appears to be seeking redemption, to regain his lost heart, he is in fact seeking the exact opposite. Since it is his weak heart that torments him and allows him no rest, he sets out to kill his heart. In the end, like the true obsessive, he is heroically fated to succeed.

As a schizophrenic in denial, Scottie is naturally and inevitably (as if by Fate) drawn to a schizophrenic mystery to investigate. An old college acquaintance, Gavin Elster, emerges from the past seeking Scottie's aid. An emissary from the unconscious, a trickster figure of basest intent, Elster is an omen of things to come. Scottie will be taken on a mystery journey into Wonderland, but it will all be fake. (He is taken not to Wonderland but to Disneyland, where all the sights and sounds, the magic, are simply meant to distract him and keep him from being "disillusioned.") Elster spins a dime-store novel yarn about his wife: that she is suffering from delusions of being taken over by an ancestor from her past, a beautiful woman whose torment led to her suicide. Like Scottie after her—works of fiction seeking a semblance of reality!—she is caught in an endlessly recurring spiral that leads to a single act; she relives her life over and over and each time it ends in suicide. The wheel of karma has become the hub of damnation.

No wonder Scottie buys this fairy tale hook, line and sinker: he is caught on the same wheel himself, and eager to get to the hub. Scottie's job is to follow Madeline (who believes she is Carlota, but is really just Judy, acting a role), to *go wherever she goes*, and this is quite literally (and fatally) what he does. She is the white rabbit that pops out the hole and drags Scottie (by the balls) down to the lower world. He is powerless to resist, all he can do is keep on her tail and make sure nothing happens to her. He has no idea that he is merely a pawn, and that a white rabbit is no lady, merely a ruse. Elster has designed his plan to engage Scottie as an unwittingly *false* witness: Elster intends to murder his wife and make it appear suicide. To do this he uses Scottie — the passive bystander with the fear of heights — knowing that he will be powerless to prevent the act or even to properly witness it. Scottie will testify to what he saw: Maddy going up the bell tower and a second later plummeting down. He won't see the switch, will never realize that another woman was murdered; he will not look at the body. (Even more improbably, no one will show him a photo of the real Madeleine during the investigation.) Scottie will remain in the dark for the majority of the movie, and all this time of unknowing, of being deceived, is time for his psychosis to advance, until it explodes into tragic action.

The Hero pursues the Heroine like a shadow, only from a safe distance. He becomes a stalker, passively spying on the object of his desire, until it grows into total obsession. From the very first, the "romance" exhibits schizophrenic qualities: passivity, distance, morbid fascination. Scottie is unconsciously seeking his anima, and the dreamlike sequences that take over the film are enactments of that human myth-drama *par excellence*— the longing of the soul for its mate. The dogged and tormented knight questing after the phantom lady in white, keeping ever out of sight; too shy to approach her, he yet pursues her, through art galleries and graveyards, an elusive vision of beauty and whispered promise of happiness. He repeatedly loses sight of her, but never for long, and each time she returns, his heart quickens; she haunts him, enslaves him, ensures (as she is paid to do) that he never shake the spell by which she holds him. He is caught in a snare and doesn't even know it.

These sequences are some of the loveliest and most hypnotic, the most purely cinematic, ever captured on film. They reveal Hitchcock's intentions as far outside the limits of the ordinary thriller, or even the psycho-thriller. Hitchcock is aiming for the quality of dream, of trance, and by so doing he is deftly suggesting the dissociation and growing psychosis of his protagonist. Scottie is drawn into the illusory melancholy of his assignment, and he quickly moves from being the stalker to the stalked. The fact that the heroine's elusiveness, her mystery and desirability, are all related to her melancholia, her being lost (which in turn relates to her insanity), is what makes Scottie's fascination so fatal. Many a man has fallen for the allure of the lost or fallen woman and made insane bids to save her (and so win her for himself), without ever paying for it with his life (or even his sanity). But Scottie is not so lucky. Heartbreak is not generally fatal, but it can be. *Vertigo* is one of those cases.

The schizophrenic obsession goes beyond mere romantic-sexual infatuation, however, because the schizophrenic obsesses not over the love object itself but rather its "fallen" nature. He seeks not so much to save the beloved as to damn himself *through* her. The fact that the heroine's mysterious allure is entirely based on *deception*, on false impressions (so characteristic of the schizophrenic experience), is what makes Scottie's falling in love a sublimated death wish. Yet Judy plays this part beyond the realistic capabilities of any actress, even one complicit with a murder plot. (Judy's performance goes way beyond Kim Novak's; for one thing she has to improvise; for another she doesn't get a second take.) There seems no doubt that Judy *becomes* Madeline, just as her Madeline gets lost in the memory-role of Carlota. All these layers of illusion exist in Scottie's mind; they are symbolic (symptomatic) of the mystery itself—the elusive, unknowable female as it recedes ever further out of his reach. From the start, Scottie is doomed by his predilection, his desire not merely to attain the unattainable (all quests come down to that), but rather to claim *what does not even exist*. Madeline is the concatenation of Scottie's own schizophrenic mind. When Judy-Madeline throws herself into the San Francisco bay, Scottie is there to save her: he does not hesitate for more than a heartbeat. But he merely saves the actress, who, aware of his presence all along, knew he would come to save her. This is not a feigned suicide attempt that is really a cry for attention; it is a subterfuge to ensnare Scottie into a murder plot. (Meanings abound: suicide is sublimated impulse to murder; murder is the last resort of failed suicides.)

Had Scottie turned away, or simply sat down and watched idly from a safe distance (as he has done until now), Judy would have been forced to save herself and Scottie would have perceived the truth (though Judy's wiles and Scottie's gullibility make a powerful combination for deception, so that's debatable). In true schizophrenic fashion, Scottie is passive when he needs to act and acts when he should stay put. Like any man whose brains have been scrambled by sexual infatuation, only more so, Scottie can only act compulsively. He gets into trouble no matter what he does or doesn't do. His first act is to take the unconscious heroine home, lay her on his bed, and take her clothes off! *Vertigo* must have been, at the time of its release, the only American movie in which the hero undresses the heroine before they have even formally met. Beyond any doubt, this is the real beginning of Scottie's obsession. Scottie is allowed to lay eyes and hands upon his naked desire, to have it in front of him for the taking, and yet be forbidden (and not just by movie codes) to act. And since Judy is acting a role, it seems likely she is feigning unconsciousness and is fully awake the whole time Scottie undresses her and puts her into bed. This only adds a further layer of perversity to their budding relationship, as it moves inevitably from physical infatuation to sexual intoxication. Scottie is not merely ensnared, he is poisoned. Yet his pathetic need to sustain the illusion of being

3. Scars: The Hero as Psychopath

Scottie (James Stewart) falls under the spell of the *anima* (Kim Novak) in *Vertigo* (1958, Paramount).

the hero (his conscious motivation at this time) once again renders him impotent. Instead of allowing himself to be seduced by the wiles of the lying female (so canceling her spell and ending her dominance), he remains "strong," intent on saving the person who is herself intent on destroying him. And so the evil scheme (of which they are both now part) begins to unfold.

Of course, nothing is ever so simple, and the best-laid plans of monomaniacs (Elster's two-bit schemer with a genius for psychology) never seem to take into account the weirdness of the human heart and its capacity to snarl things up. Scottie and Madeline (and Judy) fall madly in love, despite or perhaps because of the deception. Naturally, their love is doomed, since both fall in love with illusions. Scottie believes he is falling in love with Madeline, who is herself no more than a role out of a pulp novel. Judy falls in love with Scottie even though he is, or must appear to her, a complete dupe. Hence she falls in love with a Scottie who is operating entirely under false assumptions (about her), a Scottie who is kind and fatherly, who wants only to save her (though in fact he is ensuring the real Madeline be murdered). In every way, since he is unaware of her deception, or even of who she really is, Scottie is in an inferior position to Judy. Of course, Scottie is counting on getting to fuck Madeline once he has saved her, so his motives are hardly pure; this is why the missed opportunity of sex between them is so crucial. Once Scottie's sexual needs had actually been met, even if only momentarily, his head would have cleared, his obsession dwindled, and he would have gotten the truth out of Judy. Only by keeping him in the inferior role can the deception be maintained.

In his own way, Scottie is deceiving Judy too. From the moment he sees her naked, it is possible he sees through the whole façade but is too enamored of the illusion to give it up; if so, he feigns ignorance. From this moment on, he is really only thinking of one thing, and it isn't Madeline's soul. Like all romantic obsessions founded on deception (where egotism disguises itself as altruism), Scottie and Maddy's romance is doomed to failure, and finally to tragedy. The tragedy kicks in when the deception is allowed to continue even after the romantic illusion has been destroyed. Even after her "death," Scottie is allowed to go on believing in Maddy's goodness — and her madness. This is bad enough, but add to it the fact that he believes she died due to his own weakness and inadequacy and, under such a hideous weight, it seems that Scottie will never be a fully functioning human again. Undone by his character flaws, he has been cut down and trampled underfoot by the horses of love and lust. Nothing short of a miracle could bring him back to himself.

Until this point, *Vertigo* has kept its schizophrenic subtext occulted, and remains, though by far the most mesmerizing, melancholic work of the genre, a more or less traditional mystery thriller. From the first shots of a catatonically traumatized Scottie sat in a rest home "listening" to Mozart, however (he sees and hears nothing outside his own internal anguish), the movie veers off into wholly unmapped terrain: the chaotic terrain of schizophrenia. How many movies (at that time or since) have depicted their ostensible hero in a state of total despair and impotence? The normal thing at this point would be to show the hero in a bar, unshaven, getting drunk, drowning in self-pity and self-hatred, before some clue falls into his path and he regains the momentum of the quest. Instead, Hitchcock allows Scottie to wallow and fester in his melancholy for an unspecified period of time; he shows him to have well and truly given up the chase, to be defeated by the harsh reality of his inadequacy and succumbed to (or taken refuge in) the passivity and misery of schizophrenia. Nor are we given to understand that Scottie actively "recovers," only that, over time, he gets his wits sufficiently together to climb out of his easy chair and put the pieces of his life back together (at least to the point of changing his underwear and fixing his dinner). During this time, Barbara Bel Geddes' Mitch has taken care of him. Mitch represents the earthy, dependable female, the real flesh-and-blood woman who loves Scottie selflessly (they were formerly engaged

3. Scars: The Hero as Psychopath

but Mitch broke it off). Consequently she is of no interest to him. Her availability to Scottie, and her resulting undesirability to him, offers further proof of Scottie's self-destructive need to chase phantoms.

In any case, were it not for the perverse whims of Fate, we might reasonably assume Scottie would have settled into a bitter, melancholic life (perhaps even with Mitch), and so passed the remainder of his days content in his ignorance. He would never have known that the woman he thought he loved and lost not only never died, but never existed to begin with. Instead, he runs into Judy. There's more to this than mere chance: since Judy is still in love with Scottie she chooses to stay close by him, for the chance of seeing him again. Scottie doesn't recognize her, of course, but he is struck by the resemblance, and once again is fascinated by her beauty, and begins to obsess all over again. Since he believes Judy is a completely different person to Madeline, he believes that he has been given a second chance. In a way he has, but since he is once again blind to the truth (proving that for all his traumas he has learned nothing), he proceeds to repeat the same mistakes all over again.

Essentially *Vertigo* deals with the schizoid experience as it relates to "romantic love," i.e., sexual obsession, the desire of the fragmented psyche to find completeness outside of itself in a perfect opposite match, a sexual partner. To this extent at least, we are all practicing schizophrenics, caught up in the great lie of romantic love, the lie that places happiness and completeness outside of ourselves. Obviously no amount of companionship, no single human being, no matter how deep and lasting our connection to them, can fill the void within us. When we are seeking a *match*, seeking the equivalent of our own selves in the opposite sex, we can only perceive the differences, the ways in which the object of our desire fails to match up. Scottie first begins chasing phantoms out of an unconscious drive to find the part of himself that will give him wholeness, that will allow him to feel alive again. He is seeking to rediscover his strength and his courage, his *heart*. He has become aware of this need only by being forced to confront his inadequacy, his desperate lack of a will to live. It is only natural that such a realization lead him on a quest for wholeness, for integration of his psyche, his heart, and his mind. It is also perhaps inevitable that he be drawn towards the mysterious female as the image of everything that he is not. Woman, as the embodiment of male desire, is what gives a man courage, what makes his heart beat with renewed vigor. The fact that Scottie is unconsciously (by "sheer chance") drawn to the mysterious case of this ghostly female, a female who is lost in the past and lost to herself, shows that he is dimly aware of the true nature of his desire. He is seeking not sexual satisfaction but spiritual communion; for a time, he even seems to be finding it.

The time Scottie spends with Madeline — after he "saves" her and before she "dies" — most especially their trip to the forest where they gaze at the concentric circles of the cutaway tree trunk and Scottie glimpses his place in eternity — is about as close as Scottie gets to happiness, to the truth about himself, and to self-knowledge. For a brief moment, he and Maddy are united, not just physically but spiritually, in the shared understanding of their mortality, their insignificance. They are ghosts in search of solidity, strangers in eternity, meeting briefly, just long enough to find themselves for an instant, in love. But Judy and Scottie are both too greedy to be satisfied with a mere moment, and so they play out the deception all the way to its inevitable, tragic denouement.

When Scottie begins to remold Judy in the image of Madeline, she complies. Most of all it is out of a conscious desire not to lose him; but also perhaps from her unconscious knowledge that this is no more than she deserves after her own selfish manipulations. Judy is allowing herself to be dominated by Scottie where once she was the dominant one. For his part, Scottie is taking unconscious revenge upon Judy, and it is in these sequences that he becomes openly psychotic. He is a pathetic figure, desperately struggling to reassemble his shattered illusion, to recreate a dead woman using the components of the living — a fitting revenge indeed, for this is exactly the nightmare situation which Judy acted out for Scottie in her role of Madeline! In the process of enacting his revenge, Scottie is busy reducing the flesh-and-blood Judy, once again, to the pale ghost Maddy.

Hitchcock remarked how, essentially, Scottie becomes a necrophiliac, desiring to have sex with a dead woman; but although this adequately exposes the perversity and dementia of Hitchcock's hero, it is far too simplistic a description of Scottie's behavior. Scottie is not trying to fuck a dead woman, he is trying to breathe life into his fantasy, to project the longing of his tormented psyche onto a living person, even if he must destroy her to do so. It is the classic quest for the anima, mixed up fatally with fear of the Other. The Other is a close cousin to the anima, for both concepts relate to the dark side of the psyche, internally speaking, and to the opposite sex when manifested externally. With the anima, the paradox of the Other — as what is both feared and desired — becomes clear. Scottie wishes Judy to become Maddy, the idealized female: both phantom and human, unattainable spirit and irresistible flesh combined. Since he was never able to *possess* Madeline before she was taken from him (despite ample opportunity), he is haunted and tormented by regret, by the desire for a second chance. But Scottie never dared let himself be seduced by Maddy above all because of her terrible, unfathomable *otherness*. She was never really his, and so he never really lost her, only his fantasy of having her. This is the fantasy he wastes no time resurrecting.

Judy, on the other hand, belongs to Scottie, body and soul, from the first moment he sees her. Although so far as Scottie knows, they never met before, Judy has been hopelessly in love with Scottie for who knows how many lonely, anguished months (while Scottie has been pining for ghosts). As a result (and as with Mitch), Scottie has no real interest in Judy except as a passive object whom he can mold and shape into the image of his desire. This image is effectively his own creation, his own *self*. At this point, romantic obsession comes clean and reveals itself as runaway egotism. Scottie couldn't care less about Judy; he is only interested in satisfying his own longing. *Vertigo* illustrates, better than probably any movie ever made, the underlying, destructive nature of romantic love, making it one of the dozen or so most enduring and profound movie texts in existence. But the film goes beyond a mere denunciation of romantic desire into more bewildering terrain — that of exposing the schizophrenic impulse that lies beneath the ego-drive to destruction.

Scottie, like every other fractured soul on the planet, desires communion with the Other. Like the rest of us, he is tormented by the rift in his psyche, by the strangeness, unfamiliarity, and sheer panic which this Other invokes in him. As a result, he seeks ways and means to make it familiar, non-threatening, controllable; he seeks to dominate it. He desires to possess the anima, but he is compelled by his own fear to first strip it of its otherness. In order to possess it, he must first destroy it. And so he is left with nothing. Scottie successfully turns Judy back into Madeline, but rather than resurrecting Maddy (which he can never do), he merely eradicates all traces of Judy, denying her her true nature. At this point, Scottie has successfully reduced her to a mere actress again, only this time at *his* command, his creation to do with as he will. Does he finally possess her, now he has made her into his likeness? We never find out, since this is also the moment that — as a result of Judy's all-too-Freudian slip of wearing a necklace that belonged to Madeline — Scottie realizes the truth and his perfectly assembled fantasy crumbles to dust, in the blink of an eye. Presumably, this was Scottie's unconscious intent all along: to expose Judy, by forcing her to go through the same process of transformation-deception as before. Into the bargain, he also exposes his own fantasy (to himself): that his beloved female dream-anima is a false and lying thing, a betrayal of all he longed for. Both Scottie and Judy are exposed in this moment, utterly and irrevocably. Love dies.

What had been theirs (for one brief moment among the trees) was the love of soul mates. This love was reduced to mere sexual obsession and, as a result, finally exposed as out-and-out hatred. At which point, Scottie can only, tragically, see his madness through, complete his work of revenge upon the lying female, and bring about Judy's death. The alternative would mean admitting to himself his own complicity in the betrayal and deception, thereby acknowledging the schizophrenia behind every last one of his acts. This, plainly, he is too far gone to do. Once denial and fragmentation have reached a certain point, they attain a momentum of their own, and any attempt at facing the truth, of putting the pieces together again, is futile. Hence total schizophrenia (madness or death) is the only conceivable result. This is where *Vertigo* leaves off, with Scottie on the brink.

This time he makes it up the bell tower, dragging Judy along with him. As a result — though he proves his own potency, once again acting when he might better have remained passive — Judy falls to her death. It seems debatable, and also perhaps irrelevant, whether Scottie takes the plunge this time. Either way he is a broken man. He has freed himself from fear, but at what price? What does Scottie have to live for? If he is finally cured of his vertigo, it is perhaps only and wholly in order to jump. Death ends all traumas.

Vertigo is a work of unparalleled bleakness, melancholy and despair. It is a profoundly affecting work, and yet also an oddly cold one. It was not a great success with audiences at the time, and its director, Alfred Hitchcock (who tended to judge all his works by the public's reaction to them), considered the film one of his failures. Since then it has assumed classic status and remains a watershed in American cinema, one of the very first truly "modern" American movies. Of course by "modern" (since all movies are by definition that) what I really mean is *post*modern. Or schizophrenic.*

Vertigo can be accused of being many things, from over-ponderous to slow and stolid to outright tedious. It's a movie that has to be succumbed to be appreciated. Like hypnotism, it depends on establishing trance to achieve its effects. Of Hitchcock's films, *Vertigo* is not merely the most personal, but the only one which can really be called personal at all. Hitchcock never put much heart into his movies, probably because he didn't feel his heart belonged there. Movies were games to him, and though he took his games desperately seriously, the bottom line of all his work was always the question of *audience response*. To have one eye on the audience while creating an art work may not necessarily be cynicism, but it involves a degree of calculation that precludes heartfeltness or abandon. Though Hitchcock understood the implications of his protagonist's obsession in *Vertigo*— the folly and the tragedy of his actions — it seems doubtful he fully empathized with them. Hitchcock was, after all, making a suspense thriller, and what makes *Vertigo* unique in the Hitchcock oeuvre is that, for once, the themes came to dominate the story. Also uniquely, these themes were tied into an emotional subtext, or undercurrent, that Hitchcock almost certainly did relate to. (He was a sexually obsessed male himself, by most accounts.) But I think Hitch held back at least half of the time (which still gives *Vertigo* twice as much heart as his other movies) and, as a result, it's

---

*For whatever reasons, 1958, the year of *Vertigo*, was something of a watershed year. *Touch of Evil* ended the noir cycle; *Left-Handed Gun* introduced the existential Western; and *Vertigo* gave us our very first unequivocally psychotic hero. All of these were early expressions of the schizophrenic cinema as it approached adulthood. In the UK, Hammer studios began its hugely influential cycle of garish, blood-soaked horror movies with *Horror of Dracula* and *The Curse of Frankenstein*— the id's return in triumphant Technicolor.

3. Scars: The Hero as Psychopath

a movie that leaves some people completely cold. Scottie is not an easy protagonist to identify with, not because he is so far from us but because he is so far from how we want to see ourselves. If Scottie Ferguson is the first fully realistic movie hero in modern American cinema, it is because he is the first unmistakably schizophrenic personality to function as the protagonist in an otherwise "standard" genre movie.

Although it was *Psycho* which got the credit for proving that American movies (especially the horror movie) were growing up, *Vertigo* is by far the greater work, the more mature one. In actual fact, Scottie can be seen to anticipate Norman Bates in several crucial ways, but we will get to that later; between *Vertigo* and *Psycho* came *North by Northwest*, and if *Vertigo* is Hitchcock's greatest work, *North by Northwest* is probably his most enjoyable. Less a thriller and more a blissed-out comedy of paranoia (an early, *early* forerunner for the Yuppie Deconstruction movie of the 1980s), *North by Northwest* is a movie Hitch could put everything into, being nothing *but* games. In the movie, Roger Thornhill (Cary Grant) is a businessman who is mistaken for a CIA agent and hurled into the kind of intrigue (and absurdity) that is Hitchcock's idea of character building. This was Hitch letting off steam, flexing his muscles between the schizophrenic angst of *Vertigo* and the gothic gloom of *Psycho*. And yet, sunny and superficial as it is, *North by Northwest* retains some of the same underlying anxiety — above all the crisis of identity — that characterizes the other two films.

The twist to the situation in which Thornhill finds himself is that he has been mistaken for an agent who does not exist, who was invented by the CIA as a red herring to distract the enemy's attention, while the real agent (blonde beauty Eva Marie Saint) can work from the inside. Thornhill fills the empty shoes of the phantom agent and effectively becomes him, despite all his efforts to the contrary. (By trying to locate the real agent, for example, he winds up in his hotel room, and even wearing his clothes.) Thornhill falls in love with the real agent and, since he has put her in jeopardy with his bungling, is forced into ingenious and courageous action by which to prove himself to her. Naturally he turns out be a good spy after all. He saves the heroine and — despite the deception on which their relationship began — marries her. This is the happy ending Scottie never got, the reverse image of *Vertigo*, in which the hero comes through the schizophrenic experience whole and finds himself again. By navigating his way through the maze of illusion, he overcomes his loss of identity and wins himself a sex object into the bargain.

After this temporary respite, *Psycho* plunged audiences back into the abyss, this time all the way. If Norman Bates (in the absence of anything besides John Gavin as a hero) is the real protagonist of *Psycho*, then his relationship with the heroine Marion Crane — whom he murders — and his non-existent mother (the anima figure who takes him over entirely in the end) can be seen as a direct, though extreme, development of Scottie's relationship with Madeline/Judy in *Vertigo*. Norman is a textbook schizophrenic, and the severest weakness of *Psycho* is the manner in which it reduces its carefully established, macabre fatalism to mere psychological platitudes. The explanation of the final scene may be convincing enough on its own terms, but it adds nothing to the movie either in power or depth, and only deprives us the opportunity of figuring it out for ourselves. (It effectively robs the movie of its subtext by putting it all on the surface.) *Psycho* is not a great work (it's half a great work, half a banal one), but it is certainly a key one, and not only in the horror genre. Bates is an archetypal figure of the period, and if he is also part stereotype, then this is due, once again, to the film's falling back on the conventional psychology of the day.

What *really* drives Norman is never touched upon by this hand-me-down psycho-dribble. But it is hinted at by Hitchcock's brooding camera, the loaded dialogue, the symbolism of the stuffed birds, the shower drain, the swamp, and so forth. What makes the expositional scenes of *Psycho*'s second half so dreary (and bewildering) is that Hitchcock has worked so hard during the first hour to establish a surrealist, metaphysical feel to his American gothic, and then he willfully throws it all away. In any case, the film's weaknesses are less relevant here than the manner in which it brought clinical insanity to the mainstream. Certainly, without the "pedigree" which it displayed in its final scene, though it would certainly have been a better movie, it's doubtful if it would have received the serious attention it did, or become so "respectable" a work so quickly.

Psycho introduced the notion to the American public of psychosis as something lurking beneath the most innocuous of facades. It helped consolidate the idea that the boy next door — who seemed so shy and considerate — might just turn out to be a homicidal maniac.* Appearances were deceiving. Before Norman, there was the true-life case of grave-robber and murderer Ed Gein, apprehended in 1957 in Wisconsin, who spent the rest of his life in a mental hospital. Gein was hardly anyone's idea of a white-bread American youth, however.

Gein's grew up in a desolate location which he left only to go to school, His mother, Augusta, was a fiercely moralistic Lutheran; determined to keep her two sons isolated, she indoctrinated them with a fanatical distrust of the world, and specifically of women (every last one of whom she denounced as prostitutes). Every afternoon, she read to the boys from the Bible, favoring Old Testament passages relating to divine retribution. She verbally abused her sons, and insisted they were destined to become failures like their father, George.

---

*Six years after *Psycho*, in 1966, Charles Whitman climbed a water tower on the Texas University campus one day and began firing randomly on the crowd. It was Whitman who pretty much single-handedly introduced the idea of the psycho-next-door to the world.

George died of a heart attack in 1940, and shortly after, Ed's brother died in a fire. Ed lived alone with his mother until she died in 1945, whereupon Gein lived alone on the farm, supporting himself with odd jobs. He closed off the rooms mostly used by his mother, the upstairs floor, and downstairs living room. Gein developed a fascination for death-cult magazines and adventure stories, and began to make nightly visits to the graveyard. In 1957, police found a headless female corpse on Gein's property; it was hung upside down with ropes. The ribcage was wide open and the body stripped like that of a deer. Human skulls were found mounted upon the corner posts of Gein's bed, and lampshades made from human skin. Skin from the face of Mary Hogan, a local tavern owner, was found in a paper bag, as well as a window shade pull made up of human lips, a vest crafted from the skin of a woman's torso, a belt made from several human nipples, socks made from human flesh, a sheath made from human skin, and a box of preserved vulvas which Gein admitted to wearing. Subjected to questioning, Gein eventually admitted to digging up graves of recently buried women, all of whom were middle-aged (women Gein said resembled his mother). He took the bodies home and tanned their skin to make his trophies. During interrogation, Gein also admitted to killing Mary Hogan, who had been missing since 1954. According to the psychiatric reports, shortly after his mother's death, Gein decided he wanted a sex change and created a "woman suit" to this end. After his arrest Gein was found "mentally incompetent" and considered unfit to stand trial.

Scratch the surface of American society and underneath was a seething mass of pathological impulses just waiting to come out. Norman Bates was a far cry from Scottie Ferguson as the active hero, or even protagonist, of a movie; but he certainly was sympathetic, a fact that made *Psycho* all-but unprecedented in the American horror genre. Certainly the movie monster — be he King Kong or Frankenstein's creation — was entitled to our sympathy; but Norman was plainly no monster, and he had no such convenient excuses for his behavior as King Kong and the others. Until now, the psycho-killer had rarely played so central a role in the movies; mostly he had been little more than a heavy (Robert Mitchum, for example, in *Night of the Hunter* and *Cape Fear*). The point of this heavy, this bogeyman (as he would become known years later, with *Halloween* and its spin-offs), was that he was "pure evil"—we didn't expect or desire to understand him, much less sympathize. He was simply the means by which the other characters were put in peril, to be disposed of as soon as he outlived his purpose. There was never any question of what motivated him, it being generally as simple as monetary gain, power, or sheer sadism. *Psycho* took the almost childlike irresponsibility of King Kong and Frankenstein's monster and attributed it to the erstwhile villain, thereby turning him into something else. Norman Bates couldn't help himself— he *wasn't* himself when he committed his acts, and though he was certainly accountable for them, he wasn't responsible. The film introduced the idea of evil as sickness, not merely character bent or predilection. Like Mary Shelly's monster (who was articulate in the novel as he never could be on the screen), it was misery that made Norman a fiend.

In his own way, Scottie Ferguson murdered Judy as surely as Norman murdered Marion Crane, and for similar reasons. Both were tormented by images to the point of acting blindly, irresponsibly, outside themselves; and both were equally horrified by the consequences. Ironically, Norman survives better (at least at first) for the simple reason that his schizophrenia is so far gone that he really *doesn't* know he is responsible for Marion's death. Scottie can push the horrible truth of his responsibility away all he wants to, but deep down he knows the score, which is how we know he is doomed. Norman, on the other hand, has the dubious luxury of taking refuge in oblivion. He believes that his mother is alive and that she is capable of murdering to protect her baby boy (above all from the sin of lust).

Like Scottie, Norman has externalized his anima and projected it (this time literally) onto a corpse. This corpse, stuffed and kept in circulation by Norman's own hand, is then animated by his runaway id. Apparently Norman's mother played such a dominant (and malevolent) role in his childhood that he was literally possessed by her, and haunted by her ghost after she died. His mother became the only image of the female — the Other — that he could conceive of or tolerate in his life. (Whether Mrs. Bates deliberately intended this is irrelevant.) Her oppression of Norman's sexual instincts and of his sexual identity was so profound that it allowed no room for his psyche to develop in. He remained a little boy, and when his mother died he was forced to keep her alive — not only in his head but in his life — as the only means to keep his sexuality under wraps. By now, it would have become terrifying to him.

As long as his mother remained alive and in control, Norman need never grow up. He had the most treasured luxury of the schizophrenic — irresponsibility. In Norman's safe, secluded, schizophrenic world, there is no Other and there is no anima. There is only mother and child in eternal, loving congress — or, as invariably happens, mortal combat. But although Norman's psychosis causes him endless suffering, he is able to blame it all on his mother and so remain content and secure in his misery. He doesn't have to look at the fiend he has become, for in his world there are no mirrors, no reflecting surfaces, everything — from his mother to his birds — is a creation of his own hands and mind. They are all his familiars.

It's no wonder that Norman reacts with such barely concealed contempt to Marion's innocent suggestion that Mrs. Bates be sent away to a home. "I meant well," Marion says contritely. "People always mean well!" snaps Norman. His psychosis is finally beginning to show, and the words reveal suspicion, fear, and hostility for the outside world, a pathological refusal to allow it to encroach upon his fantasy life. The thought of losing his mother forces Norman to consider, even if only for an instant, the idea of being alone with his own self, and of assuming responsibility for his actions. Norman believes he is taking care of his mother when in fact he is taking refuge *in* her. Marion represents Norman's temptress and seducer. She threatens to awaken the repressed desires that he has worked so hard to keep in check. By giving in to these desires, Norman senses he would be set free from his misery and bondage, casting out the spirit of his mother. This would potentially begin the process of healing his damaged psyche. What's tragic is that not for a moment does Marion betray the slightest sexual interest in Norman: she is as unattainable to him as all women must be. (No woman could be attracted to him save through pity.) And yet, the mere presence of desire in Norman is enough to set alarms bells ringing in his head. By awakening Norman's libido, Marion threatens to tear down the illusion of his infantile nature, his irresponsibility, and to challenge the authority of "mother" (which she does directly). So she becomes the embodiment of all which he denies in himself; in a word, the Other. (Above all, what Norman sees in Marion is wanton sexuality; the fact that Marion is a thief and not a seductress is part of the ironic game of morals that Hitchcock plays throughout the movie.)

It is at this point that it becomes necessary for Norman to destroy Marion, to dispose of the evidence with impeccable thoroughness, and allow the black swamp to swallow it all (white car, suitcase, newspaper and stolen money). The swamp signifies the unconscious mind; the forces of repression reign supreme. Sex repressed must come out willy-nilly, and since it is such a powerful (creative) force, it almost invariably comes out as violence: wanton, irrational violence, as often as not aimed at the object of sexual desire that awoke the forbidden impulse in the first place. All this is basic, textbook stuff, and *Psycho* diagnosed the American nation (on the very brink of the assassinations and the Vietnam war) as suffering from a chronic and crippling mother complex, a case of terminal repression that could only lead to explosive results.

Family values do not enter much into Hitchcock's films. Of these three, only in *North by Northwest* is the idea of marriage allowed, as the cherry on top of a great big, gooey meringue. In *Vertigo*, Scottie appears to be an incurable bachelor who drifts through life without roots or ties, the perfect patsy for Elster's twisted plan. The only hint of a family or matrimonial life in the film relates to the tragic past of Carlotta, driven to suicide by her miseries. By the film's end, Scottie has dragged his true love to the bell tower, not to marry her but to hurl her to her death.*

---

*Admittedly his intentions are unclear at this time, and at worst he only drives her to suicide. In this he is aided by a phantom-like nun, dressed in white, who appears at a crucial moment and panics Judy, causing her to fall. The nun herself suggests the denial of sexuality and motherhood.

In *Psycho*, Marion Crane is stuck in an illicit relationship with Sam, who is still tied to his ex-wife by alimony payments, making marriage between the lovers impossible. It is this desire for legitimacy, in fact, that drives Marion to commit the fatal act of theft that leads to her death. She flees the scene and goes driving through the darkness and rainfall to be reunited with Sam, strays from the main road and winds up at the Bates motel. The heroine of *Psycho* is not herself psychologically disturbed, however (she is in fact one of Hitchcock's many capable and resourceful female characters). But she nonetheless acts compulsively, out of frustration and desperation, and so sets in motion the events that lead to her death. Her bid for freedom (both sexual and financial) is selfishly motivated; through it she sets herself at odds with the world (once on the run, she becomes at once suspicious, hostile and impatient); more importantly, she becomes prey to her conscience. It is both ironic and fitting that the psychotic mommy's boy Norman — with a morality so rigid it is pathological — is the person who awakens Marion's conscience. By speaking of "personal traps," he inadvertently inspires her to turn back and undo the damage she has done. But by now it is too late: by failing to act immediately on her decision, Marion fails to perceive the urgency of her situation. Her conscience has been awoken, but so has Norman's repressed libido. Marion will become prey to both.

The psychological intimacy — the bond — created between Marion and Norman (whose very names reflect one another) is profound, and can only be consummated through violence. Norman, being a victim himself, is compelled to victimize others; Marion, having chosen the role of the hunted, naturally assumes the role of prey. And in all this the specter of the family, like the allure of sex, is no more than a fragile dream for Marion, a freakish nightmare for Norman. Marion becomes a victim because of her unwitting complicity — not as a harlot but as a thief — in Norman's dementia.

It is interesting to compare all this with the schizophrenic females of Roman Polanski's movies a few years later, most specifically *Repulsion* and *Rosemary's Baby* (though *Knife in the Water* and *Cul-de-Sac* are also part of the pattern). In *Repulsion*, Carol is every bit as oppressed by the licentiousness she perceives around her as Norman. Like Norman, something in her childhood has given her a deep-seated loathing of sex, causing her to fiercely repress her own desires and needs, disconnecting not only from her nature but also from the world at large. Carol, like Norman, is a textbook schizo, and *Repulsion* (which bears some superficial resemblances to *Psycho*) is a grisly, joyless film that nonetheless works its effects ruthlessly and remains one of the most complete depictions of schizophrenic breakdown which the movies have given us. (Polanski's later *The Tenant* is infinitely more enjoyable an experience, however.) The common thread that runs through these movies is that of repression of sexuality leading to disconnection and fragmentation, schizophrenia, psychosis, and eventually murder.

3. Scars: The Hero as Psychopath

Rosemary's Baby is a definite deviation of the theme, being a supernatural horror story in which the heroine only *appears* crazy but is, in actual fact, the victim of a satanic conspiracy. Nor does Rosemary ever commit any acts of violence (though she does pick up a kitchen knife at the end): she is from the start seen as a healthy woman with normal sexual appetites, adequately expressed. Even so, the movie ties in with (and ties up in a blood red, satanic ribbon) all these other movies by linking up the source of schizophrenia, of breakdown, with the family itself. By repressing the truth of sexuality, the Woodhouse family literally becomes a lair for Satan, the feeding ground for demons.* The same could be said of the Bates home, clearly. The family is the immediate stand-in for society, the microcosm of the Western world, which bases its existence on matrimonial values, licensed procreation, child-rearing, and sexual repression. It is here, under precisely controlled conditions, that schizophrenia reaches full expression.

---

*In this case it is the husband, Guy, lying to Rosemary and making a deal with the devil, who is the agent of repression, though Rosemary is also complicit in the lie, having married Guy in the first place.

4

Weeping Alone: The Counterculture Fails to Communicate

The Searchers and *Vertigo* (and to a lesser extent *Psycho*) were harbingers of the schizophrenic experience. They were forerunners, and it is this that makes them great (or at least lasting) works in American cinema. It would be ten years or more before American movies were dealing with social (and individual) breakdown in anything like so unflinching a fashion, and twenty years before *Taxi Driver* finally diagnosed the American hero as a runaway psychopath. The symptoms were as yet unobservable to the untrained eye, but little by little, over the 1960s and the early 1970s, the angst-ridden teens of James Dean became the disconnected sociopaths of *Bonnie and Clyde*, and finally the schizo killers of *Badlands*. This process of transmutation (or derangement) made invaluable use of the 1960s counterculture movement, through which the rebel found himself a cause, became a flower child, a freedom fighter, and finally a homicidal maniac with no more need for causes than a great white shark.

James Dean was the oversensitive youth whose parents and peers (with one or two exceptions) simply could not understand his suffering. He wasn't rebelling so much as *emoting*—expressing his pain and confusion and alienation. This inability to connect to the world was beyond doubt the earliest, mildest symptom of schizophrenia (as it would soon become known). Yet James Dean's troubled youth wasn't "sick"; he wasn't psychotic, and if he was disconnected and disturbed it was only because he found nothing to connect to and a whole lot to be disturbed about. He *felt* more deeply than other people, and as a consequence he was baffled and confounded (and tormented) by the heartless, soulless world he was stuck in. His parents didn't understand because they *couldn't* understand: they were unable to feel or perceive the things that he was undergoing because they were blinded and numbed by the world. James Dean's saintly qualities related to the kind of schizophrenia that had fascinated Dostoyevsky when he wrote *The Idiot*. There was a purity and sensitivity that made

4. Weeping Alone: The Counterculture Fails to Communicate

both Prince Myshkin and Dean, on the one hand so endearing, so heart breaking, and on the other, so ultimately unfit to function in the world. Above all, it was their innocence that made them so easily exploited, and so tormented.

By the time of Paul Newman and *Hud* (1963), the schizo-saint had become something of a cad. If he was a fair deal less endearing, he was also a damn sight more wised up; no longer wounded by the world, he was world-weary and jaded instead, and quite capable of taking care of himself. By the time of *Cool Hand Luke* (1967), the misunderstood kid had become a full-fledged criminal, albeit a childlike, mischievous one. Having regained a little of his divine folly, he was once again seen as too "pure" to live — a martyr. *Hud* is an impressive work that captured the spirit of the times admirably, with Paul Newman's portrayal of the callow, lusty ranch hand in a dilapidated modern West (Texas) a career high. *Cool Hand Luke*, just five years later, was a new low — a crock.

In *Hud*, the title character is given blood for his veins and a heart in his chest; he is given real yearnings and failings, and the movie attempts, at least part of the time, to do justice to its creation. In *Cool Hand Luke*, the title character has been created — or contrived — crassly and cynically, for purely commercial reasons. He is a clotheshorse for any up-to-the-minute countercultural, anti-establishment ideas that the moviemakers can hang on him. He is also Paul Newman: smug, fey, cocky, and deeply troubled but too manly to show it. His shit-eating grin is that of a movie star who has stumbled on to the perfect vanity piece. The problem with *Cool Hand Luke* is that it is supposed to be about Luke, but it wants to be about individual freedom, purity and corruption, the futility of revolt, the failure to communicate, and so forth. And by pugnaciously communicating all these "important" ideas, it fails to leave room for its lead character to come alive in. The plot doesn't grow out of the characters here, the characters are built to fit the message; as such, there is absolutely no depth to Luke, making him a sorry schizophrenic hero indeed.

Even so, the film remains integral to the development of this hero, largely I think for the following reason: the failures of *Cool Hand Luke* cannot be laid at the filmmakers' door alone, but that of the entire counterculture for swallowing this crap. The film's weaknesses — its glib, self-satisfied air, its willingness to provide pat answers and pass them off as genuine wisdom, to diagnose false problems and then provide an equally false cure — are all symptomatic of the counterculture itself, and part of the reason why it failed to communicate (above all because it was preaching to the converted). This weakness was confirmed by its choice of movies.

The same year as *Cool Hand Luke*, the counterculture also embraced *The Graduate*, another empty, glib (but at least mildly amusing) exercise in commercial calculation with a faintly disturbed man-child at its center. And two years later, *Easy Rider*, a movie which the counterculture essentially gave birth to, once again suffered from the same prodigious failings (though it is by far the best of these three movies). *The Graduate*'s Benjamin Braddock may be light years away from James Dean or Hud, but he nonetheless shared some of their basic characteristics. Once again, we have youthful estrangement, general bewilderment (though in *Hud* this has been supplanted by indifference), and the groping quality of the suffering soul as it strives to connect with a hostile world. Benjamin is different from his forerunners in that he is anything but rebellious at heart; he is meek where Dean and Newman were wild, passive where they were aggressive. *The Graduate*'s popularity suggested that the rebellion, such as it was, was beginning to take root, and that even the square was starting to feel the toll of an oppressive society. Benjamin is an insider, not an outsider, and what makes *The Graduate* so disappointing and even dubious a work is that it never bothers to portray (or even conceive of) Benjamin's actual liberation. The movie has no third act; instead it descends into a mawkish Simon and Garfunkel montage (of lovestruck Benjamin stalking his desire), then limps to a hysterical climax. What makes Hoffman's Benjamin different from Dean's teens or Newman's Hud or Luke is that, as an insider, he adheres to the rules of civilization, and so is a far more repressed personality. His schizophrenic tendencies are almost entirely buried. For Benjamin, having an affair with an older woman (who just happens to be married, and a friend of the family to boot) is a truly subversive act, but it doesn't liberate his more rebellious impulses; though Ben gains confidence, he remains furtive and guilty about the affair, and until the finale (when Ben crashes Elaine's wedding) he remains inhibited throughout the film. The movie has no bite, no spark, and worst of all, it has no substance.

Even so, Benjamin became a hero of the counterculture and remains some sort of archetypal schmuck to this day, mostly I'd wager because he was played by Dustin Hoffman. Where Dean had been vulnerable and searching, with his puppy dog eyes and his hunched shoulders, Newman was edgy and sulky, closer to Brando in spirit than Dean, and equally sexually developed. Hoffman, on the other hand, was endearing, like Dean, but he was fumbling, anxious, and slightly dazed. Anything but a sexual presence, he was about as far from Marlon Brando (the original counterculture hero) as Benjamin was from Stanley Kowalski. Yet, two years later, Hoffman's Ratzo Rizzo (in *Midnight Cowboy*) was just the kind of part that Brando had made possible for a leading man: a pure character role. Ratso wasn't just a dropout, he was a bum and, what's more, a diseased cripple.

By the time of *Midnight Cowboy* and *Easy Rider*, the schizophrenic hero had literally split in two and the buddy movie was born. Obviously, this simplified matters so far as communicating the "message" to mass audiences. Now the lone, sensitive individual, misunderstood and persecuted by soulless society, had company in misery. Billy and Wyatt (and even Joe Buck and Ratso), by being partners in rebellion and destitution, could express freely the senti-

4. Weeping Alone: The Counterculture Fails to Communicate

ments which the filmmakers wished to communicate. And though they lost some of the pathos and dignity of solitude, they gained in its place a new degree of confidence — of wholeness through companionship. Ratso Rizzo and Joe Buck are both lost without each other, and *Midnight Cowboy* shows (at its best) the affinity between lost souls, the natural (though also bitter) sympathy that exists between people who share (for all their differences) a common bond of hopelessness: the sympathy of the damned. *Easy Rider* is essentially the same thing, only here the protagonists hold on to their illusions for a while longer, being a more complementary (and voluntary) partnership by far. Wyatt and Billy are old friends on a mutual journey who sell a bunch of cocaine and head across the country on their bikes to the sounds of Steppenwolf (a band named after Hesse's classic alienation text). In the process, they discover (at least Wyatt does) the emptiness and futility of their quest. Shortly afterwards, they are both blown to hell by hillbilly swamp trash (that damned Id again!).

Midnight Cowboy and *Easy Rider* are Hollywood enactments of the schizophrenic journey of the most simplistic and facile variety, but (perhaps for this very reason) they were enormously popular, both critically and commercially. At least they were *attempting* to map the journey and bring it to the public, which was more than most Hollywood movies were doing. Both films have dated so badly that it's hard to imagine (especially in the case of *Midnight Cowboy*) that they were ever considered classics of the cinema, much less works of art. And if both works still scrape by on the strength of their performances, their seedy, sun-drenched cinematography, and their uplifting scores (*Easy Rider* especially depends on rock 'n' roll to hold it together), it is only by the skin of their teeth. As commentaries on the corruption and despair of the times, they are distinctly uncomfortable experiences in all the wrong ways.

What was most surprising and disappointing about the counterculture (at least judging by its choice of movies to represent it) was that, under the guise of scathing realism and subtle ironies — and in its smug cynicism at the uselessness of old values — it was at heart every bit as sentimental and simpleminded as old Hollywood had ever been. In fact, from this period (1962 to 1969, roughly), and with the partial exceptions of *Bonnie and Clyde* and *The Wild Bunch*, there is only one movie that comes to mind that is truly subversive and that truly embodies the spirit of revolt (rejection of old values) which the counterculture claimed to stand for, that is a genuine, no-holds-barred expression of the schizophrenic experience and the breakdown of American society: *Night of the Living Dead.*

Hud appeared right on the heels of Stanley Kubrick's *Lolita* (1962), a movie in which the hero is a passive-obsessive driven by the most powerful and forbidden of lusts, at the same time hopelessly, derangingly inhibited by the fear of getting caught. Few commentators would cite Humbert Humbert as an exemplary of moral behavior, and what torments Humbert is not his conscience but the nigh impossibility of satisfying his illicit passion. But whether the conflict is caused by the repression of an inner moral sense or by the oppression of an external social code, the basic itch that needs to be scratched is the same: once again, sexual desire is at base of it all. Humbert Humbert was a true schizophrenic hero, and as a result proved unsympathetic to most audiences. Even the demented, ingenious Quilty (Peter Sellers) was more appealing. Humbert, with his mincing, ingratiating deviousness, and his fawning, sickly desperation, was repulsive to us not because of his perversity but because of his weak character, his lack of courage. He didn't even have the integrity to be an honest cad, like Quilty; and by striving to retain his facade of decency—even in his own eyes—he was not merely a heel but a hypocrite to boot. Audiences can tolerate all kinds of sin in their hero, just so long as it's shameless. One thing they won't go along with, however, is a hero who is also a creep (witness the utter failure of *The King of Comedy*).

Hud was a very different cinematic endeavor. Hud was an unregenerate cad who was, for all his callousness and egotism (and sexual voracity), irresistible to us. Of course that had a lot to do with Paul Newman, and the difference between Newman and James Mason (who played Humbert) is the difference between sympathetic and despicable to most viewers. While there's really nothing that Mason can do in order to become sexy, there is nothing the filmmakers could do to de-sex Newman. No matter how unlikable his character might be, he is still going to be Paul Newman.

Pauline Kael called *Hud* "just possibly the most completely schizoid movie produced anywhere anytime."[1] The split she was referring to was that between the filmmakers' "moral" intentions and their (considerably more sound) artistic ones, but this split can also be perceived between the movie's *ostensible* message and its actual *effects* (the two splits are actually one and the same). It goes deeper, too. Hud is supposed to represent the selfish materialist drives of the individual, while crusty old Homer (Melvyn Douglas) and decent young Lon (Brandon de Wilde) stand in for the old, solid, "spiritual" values of community, family, and so forth. But of course this was the 1960s already, and by now such homegrown values were beginning to sprout mold (just like Homer). It's hard to imagine the filmmakers (director Martin Ritt, et al) were unaware of how tired and outdated their values (especially as embodied by these actors) had come to seem to younger viewers (and wised up older ones, too). It's even more inconceivable they wouldn't have known that Paul Newman playing a heel is still Paul Newman, and that, even besides the low cunning of the casting (which made sure we side with Hud no matter what he did), the character was *conceived* to be attractive to younger viewers — not because of his materialism, or even his coarseness (though this had appeal too), but because of his individuality, his not giving a damn about what anyone thinks.

A few years earlier, Newman had officially taken over the mantle of James

Dean by playing Billy the Kid in Arthur Penn's hip, angsty *The Left-Handed Gun*. In the process, he helped consolidate the marriage between the confused, sensitive urban teenager of Dean (the first real movie role model the younger generation had been given) with the rugged and assured (though still sensitive) Western hero. This combination amounted to a new kind of hero: a schizophrenic hero. Brando certainly played his part in introducing the new, confused (but still noble and photogenic) man-boy to the screen with his rather effeminate *Wild One* and his Terry Malone of *On the Waterfront*. But I think it was Newman's Hud who really accomplished the transformation, and it's not hard to see Dean's characters in Hud (just as Dean's performance style had influenced Newman's); Hud is not really coarse or callow *by nature*, he has only come to *act* that way out of a mix of bitterness and self-preservation. Once upon a time, he was probably a-hurting just like Jimmy Dean was; and we can glimpse in him the anti-social, predatorial qualities of Billy the Kid, and of the anti-hero already on the horizon (around this time, Clint Eastwood was making *A Fistful of Dollars* in Spain).

And yet Hud was never *meant* to be the hero, not even as a suffering soul seeking redemption (or at least the understanding of a good woman). In the movie there is no middle ground where the insipid goodness and deadening rectitude of Lon and Homer can meet up with the unapologetic selfishness and alienation of Hud. Watching the movie and trying to fathom the filmmakers' intentions, one would think that James Dean had never existed. In *Hud* everything is standing on its head. Homer et al (who represent the status quo) are made so faultless that they are inhuman to us, and though this seems principally in order to ensure we don't ever mistake Hud's selfishness for rebellion, the way it's set up, who can blame him for rejecting such stuffy, lifeless values (most especially if they turn you into someone like Homer)? Fortunately *Hud*, as Kael wrote, is "redeemed by its fundamental dishonesty," and since Hud himself is the most vivid and likeable character in the film, all the finer efforts of the filmmakers to give us a serious social commentary and a moral drama for the times fall flat. What's left is Paul Newman and Patricia O'Neal's sculpted beauty and jaded *noblesse*, posed like fallen Greek gods in the dust-blown, wind-swept wasteland of the erstwhile West. Whatever Ritt and his collaborators intended, what they got, or at least what audiences responded to, was an unsentimentalized portrait of small-town conflicts and deep-rooted *ennui*, the frustration of big people with big dreams who are forced to knuckle under by small minds and live an appropriately petty, "decent," *small* life. Hud was James Dean's rebel without a cause grown up; he had found a cause all right, but by now he couldn't give a damn. *Hud* was a cause without a rebel.

It could be that Paul Newman — who had some of his best roles playing either unrepentant heels or unredeemed losers, men broken by the game of life, as in *The Hustler*— felt the need to find the rebel within and so appeal more directly to the budding counterculture. At any rate, over the next few years he abandoned the dubious integrity of the loser for the commercial viability of the winner: the cocky rebel-martyr figure (whose death makes him a winner) of *Cool Hand Luke* and *Butch Cassidy and the Sundance Kid*. These are two movies that are anything but redeemed by their fundamental dishonesty, since in this case there is no conflict, no schizophrenia, at the heart of the filmmakers (or of their lead characters), but only crass opportunism. No actor, no matter how dedicated to his craft, can resist the opportunity to play the martyr, and these films glorified the suicidal impulse with glib simple-mindedness devoid of sympathy for the schizophrenic experience. In *Cool Hand Luke*, there is never any question who the hero is, nor is there any attempt to create the least ambiguity as to Luke's basic superiority to everyone else in the film. Unlike Hud and Eddie Felson (Newman's best roles of the period), Luke is two-dimensional: he's a throwback to Newman's Billy and to James Dean's anguished teens, only this time, he's *all* victim. By now, the novelty of the vulnerable, oversensitive, and finally doomed hero had worn pretty thin, and with *Luke*, the process of turning the rebel into the martyr was well on its way. Unlike the schizophrenic heroes, Luke appears fully in control of his actions, and hence his destiny. (It makes no difference that in the first scene we find him drunkenly destroying parking meters—government property—in what appears to be a childish prank; Luke is clearly *making a statement*, albeit on the part of the filmmakers. Whatever it takes to get him incarcerated seems to be the point.) He is a Christ figure come to show the truth to unrepentant sinners, to die for them in the name of truth. His "mission" (which belongs to the moviemakers, who ought to be stoned for hubris at this point) is two-fold: to reveal the sordid corruption of the world, its antipathy to the individual "spirit" of man; and to demonstrate, in glorious contrast, the purity, nobility, and selflessness of Luke, the only man with the courage to reject the corruption of the world.

This is all very well if you are forming a new religion, but since *Cool Hand Luke* is just another prison flick, complete with the usual scenes of male camaraderie, torture, and so forth, it's a rather grotesque kind of pretension. Of course in Hollywood (where the gods are all movie stars), there's really no such thing as hubris; there's only shameless exhibitionism and runaway ambition, both of which *Cool Hand Luke* stands accused of. Beyond that (and considerably more damning), the movie drags Newman down to its level of catering to the audience with a spoon-fed, watered down, commercialized version of counterculture beliefs. *Cool Hand Luke* doesn't merely romanticize but outright sentimentalizes the rebel-schizophrenic hero, reducing him to asinine dimensions. By making him into a saint, it trivializes the suffering and uncertainty that defines his experience. There is no real sense of the loneliness, alienation, and fragmentation that give rise to the rebel-figure (with or without a

4. Weeping Alone: The Counterculture Fails to Communicate

cause), because the character is so blatantly set up as superior to everyone else. He has our sympathy, our support, and our admiration from the start. Martyred or not, Newman makes being a rebel outcast look so easy and sexy that by now everyone wants to be doing it.

Already the pop culture was doing its damnedest to assimilate the counterculture — and the schizophrenic experience that lurked beneath it — by stealing its beliefs (and its heroes) and selling them back to us in a debased form. It's a sad fact that men like Paul Newman, men who should know better, wind up betraying the very audiences they once served so admirably without even being aware of doing so. The fact was that Hud, with all his moody egocentricism, his barbarity, and his brute nature, was a hell of a lot closer to the truth of the matter (the angry youth as it grew up) than Luke or Butch could ever be; these latter characters were cynical attempts to turn the clock back, as it were, to nip this "new man" in the bud and replace it with an older, more reassuring, imitation model.

In a few years, Jack Nicholson would for a time do what Dean and Brando and Newman had done before him and become a kind of idealized, archetypal embodiment of American maleness, with all its encroaching schizophrenic qualities. At that time, the movies virtually exploded with new and dynamic male energy — Malcolm McDowell, Al Pacino, Robert De Niro, James Caan, Eliot Gould, Gene Hackman, Jon Voight, Jeff Bridges, and — lest we forget — Woody Allen. But in the meantime, with Newman's selling out the cause, Dean dead, and Brando already a burnout, the counterculture was briefly lacking a representative. Maybe it had something to do with disillusionment over these actors' past records, but the emergence of Dustin Hoffman (as this representative) suggested a rejection not only of machismo, but of all the conventional attributes of maleness that had until now held sway in Hollywood.

Hoffman's Benjamin (a part that might have initially gone to Robert Redford) wore his neuroses on the outside. He was not merely a sensitive and vulnerable hero, he was *all* sensitivity and vulnerability; these were his only "heroic" qualities. Beyond that he was simply a nebbish. By the time of *The Graduate*, the very idea of heroics defining the protagonist had lost all meaning. Benjamin's appeal lies not in anything he does — or in any noble qualities he may possess — but simply in what he *is*. Above all he was a stand-in for younger (and more bewildered) movie audiences everywhere. As such, by being the least heroic and most unremarkable of figures, he was also the most sympathetic.* Hoffman's acting style — a revelation at the time — invoked a mixture

---

* Pauline Kael: "The small triumph of *The Graduate* was to have domesticated alienation and the difficulty of communication, by making what Benjamin is alienated from a middle-class comic strip and making it absurdly evident that he has nothing to communicate — which is just what makes him an acceptable hero for the large movie audience. If he said anything or had any ideas, the audience would probably hate him." *Going Steady*, pg. 125.

of pity (and embarrassment) and amused fascination in the audience. Above all audiences were delighted by the fact that anyone so basically unsure of himself — so gauche and ungainly, and so homely — could ever become a movie star. This worked perfectly for the role, since it was above all discomfort and anxiety — a general out-of-placeness — that Benjamin was communicating; as such, Hoffman was the perfect choice. Without him it's safe to say *The Graduate* would have proved a wholly forgettable movie experience. It's also fair to say I think that without *The Graduate* as his debut movie, Hoffman might never have overcome the obstacles of his physical nature, and at best would have gone the character actor route of Duvall and Hackman (Hoffman's friends at the time).*

The first forty minutes of *The Graduate* (up to the part where Benjamin begins to fall for Elaine) are touched with genius, all of it Hoffman's. It's no wonder, watching these scenes, that younger audiences identified so deeply with the fumbling, bewildered Benjamin. Benjamin is so numbed and repulsed by the hypocrisy and inanity of his surroundings that he will take any opportunity to escape, to *rebel*, even if he feels secretly ashamed of doing so. If the rest of the movie measured up to these early scenes, then one could understand why it's considered a classic today (AFI voted it the seventh greatest American movie of all time); as it is, there is no movie once Benjamin finds romance and the thrill and anxiety of his transgressions give way to the banality of unrequited love. At this point, the darker, more troubled waters of adultery, deception, pathological sex drives, and so forth, are abandoned, and what had promised to be a lacerating sex comedy turns into cotton candy. Once again, the counterculture had been fobbed off with faulty goods — a hollow facsimile. As Pauline Kael noted at the time, "What's interesting about the success of *The Graduate* is sociological: the revelation of how emotionally accessible modern youth is to the same old manipulation."[2]

---

*Instead he became a movie star, and it may have been the worst thing that could have happened to him. With a bare few exceptions (*Straight Time, Tootsie*) Hoffman's later work (his career post *All the President's Men*, at least) was (like Nicholson's career post–*Cuckoo's Nest*) remarkable for being entirely devoid of either interesting roles or memorable movies. And yet for a time (up until *Straight Time*, and briefly again with *Tootsie*), Hoffman was certainly one of the four or five most exciting American movie stars around. With *The Graduate* he went from a total unknown to an international celebrity, and for someone as apparently shy and private as Hoffman, this must have been anything but easy. Hardly any wonder, then, that for a while he strived to take refuge in character roles, complete with handy props and physical deformities (most notably in *Papillon* and *Midnight Cowboy*). Hoffman's improbability as a leading man wasn't entirely due to his physical appearance, however. Al Pacino resembled Hoffman but that didn't stop him from becoming a romantic lead. It was more something in Hoffman's manner, his shuffling duck walk, his nasal whine, his palpable tenseness and constant fidgeting, that made him a natural either for comic or character roles (or both). Yet more than any of these other actors, more than any actor of the period in fact (with the possible exception of Jeff Bridges), Hoffman had a natural rapport with the audience — his sheer appeal was formidable.

4. Weeping Alone: The Counterculture Fails to Communicate

Benjamin may have disappointed his parents, he may have betrayed their oppressive dreams for him, he may have turned down a career in plastics and rejected the hypocrisy and banality of the materialist life as lived by his elders and peers; but by the end of the movie he has only opted for another version of the same. By what species of doublethink can pursuit of a mate and romantic partnership constitute the be-all and end-all of self-fulfillment? More to the point, how can the filmmakers pass this off as an act of rebellion? How can *The Graduate* claim to be about rejection of the old social values and a quest for new meanings and give us the hero and heroine riding off into the sunset? (The only twist to all this radical marital bliss is that the hero just stole the bride from another man.) As if the schizophrenic experience could so easily be resolved as this; as if it had only been that same old loneliness and heartache, after all, and all the schizo needed was the love of a good woman. What a relief!

It's true that Mike Nichols ends the movie on an ambiguous note: Benjamin and Elaine on the back of the bus, no longer smiling, apparently wondering what the hell they have gotten themselves into. But this hardly proves the integrity of Nichols' vision, only his doubts about it in the final hour. *The Graduate* puts all our problems into a single, worn old bag — call it society or call it Mrs. Robinson — and then conveniently does away with it. Did the filmmakers never hear of the sins of the fathers (or the mother)? As if making Miss Robinson into Mrs. Braddock would change anything! However far Benjamin runs, he's still left holding the bag, only now we're supposed to believe it's a prize. That's the trouble with blaming our problems on society — no matter how far we run, they're still with us.

Midnight Cowboy (AFI's 36th greatest American movie) wasn't really much better, but at least it had a complete dramatic arc to hang its rags and bones on. It's a little difficult to see the natural progression from Hoffman's Benjamin to his Ratso Rizzo two years later. (As Kael pointed out, Hoffman's David from *Straw Dogs* was a lot closer to how Benjamin might have ended up.[3]) All that came between the two roles was the disappearing whimsy *John and Mary*, which took the lamest aspects of *The Graduate* and extended them to feature length. Even so, it's doubtful *Midnight Cowboy* would have resonated quite as strongly as it did with audiences if they hadn't had Hoffman's familiar presence to help them through it.

Midnight Cowboy rejected the affectionate, empty-headed satire of *The Graduate* in favor of "scathing" social critique — it was a "message" movie in the old Hollywood tradition, all done up (or dirtied down) for new audiences to feel hip to. If *Midnight Cowboy* took risks, broke taboos and tapped into the more "grown-up" potential of movies (it was the first and last X-rated movie to win the Oscar for Best Picture), it did so not so much out of artistic imperative but knowingly, with one eye on the market. The director, John Schlesinger (as he proved over the years, with *Marathon Man* and other thumbscrew movies), has the ruthlessness of a good hack. Though he has the eye and occasionally the touch of a genuine artist (he certainly has film sense), it generally takes a back seat in his films to getting the desired effects (whether for visceral excitation or social indictment). Crude and manipulative as it is, *Midnight Cowboy* does get its effects, and like *Easy Rider* of the same year (equally crude and manipulative a work, but considerably more honest), it connected with audiences in ways that movies had rarely done before.

As Kael wrote at the time, "It's cool to feel that you can't win, that it's all rigged and hopeless. It's even cool to believe in purity and sacrifice." There was no longer the need to provide audiences with a reassuring moral coda, the same need that had made *Hud* such a schizophrenic affair and such a conflict of interests. Now the reassuring coda was not that the old values held good but that they *didn't*, that nothing was holding up, that society was a sinking ship, a rat-infested hell-hole, and that it was a *good* sign if you felt alienated, lost, helpless, defeated. That was the new reassurance, and it was being sold to the counterculture as true revelation and not just more humbug. Beautiful losers were in. Ugly losers were in.

It was a natural urge for the alienated, fragmented psyche — unable to connect to reality — to want to disconnect from society too. This was a preliminary step towards seeking some alternate means of identification, some alternate place to belong. (In a word, dropping out.) It was becoming a popular belief (even in the light of a failed sexual revolution) that repression was at base of all our ills, and that society itself— by oppressing us from without and inculcating us with neuroses within — was to blame. It followed that the logical thing to do was to reject society's program and seek an alternative one. At first glance, this might seem feasible; but essentially this desire is no different from the schizophrenic quest for a different reality to live in. The rebel-outcast's urge to destroy, reform, or at the very least reject the society that made him is nothing but an early symptom of the schizophrenic's estrangement from — and ultimately rejection of— reality itself. Both the rebel-dreamer and the schizophrenic are seeking refuge in fantasies. Society, as much as reality, is all we have — it's inescapable. As a result, "dropping out" became the only viable option besides out-and-out madness; realizing this, Hollywood began to flirt with the notion, giving birth to the drifter hero, usually two buddies who drift together, one or both of whom die in the end. It would be a while before the genre really took off (with movies like *Scarecrow, Thunderbolt and Lightfoot*, etc.), but the cycle really began in 1969, with *Easy Rider* and *Midnight Cowboy*.

Usually the buddies were contrasted in personality and even lifestyle: they were "complementary" in the sense of being opposites. Also, one supposes, their differences were meant to compensate for (and disguise) the fact that these were two *males* ostensibly involved in a romance usually reserved for the opposite sexes. In *Midnight Cowboy*, Joe Buck (Jon Voight) and Ratso Rizzo are about as different as two American males in their twenties could possibly be; yet they are drawn together by a common rootlessness. Joe, despite his small-town charm and good looks, is hopelessly unversed in the corrupt ways of the Big City; he is already disillusioned and corrupted before he even realizes his mistake. He sets out to be the predator (taking advantage of sex-starved older women) but winds up the prey (doing tricks for bucks in movie houses). Ratso, on the other hand, is the opposite end of the scale: filthy and diseased and charmless, he is reviled wherever he goes and yet possessed of enough animal cunning and street smarts to make his pariah-like status work for him. Instead of charming his way through this sleazy social underbelly, he *exasperates*. Ratso is the kind of person who gets his way simply because no one wants to spend the time it takes to argue with him: people accommodate him just to get rid of him. Ratso knows he is despised and doesn't care. He holds the rest of the world in such disregard that there's not much it can do to affect him. Ratso sees Joe as an easy mark, but despite this develops an affection for him. And Joe, in turn, despite finding Ratso repulsive and maddening in equal measures, somehow becomes attached to him.

In *Easy Rider*, Wyatt (Peter Fonda) and Billy (Dennis Hopper) are both hippies, potheads, and aficionados of Harley Davidson and Steppenwolf. They are certainly from a common "tribe," but beyond this their personalities (and physical appearances) seem to be diametrically opposed. Wyatt is tall, rangy, clean-shaven, a man of few words, taciturn and serene, thoughtful and mysterious (as mysterious as Peter Fonda can manage). Billy, on the other hand, as much a side-kick as a partner, is short, hairy, hostile, aggressive, profane, and talkative, making him something of a clown figure to Fonda's saintly dude.* The two traveling schizos head to New Orleans for the Mardi Gras, a carnival of drugs and debauchery that presumably suits the needs and desires of both men. The quest of *Easy Rider* is not a quest for greater meaning, or even belonging (when they find a genuine alternative in the commune lifestyle they don't stay long). They already have money from their cocaine deal, so their whole journey is really no more than recreational. To say that two men went looking for America is really a crock — in what sense are they seeking? By going to whorehouses and the Mardi Gras? Only when they drop acid in the graveyard and begin to lose their minds is there a hint of experience beyond the everyday material quest for distraction (the very thing they are supposed to be getting away from). But the acid trip is anything but enlightening: it's enough

---

*Fonda and Hopper, being the producer and director of the film respectively, probably shaped these roles for their own qualities. Fonda is given a role not too demanding in which his good looks and height should be enough (Fonda invokes a physical type most of all, that of Gary Cooper and of Peter's own father, Henry). Hopper is able to more or less play his own jittery, hyped-up and drugged-out self.

to put the un-experienced off taking LSD for life; all it really seems to offer is a heightened sense of incoherence.

Whatever they are seeking, Wyatt and Billy find it — if they find it at all — only at the barrel of a shotgun. And enjoyable, even affecting, as *Easy Rider* is, it really doesn't mean much as a movie, much less an experience. It may expose the schizophrenic under layer of American society, but in such a prosaic, unsophisticated way that it's preaching to the converted. The film's simplemindedness undoubtedly served it well, however, so far as reaching a larger audience and disseminating paranoia far and wide. It framed its message in neon and laid the signs out in black and white; as a result, it changed the face of American cinema. Schizophrenia was ready to go mainstream.

5

The Revolting Male: Jack Nicholson and the Schizophrenic Journey

> The man who lives more lives is in a better position than the guy who lives just one.
> — Jack Nicholson, 1986

"Doing a Jack" was a phrase that an old (now dead) friend of mine and I adopted in our early teens in recognition of a quality particular to one of our favorite actors. The qualities of assertiveness and fearlessness were most fully embodied in the leering, satirical machismo of Jack Nicholson in his earliest roles. Nicholson — "the people's freak of the new stars"[1] — didn't take any shit, and if the reason was that he was so full of shit himself that he had zero tolerance for anyone else's, that just made his stance all the more ironic. The key scene that epitomized this (essentially male) quality of "no bullshit" occurs in Nicholson's first leading role as Bobby Dupea in Bob Rafelson's *Five Easy Pieces*. The famous diner chicken salad scene, significantly enough, was (according to screenwriter Carole Eastman, writing as Adrien Joyce) taken directly from Nicholson's wild youth. (Not to suggest that Nicholson mellowed with age: many years later he was brought up on charges in LA for attacking a motorist's vehicle with a baseball bat.) There were other scenes, of course, specifically in *The Last Detail*, but this early example pretty much set the stage for the Nicholson persona as we would come to know it.

Nicholson/Bobby's coldness and contempt in *Five Easy Pieces* is not mere cynicism; it is closer to jaded wisdom and world-weariness. Bobby — the role which consolidated the Nicholson persona of the period — doesn't budge for anyone's feelings, including his own. He's detached from, and contemptuous of, his own actions as much as everyone else's; that's what makes him so good at playing the piano and bowling and fucking, but so useless at intimacy of any kind. He lacks sweetness. It's also this schizophrenic detachment that allows him to jump on the back of a moving flatbed truck and play a Mozart concerto. He is "deranged," or derailed, all for a moment of bliss, of forgetfulness. This, along with the diner scene, is the movie's emotional highpoint, a sort of epiphany; yet like the rest of the movie, like Bobby himself, it is cold, ironic, detached. It partakes of an odd mix of passion and passivity characteristic of schizophrenia.

When we first meet Bobby he is ensconced in his dreary routine—working on a drilling site, bowling with his workmate, his workmate's wife, and his lover Rayette (Karen Black), a lousy bowler with whom he seems to be in an almost constant battle of wills. It may seem strange that Eastman should have written for Bobby such a weak and unappealing female, but then *Five Easy Pieces* is anything but a feminist tract. What it is is a study of machismo. Bobby is Eastman's case study, and Rayette is just the sort of female that Bobby *would* be drawn to. Bobby despises her whining, her excess femininity, her constant need for reassurance and affection, and he despises himself for putting up with it. One of their first dialogues ends with her telling him, "You're never satisfied," to which Bobby replies, "That's right!" Why *should* he be satisfied, his defiant tone implies, with this empty sham of a life? But Bobby doesn't know of—cannot even imagine—a viable alternative. He rejects the falseness of his more refined, "civilized" upbringing—his musical vocation and all the rest—and opts for a crude, blue-collar life, presumably feeling less of a phony for rejecting the life that is expected of him. But Bobby's twice the fake as a blue collar worker that he is as a pianist: the only difference is that now no one expects *anything* of him. He has the dubious luxury, the "freedom," of being a phony that everyone *knows* is a phony (starting and ending with himself). But this pseudo-life is stifling Bobby, and when he learns that Rayette is pregnant he seems ready to toss it all away, baby and all.

Bobby is an outsider vainly attempting to blend in, to disappear into a "normal" existence. Even though he knows it's futile, even fatal, to try, he has run out of options. Bobby despises his job, he despises his friends, he despises his mate, he despises himself. This, perversely enough, gives him a certain integrity, or at the very least volatility, that the other characters are lacking. In a sense it's incorrect to say (as Catherine does) that Bobby doesn't care about anyone or anything; in a sense he cares too much. What he can't bear to see is people that he wants to care about settling for such dull and pointless lives, becoming so accustomed to the lie, the façade, that they wind up with nothing to live for. What makes Bobby dynamic, charismatic, and attractive to us is also what makes him volatile, desperate, unstable, and finally schizophrenic: his capacity to see beyond the surfaces and feel the deeper undercurrents of an apparently placid existence. What Bobby feels above all is rage and despair—exasperation, disgust, contempt. But there's little doubt by his displays that

5. The Revolting Male: Jack Nicholson

Bobby feels these things more deeply than anyone else around him feels *anything*. (Bobby is the only character who really expresses any emotion beyond self-pity or mild amusement, save perhaps for his sister.) Bobby is on an ironic quest, seeking numbness, absence of feeling (hence of pain); yet the further he goes into this living death, the profounder and more tormenting his despair becomes, the greater his rage and contempt for himself and for all those who have accepted their deathlike lives as natural and inevitable. It's a schizophrenic quest: the more Bobby tries to deaden his heart and mind to the world, the more desperately alive his need for something greater becomes.

During this period Nicholson represented the outsider, the rebel outlaw/existential man, in revolt at the most mundane, restricted level. Bobby, Buddusky in *The Last Detail*, David Locke of *The Passenger*, and finally Mac-Murphy of *One Flew Over the Cuckoo's Nest*, are all ordinary men with extraordinary levels of energy and passion (albeit of the negative variety) who lack the insight or the imagination to express themselves in anything but petty, occasionally poetic but finally impotent acts of revolt. Above all their frustration takes the form of an absurd kind of posturing, what Pauline Kael called "a satirical approach to macho."[2] Kael was referring to Nicholson's persona rather than that of his characters, and yet (as she also pointed out), the two often seem inseparable. It is the knowing manner in which Nicholson inhabits his roles, while at the same time staying outside of them, as if winking at the audience, that make so much of what he does a kind of "turn." Nicholson mocks his characters' frustration, their impotence, but he also gives them enough self-awareness to appear to be mocking themselves. The machismo of his characters is the machismo of a male too sophisticated not to know how hollow and childish such posturing really is. At the same time, they are too contemptuous of their own sophistication and awareness to do anything but mock and degrade it with empty acts of machismo.

Nicholson — whose "specialty is divided characters"[3] — was the necessary counterculture hero who mixed the sensitivity and vulnerability of James Dean with the uncouthness, roughness, and virility of Brando, while adding something entirely his own to the mix — irony and satire. It is there in the devilish leer of his grin and the mischievous tilt of his eyebrows. At times, this deviltry was indistinguishable from mere clowning, the wild, unpredictable, possibly psychotic (definitely dangerous), but undeniably seductive *mystique* that made Nicholson the biggest star in the world (perhaps not in box office terms, but in terms of status as a movie actor). Of course, "mystique," so far as any actor has such (and it's what makes a mere star into a kind of legend, along the lines of Brando, Dean, and few others), is entirely particular to the *method* of the actor in question; above all, I think, it depends on the feeling that we are seeing only and exactly what the actor intends us to see. On the one hand, it's the undisclosed depths — and early Nicholson suggested this as much as early Brando — on the other hand, it relates to the superficiality of what the actor is actually doing, the awareness that he is greater than the role, that the role is but a single facet of the actor's total *personality*.

When we think of Brando we think of Terry Malloy and Stanley Kowalski, or we think of Don Vito, Paul from *Last Tango in Paris*, and of other, more peripheral performances that added body and texture to these personas (young and old Brando, respectively). Nicholson never really succeeded in creating a second, more mature persona after his 1970s peak, but during the seven years between *Easy Rider* and *Cuckoo's Nest*, he attained a consistency and integrity of performance that perhaps no other movie star ever has before or since. All these portrayals — George Hanson, Bobby Dupea, his less successful but still noteworthy turns in *The King of Marvin Gardens* and *Carnal Knowledge*, Buddusky from *The Last Detail*, David Locke in *The Passenger*, Jake Gittes in *Chinatown*, and finally MacMurphy of *Cuckoo's Nest* — fuse into a single persona. Nicholson, in a sense, completed the work of Brando and Dean in bringing the once-untouchable male movie god into the everyday milieu of our lives. Via the "method performances,"* and the sordid anti-romantic nature of the movies themselves (at least compared to old Hollywood product), Nicholson ensured that the aloof, superior perfection of Cooper, Gable, and Grant became forever a thing of the past. Those actors who upheld the more mythical or idealized image of the male — Newman, Eastwood, Redford, Beatty — may have had more commercial clout, but they lacked the authenticity and credibility of the new, post–Brando breed — Hoffman, De Niro, Pacino, Hackman, Duvall, et al. — none of whom were really "leading men" in the old Hollywood sense. Of this new breed of anti-heroes, it was Nicholson who was the closest to being conventionally handsome, and beyond doubt he was the most sheerly charismatic. One felt with Nicholson that, although he was certainly capable of the same depth and subtlety as these other performers, he tended to opt instead for the more theatrical "turn," partly, one suspected, to draw attention to the illusory process of acting in which he was involved. To this extent, Nicholson, by both portraying and embodying a rejection of hypocrisy (lies and facades), spoke directly to his audience. He was the male in revolt, and what Nicholson communicated, once the excitement of revolt had died down and the sober reality of impotence had sunk in, was fatality, resignation, and despair.

In *Easy Rider*, George Hanson enjoys a brief "initiation," a temporary enlightenment, before being sacrificed on the proverbial altar of conformity.

---

*It's true that in many ways Nicholson was anything but a method or naturalistic actor during this period; and yet his style certainly takes off from the "scratching and sniffing" improvisatory naturalism of Brando, Clift, and Dean, even if it adds a new "Brechtian" layer of irony and self-consciousness to the mix.

Hanson never had it in him to be a true rebel; he was really no more than a dilettante. Consequently, when things got apocalyptic, he was the first to go. Bobby Dupea is considerably more committed to the idea of freedom and revolt, even if he has little idea of what it might consist of. In *Five Easy Pieces*, Bobby undergoes your basic, preliminary "apocalypse," the schizophrenic journey of awakening. His frustration with the endless and meaningless cacophony of his life is symbolized — poetically rather than dramatically — when he gets caught in an early morning traffic jam. Godard, in *Weekend*, used the same symbolism (traffic and the cacophony of horns) to symbolize the same thing: the futility and arrogance of man, forever complaining about his own stupidity; but here the device feels less indulgent and as a result is far more effective. Bobby mounts a furniture truck in front to see how far the jam extends; once up on the truck, he notices a piano under a blanket, pulls back the blanket and sits down to play one of his "easy pieces." The sound of the car horns renders his music inaudible, useless, an act wholly for himself; yet this is one of Bobby's rare moments of genuine self-expression, and the only one of his acts of revolt that is creative and not destructive. The fact that the jam unclogs as soon as he begins playing (and as a result, the honking fades out and the truck begins moving, Bobby still on it) signifies that here and here alone is the solution to Bobby's problem, the means for his "unblocking." The fact that, as a result of his gesture, Bobby winds up miles from his destination and so misses his workday needs no interpretation. The symbolism of the movie is not heavy-handed, exactly, but it is certainly simplistic; and at times the film sinks to the level of a facile, slightly self-satisfied social critique. Mostly however it sticks to its humbler and more honorable intentions as a straightforward character study.

In any event, it's not until news of Rayette's pregnancy arrives that Bobby's safe, uncreative (though still revolting) existence begins to crumble. Bobby is disgusted when his workmate Elton gives him advice as to the consolations of fatherhood, and reacts with vitriol to having "some cracker asshole compare his life to mine!" Nicholson plays these kinds of scenes better than anyone ever has. He communicates Bobby's disgust and frustration, his pent-up rage and hostility, so directly and with such an eloquence of expressions that in these few moments it's as if we are under his skin. No other actor, not even Brando, took us quite this close to visceral identification. And what we identify with here is not merely Nicholson's joy of acting but Bobby's horror and revulsion at the thought of becoming just another statistic, at finding himself caught in a life that has nothing at all to do with his actual desire or needs as an individual. This horror and revulsion (that leads finally on to actual revolt) is the first awakening of Bobby's unconscious, the first rumblings of schizophrenic crisis. He storms off and quits his job. Moments later he sees two men attacking Elton and runs back to his aid. It turns out that the two men are govern-

White trash blues. Bobby Dupea (Jack Nicholson) gets ready to blow in *Five Easy Pieces* (1970, Columbia).

ment agents and that the complacent husband/father Elton, who has just been defending the sanctity of the "good life," is wanted for petty robbery and is in violation of his parole.

By this time, Bobby is ready to cut out on his responsibilities, whatever the toll on his conscience may be. When Rayette asks him one more time if he loves her, Bobby says dryly, "What do you think?" He means it as an affirmative, or at the very least he means her to take it as such. The suggestion is that, if he didn't love her he wouldn't be there, and certainly wouldn't put up with all her crap (this is the inflection Nicholson gives the line anyway). But in fact Bobby is asking himself—Why *do* I put up with this? The answer is that it's not love that keeps him around. Since it's plain Bobby doesn't much like Rayette, and certainly doesn't respect her, where does love come in? There is an element of need—in terms of the emotional security and support that she gives him—but the price of having to constantly pamper, flatter, reassure, and indulge Rayette in her insecurity and self-pity is getting too high to make it worth Bobby's while. His patience is already worn to nothing when news of the baby arrives, and it's at this juncture that Bobby visits his high-strung sister and she tells him that their father has suffered a double stroke and been incapacitated. She asks Bobby to come home and make his peace with him.

Five Easy Pieces doesn't make pretensions towards a plot, as such. It's a

5. The Revolting Male: Jack Nicholson

situational drama, and however hackneyed this device (that of an illness in the family), it is thematically correct. Bobby can't simply run away anymore: he must "look within" first in order to know what it is he is running from and (most importantly) where to run to. Hence there arises, as if from nowhere, the obligatory "journey into the past" which Bobby must make in order to get free to face the future. In simple terms, the return to roots to confront past sins or sorrows represents the necessity (on the schizophrenic journey) of examining one's conscience in order to discover the sources of one's discontent. Bobby is fleeing his own familial future as a father-to-be by taking reluctant refuge in his own family past. Were he not so desperate for an "out" at that precise time, it seems unlikely he would be so ready to make the journey. Certainly it's not sentimentality that takes him back to see his father; and if it's duty, then it's duty based not upon any morality but on sheer survival instinct. Bobby knows there is something he must confront. The idea of his own fatherhood is intolerable to him; logically enough, then, it's his role as a son — an irresponsible child — that comes back to haunt him. At first he plans to use this opportunity to abandon Rayette. His conscience at her pathetic display of self-pity (his fear that she will commit suicide once he leaves) does not allow him this easy escape, however, and he ends up taking her along for the ride (though only part of the way, as he installs her at a motel before reaching his family home).

On the way, they pick up an obsessed hippie and her companion and are subjected to an endless diatribe on the "filth" of modern (male-orientated) society. Although Bobby shows anything but sympathy or interest for the woman's point of view, somehow or another it plants a seed in his mind. His own sense of psychic pollution — of being stifled and choked by the filth of society's lies, chin deep in bullshit — obsesses him every bit as much as mass consumerism obsesses the hippie girl. She is externalizing, while he internalizes. She is hysterical, where Bobby broods. Yet it's Bobby who explodes in the diner, who "takes a stand" against the ever-encroaching bullshit, delighting the hippie girl and impressing her with his integrity. Of course, the fact that Bobby takes out his frustration on a mealy-mouthed and tight-assed but otherwise insignificant waitress makes his stance little more than a show of impotent rage; but this fact is lost on the girl. When Bobby points out sourly, in response to her admiration, "I didn't get the toast, did I?," he reveals that he is not interested in the aesthetics of revolution, but only in getting results. He's not out to prove anything to anyone, or to convert anyone to his point of view (he doesn't have one).

When Bobby says to the waitress, "Do you see this sign?" — before sweeping the water glasses off the table in a magnanimous act of destruction — he is being wholly ironic. It's a bitter, hostile response to the waitress' bitter, hostile manner in refusing him a simple slice of toast. He's not concerned with making a point, however; he's just letting off steam. It is this ingenuousness, this lack of regard for the effects of his actions or for anyone else's opinions about them, that makes Bobby at least less of a fake than he believes himself to be. He is real enough to know that he's a fraud, that none of his acts matter, hence he may as *well* piss over everything; not in order to get a reaction but simply because he *feels* like it (most of the time at any rate). The return to the family fold — though there is not the slightest chance of his belonging there, even for a second — demands a limited amount of restraint, even courtesy, on Bobby's part. Bobby may be desperately hostile but he is not malevolent or spiteful; besides which, he is, perhaps despite himself, hoping to find some kind of refuge or respite in the "lunatic asylum rest home" of his childhood. If Bobby stays considerably longer than he had planned, it's less to do with his feeling at home there than with the presence of a desirable female, Catherine, whom he is intent upon seducing.

Bobby's seduction technique hardly merits the term; the most one can say is that, in his behavior with Catherine, Bobby displays a degree of tentativeness, even sweetness, that at other times he seems incapable of. It's plain when he succumbs to Catherine's wish and plays piano for her that he is only eager to please her: nothing but the desire for sex could ever persuade him to "compromise" himself in this way. For a while it even seems that Bobby may be capable of inhibiting his baser feelings and of feigning a civilized veneer of warmth for Catherine, at least long enough to get her into bed. But he is finally unable to maintain the façade, to be the pretender, and, by mocking her admiration for his playing, he lets her know he has conned her. Bobby is too "honest" (or embittered, depending on how you look at it) to enjoy a simple seduction. He pulls all the right strings but then he comes clean by making Catherine aware of how she was falling for his ruse. Hence he pushes her away again. After this, they have a confrontation in which Catherine tells him how low he is and asks that he leave so she can take a bath (hint hint). And all the while, under that civilized, icy veneer of rejection, her true desire is screaming out through every hormone in her body. Bobby responds to the hormonal plea and not to the icy words; he smashes her perfumes with contempt and then, a moment later (since she continues to stand there), he attacks. The last thing she says to him before he moves in for the kill is, "No inner feeling?" Of course: when Bobby plays his "easy piece" for Catherine, he *believes* he is faking it (hence "easy"), that he feels nothing. And as he plays the camera pans over family photos, as if he were erasing his past with his concerto. But Bobby has been faking his fakeness. At the same time, he's got so good at feeling nothing that he's barely able to express a real feeling when he has one, save through hostility. The result is the same, in any case, and once the sparks are allowed to fly in a more creative fashion, Bobby becomes (briefly) a puppy dog again. He wants Catherine to love him, but she knows better. She knows that the moment she gave herself to him emotionally, he would begin to despise her.

Bobby's lust/love for Catherine allows him to experience his first really cathartic outburst. By coming to her defense and attacking the frigid intellectuals as they glibly discuss primal instincts and latent aggression (whereupon Bobby gives them a spontaneous display of just that), he brings the situation to a head. No explanation is given for the intellectual middle-aged woman's presence in the house; apparently she is a friend of the family, though no one seems to like her much. She holds forth on repression, innate aggressivity, "the adversary" (presumably referring to the atavistic side of ourselves), and the inadequacy of reason to do any more than placate and distract this primal side of our nature (like TV, she adds). Her argument is fascinating; despite the fact the filmmakers wish to present her as a sterile and pompous bore, they can't resist putting words of profound significance in her mouth, most especially in the context of the film itself. But the woman's manner of delivery is glib, facile and condescending, and she manages to alienate everyone in the room with her superior tones. As a result, when Bobby explodes on her (for pointing her finger at Catherine) and tells her she's "full of shit," he seems to be the voice of reason (or atavism!), and wholly justified. The guests sit meekly while she pontificates (one of them says drolly, "Isn't that a little apocalyptic?"), but Bobby acts where the "pompous celibates" only talk. What gets Bobby's goat most of all is the veiled aggression of this civilized society, the unbearable repression; and this is where Bobby, "the adversary," comes in — apocalyptically — to cast all the lies aside. Bobby is an iconoclast in a mundane, sterile time where the only things left to smash are the petty baubles of people's egos. There are no gods, much less icons — this is all academic; even Bobby's outburst is somehow half-hearted. Bobby is a destroyer, and that is exactly why he must withdraw from "civilized" society. His presence is intolerable to it, since all he can communicate is disgust. But even his disgust is not enough to sustain him anymore. This society is not even worth the trouble of destroying.

What the pompous celibate is talking about applies directly (and perhaps threateningly) to Bobby himself, who seems above all to be stifled by the "reasonable" demands of civilized behavior. He was just waiting for an opportunity to let rip like this, and the fact he sneers at the woman as a *celibate* is apropos. Bobby is incapable of expressing his brute, animal side save through sex, and through these passionate but petty fits of rage. Unconsciously, this sexless intellectual has hit a nerve in him. *Something* strikes him anyway. Following his violent denunciation of everyone in the room, he chases after Catherine, who has already fled in disgust, not at Bobby's outburst but at the cold aggression of the intellectuals (though Catherine — as played by Susan Anspach — is rather pompous and icy herself). Bobby goes charging through the house shouting her name, thereby revealing to everyone present the illicit nature of their relations. Unable to find her, he stumbles upon his sister in sexual congress with the male nurse Spider (a most bizarre peripheral character, a body builder who dresses all in white, played by John P. Ryan). Bobby, too pent-up to act rationally, falls back into the (wholly inappropriate) role of protective brother. Even though earlier he had been nudging his sister gently in Spider's direction, he is enraged at seeing them together, and ends up wrestling with the far bigger and stronger Spider. Eventually he is subdued by force, by which time everyone in the house has arrived to witness the scene. Bobby has had his explosion, his breakdown, and his melodrama, all in one; the experience has culminated in an inevitable paroxysm of impotence by which Bobby effectively renders his presence there impossible. All that now remains is Catherine's gentle rejection, and Bobby's final face-off with his father.

It's necessary and natural that Bobby must be both beaten into submission by Spider and then pushed gently away by Catherine (away from the possibility of love, refuge, belonging), before he can finally approach his father. No longer desperate, finally humbled, he is quite literally out in the cold, frozen out by his own bitter inability to communicate. At this point the mute, unbudging father figure — a figure of stone that the film hardly gives more attention to than a piece of furniture — becomes such an overtly symbolic cinematic device that it seems superfluous to write about it. He symbolizes the proud silence of the afflicted. He has been struck down, one supposes, by his own hard-heartedness. The fact that (we are told) he never was much of a communicator to begin with — and now that he has been sufficiently humbled to want to do so, he is incapable of it (besides the occasional belch) — all this serves to underline the futility and hopelessness of Bobby's life. Any and all attempts at communication must end in failure. As Bobby says (as it were to the dormant right side of his brain): "If you could talk we wouldn't we talking."

Plainly Bobby is a chip off this old block, and his searching, struggling attempt to express his sorrow and his regret to the old man are, if genuine, no less futile for that. Bobby is simply getting a load off his chest, and it seems doubtful if his father gains much from Bobby's admissions, though perhaps there is some relief (assuming he understands at all) in the thought that the son may be learning from the father's mistakes. In any case, the face-off, the entire relationship here, is purely symbolic. This is the commencement of Bobby's true journey. Whether or not he will ever attain peace or understanding, much less the companionship he secretly longs for, cannot be known. All that seems clear is that, in this penultimate scene, the schizo finally initiates dialogue with his unconscious, his "Other" — the silent, atavistic side of his psyche represented, aptly enough, by his father. It is of course a one-sided dialogue, because Bobby's unconscious has been so long ignored, rejected, and despised that it is slow indeed to answer. But it listens, and if Bobby's desire to communicate is true, and if his will is strong, then eventually, one supposes, he will get through. Bobby doesn't make peace here so much as put to rest his ghosts. He comes clean, so far as he is able. The whole movie is a mundane enactment of the crazed hippie girl's metaphorical pilgrimage to Alaska: to get clean means to seek out the cold, to uncover one's own heartlessness. Bobby's ruthlessness (what is perceived as his lack of concern for other people and for himself) is in actual fact his sole, saving virtue. But only when he applies it fully and squarely to himself (following his attack of conscience) and faces that cold, North wind does it actually begin to serve him as such.

In *Five Easy Pieces*, Bobby faces off the anima (Catherine) and then he faces up to the Other. Bobby's heading off to Alaska symbolizes this journey into the realms of the unconscious. It is his opting for silence, even possibly for death, over the endless, mindless chatter of his life. By the end of the movie we may feel that Bobby has attained, if not peace exactly, then at least resignation, acceptance. His petty battles with a petty world are over, and his true battle — a simple battle for survival — has begun. It's hard to imagine a future for Bobby, however, to picture him as some Jack London hero, silently struggling through the wilderness. Has he integrated his primal self sufficiently to let the id carry the day, to find a new purpose unencumbered by the trappings of civilization? It seems more likely that, whether in Alaska or somewhere else, Bobby will wind up getting trapped in the same petty struggles for his dignity and freedom.

Bobby thrives on contempt and revolt, and by the end, with it all apparently beaten or drained out of him, he seems dazed, more dead than alive. Probably his trip to Alaska, abandoning his car, his lover, even his jacket and wallet (which he leaves in the men's room), is no more (though also no less) than a glorified suicide. But if so it is the only honest recourse left open to him. Bobby had always taken the easy path, the path of the complacent, inferior man, and as a result his conscience never gave him any peace. He was forever dogged by self-contempt for selling himself short, for backing away from his greater desire, his true will. Now that he has finally embraced a life of solitude, hardship, and danger — even if it means premature extinction — he can at last find peace.

This is more than can be said for any of Nicholson's following (key) incarnations, who get to choose between death (*The Passenger, Cuckoo's Nest*) and bitter resignation to cruel fate (*Last Detail, Chinatown*). Part of Nicholson's motivation for choosing his roles in this period seems to have stemmed from an affinity for the "beautiful loser" ethos of the (now lost) 1960s counterculture: the doomed generation. The essence of Nicholson's appeal may well have been his uncanny instinct, and his empathy, for the despair, rootlessness, and lack of direction of the younger generations in increasingly schizophrenic times.

Yet although Nicholson played what are essentially doomed, or at least unredeemed, protagonists, he never lost his dignity in the process. Nicholson's characters never seem like losers (even until the bitter end) because they never stop struggling. Like Buddusksy in *The Last Detail,* Nicholson kept up a show of bravado to cover his center of self-doubt and self-loathing. To different degrees — depending on their level of self-awareness — Nicholson's schizo heroes are all driven by suicidal urges, or at the very least by self-hatred; but they are also involved in a personal journey of revelation (even if the revelation, when it comes, is of their own suicidal impulses).

The Passenger is the quintessential schizophrenic journey movie, but also one of the most boring films ever made. It is a study of alienation that so thoroughly alienates the viewer that its deeper meanings get lost beneath the relentless banality of the surface. Nicholson's desire to do the film was above all a desire to work with the director, Michelangelo Antonioni (out of favor in Hollywood since the disastrous reception of *Zabriskie Point*); it was also, one presumes, to further his credentials with the counterculture (what was left of it) as an "experimental" performer. But Antonioni's style so effaces the actor's as to all but erase any positive attributes he has, making one wonder why Antonioni wanted Nicholson in the first place. At the same time, what negligible watchability the film has comes solely from Nicholson's presence. Once Antonioni's technique has ceased to pass for "hypnotic" and become merely numbing, once the obligatory plot has taken over from the director's themes, there's nothing there to hold our attention save the actor's eyebrows and hairline.

The Passenger begins where it might reasonably have ended — where in fact *Five Easy Pieces did* end — with the Nicholson character's decision to erase his identity and assume a new one, in a word: to disappear. Both Bobby and David Locke appear to be fleeing reality — the trap of their own identity — but whereas *Five Easy Pieces* went to the trouble of showing us the why and wherefore, *The Passenger* takes our comprehension of such a quasi-suicidal step as a given. Perhaps this was the reason Antonioni wanted Nicholson for the role, since by this time the actor had come to embody, more than any other actor, the traits of alienation, impotence, and schizophrenia which Antonioni wished to communicate. Nicholson, for his part, seemed to be at least partially conscious of his intention, and methods, in choosing role after role that combined these particular traits.

For so dynamic an actor it's curious to note just how passive his characters from this period really are. George Hanson takes the initiative, it's true, but thereafter is simply along for the ride, a sitting duck for Fate. Bobby Dupea opts out of his own life; he denies and scorns all the things that might give him a sense of purpose, integrity, or contentment. The sex-fiend/male chauvinist of Mike Nichol's puritanical *Carnal Knowledge* is shown to be doomed by his own caddishness, a victim of bitterness and self-loathing and an inability

5. The Revolting Male: Jack Nicholson

to change. Buddusky in *The Last Detail* is likewise trapped in his blue-collar drudgery life, confined to empty displays of bravado and machismo to assert his independence. Though he takes pleasure in initiating the young sailor Meadows (Randy Quaid) into "manhood" before his eight-year incarceration, this is a largely selfish gesture on Buddusky's part. Not for a moment does he seriously consider setting Meadows free, despite his contempt for the injustice of the system that has sentenced him, and despite his apparent regret. To do so would mean jeopardizing his own position in the Navy, but this is exactly what makes his cowardice, his passivity, so contemptible. Since Buddusky none-too-secretly despises the system to which he is (voluntarily) enslaved, since he privately yearns for something more meaningful, his incapacity to break away from it — by "doing the right thing" and releasing Meadows — only intensifies his sense of impotence. Any punishment for letting Meadows go — such as being expelled from the Navy — would in effect be Buddusky's reward: by breaking away from the oppressive military program and letting Meadows escape, he would also be freeing himself. Buddusky is not an *overtly* schizophrenic figure like Bobby Dupea, however, because he lacks Bobby's awareness and sophistication. In a sense he is the reverse image of Bobby: Bobby hides his sophistication under a guise of blue collar brutishness, while Buddusky affects a certain sophistication, or at least elegance, to cover the fact that he is little more than a Navy thug. But both characters are divided by their own assumption of facades, or masquerades, and their incapacity to assume responsibility.

In *Chinatown*, J.J. Gittes is a different kind of putz and a higher class of loser. Gittes has compromised on his own terms, and within the Hollywood framework of the private eye, he is a far cry indeed from Bogart's Marlowe. For one thing, he does divorce work, and though he has fancy suits and shoes to show for it, he also has the shifty look and cynical whine of the sell-out. Gittes — unlike Buddusky, who knows his limitations all too well — overestimates his abilities — his "finesse" and cunning — to an almost fatal degree. He is finally shown to be incapable of fathoming the corruption which he investigates, and as a result he is powerless to save Evelyn (Faye Dunaway) from the forces of evil (symbolized by Chinatown, where her sordid death occurs*).

Gittes is a private eye, a voyeur, and all he really does in the film is snoop, peep, and sniff, passively, through the labyrinth of iniquity, very nearly losing his nose in the process. If Gittes' sanity is never in doubt, his integrity and his potency are not so vouchsafed. By the end of the movie (and it's a muggy,

---

*Chinatown of course is a symbol not merely for "evil" or corruption, but for the hero's past, and by extension, his unconscious. Above all, it signifies that part of Gittes that he is unable to confront, or even to look at directly. As such it is (by the schizophrenic formula) as inevitable as Fate that it will eventually return to undo him.

oppressive movie, perhaps the most unenjoyable "classic" of the genre ever made), Gittes has been overwhelmed by circumstances; and if he is not permanently unhinged by what he has seen (like Det. Mills at the climax of *Seven*), then it can only be due to his complete lack of sensitivity. In this regard also (his apparent lack of personal concern, the absence of heroic qualities), Gittes is a quintessential schizophrenic hero of the period.

Nicholson's final and best role in this seven-year excursion into schizophrenia was the full expression of the actor's preoccupation and the most complete realization of his talents to date. It has been thirty-five years since *One Flew Over the Cuckoo's Nest* and, with the exceptions of *The Crossing Guard* and *The Pledge*, the actor has never even come close to the degree of intensity, commitment, and depth which he showed in his earliest roles. In fact Nicholson's career has been something of a travesty from this time onwards, almost as if the passivity of the schizophrenic roles which he embodied so superbly left him at the mercy of greater forces, helplessly swept away on a tide of mediocrity.*

With *Cuckoo's Nest*, Nicholson became for a brief moment more than a mere actor, he became an archetype, a symbol (specifically, the Nicholson seen on the movie poster, straining upward as he attempts to lift the marble shower unit). What this archetype symbolized was freedom, revolt, the undying will to prevail no matter the obstacles, and no matter how impotent the revolt may initially appear to be. ("At least I tried, goddamn it!") Despite his grandstanding and rebelliousness, however, MacMurphy was also in a sense a passive character. He enters the lunatic asylum not on a mission but simply taking refuge from the hardships of prison life, expecting an "easy ride." Once there, something takes over and he becomes, against his own better instincts (and certainly against his interests), a sort of schizophrenic crusader. Finally (as Kesey's novel has it), he becomes a martyr. Nicholson/MacMurphy was the schizo trickster who unwittingly sacrificed himself for a cause he never believed in. It was something that Bobby Dupea had to head for Alaska to find, something that Buddusky and Gittes in their world-weariness lost sight of altogether. This "cause," most simply encapsulated under the banner of "Freedom," relates to the liberating allure of non-conformity, which finds its apotheosis in madness. It is more subtly and obliquely signified by the emblem of *silence*—the

---

*Perhaps this is the price that Nicholson paid for his earlier, phenomenal success, and for his at least partially realized Brechtian aspirations? After *Cuckoo's Nest*, Nicholson moved steadily further into a kind of self-parodic style of acting which—much like Brando before him—helped to distance him from the paucity of his material but also consigned him to the reluctant, if not entirely unintentional, role of clown. Nicholson's clowning was up there with most other actors' sincerest efforts, however, and somehow he survived with his legend—if not integrity—more or less intact. It seems a given, however, that he will never again regain the kind of power, or artistic relevance, which he enjoyed in his heyday.

unconscious. In *Cuckoo's Nest* this alternative, the possibility of freedom, is represented by the Chief, the Indian, the Other, who is for most of the movie passing himself off as a deaf-mute. The Chief abides in silence partially because he has nothing to say, but mostly because he knows whatever he says would be wasted on the world. He has taken refuge in the appearance of imbecility, and this is his greater wisdom. Knowing that in an insane world any sane man will be thought mad, he feigns insanity instead. But of course he gets locked up anyway, and this also is his refuge, the madhouse offering a more organized, peaceful kind of insanity than that of society at large. The Chief (read: unconscious) abides in silence until MacMurphy (the ego) comes along to stir his inner fire into life again, to reawaken his will to live, to partake in the madness rather than simply observe it passively from a safe distance. The chief, by biding his time, is also (as the film has it) gathering the power to act, while MacMurphy, for all his conscious striving, is impotent. But it is MacMurphy's (the ego's) powerlessness — or more precisely his struggling in spite of it ("At least I tried!") — that serves as an example to the Chief and an inspiration, an incentive, to the unconscious to *move*. It's MacMurphy's insane bid to accomplish the impossible that inspires the Chief to act, and so (with the strength of silence behind him) make the impossible possible. This in turn stirs up the fires of revolt in the other inmates (though in the movie they stay safe in their incarceration, they at least cheer the Chief on his way), and, potentially at least, it starts a chain reaction by which (ego overrun by Id) the lunatics take over the asylum.

MacMurphy's example is an unstoppable motion. What makes him an authentic martyr, and *Cuckoo's Nest* a genuine parable of its time, is how he uses the (growingly collective) schizophrenic experience as a cover for his messianic (apocalyptic) pretensions. Society *is* a madhouse. The sane man is called mad, and crucified — or lobotomized — by such a society. This is *ostensibly* to suppress his message, but it also allows the other inmates to see for themselves the truth (that society is a madhouse), so that, potentially, this truth may set them free. When the Chief breaks out and returns to the wilderness, swallowed up by darkness, it's the unconscious taking over again, the stirring of the Other, the awakening of the Id, by which the ego is inevitably and fatally smothered, and so finds release. Now the trickster's mission has been accomplished, he is no longer of any use and must return whence he came: to nonexistence.

It's no wonder, perhaps, if Nicholson's career seemed to be smothered in its cradle after this. As spokesman for the schizophrenic experience and avatar of impotent revolt, his work was done.

6

Into the Wild: John Boorman's Explicit Myths

> I suggest that being uncomfortable in my own skin, feeling the world to be an alien place, I have sought out actors, surrogates, to send out into worlds of my invention.
> —John Boorman, "Bright Dreams, Hard Knocks"

I doubt if any moviemaker ever lived who has such a natural affinity for the schizophrenic experience as John Boorman. More than anything else, such an affinity relates to Boorman's penchant and predilection for mythology, and the fact that most myths—in addressing indirectly the fragmented state of the human psyche—are, at least in part, diagnoses of our collective schizophrenia. In myths—be they those of classics or children's stories or comic books—the various characters tend to be defined, as archetypes, by their specific *natures*, ranging from good to bad to ugly and everything else in between. In this way, the characters all *add up* to a single composite, they are facets of a non-unified psyche (as we saw with *The Good, the Bad, and the Ugly*). In myth, the characters complement each other, even as they occasionally conflict, to form a more or less harmonious community (or, in many myths—such as that of Camelot—a community in a state of collapse). In simple terms, the various characters serve to alert the Hero—the ego—as to his various unconscious urges, weaknesses, obsessions, and so forth. In a word, the undercurrents of the Id. By becoming aware of them, and by being forced to confront them, the Hero is given the opportunity of integrating them into himself (i.e., making the unconscious conscious) and becoming whole. This process is described by Jung as "individuation."

In the Arthurian myths, there are two primary factors that bring about the collapse of Camelot: on the one hand, Arthur's illicit tryst with his half-sister Morgan Le Fay, which gives birth to the demon offspring Mordred; and secondly, Lancelot and Queen Guinevere's secret affair. In both cases, it is not the indiscretion itself that is so fatal but rather Arthur's willed *denial* of it, his refusal to accept responsibility for it. With Lancelot/Guinevere, he refuses to look at his own complicity in the "betrayal," his own untrustworthy nature, and above all his fallibility, all revealed by his selection of Lancelot as "first knight." Likewise with Arthur's succumbing to the sexual wiles of Morgan and rearing the bastard Mordred (who will be instrumental in Camelot's ruin); it is not that Arthur is *punished* for this moment of weakness, rather that, by ignoring it (by failing to deal with the consequences at the time), the problem is allowed to fester and grow. Just as Mordred grows in Morgan's womb, Arthur's personal flaws take on an autonomous nature and eventually undermine all his nobler qualities. The result is that Arthur's Kingdom — his soul — is brought to ruin.

The myth of Arthur is an enduring myth which Boorman was bound to be drawn to sooner or later; long before the divine folly of *Excalibur*, he had already been dabbling in his own brand of mythmaking, with the ludicrous *Zardoz*, the somewhat more successful but incoherent *Point Blank*, and the primitive *Hell in the Pacific. Point Blank*, in Boorman's own words, was "based on a pulp thriller that I tortured into an existential dreamscape."[1] The film takes Lee Marvin and a more or less standard revenge/chase thriller plot and transforms it, by a mix of audacity and folly, into a largely impenetrable, quasi-surrealist psychological text. As Boorman has it, Walker (Marvin) is a wandering ghost trapped by unfinished business, condemned (as legends, myths, and New Age lore has it) to act out residual desires from his former life. At the same time, he is a hitman on the trail of his betrayers, looking for revenge and reimbursement — the $93,000 that was stolen from him (*Payback* in both senses of the word, as the title of the more prosaic pulp Mel Gibson remake had it).

The simple plot and the mythical themes of *Point Blank* would certainly seem to mesh seamlessly enough, at least on the drawing board; but Boorman lacks the necessary skill to pull it off. As a director, he is fatally tangled up by his pretensions as a writer, his almost hysterical ambitions as a "Jungian" filmmaker. This is a general flaw of most of Boorman's movies, and one that he himself admits to: "The writer's unfettered imagination irresponsibly puts down scenes that are impossible to shoot."[2] As insightful as he is (and considerably gifted as a director), Boorman is only ever as good as his material, and sometimes considerably less so. He's probably the most awkward and amateurish of accomplished moviemakers; it's as if his passion for ideas gets the better of his levelheadedness as a craftsman, and when it comes to translating his ideas to the screen, Boorman often seems hopelessly at sea. As Pauline Kael observes, "Without a strong writer to supply emotion and a coherent level of meaning, Boorman's movies disintegrate into shots and sequences."[3] Of all his movies, those that he also wrote (with the marked exceptions of the autobiographical *Hope and Glory* and the playful *Where the Heart Is*) seem to be the biggest messes. Yet Boorman himself makes no bones about this: "All movies are bad," he says. "Mine are often acutely embarrassing."[4]

Boorman's movies must look great on paper however. They are thematic enactments of his personal, none-too-private obsession: the split between man and nature, between conscious and unconscious. Boorman laments man's estrangement, not only from his animal roots, but also from his higher (or divine) calling. This is a theme most overtly dealt with in *Hell in the Pacific, The Emerald Forest,* and — still perhaps Boorman's best-known and influential work — *Deliverance*. In *Hell in the Pacific,* Boorman forgoes plot and opts for metaphor instead: an American and a Japanese solider during World War II are trapped together on a desert island. The film is a vignette, using the circumstantial (though nonetheless profound) antagonism of war as a means for addressing the more fundamental human antagonisms, those of the self with the "other." It posits not merely the differences of East and West but also "primitive" and "civilized," unconscious and conscious, quickly exposing the fallacy of our assumptions about each. The Western man, played again by Lee Marvin, is anything but "civilized," while the Eastern Man — Toshiro Mifune — is far from being a savage. Nonetheless, these stereotypes (which audiences had grown to accept blindly, in large part thanks to anti–Japanese war movies) still prevail to a certain degree. Boorman pits the two men — the two opposing sides of the psyche — against one another in a sort of microcosmic world war, reducing it to, and exposing it as, the petty bickering that it is. At the same time, he is intent on getting at something deeper, namely, a recognition that the two sides are in actual fact complementary, even though opposed (hence equal), and that, reduced to the basics, "all men are the same." Through this realization, Boorman hopes to effect a reconciliation with his protagonists, and presumably also in his own psyche and, by extension, that of the audience.

Hell in the Pacific is a terribly dull movie, however, despite having two such physically charismatic actors. The natural setting is simply too confining; not because the characters are restricted to an island, but because they are trapped inside the confines of Boorman's humanistic conception — his conceit — by which he turns them into archetypal signifiers instead of people.*
Nature is central to Boorman's movies, and it *can* be the perfect backdrop to human drama, provided — as in *Deliverance* — that it is a dynamic player itself, an actual threat and not merely a pictorial setting. From Westerns to war movies, the desert or mountains or the jungle have been the perfect milieu for suspense and drama — not merely a place for the enemy to lurk in but as an

---

*Is there any desert island movie that doesn't become tiresome, once the initial premise has been assimilated and we are forced to simply wait to see if — or how — the character(s) will escape? I can't think of one. A desert island setting has the static quality of a one-room drama but lacks the claustrophobic tension — the mood — that is built into a theater-based work. Nature just isn't as cinematic as a courtroom.

actual, physical embodiment of the protagonist's fears. Such terrain stands in for the strangeness and hostility of the unknown, the psychological terrain through which the hero must journey. (Walter Hill's *Southern Comfort* is a striking example, and the film owes a large debt to *Deliverance*.) But there are few directors with the guile and the cunning to communicate the ruthlessness of Nature. It is not a human ruthlessness; on the contrary, it is Nature's very lack of human qualities that makes it seem so ruthless to us. To effectively depict the awesomeness of Nature — and at the same time convey man's helplessness (though also his freedom) within it — a filmmaker must align himself with both the civilized and the wild, the conscious and the unconscious. There is no room for sentimentality: such things are deadly weakness in a jungle where only the strong survive. But there is also no place for cruelty or capriciousness. These are equally human traits that Nature does not indulge in. Nature, however harsh she may seem, is nothing if not just.

When a filmmaker like Terence Malick makes a war movie from the point of view of Nature (*The Thin Red Line*), the human characters are reduced to inconveniences; they are stripped of not just their significance but of their character, and hence are of no interest to us; the result is a movie that allows no access — it's one big, bloody travelogue, with philosophical pretensions. At the other extreme, Boorman's *The Emerald Forest* is an example of how a filmmaker's sentimentalism (for the "lost heritage of Nature") can blur his creative faculties and turn a potentially powerful mythic adventure story into New Age pap. Boorman stacks the deck too heavily on the side of the wild, and in the process (conversely) he *humanizes* it to an almost ludicrous degree. He shows the allure but not the terror. Likewise, his depictions of modern civilization as grim, gray, and soulless fail to account for why anyone would ever want to live there in the first place.

As Boorman himself writes — in *Money into Light*— after spending some time in the Amazon making the movie, he began to miss the comforts of civilization, magazines, TV, etc., and to long to get back to his "soulless" but familiar world. Wouldn't we all feel the same way? But in his movie he never bothers to show us the things that the Western family enjoy about their world, the things they are giving up to be in the jungle, and that the abducted boy is deprived of; in a word, the price he pays for his newfound freedom as a (not just noble but *sacred*!) savage. It's as if Boorman kept from his movie what he admitted so freely in his journal: that he is as much a modern world junky as the rest of us. That basic dishonesty — which shows his lack of ruthlessness as an artist — is what makes Boorman's vision of Nature (and hence the whole movie) essentially bogus. It's sentimentality where sentimentality no longer applies — which is every bit as true of Art as of Nature.

Deliverance is another matter, however. The movie has a lot in common with Lee Tamouri/David Mamet's *The Edge* (which in its own way was as bogus as *The Emerald Forest*, but worked a lot better as a visceral adventure story). It offers up the pleasures of a classic survival story: city boys pitted against Nature. *Deliverance* is less bogus — if less entertaining — because it was written by James Dickey who, unlike Mamet, knew a little of what he was writing about. Unlike *The Edge* (or *The Emerald Forest*), *Deliverance* (the book) is not the work of an armchair dilettante but of a man genuinely enamored of — and intoxicated by — the beauty and brutality of Nature. It's curious, then, that Dickey chose to make his protagonist, Lewis (played in the movie by Burt Reynolds), if not into a dilettante, still something of a fraud, a hollow man. Dickey appeared to have suffered doubts about himself as a "man's man," and it's probably these doubts that give him whatever integrity he has (as both an adventurer and as a writer). His awareness that, for all his macho expertise, his civilized skills — and his human reason — he would never be a match for the wild. Lewis is the exact opposite of this: for all his pompous pontificating about the supremacy of nature, it's clear he considers himself its equal, a superior man, a natural hunter and survivor. This arrogance is Lewis' undoing. In Dickey's view there is no sin greater, no weakness more fatal, than man's assumption of supremacy. In contrast with Mamet's contention in *The Edge*— that most men in the wild die of shame — Dickey's Lewis is defeated by the sin of *hubris*.

Deliverance is a primal fairy tale for adults, a visceral and macabre adventure story with its very own "moral" subtext. It was such a big hit with audiences, I think, partly because it serves as a more sophisticated version of the kind of gothic horror story audiences never tire of (it has "the formality of a nightmare"[5]). Boorman indeed comes clean in this regard at the end of the movie, when all pretenses at social commentary are swallowed up by the simple desire to chill and thrill us. Ed's nightmare of the resurfacing dead, the unkillable demons of his unconscious (and conscience), is a hokey, effective device, and belongs firmly to the horror genre.

In the supernatural horror movie (for example, *The Haunting*), the protagonists find themselves being drawn ever deeper into a strange and terrifying world in which the rules of nature (and of reason) no longer apply. Without ever taking recourse to the supernatural, *Deliverance* gives us the same basic shtick. It gives us four urban professionals heading to the mountains for a male-bonding/initiation-into-nature experience. Lewis is the instigator, though it seems likely that it is Ed, Lewis' friend — and the only one who seems to "understand" Lewis — who talks the others (Bobby and Drew, played by Ned Beatty and Ronnie Cox, respectively) into it. Lewis' plan, his "vision," is to take one last, death-defying trip down the rapids of the river before industrial developments render it inaccessible. The other three men, to varying degrees but most especially Ed, look up to Lewis as a superior specimen of manhood and put their trust in him as their guide through the wilderness. They expect him not only to show them a good time, but to initiate them into a more primal kind of experience.

6. Into the Wild: John Boorman's Explicit Myths

None of what happens (when these best-laid plans go awry, leading to the kind of initiation that no one in his right mind would volunteer for) is actually Lewis' *fault*; but it's his inadequacy as an initiator, and the other men's misplaced trust in him (symptomatic of their combined folly), that leads them to disaster. Despite Lewis' posturing, they have between them failed to make the necessary preparations for their venture into the unknown. All of them (including Lewis) are flirting with the elements; they are treating an excursion into the primal depths as a simple weekend trip, as recreation. Here we have the familiar shtick: the protagonists are undone by their lack of respect or understanding for the forces of the supernatural. The supernatural and "Nature" stand for the same thing: the Id, with its unreasoning power that cannot be placated, and that (according to the generic pattern) is to be underestimated only at severest cost.

Like the unconscious, Nature appears to be largely passive until the moment it is roused to act. Once stirred to attention by the rash flirtations of the ego, however, it becomes a brutal consort. In the case of *Deliverance*, it leaves one of the team dead (Drew), another (Lewis) crippled, a third (Bobby) raped and humiliated, and the fourth (Ed, played rather joylessly by Jon Voight, as the ostensible "hero," the practical man) severely traumatized by his brush with Reality. The excursion, and the flirtation, begins harmlessly enough when Drew initiates the famous "dueling banjos" set with the large-skulled swamp boy at the gas station. This scene (initiated by Dickey, and barring Bobby's rape probably the best in the movie) serves a dual purpose. On the one hand, it appears as a lighter (musical) interlude by which Boorman can ease us unsuspectingly into the action by giving us a false sense of well-being. It suggests that communication — even a kind of communion — is possible between the (soft, arrogant) city dwellers and the (cold, hostile) mountain folk; it offers a common language, that of music, the language of the unconscious, through which it *appears* that mutual respect, even affection, is possible between the different peoples. This is illusory. The swamp boy responds to Drew's playing, but not to Drew. He refuses contemptuously to shake Drew's hand when it is offered, and later, when the four men pass under the bridge in their canoes, the boy's cold, inhuman gaze reflects the gaze of the wilderness. This crew is not welcome here, they do not belong; they can expect nothing but hardship.

In Boorman's treatment of Dickey's story, the characters become secondary to the *myth*. Each of the men signifies a *type*, a facet of the ego.* There is the vain, narcissistic Lewis, with his overconfidence, his animal-man poses,

---

*This is confirmed by Christopher Dickey (James' son)'s account of the making of the movie, in which he observes, "The four suburbanites, the narrow-eyed rednecks — all those men were James Dickey." From "Summer of Deliverance," *The New Yorker*, July 13, 1999, pg. 41.

and his cryptic remarks full of empty portent (Reynolds is perfectly cast here, maybe for the first and last time). There is the shy, uncertain family man Ed, a coward perhaps, but certainly not a faker. Drew is the feminine, mealy-mouthed banjo-strumming nice guy; and finally there is Bobby, the fat, whining buffoon, the figure of fun. Between them they make up a pretty sorry bunch of adventurers, but if Lewis' silent, quasi-mystical pose were any more than a pose, they might have stood a chance. As it is, it's the vain leading the blind: there's no integrity to the group. It is (in our present terms) a fragmented psyche, the lines of communication are down. There is little respect and even less love between the men, and as such, the group quickly disintegrates into a bunch of (not warring but whining) fragments. Since there is no integrity to the whole, no *cohesion*, it's wide open to attack from without. This is an eventuality that even Lewis, with all his survivalist blather, is unprepared for: he never once considers the possibility of a *human* threat.

This is the irony of Dickey's fable: it is not Nature that undoes the men (though the river will soon join in the attack once morale has begun to crumble) but its denizens, the subhuman, sexually depraved mountain men. Such id-monsters represent the embodiment of Nature in its most hostile, aberrant, anti-human form. They are reflections of the men's worst natures. By venturing into the unconscious without realizing the stakes, and without first mapping the terrain, they have left themselves wide open not just to the elements, but to the "elementals." They have made the most common mistake arrogant adventurers can make when wandering uninvited into the wilderness: assuming it to be uninhabited. (The psyche, just as much as these mountains, is certainly populated by all kinds of unfamiliar forms, not all of which are friendly.)

When the mountain men get a glimpse of the city dwellers, they are unable to resist the allure of their soft, white flesh. They stalk them and snare them, treating them as they would a sacrificial virgin, or, for that matter, a tamed boar. Bobby's rape at the hands of the lascivious mountain men — in Boorman's vision at least — amounts to fitting, if extreme, retribution for "White Man's rape of the land." It's the unconscious getting its own back: having bided its time, it now seizes its opportunity. The sequence is genuinely appalling, maybe the most erotic anti-erotic sequence ever filmed in a mainstream movie. Boorman shows an astonishing aptitude for wringing all the queasy dread from the scene; with what Kael called his "hypnotic talent for charging an atmosphere with fear,"[6] he puts us square inside the scene with no option of escape: every white man's worst nightmare coming true. He gets us not just inside poor Bobby and Ed's skins (Ed is strapped to a tree with a knife at his throat, forced to watch as Bobby is stripped and sodomized) but also — far more disturbingly — inside the leering, bestial mountain men. As a result, we are forced to *feel*, quite palpably, the thick pleasure they take in terrorizing their victims. Like nasty children pulling wings of flies, they revel in

6. Into the Wild: John Boorman's Explicit Myths

the power, the heady thrill, of playing gods. The eroticism of the scene comes not from Bobby's wobbling white flesh or his piglike squeals, but rather from his complete subjugation to the will of his tormentors, and in their obvious relish at having complete mastery over him. Here Boorman depicts, as guilefully and powerfully as anyone ever has, the nature of sadism and of violence. At this point, the excursion into the wild has become a trip to hell.

Boorman said how he shot "the mountain men as though they were emerging from trees: like malevolent spirits of the forest coming to rape these city men who had in turn ravaged the forest."[7] And he cast the roles so astutely that — as with Hooper's casting of the Hitchhiker in the thematically similar *Texas Chainsaw Massacre*— we may be in doubt as to just how much these bumpkin perverts are *acting*.[8] The scene is soaked with such grisly authenticity that, for all its repulsiveness, it's mesmerizing to watch; and it's the searing, sickening power of this scene, I think, that accounts for *Deliverance* becoming so successful and influential a movie of its time.[9] Boorman was showing us something which movies had never dared (or cared) to show us before (or even since). He depicts a level of degradation that is very nearly traumatic to watch.*

Law of the Primal: Ed (Jon Voight) falls prey to the swamp demons (Bill McKinney and Herbert Coward) of the id in *Deliverance* (1972, Warner Bros.).

---

*The Texas Chainsaw Massacre— a horror film — can perhaps compete with the traumatic intensity of Boorman's rape scene, but being in the more "disreputable" genre of horror somehow makes it less remarkable, and less shocking. Lynch's *Blue Velvet* and De Palma's *Casualties of War* offer moments with a similarly traumatic quality to them, but such cases are certainly exceptional. None of these other examples deal with a man being anally raped, which, as taboos go, must be one of the deepest and most enduring. All in all, at least by today's standards (actually more puritanical and "repressed" than in 1971), one wonders how Dickey and Boorman got away with it.

Following this sequence, Lewis comes to the rescue just in time to save Ed from being forced to perform fellatio on the second swamp demon. Lewis appears not in the traditional, swashbuckling manner of Robin Hood but stealthily; he strikes from a distance, killing one of the mountain men with an arrow through his chest. The other flees, and the four men debate what to do with the body. Drew becomes the voice of "reason," the civilized appeal. His mincing pleas to the others to uphold "the law," woefully out of place here, meet with scorn from Lewis, who has by now taken full charge. He is the hero (and the killer) he always wanted to be. He sneers at Drew, raising his arms to the wilderness: "The Law? What law?!"

The law of civilization (repression) is now obsolete. This is the realm of the unconscious, where reason does not prevail. All laws have changed and a new order has emerged. Bobby, of course, doesn't want anyone to know what happened; that's all *he* cares about. He is in no mood to be either sentimental or picky about the finer points of "the law." And so Ed becomes the arbitrator: the deciding vote is his. Yet this little enactment of "democracy" is little more than a sham, since Lewis would almost certainly have gone ahead with his plan regardless of the others' decision; it's physical support he requires, not moral. And at this point the whole initiation journey comes off course. The group is now divided, there is no longer even the *appearance* of harmony. The forces of the unconscious are moving in. Through the "chinks" in the armor, it is possible to infiltrate the whole and break it down into parts; these parts will then be undermined and overcome in an inevitable process of disintegration. Schizophrenia has taken root.

Drew, the "conscience" of the group, is the first to go; he is nothing but a "drag" on the rest of them. (It's unclear what happens to Drew in the movie; he appears to suffer some sort of attack and falls from the boat, but Lewis becomes convinced he was shot by the second mountain man whom he believes — rightly as it happens — is stalking them.) Moments after Drew falls, Lewis, the ostensible "ego" or controlling intelligence of the group, is rendered impotent when the rapids capsize his boat and his leg is torn open. At this point Lewis loses not only his authority but all credibility also. Horribly injured, he falls apart and begins to howl and whimper like a child, thus revealing himself to be a man of straw. Bobby, ineffective to begin with, is now worse than useless; he's outright hostile from the misery and shame of his ordeal. That only leaves Ed, whose story this is. Ed is the true ego, or Hero, to Lewis' pretender. This is *his* initiatory journey, and exposing Lewis' inadequacy is a central part of it. Through the process of disillusionment, Ed must assume responsibility and claim his independence.*

---

*Unfortunately, from this point on, Boorman's handling of the movie becomes less and less assured, just as if he were suffering a corresponding crisis of confidence along with his hero.

6. Into the Wild: John Boorman's Explicit Myths

In 1991, Boorman made a documentary about himself (I have read the script but never seen the finished product), called *I Dreamt I Woke Up*. Besides the (appropriately schizophrenic) premise of the movie as summed up by its title (that of the conjugation of myth and reality, art and life), Boorman's most recurring contention is that he is a man forever at odds with his sense of self. He begins the movie with the words, "Soon I would have to re-enter the waking world and resume the pretense of being one person ... a ridiculous man, a stranger to himself ... I am not comfortable in my own skin.... Fortunately, making movies has allowed me to engage the charming, handsome, rugged men I ought to have been and to send them off on my adventures."

Boorman's movies are his own means of coming to terms with himself, of finding an outlet for his fantasies, and perhaps this is in large part the reason why they are so uneven: so passionate but so indulgent. As Boorman writes, "There is an intensity about my work which often makes it painful to watch, but also gives the films an integrity. There is also a silliness which crops up with irritating frequency. I recognize this in my character.... It comes from a fear of being serious, of embarrassment, of a lack of belief in self, not being rooted in a strong cultural tradition."[10]

Boorman is a wonderful observer of the flaws of human beings (starting with himself), of the quirks and catastrophes, the ups and downs of our existence. As a writer (not of scripts, I mean, but of prose journals) he draws you effortlessly into his dreamy, almost childlike perceptions. He has a wonderful, easy style, poetic but insightful, direct, almost beguiling. It's his gentleness — his humility — that makes Boorman a born poet, a natural visionary, but also I think a hugely flawed filmmaker. He's at the opposite end of the spectrum to Oliver Stone, who also aspires to mythic proportions in his art (and likewise suffers from shamanic pretensions) but who has a basic obtuseness, a pigheadedness as an artist, that often sees him through, however false his

(Continued.) Unlike Ed, however, Boorman doesn't pull us through. His staging of the supposedly definitive climax, in which Ed scales the sheer cliff face at night then waits till morning for the second mountain man to arrive and finally dispatches him, is sloppy and unfocused. It lacks either visual or emotional clarity, and has none of the visceral power of climax. We do not feel Ed's terror climbing the cliff face, and though we certainly feel his relief when he is finally able to let fly the arrow and (despite his appearing to have fumbled at the last minute) kill the adversary, it is far from a cathartic moment. As a result, *Deliverance* is only half successful; like so many of Boorman's films it fails to deliver on its early promise, and seems to fizzle out rather than reach a climax. "[G]ifted as he is, Boorman doesn't have much common sense." (Kael, "O Consuella!" *Reeling*, pg. 276.) As a director, he seems to suffer from excess imagination and not enough focus. His attention tends to waver just when he needs to be applying it, and as a result many of his movies seem unfinished, bungled. Boorman — with his predilection for mythic undercurrents and his passion for "ideas" — is more of a conceptual artist than anything, or at least he seems to aspire in that direction. As a result, his films tend to get swallowed up by their own themes without ever coming to grips with them or finding an adequate structure to house them in.

aspirations may be. If Stone is all ego, Boorman is too much ruled by his id. His vision is all-embracing, and as a result it's diaphanous, fuzzy. Where Stone takes depressingly mundane subjects and inflates them up to mythic dimensions (such as his epic indulgence *Any Given Sunday*, or his film noir piffle *U-Turn*), Boorman takes huge, universal themes and flattens them, renders them impotent.

Kael wrote of Boorman, "Maybe if he got his fill of communing with a past that never was he could move on to making movies."[11] Boorman does seem (by his own admission) unable to fully engage in the present and to give himself wholeheartedly and ruthlessly to the business at hand.* And for a moviemaker (Boorman's business), this entails not only passion but also a sort of ferocity and brutality — a ruthlessness that can easily be mistaken for mere egotism — of which Boorman seems to be incapable. In a word, he may be just too nice a guy.

It's curious to note (in regard to this) how in his journal "Bright Dreams, Hard Knocks," Boorman recalls a dream he had the night before starting filming his auto-documentary, in which he hears a voice telling him, "You are an absolute shit, and that should be in the film."[12] I'm sure that Boorman, like the rest of us, can be an absolute shit when he wants to be, but if anything this dream — or Boorman's reporting it — seems to point out just the opposite: how inhibited he is by the possibility, not so much of being a shit, but of being seen as one. In a word (and again by Boorman's own admission) — his self-consciousness. This I'd wager is at the root of Boorman's struggle to get comfortable inside his own skin, and to make movies in the modern world without betraying what he sees (perhaps) as his sacred allegiance (and alignment) to the past. Another way of putting it would be to say that his conscious goals as a filmmaker tend to be at odds with his unconscious needs as an ordinary human being. Part of him seems to feel that what he is doing is not only phony, spurious, and ineffective, but that it is also somehow immoral or deluded. And of course he may be right.

This disharmony between personal ambition and philanthropic desire, this split between ego and id — is potentially the source of friction from which

---

*"To be totally present, to be here and nowhere else, to exist in this very moment without referring to past or future, without a rogue corner of the mind flitting hither and thither, stepping out of that moment and the self, looking back at us, making us self-aware, self-conscious and therefore unable to be entirely present — that is a wondrous thing. It means to be completely alive.... But to dream it is necessary to be free of here and now; in the unconsciousness of sleep we are liberated. In day-dreams only partially so. There are few people who can achieve a total 'waking absence,' but, for most of us, we only experience something like it at the movies, which approximate the condition of dreaming.... How can we be utterly lost in a movie, yet still be aware that we are sitting in a theater? That is day-dreaming: to be both absent and present at the same time. So the movies can transport us into a trance of dreams." "Bright Dreams, Hard Knocks," *Projections*, pg. 73-4.

6. Into the Wild: John Boorman's Explicit Myths

creativity emerges. But it can also, if dwelled upon too much (or conversely, if not sufficiently acknowledged, as is the case with Stone), work to the detriment of the artist. Stone has lost sight (lately at least) of his better instincts as an artist and taken to indulging in the heady thrill of his talent and his "reputation"; he's become what he always had the potential to be, an empty showman. Boorman — whose career trajectory is so uneven it can hardly be called a trajectory at all — continues to fluctuate and vacillate between spectacle and dialectic. He has the same preachy tendencies as Stone, and is certainly his equal when it comes to natural cinematic gifts, but he lacks Stone's assurance, his confidence, his arrogance. As a result, he's infinitely more appealing in his appeals (which are less political than Stone's and more mythical, or at least ecological); but he is also, for the most part, considerably less effective in his effects.

It's hard to say where Boorman's unique (and uniquely endearing) brand of creative schizophrenia will lead him. If he lacks the endurance — the undauntedness — of a Stone, he retains the kind of integrity that few directors (certainly not Stone) can lay claim to. Boorman may be incapable of making a movie that comes close to realizing his ambition as a filmmaker/mythmaker. But he also seems incapable of giving up the struggle, of selling out and opting for the glory without the scars. In which case, his apparent schizophrenia as a filmmaker really singles him out as being that much more healthy as a human being. And there's the irony — the rub — in a nutshell.

Boorman is an "apocalyptic" director with an unparalleled respect for the chaotic revelations of the unconscious. When he applies himself to a straightforward (often non-fictional) narrative such as *Hope and Glory* or *The Taylor of Panama*, he is as assured and accomplished as any filmmaker needs to be. But when he goes with his more visionary impulses — as with *Zardoz, The Heretic, Excalibur* — the results range from the sublime to the ridiculous, without any apparent awareness (on the director's part) of the difference between the two. Boorman's critical/aesthetic faculties (by all other accounts quite finely tuned) seem to desert him at these times, and the only film of his in which his visionary imagination and his narrative technique seem to be more or less in sync is — my own personal favorite — the eccentric crisis comedy *Where the Heart Is*. This is something of a director's whimsy perhaps (he wrote the script with his daughter), but it's a genuinely inspired whimsy: intriguing, affecting, often hilarious, it successfully incorporates all of Boorman's major preoccupations — magic, creative imagination, community, pagan ceremony, growth through adversity, etc. — and offers up a convincingly happy reconciliation between the past and the future (here represented by the two generations of parents and children*).

---

*The film depicts an irate father (played by Dabney Coleman) who forces his almost-grown children to move into a decaying house on a wrecking site and learn to make it on their

All of Boorman's movies — give or take — involve excursions into unfamiliar, generally hostile terrain. It may be for simple mercenary gain (*Point Blank, The Emerald Forest, The Taylor of Panama*), or through sheer necessity (*Hell in the Pacific, Zardoz, Hope and Glory*), or else the simple thirst for experience (*Deliverance, Beyond Rangoon*); but invariably there are transformative results. Boorman sees movies as a tool — like myth itself — for plumbing the depths of his own unconscious, a flashlight for discovering new nooks and crannies in the human psyche. As such, all journeys for Boorman are expeditions into the chaotic landscape of the unknown; they are field trips from which no guarantee of return is possible, but on which, if we stick the course, some degree of enlightenment is promised. In Boorman's world there is no madness that does not offer at least the possibility of vision, no schizophrenia that doesn't hint at shamanic reality, and no wilderness that isn't populated as much by wonders as by terrors.

If Boorman ever gets to produce his definitive schizo journey, a movie that sees the reconciliation of subject with object, dream with waking, madness with illumination, it will surely depend on his effecting such a reconciliation in his own psyche. Meantime, he remains "lost" in his own darkness, on an expedition all his own. He is still mapping the wilderness of his unconscious: no easy task when he has to keep one eye on the camera and the other on the compass. It's perhaps no wonder if he seems to be going round in circles half the time: Boorman can go from shaman to schizo and back again in the course of a single sequence. But if he ever does strike up a balance, he may just find there's no difference between the two. Didn't Merlin walk with one foot in the past and the other in the future? That may be the curse of the schizo, but it's also the art of the shaman.

(continued) own. He calls their bluff and gives them independence, in order to get them out of his hair. The kids are anything but thrilled by this new "opportunity" (read: crisis) but, once they realize their father isn't bluffing — that they are on their own — they make the most of their grim new circumstances and get creative. Before long they have turned their dusty squat into a kind of New Age creative community madhouse, where practical needs are met with imaginative — often batty but nonetheless effective — measures. Meantime of course, the father's own world of corporate greed begins to backfire on him, while that of his children blooms. Once he suffers complete financial ruin, they take him in.

7

A Glass Darkly: Brando and Bertolucci's *Last Tango*

> I think that I am a repressed person. I think I can express my energy, my libido, my aggression, only in my work. We are all Dr. Jekyll and Mr. Hyde. We know our ghosts. And we don't tell anybody, not even our partners, about our ghosts. We live with our ghosts. We keep our ghosts inside in our life. It's just in the moment that Jekyll becomes Mr. Hyde that I can put my ghosts on the screen.
> — Bernardo Bertolucci, 1977

Bernardo Bertolucci hit a creative peak in 1972 with *Last Tango in Paris*, and attained a level of emotional honesty and visual poetry that would set a new standard for filmmakers thereafter. Perhaps he put so much of his inspiration— his "life force"— into this one movie that he never fully recovered? *Last Tango* is such a full-blooded work that it's likely that *anything* Bertolucci did afterwards would have paled by comparison, but the fact is that his movies since have been pretty pallid by any standards. He followed *Tango* with an epic folly, the sprawling but engaging *1900*, a sloppy work imbued with passion and intensity. The same could hardly be said for *La Luna*, a tawdry tale of incest and heroin addiction, or for his vacuous and spiritless "Eastern chic" trilogy, *The Last Emperor*, *Sheltering Sky*, and *Little Buddha*. By the time of the adolescent *Stealing Beauty*, there was really nothing left in Bertolucci's movies to suggest the impassioned sensualist and master composer, painter, and poet of *Last Tango* and *The Conformist*. Only with the more recent *Besieged*— in which Bertolucci seems to be deliberately stripping away the pomp and circumstance of his previous few films— did some of the intensity and integrity return to his filmmaking.

Judging by *Besieged*, Bertolucci was himself aware that something had been lost in his progression from revolutionary poet-filmmaker to Oscar-winning showman. A master movie seducer, he had allowed himself to be seduced by images. In 1973, just after *Tango*, he spoke of filmmaking as follows:

I do not like to talk alone, and I do not talk alone. I do not talk for myself, I mean. This, by the way, is how the cinema becomes a way of weighing reality, that is, it becomes an instrument for understanding the world. And I think this is true for both creator and viewer.... And as far as the public is concerned, the only thing I know is that I seem to be seeking an ever bigger one ... perhaps part of my process of liberation was the acceptance of the fact that I had always wanted to create a *specttacolo*.[1]

Certainly *Last Tango* was the last of his films, until *Besieged*, that had the content to match — to justify — its excess of style. Spectacular as it was, it was anything but a *specttacolo*. *Last Emperor*, *Little Buddha*, and *Stealing Beauty*, on the other hand, for all their scope and technical ambitions, are whimsies, the work of a man with no obvious fascination for anything but the beauty of images and the technical challenges of his craft. *Sheltering Sky*, based on the book by Paul Bowles, had the potential to be a searing addition to the cinema of schizophrenia, but it's a film which to this day I have been unable to sit through. In its own way, Bowles' novel is as influential and "seminal" a piece of schizo literature as Kesey's more celebrated *One Flew Over the Cuckoo's Nest*; as much as any novel of the period it translated the existentialist affliction — the *nausea*—diagnosed by modern European authors such as Kafka, Camus, Sartre, Hesse, Gide, Hamsun, et al.— to American pop culture. (Bowles was something of a spiritual godfather to the Beats, who in turn anticipated the wild experimental rebellion of Leary, Kesey, and the rest.) I have refused to watch Bertolucci's film because, in the first three minutes alone, it was painfully obvious how mistaken his approach to the material is. Bertolucci Europeanized it, tried to give it a classic sheen, when the novel, for all its depth, is a *sensationalistic* work, a pop *Heart of Darkness*. Bowles' psyche was one of the most authentically delirious psyches in modern literature, and Bertolucci would never have been the right director for this book, not even at his peak (it's more suited to Lynch or Cronenberg); but at least in his *Tango* days he might have connected to the sleazy, psychedelic despair of the novel and been inspired by its themes of alienation and schizophrenia. By the time he came to it, however, his empty aestheticism had taken over and he seemed to have no interest in the characters save as figures in the landscape. He renders them (judging by the first ten minutes alone, which is enough) puppets for Bowles' anguished prose, posing absurdly, tourists at the abyss. (He also puts Bowles in a commentator role, and so manages to embarrass the author as *well* as destroying his work, probably a first in movie history.)

The film only confirmed what was by now already clear, that Bertolucci had lost his "edge." His case is illustrative of the pitfalls of the kind of divided sensibility that most — if not all — major artists (and especially filmmakers) seem to suffer from. This "split personality" is something Bertolucci freely admits to: "I am condemned to be divided. I have a split personality and the

7. A Glass Darkly: Brando and Bertolucci's *Last Tango*

real contradiction within me is that I cannot quite synchronize my heart and my brain. One of the two is always ahead of the other one." Bertolucci here simplifies his schizophrenia as a heart-and-head conflict, but it might just as easily (for our purposes) be reduced to a question of style over content. Of course, in Bertolucci's case, his heart yearns for the simple (indulgent) delights of visual imagery: he is a filmmaker-poet who barters in images. If he can satisfy his poetic instinct and his painter's eye with the mesmeric sweep of his "vision," what does the head have to say about it? The answer is that his head — with its at least partially developed philosophic insights — demands, above and beyond the empty pleasures of style, some sort of *substance*. Bertolucci is something of an Italian Spielberg, a man whose tastes — his judgment — seem to be woefully unequal to his talents. How could a man of Spielberg's gifts serve up a bowl of slop like *Always*? The same way Bertolucci could dedicate himself with apparent conviction to a piece of fluff like *Stealing Beauty*. These men have become intoxicated by cinema, and convinced themselves that, merely be making a movie of it (whatever "it" may be, whether some old Spencer Tracy weepy or a tale of adolescent lust), it will somehow be transformed into art, or at the very least magic.

Last Tango in Paris is Bertolucci as a genuine alchemist. The film is full of glass partitions and reflections, a favorite signifying device of existentialist filmmakers all the way from Welles to Greenaway. But here they are not used to signify (at least not primarily), but rather to beguile and mystify us with their beauty and strangeness. This is Bertolucci's strength, and the occasional paucity and familiarity of his "message" (existential cinema was already getting old in 1972) never undermines his mastery of the medium. *Last Tango* is not a film with a message. Its meanings are far less interesting, finally, than the manner in which Bertolucci and Brando communicate them. But, so long as we are on the subject — seeking schizo themes in occult texts — they certainly abound.

Last Tango is about a man (Marlon Brando's Paul) seeking non-entity, looking for a womb he can disappear into, a place where he can forget his name, his pain, his past. Paul's thoughts torment him with their meaninglessness, their repetition, their lack of purpose, and their incapacity to make sense of the world. His wife Rosa's suicide is but a convenient excuse to succumb to despair and retreat into the bleak corner of his philosophy. One never gets the impression that Paul actually *misses* Rosa, only that he resents her for what he sees as her ultimate act of contempt. Perhaps even he resents her for "outdoing" him, for taking such an easy way out (and cheap: as Paul rails against her corpse, as cheap as the razor with which she cut her wrists). Suicide is the one act that Paul is too afraid or too stubborn to commit; yet he longs for death.

Paul's grief seems to be inseparable from the guilt he feels. It's not simply that he has failed to save his wife, it is as if he has willed her death. As

Bertolucci and Brando have conceived him, Paul is a nihilist, a destroyer of values, and a coward. His weakness is his fear of death, his hatred of a God in which he refuses to believe out of pride and anger (Paul might agree with Keating in *The Usual Suspects*, who says, "I don't believe in God, but I'm afraid of Him.") And Paul's incapacity to destroy himself— his constant torment — turns

Paul (Marlon Brando) and Jean (Maria Schneider) share a primordial courtship in *The Last Tango in Paris* (1972, United Artists).

him into a sociopathic personality, driven to tear down everyone and everything around him. But Paul doesn't do this through brute force (like Brando, he is an intelligent man tormented by his intelligence), but rather through subtlety and wiles.

Besides being an atheist and a nihilist, Paul is also a sensualist. He seeks the comfortable oblivion of impersonal sex. Yet beyond this, at a deeper level, he is seeking a worthy opponent to expose himself to, so as to reveal the hypocrisy on which is life — his identity — is founded. This entails our classic (schizophrenic) search for Anima — the Other — which comes — in good Hollywood fashion — in the shape of the soft, yielding but deadly *femme fatale*, Jeanne. Jeanne (Mara Schneider) is Paul's Adversary, his downfall. Since he is really seeking his death, he finds it in Jeanne. Paul is an isolate man, lost in his own dreary, desperate, self-reflecting universe. Like Narcissus gazing at the lake, he is compelled finally to break the surface of the waters, to destroy the illusion and find himself alone.

If Paul is as adrift as Rosa, then so is almost everyone else in the movie. Whether it's the morbid self-loathing of Paul, the vapid dissociation of Jeanne, or the fevered egotism of Tom, Jeanne's moviemaker lover (played by Jean-Pierre Léaud), they are all lost in their own clouded bubbles of self-attention. Tom in particular — though he becomes quite wearisome after a time — serves to illustrate Bertolucci's schizo themes best of all, perhaps because he is a stand-in for Bertolucci himself. Tom films everything, everywhere he goes; like Madonna in *Truth or Dare*, he cannot exist off-camera. His reality is creating illusions, his purpose in life is to distort life, to rearrange it until it *has* meaning, until it has a purpose all his own. Tom is the craziest of the bunch, the most narcissistic, destructive, and unpleasant character in the movie. He is Paul's "double," even though they never meet, because they are both seen — through Jeanne's eyes — as being oddly alike. Tom is intent on doing exactly the same to Jeanne as Paul is, albeit in a different — less honest or primitive — way. (As she shouts at him from the other side of the metro tracks: "You're taking advantage of me ... you force me to do things I've never done before ... I'm tired of having my mind raped!") Paul wishes to dominate, to violate, but also — in his own twisted way — to liberate Jeanne. Through his oppressive, animalistic rituals, his perverted sexual demands, and his mysterious, almost childlike refusal to give up his "essence" to her, he shows an almost paternal desire to act as an authority in her life. Paul is a kind of negative father figure to Jeanne: he wants to "unprogram" her rather than educate her, to expose rather than protect her. On the other hand Tom's demands upon Jeanne seem to be wholly selfish: he wants to "rape her mind" with his relentless, pseudo-romantic cinematic courtship, but it is all for his movie, all for the sake of image. Neither Paul nor Tom are comfortable with "reality," or with relating to other people. Paul creates his own, hermetic world where names are not allowed, a world in which he can erase the past and return to the primal, infantile state of pure sensuality. He takes refuge there, but like any womb it is only good for a limited time. In the end, his illusion becomes suffocating for Jeanne, who cannot even escape Paul by being with Tom, since Tom's obsession is even more restricting for her, even more oppressive. (Tom can only relate to Jeanne as his creation, a character in his own solipsist fiction.) Jeanne of course is more than a match for both of them.*

Simply by existing, by continuing to endure despite all Paul and Tom's efforts to reduce her to a fantasy (to debase her by idealizing her), Jeanne must eventually tear down their illusions and force them to confront the truth about themselves. In Tom's case, he is as unreal as his movies; if he can't have Jeanne then he will undoubtedly find another waif to seduce and enslave, and so on, until they have all left him and he is a vain and ridiculous old man (perhaps not unlike Marcel†). With Paul, the "truth" is more simple. He is not seeking a womb to be reborn through; he is seeking the womb as the closest thing he knows to death.

When Jeanne tells Paul that she has found a man to love, he assures her that she will never find such a man, that until she has gone "right up the ass of death" and found "the womb of fear," she will always be alone. The womb of fear is where Paul resides; it's the fantasy world he has built for them, a world (or womb) modeled not on life but on death. When Jeanne admits to Paul that *he* is the man she is talking of, that she loves *him*, he doesn't hesitate to test her love in the most degrading fashion he can conceive of. He gets her to cut

---

*Pauline Kael grasped the Maria Schneider/Jeanne character best when she wrote, "She carries the whole history of movie passion in her long legs and baby face.... When she lifts her wedding dress to her waist, smiling coquettishly as she exposes her pubic hair, she's in a great film tradition of irresistibly naughty girls ... the pliable, softly unprincipled Jeanne of Maria Schneider must be the winner [of this sexual battle]: it is the soft ones who defeat men and walk away, consciencelessly." (Kael, "Tango," *Reeling*, pg. 33-34.) Bertolucci seconds this point of view. "Physically she is reminiscent of a typical French woman, like those painted by Renoir father and son; those women who can walk serenely over the corpses of the men who fall in love with them." Thompson, *Last Tango in Paris*, pg. 71.

†Paul has not one but two doubles or *Doppelgängers* in *Tango*. (One of Bertolucci's earliest works was Partner, based on Dostoevsky's *The Double*, a rendition of the *Doppelgänger* myth.) The first and lesser one is Marcel (Massimo Girotti), Rosa's lover. In their scene together Paul and Marcel wear matching robes: Rosa made sure they had the same robes, as if something in her wanted this familiarity, or as if she were collecting lovers. When Paul visits Marcel and they share a bourbon (also bought by Rosa), Paul cannot resist comparing himself to the other man, hoping to come out favorably. He notes how Marcel still has a full head of hair, which pleases Marcel. He's a vain man, while Paul only falls back on vanity, as if for relief (like a drowning man clutching at straws). Marcel explains to Paul that he washes his hair every day, and when Paul asks how he keeps his stomach trim, Marcel shows Paul his "secret": thirty pull-ups every morning. By this time, Paul has lost interest in his own pretense; he looks at Marcel with disgust and says, "I wonder what she ever saw in you." The question echoes back on himself, as does everything Paul says and does.

7. A Glass Darkly: Brando and Bertolucci's *Last Tango*

the nails on her right hand and to force her fingers up his ass; then — in a perverse variation on the lover's sweet nothings — he has her imagine she is fucking a dying pig, eating its vomit and breathing its death farts. All this is Brando's improvising, no doubt, and worthy of Colonel Kurtz at his scatological best. Paul *is* death, and she is going right up his ass, to find the womb of fear, the hollow heart of darkness. Could Jeanne really love a man like this? Paul does everything he can to shatter her fantasy the moment it begins to impinge upon his own. And despite himself, he succeeds.

Like many post–Freud sociopaths, Paul doesn't seem to know the difference between death, the womb, and the asshole. He is scatologically incapable of owning up to his more spiritual needs, just as he is forced — by his macho-masochistic façade — to deny all his more tender, "feminine" characteristics. Paul's arrogance — his machismo — is a mask for his pain, which in turns comes from a childish need to be loved. It's perversely ironic, even poetic, that Paul perceives this need as beneath him, as "womanly," since of course (in good Freudian terms) such a need (or weakness) stems from his relationship with his mother. In Paul's monologue about his past, Brando was drawing on his own recollections of his father ("whorefucker") and of his mother (after whom Brando named his autobiography, *Songs About My Mother*).

(To say that Brando *is* Paul is a simplification, and meaningless besides, since Paul is largely unknown to himself—and certainly to the director. It's safe to say however that Brando is the only person involved in the movie who really understands Paul, that Paul is essentially Brando's creation. Much as he would do — to considerably lesser effect — in *Apocalypse Now*, Brando draws Paul out of himself through improvisation: he conjures him, on Bertolucci's stage, out of his psychic hat. Paul is the full creation of an empty man. He reflects I would guess many of Brando's own insecurities, neuroses, and pathologies, his obsession with sex, death, despair, and godlessness, which essentially are the themes of the movie. Also, Brando's own conflict as an actor: his schizophrenic need to be anonymous, on the one hand, and to be all-powerful, adored, worshipped, on the other.)

Brando's Paul is himself caught in the vicious cliché of the macho clown who deep down is just a momma's boy (think of all those sailors with "mom" tattooed on their biceps). His longing to be loved is his longing to be a child again, his yearning for his mother's caresses and for the safety and warmth of the womb. But since all this is "beneath" him, unthinkable to him, he can only seek such affection and reassurance through sex, and finally through death. This is why he chooses the unbalanced, suicidal Rosa, on the one hand, and Jeanne on the other; in Jeanne he attains — however briefly — the perfect impersonal love slave to be master of, and so becomes a father rather than a child. Both women are intrinsically connected to death, however: Rosa commits suicide, Jeanne commits murder (Paul's). Both symbolize and enact Paul's longing; they are the realization of his romance with eternity.

It's significant that Paul only speaks briefly of his mother (again, Brando is speaking of his own mother here), calling her "poetic," and remarking how she taught him to "love nature" (as well as wandering about naked in public). At one point, Paul expresses to Jeanne his intolerance for females: "Either they think they know who you are, or they think you don't know who they are." Then later he laments to his dead wife: "I might be able to comprehend the universe, but I'll never discover the truth about you. Never." Women signify both the restriction of the mundane, the material (maternal) coils of nature, and — its precise opposite — the unknowable mystery of existence, the boundless. Paul cannot reconcile his two opposing perceptions of women/sex/death, because he cannot acknowledge in himself his own conflicting needs: to be free and yet to be loved and nurtured. He can't cut the umbilical cord and he can't return to the womb. All he can do is to hang himself, using the female (and his ties to her) to do it.

When Paul finally "cracks" and tells Jeanne he loves her (revealing his age and his predicament, but still neglecting to tell her his name), he has perhaps decided, like his namesake St. Paul, that "it is better to marry than to burn." But by now it's already too late: he's already burning. He has destroyed her fantasy, and the truth of himself, deprived of the mystery, is that he is a run-down, washed-up, middle-aged loser — a buffoon. He has nothing to offer Jeanne save some ephemeral "life in the country," another fantasy, only now they are outside the womb, it is unthinkable to her. Jeanne remarks that she didn't know that Paul liked nature, revealing how little attention she has paid to his words. Her only interest — as Paul pointed out — was in his cock ("your happiness, and my ha-penis"). Jeanne tells him that she hates the country, betraying her own anti-nature, anti-life tendencies. She can never be the mother of his imaginary "children" or the custodian of his impossible "happiness." She can't nurture or care for him, she can only expose and destroy him as the hopeless blowhard and helpless infant that he is. Since this is exactly why Paul sought her out in the first place, she is only being true to her calling (not only to her nature but to his own instructions). Although Jeanne feels little when she kills Paul, her resignation is surely tinged with regret, her indifference leavened with the sadness of inevitability.

Paul chases Jeanne back to her mother's apartment, where she finds her father's army pistol (Bertolucci has prepared us for his melodramatic — but necessary — climax by showing us the pistol in advance). Paul is drunk from his "last tango" (in which he bares his ass at the irate judge, who tells him to go seek love "in the movies"). He puts on the father's legionnaire's cap and asks Jeanne how she likes her hero: "Over easy or sunny side up?" The answer of course is "over easy." Since Paul can only do this the hard away, however, Jeanne has to kill her erstwhile hero and father surrogate simply to get free of him. He asks her for her name and gets a bullet to the gut in response. This is justice, as well as Jeanne's revenge on Paul and on her father (and even on the first boy she ever had sex with, also named Paul), a revenge that, in the best Arabian tradition, she serves cold.

Paul staggers to the terrace and takes out his gum, sticks it under the railing, in a last, childlike act of unburdening. He gazes onto infinity, as onto a long lost beloved, his blue eyes fading. He murmurs something indecipherable (Brando improvised again here, apparently the name of his Tahitian island—"home") and gives up the ghost. The next shot is of Paul curled up in a fetal position as Jeanne prepares her alibi ("I didn't know him"), making Bertolucci's parallels (those of life and death) unequivocal. Paul has come full circle, from womb to tomb. He has conquered the last of his illusions and found the truth at last. If it takes two to tango, then death invariably takes the lead.

8

The Man Behind the Mask: Roman Polanski's Dementia Tales

> At what precise moment does an individual cease to be the person that he, and everyone else, believes him to be?
> — Trelkovsky, *The Tenant*

Roman Polanski was the first filmmaker with whom, in late adolescence, I became infatuated. It's hard to say exactly why Polanski. I think his mix of European "respectability"—his modernist/ surrealist/existentialist credibility with the art house—combined with his obvious affinity for the grand guignol of Hollywood—his glee for violence and sensationalism—made him the perfect choice for a still-forming, cheerfully perverse, adolescent film buff. Polanski was the most overt and easily identifiable of "auteurs": his obsessiveness—the recurring themes of his films—was so obvious that even a child could spot it. His vision was dark, pessimistic, macabre, but leavened by a sense of the absurd and by wicked, mischievous humor. Polanski took delight in appalling and disturbing audiences with his perversity, and in mocking and deriding us for our susceptibility to his devices. He was a postmodern master of suspense, torturer as entertainer, Hitchcock by way of the Marquis de Sade.

In my adolescent days, I was even taken with Pinter for a time, and Polanski no longer seems to me the authentic maestro of movie art I once considered him to be. Certainly, in his prime (the period from *Knife in the Water* to *The Tenant*) he was a genuine wizard of the cinema; his instinctive grasp of the medium was second to none, and matched only by his consistently twisted, often inspired, choice of material. But by and large I now feel that his movies lack emotional substance or depth. They are intricate studies in paranoia, persecution, dementia, delirium, and psychosis in which the characters are as often as not at the mercy, not only of unseen forces (*Rosemary's Baby, Macbeth, Chinatown*), but of their own perverse drives and unconscious fears (*Repulsion, Cul-de-Sac, The Tenant, Bitter Moon*). But they are also subject to

8. The Man Behind the Mask: Roman Polanski's Dementia Tales

the torturous scrutiny of the director's ruthless hand and eye. With the exception of *Dance of the Vampires* (my personal favorite of his movies), Polanski doesn't seem to spare much affection for his protagonists. He seems to enjoy creating circumstances and environments — rather like Descartes in his laboratory — through which he can inflict the maximum amount of suffering upon them. (Polanski's closest peer as torturer-entertainer is probably not Hitchcock — who seemed quite fond of his characters — but Brian De Palma, who also makes movies like mouse-traps for his hapless creations to fall into.)

This characteristic of viciousness was present in Polanski's work from the very beginning, but it can only have been exacerbated by the personal catastrophe he suffered at the peak of his career, in August of 1969, when Polanski's wife Sharon Tate and their unborn child (already named Paul) were murdered, along with several others, in an apparently senseless act of violence. This was seen by the media as Polanski's "karma." He had come all the way from the concentration camps of Poland to the land of opportunity to conquer Hollywood and become a star, with a movie that just happened to be about Satanism, sacrifice, and unborn babies. Polanski embraced the Hollywood Industry, and it swallowed him up.

It's impossible to imagine how Polanski's career would have evolved if the "Manson murders" had never occurred, but it's unlikely he would have made *Macbeth* as his next movie.* Polanski was hurled by circumstances (the conspiracy of events, coincidentally or not) through the looking glass of the movie screen, into one of his own nightmare scenarios. He arrived at that forbidden zone in which life really *does* imitate art, where truth reflects fantasy and reality itself is but a by-product of a greater, collective Fantasy. At this point, Polanski's role as a filmmaker took on new, more horrendous proportions. What was his "responsibility" now? After the killing of Tate, as Barbara Leaming writes (in *Polanski His Life and Films*, pg. 76), Polanski "could not direct just *anything*—for whatever he did would be received in terms of the crime that had infected him. Polanski was no longer making films to create an image. From this point on, his films would respond to an image he no longer fully controlled. Obviously he could not return to his earlier project about cannibalism."

---

*Manson was not there at the time of the murders and claims innocence to this day. Manson was a graduated Scientologist with a scheme for "immanentizing the eschaton" by starting a race war, or spreading paranoia amidst the rich and famous (or all of the above). He targeted Hollywood specifically for his first act of theatrical terrorism, and the Tate/Polanski residence *apparently* at random. Whether Manson adopted techniques for "clearing" from his Scientology apprenticeship and so brainwashed his "disciples" into committing the crime, the official story is that they enacted the murders on Manson's precise instructions, following his orders to the letter, and so fulfilling the spirit, also, of his "vision" — blood sacrifice in Hollywood.

Why obviously, I wonder? To prove to the world that he had learned from the killings, that he had "repented"? Make a sweet and gentle tale of redemptive love? Not likely. Besides being perhaps what got him into this mess in the first place, Polanski's perversity was also what had made his reputation. By having life come back at him with an even greater dose of dementia and grotesqueness, Polanski could only feel all the more the necessity — the rightness — of his vision. He would be confirmed in his grisly and brutal Weltanschauung. In a sense "life" (circumstance) "chose" Polanski as its apostle of abomination; by this time, he really had little choice.

When Virginia Wright Wexman writes that "all of Polanski's films are about insanity" (*Roman Polanski*, pg. 45) she is exaggerating, but not by much. *Dance of the Vampires* is a comedy and more about zaniness than psychosis (though it retains Polanski's ubiquitously paranoid touch). *Chinatown* is about corruption, not madness; *Pirates* is about nothing at all; *Frantic* is about desperation rather than insanity, but the terrain is close enough. *Ninth Gate* is perhaps best not mentioned at all. After that, *The Pianist* was about the holocaust, and *Oliver Twist* hardly counts as a Polanski movie at all. All the rest — *Knife in the Water, Repulsion, Cul-de-Sac, Rosemary's Baby* (admittedly a madness that turns out to be all-too-sane), *Que?* (*What?* a film I haven't seen but which seems to involve sexual dementia), *Macbeth, The Tenant, Tess, Death and the Maiden, Bitter Moon*— take paranoia, psychosis, obsession, dissociation, and schizophrenia as their subject matter, if not centrally at least peripherally; they are, to a one, movie tales of madness. That's an astonishing tally for a filmmaker (more than half his oeuvre, a ratio only David Lynch can beat), even bearing in mind the natural predilection of an expressionist artist for extreme psychological states. If we acknowledge that any auteur filmmaker uses his films — in the manner of a Boorman or Bertolucci — as tools for self-analysis — the means for confronting the darker regions of his psyche — then it's safe to say that Polanski is (or would be, if not for his movies) something of a runaway schizoid personality.* Please note that, unlike Bertolucci or Boorman, I mean to suggest that Polanski is schizo as a *man*, not merely as a filmmaker.

---

*By this (loose) definition, "auteur" cannot apply to most of the work of such cherished exemplars of the auteur theory as Ford or Hawks. These men were not necessarily the *authors* of their movies, for the simple reason that their films were not necessarily the by-products of their tormented, searching psyches, but merely the products of their craft. There is a profound difference between the artist who creates recreationally (as work, or even hobby) because he can, and the artist who creates compulsively (as therapy, or catharsis), because he *must*. Herein lies the difference between a film director and a film "auteur" (though admittedly the term has changed its meaning some since the days of Sarris et al.). Hitchcock (much more than Hawks or Ford) is the prime example of an artist caught somewhere between the two "callings," with his capacity to move from one to the other and back again (as he did from *Rear Window* to *To Catch a Thief* to *The Trouble with Harry*, for example; or from *Vertigo* to *North by Northwest* to *Psycho*).

8. The Man Behind the Mask: Roman Polanski's Dementia Tales 133

This accusation was leveled at Polanski by critics from the start, as a deprecatory measure by those who couldn't stomach his films: here was a sensibility too perverse, morbid, unhealthy, and (shudder of shudders) *unwholesome* to possibly be considered artistic. Yet Polanski's vision was so original and so penetrating (and popular) precisely for these reasons: it was far closer to the American *Zeitgeist* than other, native-born moviemakers working at the time.* By the time of *Macbeth*, however, it appeared to be "all over" for Polanski. Violent as it was, both the times and the movies had caught up with his blood-soaked vision and his movies began to seem perverse in all the wrong ways. The bloodiness of *Macbeth* seemed deliberately overstated, not merely as a response to his own personal tragedy (a can of worms we will get into), but also as a more cynical attempt to keep abreast of his competition, to retain his credentials (even while taking on Shakespeare), as leading shockmeister of Hollywood.†

Polanski complained noisily when the movie came out: "What happened [the murders] was reviewed in terms of my films. Now it's vice versa. Now my films are reviewed in terms of what happened." But how could any reviewer overlook such parallels when they would only become all the more conspicuous for being ignored? And how could Polanski imagine his choice of *Macbeth*—with its slaughtered families, its witchcraft motifs tied to blood and ambition, its reference to MacDuff being "torn from his mother's womb," and all the rest—wouldn't ring bells in viewers' heads? The answer of course is that he could not have been unaware, both of his own motives for choosing the play and of how obvious these motives would be to the world.** In other words, however uncanny the effects might have been, however "divided" his consciousness,†† Polanski's *method* was as canny and calculated as everything

---

*Kubrick is a possible, partial exception, since he shared many of Polanski's traits; but Kubrick lacked Polanski's all-important, all-redeeming irreverence, his mischievous humor. Sam Peckinpah, on the other hand, could have answered this need in American movies for a new, more ruthless sensibility, but—perhaps for being native-born—he was more susceptible to Hollywood's insidious techniques of discouragement and sabotage, and didn't even get it together until 1969, with *The Wild Bunch*.

†Besides this, Polanski's *Macbeth* is a travesty of casting; it might have survived any and all of his other missteps but it cannot survive Jon Finch as Macbeth or Martin Shaw as Banquo. Also, Polanski's handling of many of the play's central scenes—Macbeth's hallucinations as he descends into madness—are sloppy and contrived. He seems to be reaching for effects that he no longer has in him; or perhaps his heart is no longer in his work?

**Newsweek* played right up to Polanski's paranoia and sensitivity, "the critic blurring crucial distinctions between imagination and reality" (Leaming pg. 88): "Is the decapitation of Macbeth and the parading of his head on a spear an indispensable reality?" he wrote. "If so, then Macbeth is a work of art-in the grand manner of Buchenwald, Lidice and, yes, the Manson murders."

††"Now it suggests either a strange form of naiveté or a *divided consciousness* for Polanski to complain that his *Macbeth* is being reviewed in terms of the Manson case." Italics mine, Kael, "Killers and Thieves," *Deeper into Movies*, pg. 399.

else he had done until now, both as an artist and an "entertainer." Polanski was putting his life, his loss, his tragedy, on display. Above all (to be charitable), one imagines this was for cathartic reasons; but one can't help but suspect more cynical ones — in order to stir up controversy and attract audiences (a failure at this point could have been fatal to Polanski's self-esteem). Whatever the case, his ploy succeeded. For all its mediocrity as a movie — the paucity of its vision and its lack of integrity to its source — *Macbeth* caused a furor of critical-media attention and, at the very least, re-established Polanski as a fully functional filmmaker and media personality. As to his own personal catharsis, no one but Polanski can say, but I can't help but sympathize with Kael when she wrote, "I came out willing to believe Polanski hates violence, but I wish he could give some evidence of caring about something else."*

If *Macbeth* was a sustained dirge of despair, Polanski's vision had certainly not lightened by the time of *Chinatown*, which besides its pessimism and its sadistic streak — already quite prominent in his previous work — was by far the gloomiest and least playful of Polanski's films. In *Chinatown* (which established Polanski in Hollywood not merely as a perverse talent but as an authentic "genius," the maker of "classics"), Polanski takes the role of "the man with the knife," the snickering, white-clad "midget" who slices open Jack Nicholson's nose as a warning to mind his own business. What could be better evidence of Polanski's canniness in exploiting his own tragedy for sensationalist effect — playing up to the public's association of him with knives and bloodshed — and of his stubborn refusal to turn over a new leaf? Polanski — an avowed atheist with a fascination for occult themes — did not have it in him to learn from his mistakes. But as a filmmaker he was beginning to seem something of a one-trick pony. Without savagery to fall back on, his vision was growing grim and empty and oppressive.

Based on Robert Towne's now-canonized script, *Chinatown* is one of Polanski's most assured works, the most technically smooth, well structured, and "solid" of all his films. It is also one of his dullest movies. If the scenes in which he himself appears, or in which (that fellow movie director with a sadistic streak of humor) John Huston plays Noah Cross, the arch corrupter, are the only scenes that have much life in them, it's because these are the only times Polanski's wicked predilection for evil gets full play. The rest — closely following Towne's script — is ponderous and stifling with its moral tone (completely at odds with Polanski's amoral glee), and its suffocating atmosphere of regret.

---

*Kael, "Killers and Thieves," *Deeper into Movies*, pg. 399-401. "Polanski is a gothic realist; his murderous carnivals have an everyday look, with no mystery, and no exaltation, either ... when Polanski converts what in Shakespeare was pathology into the normal state of affairs, he gives us a horrendous vision but also a rather complacently lucid one. It's as if the riddles had all been solved ... this dark vision goes nowhere but further into gore, and that's where it goes." (Ibid.)

8. The Man Behind the Mask: Roman Polanski's Dementia Tales

Above all, what's missing is the under layer of delirium which Polanski's best films depend upon for their kinky, queasy fascination. The mesmeric (cinematic) *effect* of creeping madness is central to Polanski's vision of the world and, one supposes, of himself. Without this under layer, the brutality and bleakness of his vision becomes meaningless (at least to me).

For Polanski, the only redeeming feature in a world in which Hitler and Manson hold sway is to be found in the absurdity, the insanity, and the macabre power of horrifying beauty. His best movies suggest vision in madness, and the enlightenment of surviving atrocity (as his own life implies). Polanski takes glee in stripping away the banal surface of the world and revealing its worm-infested, disease-ridden interior. There is relief, perhaps, in the sense of confronting an unpalatable reality, and of being liberated from the oppressive chains of illusion (be they those of decency, order, justice, or whatever). All such illusion (in Polanski's world at least) cannot withstand closer scrutiny. Polanski's movies are not revelatory, because to Polanski the hideous under layer is all there is — the final truth is the absence of meaning at the heart of (his) life. But at their best, his movies *are* apocalyptic; they serve to pull back the everyday surface and allow us to glimpse another, more horrible truth.

In this way madness, schizophrenia — the juxtaposing of subjective with objective reality until subjective wins out, as it must (just as, in movies, illusion always conquers truth) — this is Polanski's own "religious" impulse coming out the only way it can. It's his personal obsession, and at base of it I think is the fact that, for all his apparently unflinching desire to confront the dark underbelly of his psyche, to plumb the unconscious and bring forth its demons, Polanski was unprepared for these demons when they emerged. They were too much for him in his own life — not in the sense that they destroyed him (Polanski must have "survived" better than 90 percent of us would have under similar circumstances), but in the sense that they swayed him and caused the decay of his vision. There simply *is* no redemption in Polanski's work save in a complete resignation to inevitable corruption. Surrender to madness. Passive revulsion avails, but not revolt. Above all there is acquiescence to destruction, be it of the self or of the other: suicide or murder.

If enlightenment (redemption) is like a Church with gargoyles outside to keep away the unrepentant — in order that only those who can see beyond the gargoyles have the wit or courage to enter — then Polanski (who gave us depictions of madness and schizophrenia such as no other filmmaker has) never seemed to realize that his characters (as much as he) are on their own misguided quest for enlightenment. Polanski gets beneath the shiny surface, but he never makes it past the rotting under layer. He never gets past the gargoyles.

Seven years after his wife and child's murder, Polanski was embroiled in yet another personal catastrophe that would change the course of his career irrevocably. It's not quite accurate to say in this case that "events conspired" to undo him, for unlike on the previous occasion, there could be little doubt this time that Polanski brought the catastrophe upon himself. Proving his private life to be every bit as lewd, kinky, and perverse as his movies had suggested, Polanski was brought up on charges of the statutory rape of a thirteen-year-old girl, whom he had ostensibly been photographing for *Vogue* magazine. The story goes that Polanski took her to Jack Nicholson's house, plied her with champagne and Quaaludes, had her strip naked for the photo shoot, then, putting aside his camera and letting pleasure get the better part of business, performed oral, vaginal, and anal sex on her. For her part the girl (who shall remain nameless) was probably compliant, if far from willing (she claims to have been too zonked to scream). The medical report established that she had had "previous sexual encounters" (i.e., was not a virgin) at the time of the "rape," and that no "force" (i.e., violence) had been used. Technically speaking no force is required for sex with a thirteen-year-old to constitute rape, since minors cannot give consent even if they want to in the U.S. And it's a remarkable fact that, despite breaking the American taboo-to-end-all-taboos — pedophilia — Polanski is still making movies for Hollywood, and even won an Oscar in 2002 (He was unable to collect it however, since he would have been arrested the moment he landed in the U.S..) The privileges of "genius" abide, and a healthy double standard still pertains to American morality (most especially in Hollywood). Since Polanski was still good for making a lot of people lots of money, his sins were eventually forgiven.

Polanski has retained a reputation, much as did Kubrick, based on the brilliance and originality of his early work. There was only ever one Polanski, hence, even if Polanski's talents have all but evaporated, he is still the only Polanski we've got. Sentimentality and opportunism alone (two most valued qualities in Hollywood) are enough to keep him in business. But if Polanski's is a cautionary tale, it is also a peculiarly moral one — ironically enough considering how much of the thrill and intensity of his art comes from its lack of a moral slant. If an artist can't afford the luxury of ethics in his art (his unconscious urges preclude all such judgments), by the same token, he must be all the more impeccable in his private life. Artists adhere to the highest morality of all, that of assuming responsibility for their dreams. Anything less is madness.

The life of the imagination thrives on freedom and, to an extent, on licentiousness and indulgence. The further into the darkness it ventures, the more wonders it can bring to the light. An artist entrusted with such a task must take almost superhuman care not to succumb to the darkness or be overwhelmed by his demons. He must do the work of the devil and live the life of the sage. Like so many visionaries in the movie business, Polanski appears to have allowed his business and his pleasures to get tangled up, and paid the ultimate price an artist can pay.

8. The Man Behind the Mask: Roman Polanski's Dementia Tales

The Tenant is Polanski's masterpiece — as flawed and indulgent but inherently fascinating as the man himself. One of the most haunting and intimate depictions of mental degeneration ever put on film, it's schizo cinema at its best. The film is a mess, with its shoddy dubbing and its repeated bouts of excess bordering on the ridiculous. But even these flaws seem to merge — quite unnaturally — with the protagonist's dementia. Like *Repulsion*, *The Tenant* is a cinematic exercise that takes the point of view of an insane person. In this case the foreigner is Trelkovsky living in xenophobic Paris. Nothing in the movie occurs outside his point of view; it is a wholly subjective vision, and the audience is not permitted the luxury of distance. Beyond sympathy, we are forced into a state of complete, agonizing empathy.*

Polanski himself plays Trelkovsky, a meek, timid, cowardly man who passively submits to the hostile forces of his life until he is reduced to a twisted caricature of himself, a broken doll. Trelkovsky lacks a center, a sense of self. His foreignness — his displacement — is essential to the movie, as contained in the title. The tenant is one who resides in a place not his own; in this case Trelkovsky's body, and even his psyche, becomes alien to him. It is taken over by an Other. By choosing to play the lead role, Polanski was implicitly acknowledging certain affinities with the character. *The Tenant* is his most interesting and satisfying work for precisely this reason — it gives his talents, his obsession, free reign. It's also significant that there is very little violence in the film compared to his other movies. Barring the ending (in which he hurls himself out of his window, *twice*) and a brief moment when he strikes a child, the horror of *The Tenant* is wholly psychological. Trelkovsky is *passive* psychotic, a schizophrenic of no danger to anyone but himself. On the contrary, it is everyone else who is perceived (through Trelkovsky's eyes) as a threat to him, whether insidiously, in their conspiratorial attempts to rob him of his identity, or more directly, by taunting and hounding him to suicide.

The story of *The Tenant* (from a novel by Roland Topor) is simple, concise, profound. Trelkovsky finds an apartment in Paris (no mean feat in itself) but learns that it is not yet available; the former tenant, Simone Choule, threw herself from the apartment window and is critically wounded. Trelkovsky goes to visit her in the hospital and finds her swathed in bandages, like a creature

---

*And yet: "Polanski never allows us to forget that we are watching a movie. He characteristically makes us question the motives that underlie our interest in the false self of the filmic body he has created.... The analogy to Polanski's own audience is clear; for we too may be looking for an alternate, false self upon which to project unacceptable impulses toward sexuality and aggression that we consciously deny to our 'real' selves.... Polanski, with his usual contrariety, has forced the audience to face up to the squalid nature of our pleasure in the genre even as he has satisfied it. In *The Tenant*, Polanski pushes the psychology of the horror story to its limit." Virginia Wright Wexman, "The Body as Theater," *Roman Polanski*, pg. 74-5.

from a horror movie, with only the black, gaping hole of her mouth (with a missing front tooth) exposed. At Simone's bedside Trelkovsky meets Stella (Isabel Adjani) and pretends to be a friend of Simone, knowing she is in no position to deny it. (This is the first indication of his passive but devious nature; Trelkovsky is constantly lying for convenience, as when he covers his embarrassment at having to urinate by making up a story about an "important phone call.") Stella tries to solicit some response out of Simone, but gets only a blood-curdling scream. Is Simone trying to denounce Trelkovsky as a pretender? This scream — the wail of the damned — will be repeated at the end of the movie, only this time Trelkovsky is the one screaming, trapped inside the body of Simone.

Not long after the scream, Simone dies and Trelkovsky takes the apartment, and so begins his degeneration. Haunted by the memory of the dead Simone, he begins to take on her characteristics one by one, until he is doubting his own identity. At the local café, they sell him Simone's brand of cigarettes and serve him her choice of beverage. The landlady and landlord (played by Shelly Winters and Melvyn Douglas) are intent on interfering in Trelkovsky's life and manipulating him to their will. Stella (possibly Simone's lover) seduces Trelkovsky crudely at a Bruce Lee movie (aroused by the violence on the screen?), and they become lovers; yet, like everything else he does, Trelkovsky seems to be acquiescing passively to her will. Little by little, his reality becomes steadily more oppressive and he begins to hallucinate. He becomes convinced not of a supernatural plot (that Simone's spirit is trying to possess him), but of (perhaps even less likely) a mundane one: that the other tenants—*everyone* in fact—are conspiring to make him *believe* he is Simone, and so drive him to suicide.

The Tenant is a comic nightmare, a feverish excursion into the absurd, a giddying exercise in the theater of cruelty. It is our worst conceivable nightmare of hostile, meddlesome neighbors and tyrannical landlords—a dramatization of everyone's greatest fear of being unwanted, rejected, despised by the community in which we live but can never hope to belong. It is the alienation text par excellence, and its humor comes not only from Polanski's dexterous handling of the material but from its utter familiarity to us, its eerie universality. It depicts a wholly personal and yet strangely shared paranoia, the paranoia of the schizophrenic cast out of objective reality, who sees conspiracy in every circumstance. And, as in all good horror stories, Trelkovsky's persecution mania is self-fulfilling. It matters not if the neighbors really are conspiring to drive him insane, because by the end his insanity has taken over and his neighbors have become demons from Hell. If his paranoia is unfounded, by the end he has justified it himself.

Trelkovsky's loss of self—his alienation from his surroundings and finally from his own psyche—centers around his fear and loathing of his own body.

8. The Man Behind the Mask: Roman Polanski's Dementia Tales   139

Simone was working as an Egyptologist, and presumably involved in all sorts of atavistic disciplines: hieroglyphics, pyramids, mummification. Without ever referring to it explicitly, *The Tenant* posits an unconscious force such as torments many schizophrenics with its otherness, its seeming omnipotence. Deathless, eternal, unfathomable, inhuman, this force possessed Simone and drove her to suicide (she was dabbling in matters beyond her grasp), and now it is acting on Trelkovsky (he even begins to see hieroglyphs on the toilet wall). Nothing supernatural is ever suggested in Polanski's film (though it may be there in the novel) since Polanski (whom Kael called "a gothic realist") has little time for such things. He is only interested in Trelkovsky's madness, not in the possible reasons for it. The nature of madness is *un*reason, plainly, so for Polanski there can be no possible explanation that doesn't detract from insanity's terror. And this is the beauty, and the strange allure, of the movie; it skirts such questions as natural/supernatural, rational/irrational, sane/insane, with such deftness that the distinctions become blurred, and finally irrelevant — exactly as they are to the schizophrenic mind.

The "ancient, deathless force" that possesses Trelkovsky (and that dates back to ancient Egypt and beyond) is nothing less strange or mysterious (or supernatural) than his own unconscious. But this Id has its own peculiar agenda, its own "fearful symmetry," and so, for all the unreason and dementia which Trelkovsky's journey (and Polanski's movie) consists of, there is indeed a haunting pattern to be deciphered. Along with *Don't Look Now* and very few

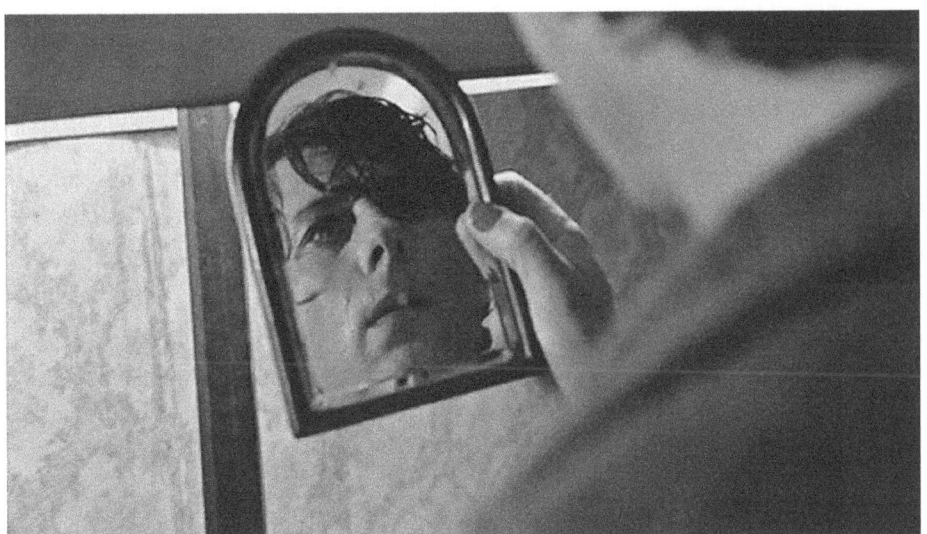

Unacceptable impulses of the false self: Trelkovsky (Roman Polanski) reflects upon his disintegration in *The Tenant* (1976, Paramount).

other films, *The Tenant* is a rare case of a horror movie that communicates a genuine sense of the *occult*. It presents consensus reality as a club from which it is possible, at any time, to be ostracized, whereupon the *true* nature of reality can no longer be avoided. This "club" provides shelter and refuge from the forces of our own unconscious, and as such, most of us (like Trelkovsky) would do just about anything to stay within it. It may be hell, but at least we belong there.

Trelkovsky sweats and frets and grows more sickly and pallid with every passing hour. He becomes a kind of ghoul, a phantom haunting his former life, trying to find a way *in*, a way back to himself, but only ever drifting further away, into non-entity. His world becomes a perceptual nightmare in which thoughts, fantasies, and fears are embodied as *living beings* around him: neighbors knocking on his door and shadowy figures watching him from the toilet window. He even begins to find concrete objects that serve to solidify his fantasy, to provide him with the necessary props to act it out: Simone's make-up case, her dress, her tooth which he finds in a hole in the wall (as if left there as a memento, some retroactive voodoo to possess him by). When Trelkovsky wakes to find blood on his pillow and his own front tooth missing, he searches everywhere for the tooth before finally accepting the inevitable and looking for it in the hole in the wall. At this point the "transference" is complete. Barring a supernatural explanation (and unless we regard the whole film as Trelkovsky's fever dream), what Trelkovsky is undergoing is a schizophrenic split-off of personalities in which he begins living an alternate life, unknown to him. This secondary personality "is" Simone, though in actual fact it could be anybody at all — or nobody — since this is simply the way the identity crumbles.

The overlap of the ego with the id initially creates the impression of an *alternate* identity that has nothing in common with — that may even be hostile to — Trelkovsky's conscious identity. Merely by existing, this id-entity threatens to "destroy" the ego, though in actual fact it merely wishes to overwhelm it and assimilate it *into* itself. But it's all "death" to the ego, and so the existing personality becomes unstable, unreal, and the new, emerging self is perceived — in good horror tradition — as a devouring force of unreason. As Trelkovsky's already passive and unstable ego begins to collapse, his unconscious takes over; he loses all "objectivity" and the line between perceiver and perceived — or better said, between the act of perception and the world that is being perceived — disappears. He enters the imaginal realms, where past, present, and future are one and nothing is fixed or solid. But this is no strawberry fields, much less a mythic rebirth. Trelkovsky is so unaware of what is happening that he is a victim of his own perceptions. If nothing is real, there is still plenty to get hung about.

Losing the tooth is symbolic not only of Trelkovsky's dissolution and decay but, at a deeper level, of his finally facing up to the truth about himself: that he is a ghost, a phantom, a collection of assumptions, all of which are coming up false.[1] Later on Trelkovsky, while drunk, babbles to Stella his existential dilemma. He speaks of losing body parts one by one (much as occurs in shamanic initiation myths); if he loses an arm, "one says, 'myself and my arm,'" but if he loses his head, "is it then myself and my body? By what right," he asks, "does the head claim the title of myself?"

This speech is central to the film. Esoterically (to plumb the depths of our "occult text"[2]), the head is aligned to the forces of death, while the body is aligned to those of life. The body strives for nutrition — food, water, sunlight, movement — the head seeks a different kind of sustenance, that of knowledge. Knowledge — associated with good and evil since mythology began — is what separates the pure, instinctual animal (the body) from its environment, and what allows it to reflect upon *itself* (self-consciousness, when the head claims the title of "I"). It is equated with the fall from grace. "Therefore is the knowledge of me the knowledge of death."[3] Yet this is all illusion, as suggested by Trelkovsky's need to question his hitherto assumed identification with the head — i.e. thoughts — as opposed to the body (physical sensation). Which is more real? Finally the schizophrenia *The Tenant* diagnoses — in its own oblique, roundabout fashion — is the true schizophrenia: the split of mind from body. "The mind" or ego is but a collection of thought processes that result from neurological firings, in turn related to the biological functions of the body; as such it is a part of the body, and not vice versa. Yet the dementia of solipsism which Trelkovsky (along with the rest of humankind) suffers from attempts to reverse this arrangement, to stand it on its head. The head claims sovereignty over the body, as if the physical universe (as many mystic teachings posit) were but a by-product of a greater, *mental* working.

For Trelkovsky death is given sovereignty over life, and his mind becomes a dis-ease of the body. His dissociated psyche then sets about slowly, inexorably, to destroy his body, to lead it (like the serpent with its wiles) to ruin with false promises and chimera. When finally the split-off is complete, Trelkovsky has "become" his head — namely his fantasy projection of Simone. He has effectively denied his body completely (signified by his becoming a woman); at this point he is ready to "translate" to the next dimension, and hurls himself from the balcony. This is also the point at which Trelkovsky enters the imaginal realm fully (not just mentally but physically) and his perceptions become unhinged. His world has become an organic, self-sustaining nightmare, a living hell. The neighbors gather at their windows to watch his final enactment and he perceives them as theatergoers in their boxes, applauding, goading him on. They are the succubae, the evil spirits of the schizo (or shaman) gathered around the suffering soul, salivating in anticipation, as they feed on his fear and despair. At this point Trelkovsky has become a spirit himself. His existence is defined by torment, hence death (self-negation, beginning with his transformation into Simone, completed by his mimicking of her suicide) is the only answer to life. Madness is the only cure for the body's disease of "mind."

What an appalling, hilarious, and sublime parable Polanski (the erstwhile genius who lost his head) has assembled! His juggling of the absurd with the tragic, the sublime with the ridiculous, the surreal with the grotesque, and the mysterious with the obscene is as masterful as his own performance in the film. As Trelkovsky, Polanski seems to be taken over by the role, a consummate actor giving an almost flawless exercise in empathy. And for once the cruel, cool malevolence of the director is equaled and balanced by the almost painful vulnerability of the actor. Polanski becomes his own victim here; not only is his suffering made real this way, but the director's torture is rendered more heartfelt and exquisite also. It is the perfect schizophrenic juxtapositioning of director-victimizer with actor-victim, the very essence of the divided consciousness. Polanski the director conceives, creates, and controls his nightmare vision with all the ruthlessness at his disposal; overseeing his own private circus of delirium, he pulls out all the stops and makes a carnival of despair. Meanwhile, down below, forever trapped inside the circle, Polanski the actor twists and writhes and squirms, a puppet on evil strings, lost in this abominable world of his own fantasy creation.

With *The Tenant*, Polanski's art is realized, his vision fulfilled. The boundaries between subject and object, fantasy and reality, art and life, have been erased, both embodied in a single body and soul. And, however at odds they may be, deep down both sides know they are complicit in the upholding of the illusion. Like the little child who dons the Trelkovsky (Polanski) mask with the jester's cap and points mockingly up at the real McCoy — a distorted image of Trelkovsky's alienated self, an offspring of his own runaway id (like the children in *The Brood*, or the red dwarf in *Don't Look Now*) — Polanski is holding up a twisted, mocking mirror to his own haunted psyche. We are all unruly children trapped in the cruel circuses of our mock existences. Caught under the shadow of some "ancient force" of darkness from which we have emerged, we are living lives that do not belong to us, unwelcome lodgers in our own bodies and psyches, longing for madness or death, if only for the chance to see what lies behind the mask. (A little child?)

Through the imitation of an illusion, Polanski is finally facing up to this truth, making *The Tenant* something to see. The schizo comes clean, and speaks for us all.

9

Beautiful Freaks: Tim Burton's Celebrations of Specialness

> Insanity is in some scary way the most freedom you can have, because you're not bound by the laws of society.
> —Tim Burton, *Burton on Burton*

Tim Burton is a runaway talent. His gloomy, autistic sensibility would seem to make him the last person to be embraced by the Hollywood industry, but this is exactly what has happened. Like one of his own misfit characters, Burton has not only retained his freakishness but been embraced for it by a community that will always see him as a freak, but continues to love him for it. Yet, like Edward Scissorhands with his potentially deadly digits, Burton at times seems unable to control his own talents. Burton's movies for the most part seem made by a precocious, particularly perverse child, a prodigy; they are inspired, visionary, dreamlike, free-rolling, but often shapeless, unruly, indulgent. At times, Burton's talents seem out of proportion with his ability to apply them, and as a result less than half of his films (*Beetlejuice, Sleepy Hollow, Big Fish, The Corpse Bride*, and his recent triumph with *Sweeney Todd*) are fully satisfying works. The rest range from inspired messes to self-indulgent duds, yet throughout them all (not counting *Planet of the Apes*) dances the idiosyncratic, perverse, visionary energy of their maker.

By his own admission,* storytelling is not Burton's strongest trait. Although many of Burton's movies may *look* like the casualties of studio interference, scrappy and shapeless and full of glaring holes in plot and logic, in fact, Burton has enjoyed an almost unprecedented degree of freedom within the industry. Burton's movie persona is dark and deranged, as befits a true artist, but in a curiously retarded fashion. His infantile tastes have led him to

---

*"In any of my movies the narrative is the worst thing you've ever seen, and it's constant." *Burton on Burton*, pg. 114.

channel his dementia into the most fantastic genres, and although Burton seems to have more in common with Surrealists such as Polanski or Lynch, his choice of material seems closer to showmen like Steven Spielberg and Robert Zemeckis. (A filmmaker who seems a kindred spirit to Burton is Joe Dante, who peaked with the camp horror classic *The Howling* and enjoyed brief commercial glory with the Burton-esque *Gremlins*.)

Burton started out in animation and to date all his movies (even the best of them) might be described (though never dismissed) as "live-action cartoons." Burton has a fascination for the twisted, unnatural, absurd side of things, the underbelly of the human psyche. He is drawn to freaks, not in a callous, exploitative way, but rather as one himself (he betrays an affinity for misfits). One gets the feeling that Burton knows he doesn't belong among the beautiful people but rather with the outcasts; this is why he is drawn above all to fantasy — his themes would be too dark, too depressing, if confined to a naturalistic milieu. His humor would be strangled in the crib, and without humor Burton's vision of the world would be nigh insufferable. As it is, within the fantasy genre and making live-action cartoons, Burton is able to adapt his singularly twisted view of humanity and turn it into something entertaining; morbid, but also darkly fascinating.

All of Burton's characters (if we exclude *Apes*, and *Mars Attacks!* which does away with characters altogether) display delightfully schizophrenic tendencies; they are either out-and-out freaks or have hidden sides to their natures by which their schizophrenia comes out more covertly (Batman being the most obvious example). There is something distinctly *other* about Burton's conception of humanness. He might almost be a visitor from another planet, attempting to make movies about this curious species he is studying and forever getting it wrong (like Vincent Price's inventor in *Edward Scissorhands*, who fails to finish his creation and leaves him with blades in place of fingers). Yet it is their very "off-ness" that makes his characters so endearing and his movies so unique. Even when Burton made a biopic of a real-life personality (*Ed Wood*), he chose a partially demented, wholly deluded, closet transvestite for his subject.

Following the short films *Vincent* and *Frankenweenie*, Burton began his movie career working with Pee Wee Herman (*Pee Wee's Big Adventure*, 1985), a weirdly androgynous, chronically pubescent, possibly retarded man-child whose weirdness is doubly unsettling for being entirely self-determined. Much more Paul Reubens' creation than Burton's, Pee Wee is a species unto himself. After Pee Wee came *Beetlejuice* (1988), in which the main characters, though normal to the point of blandness, also happen to be dead; the rest of the cast is made up of a motley crew of eccentrics, from Winona Ryder's teen queen of Goth to her kooky parents (Jeffrey Jones and Catherine O'Hara) and their bloated fag-hag interior decorator Robert Goulet; add to this the most outrageous assortment of ghouls, ghosts, and goblins, and the frenetic genius of

9. Beautiful Freaks: Tim Burton's Celebration of Specialness

A social services bureaucracy of the afterlife: Runaway ids and shrunken heads (and Michael Keaton) in *Beetlejuice* (1988, Warner Bros.).

Michael Keaton in the title role, and you have a freak show worthy of Tod Browning or John Waters, without the queasiness.

Beetlejuice is Burton's excursion into the terrible ids of a perfectly normal, sweet couple who die prematurely and then postpone the afterlife in order to hang out a little longer in the world of the living. The Maitlands (Alec Baldwin and Geena Davis) are too conventional for death, and as ghosts they are timid and straight-laced and endearingly ineffective. *Beetlejuice* doesn't have much narrative drive, or much of a plot either, but it has a doozy of a premise and a marvelous, parable-like simplicity. The Maitlands are snatched up by cruel Fate in their prime, fully embarked on a nice, quiet life when a freak accident brings it to an end. These souls are so unprepared for the loss of their bodies that at first they don't even realize they are dead. They suffer a blackout, memory loss, and return home, drawn by the power of habit to resume their lives even though they have no material existence. When they attempt to leave the house, they find themselves in a terrifying, unfamiliar dimension (sand dunes) inhabited by huge, carnivorous worms, after which, they resolve not to leave the house again. When they finally realize they are dead, ghosts haunting their former home, they aren't so much horrified as frustrated and bewildered.

The Maitlands (Adam and Barbara) find an old book, *The Handbook for the Recently Deceased*, and use it to visit the "social services bureaucracy of the afterlife,"[1] staffed by suicides. There they are informed that they are to spend the next 125 years in their home, as resident ghosts, before graduating to the next phase of Eternity. The Maitlands have no problem with this, at least until the house is invaded by the Deetzs, a tasteless and vulgar couple and their possibly autistic daughter Lydia (Winona Ryder). This New York nouveau riche pair bring along an interior decorator who proceeds to turn the house into a grotesque art work, sending Adam and Barbara into a frenzy of misery. They make such poor ghosts that nothing they do can scare this nightmare family away (they can't even get the Deetzs to *see* them; only the self-immersed daughter is sufficiently schizo to detect their presence). In desperation, the Maitlands resort to the services of Betelgeuse, a "bio-exorcist," to cast out the evil humans and make the house safe for ghosts to live in. Betelgeuse, of course, turns out to be considerably more than the Maitlands can handle, and before long he is turning *everybody's* world into a living hell. *Beetlejuice*—"an art work that has no depth but jangles with energy"[2]—is a beautiful, surrealistic farce that turns all the staples of melodrama on their head and creates a genre all its own—screwball metaphysics. It's a one of a kind movie, a comedy of schizophrenia that never gets sickly sweet or cloying but retains its bite throughout. It's death-affirming.

Betelgeuse—the shameless, lewd, obscene, and genuinely frightening ghoul which the Maitlands lack the heart to be—is the manifestation of all their repressed rage and hostility. He's the id demon, the imp of the perverse unleashed, and Keaton takes the role as far as he can go with it: he burns like a roman candle. Betelgeuse is a pinball machine, he lights up and just keeps on going. Since his time in the material world is limited, he's always racing, trying to do the most harm in the shortest possible time. The movie doesn't need much of him, either (just as the Maitlands don't). A little of Betelgeuse (and of Keaton) goes a *long* way.

The Maitlands are the conventional, bland, ordinary folk for whom even death is an inconvenience (as it happens, it doesn't upset their daily routines much). Their being confined to their home is not a punishment, on the contrary. They are not ready for the higher dimensions yet, and to them the house stands for the comfortable security of the known, their personal selves still intact now their bodies are gone. The sandy nightmare realm outside is the raging netherworld of the Id, still populated by the demon forms of fear and confusion. The Maitlands are given time to adjust to their new state of being and to get acquainted with the irrational forces of the afterlife—the fourth dimension, the world of the Id. Betelgeuse, like any good Other—the shadow trickster figure—is only so extreme, so outrageous and repulsive, because the Maitlands are so *uptight*. Their squeamishness and goodliness is a red flag to his libidinous nature: he takes one look at them and—lets rip. But, for all the malevolence of his actions, Betelgeuse is a good, old-fashioned (though rather unconventional) psychopomp, a guide for the dead. If he's beastly it's only

9. Beautiful Freaks: Tim Burton's Celebration of Specialness

because he is instructing them in the ways of the Id, helping them to develop their own natural talents, as spirits for transformation and trickery.

Betelgeuse is a trapped soul himself, apparently, hence his desire to wed the vampiric, enticing Lydia. Like Lucifer, he's contemptuous of these humans but secretly jealous and desirous of them. And as in all Tim Burton movies (even the dreary *Planet of the Apes*), the bad guy isn't really *bad*, just unruly, irresponsible, and mischievous; above all, he's *lonely*. In fact, all of Burton's characters are painfully lonely. Some are twisted and corrupted by their loneliness while others are ennobled by it, and that's what makes the difference, finally, between Burton's heroes and his villains. Betelgeuse is lovable but intolerable. He's like a genie kept too long inside the lantern: when he gets out he's so revved up and anxious to make a good-bad impression that he deranges himself (and everyone else). There's nothing to do with him but get him back in the box as quickly as possible.

Next up was *Batman* (1989), Burton's graduation to blockbuster filmmaking, a fatally flawed work but one that offers up delights just the same, and not just one but *two* runaway schizos.* Batman is the archetypal schizophrenic of the 20th century. As created by Bob Kane and Bill Finger, he's probably the closest we get to a genuine modern myth, with all the ingredients present in his conception. The fall from innocence (Bruce's parents are murdered before his eyes when he is a child), the quest for power and knowledge (in later versions, as seen in *Batman Begins*, Wayne spends years journeying in the East studying secret wisdom and occult science, training his body and mind to the peak of human potential); and finally, the actual self-transformation from mortal into mythic hero, creature of the night, dream warrior, relentless avenger. Batman was unique among comic book heroes for being consigned to the darkness and being driven above all by pain and suffering. He chose a bat as his emblem, his totem animal, because it seemed a fitting guise — an ally — by which to "strike fear into the hearts of criminals." But of course, bats are blind, so his choice also suggests other, more oblique rationales. Wayne takes refuge from pain (like Parry in Terry Gilliam's *The Fisher King*) by hiding inside a fantasy life; he creates a new identity to make sense of the madness and injustice of the world. He literally hides in the shadow of this self-created, uncon-

---

*Good as he is, however, Jack Nicholson is all wrong for the Joker. Lacking either the courtly, manic grace or the otherworldly menace that made the comic book character so memorable, Nicholson is clumsy and ungainly and out of shape (not to mention middle-aged), and as a result his antics are rather painful to watch (he turns the demonic trickster into a buffoon). Fortunately, Michael Keaton, in the role of Bruce Wayne/Batman, is more effective. Keaton has the wariness, the dark, edgy undercurrents, to suggest a man driven by inner demons. We can understand why Wayne is driven to transform himself into a bat — to become a monster in order to do battle with monsters.

scious other self, and as a result all his pain, sorrow, and confusion (and fear) is transformed into a single-minded dedication to "justice" (vengeance). Only so can he continue to live with himself, by dissociating from his grief, by separating all that is unpalatable to him and giving it autonomous existence as another Self. Hence, although Batman is a hero to many, in his own mind (and this was Burton's take on the myth), he is a desperate, lost soul living a double life as the only means for keeping his demons at bay.

Batman doesn't fight crime out of a sense of justice or righteousness; he does so as a man fights a fire devouring his home. The monster he turns himself into and the monster he is fighting is actually one and the same. This is why the movie goes to great pains to show that Batman has created the Joker, and the Joker (by killing Wayne's parents) created Batman. The Joker is an evil twin, a mirror that will not let Wayne forget his true nature. By being a reflection of Wayne's reflection, the Other to his other, the Joker gets to be everything Wayne *can't* be: extrovert, gaudy, brightly-colored and *cheerful!* He gets to laugh and sing and dance and have fun while doing unspeakable evil. This is all dictated by the nature of Wayne's psychosis: his rejection of pain and evil is only made possible by his hysterical blindness, his need to cloak himself— as a force of good — in shadows, morbidity, fear and darkness. Likewise, as the reverse, perverse, and inevitable reaction to this (within Wayne's own psyche), evil re-emerges as the very opposite: disguised in the gaudy, carnival colors and bright, laughing euphoria of "happiness." In such a way, the Joker becomes the perfect, gibbering apotheosis of the Other to Batman's relentlessly somber crusader.

The Joker is the ego here, Batman the Id. The Joker prattles, Batman keeps silence. The Joker's motivations are all-too apparent: money, glory, and personal gratification. Batman's motives remain obscure, abstract. He fights the Joker *apparently* because he (the Joker) exists, because *someone* has to stop him. But, as we've seen, he has hidden motives. They are the twin gods of Christ and Satan all dressed up for a consumer, comic book culture; and what's striking here is how the poles have been reversed. Batman — with his horns and cape and his dark, cavernous lair — is the Hero, while the Joker — with his purple robes, his perennial, life-affirming grin, and his vast array of dazzling party tricks (miracles) — is the Arch Fiend. Between them, the two dancing, parading, only partially human avatars of "good" and "evil," light and darkness, make the quintessential dyad for pop culture, a perfect double-edged emblem for our schizophrenic times.

Batman Returns (1992) is the most glaring example of Burton's shabbiness as a storyteller. The film begins marvelously, sustains itself well enough for most of its length (especially in the scenes between Batman and a latex-clad Michelle Pfeiffer as Catwoman), then collapses into incoherence in the final scenes. Burton is hamstrung by the restraints of big-budget, blockbuster

9. Beautiful Freaks: Tim Burton's Celebration of Specialness

moviemaking, and by the confines of these already established, quasi-mythic comic book characters. Although he seems to have a genuine love for the characters (and plenty of ideas for them), he is unable to give free reign to his ideas without undermining his story in the process.* The *Batman* films are perhaps no more unwieldy than *Beetlejuice*, but since the films rely on traditional melodramatic devices (such as suspense and narrative drive) to stay together, the flaws here are much more apparent. The more one sees the films, the less they stand up.

Edward Scissorhands (1990) is a movie beloved by many, but not, alas, by me. I found it tame, lame, mawkish, and rather dull. (Pauline Kael said it best: "Beetlejuice would have spit in this movie's eye."[3]) The same might be said for *Ed Wood* (1994), a proficient piece of filmmaking with an extremely touching central performance by Johnny Depp but rather a lifeless movie, marred above all by its subject matter. Burton wants here to celebrate, without irony, the life and career of a man remembered as being "the worst movie director of all time." Burton explains his interest in the character as follows:

> The thing I was taken by ... was his extreme optimism, to the point where there was an incredible amount of denial. And there's something charming to me about that.... being passionate and optimistic is great to a certain point, and then you're just in complete denial, it becomes delusional. That's what I liked about the Ed Wood character. I could relate to him that way.... One of the things I liked about Ed, and could relate to, was being passionate about what you do to the point of it becoming like a weird drug.... again, that's why I admire Ed so much, and those people — he was doing *something*. If I see something, a piece of work, a painting, film, anything, and somebody's going out on a limb and doing it, I admire them. I don't even care if I like it, I just admire them, because they're doing something that a lot of people won't do.[4]

Ed Wood was deluded into believing he possessed talent, and the problem with Burton's film is that, however touching Burton's affection for Wood may be, his treatment of such an excruciating theme is entirely at odds with the material. He wants to make his movie "up," quirky, endearing, when the truth is that it's actually an extremely grim subject: that of a lost soul struggling against an utter lack of talent, a lack which no amount of childish enthusiasm or willful blindness can compensate for. Why would we celebrate and admire a man who made some of the worst movies in history? If it was just

---

*Until *Sleepy Hollow*, Burton was unable to sustain a full-length narrative all the way through without it either sagging in the middle or coming apart at the end (or simply never finding a form to begin with). Even *Beetlejuice* is rather ungainly and tends to jerk — and occasionally limp — along to an unformed conclusion; without Keaton to give it a shot in the arm every few scenes, it would certainly have died a premature death. (I have not mentioned *Tim Burton's The Nightmare Before Christmas* in this essay because, despite the title, the film is directed by Henry Selick and only co-produced by Burton.)

because he *did it*, there are thousands of cases out there equally worthy of celebrating: talent isn't a requirement of productivity, only determination. Is it because Wood remained mysteriously oblivious to his ineptitude? (One might as well make a movie about a mass murderer who believed he was performing a public service and expect us to applaud *that*.) The idea has comic potential, of course, but for once Burton tries to play it straight. There *are* scenes and moments in Wood's movies of such unparalleled ineptitude they seem oddly inspired, and which are genuinely hilarious; but, painstakingly reproduced here, they become simply embarrassing. Burton doesn't allow us to laugh at Wood, yet he doesn't want us to feel sorry for him either. But for an untalented transvestite driven by sheer schizophrenic zeal to prove himself against impossible odds — what sort of response does that leave us? *Ed Wood* is a travesty of conception from the start, and not even Depp's beguiling performance can save it. The film is like one of those retarded nephews in horror movies: instead of wanting to celebrate it, you want to lock it away in the basement where no one will have to see it.

Yet critics embraced the movie, maybe because it was Burton's first film made entirely in earnest, about "real" people, or perhaps because he proved that his technical skills were equal to his creative vision and seemed to be finally bringing them into balance. If so, then *Mars Attacks!* soon dashed such hopes. The film is a self-indulgent bit of sticky toffee, a whimsical bombast full of poorly-shaped scenes and misdirected performances (Jack Nicholson is especially at sea in his role as a Las Vegas sleazeball). The only moments in the movie that stand out are when the brainy Martians arrive and start incinerating and Burton gets to play with his puppets. The movie is like a *Saturday Night Live* skit blown up to multimillion dollar proportions, an example of a prodigious talent being shackled to (and swallowed by) a willfully adolescent sensibility. Burton was indulging in being a boy with his train set again.

Sleepy Hollow (2000) is magical cinema at its best, there to remind us why we love movies: because they give us the kind of pleasure we can't get anywhere else (save maybe in dreams); they give form to our fantasies. Burton is a unique talent, and his particular, twisty, gothic-absurdist vision is all of a piece. But he couldn't have pulled it off without Johnny Depp — as Ichabod Crane — to anchor his movie in flesh and blood. Depp turns himself into a cartoon character for Burton, and as a result, with the pure instincts of a natural-born actor, he transforms Burton's cartoon into a full-blooded drama. Depp is as much a freak of the cinema as Burton; he's one of a kind. To get close to what he does here, one would probably have to go all the way back to Buster Keaton. Ichabod Crane is a perfect role for Depp, a return to the early antics of *Benny and Joon*, and to compare the two movies is to see just how far he had come as an actor: from an inspired novice to a master of the craft. Although he appears to do little in *Sleepy Hollow*, what he's actually doing is

9. Beautiful Freaks: Tim Burton's Celebration of Specialness 151

Tim Burton (right) and Johnny Depp on the set of *Sleepy Hollow* (1999, Paramount).

closer to mime, or silent movie acting, than the usual method performance. There are few actors with the grace and ingenuity (and humor) to pull this off without appearing ridiculous, but Depp not only brings Crane to life, he turns the movie into the most satisfying adult fairy tale since ... I can't think of another adult fairy tale that even compares. *Sleepy Hollow* is a gorgeous piece of work, on a par with Polanski's *Dance of the Vampires*—a homage to Hammer horror films that affectionately and faithfully evokes the originals while outdoing them. In its very limited genre — the camp horror movie — *Sleepy Hollow* is a bona fide masterpiece.

The amusing thing about Ichabod Crane is that, however sweepingly dismissive he is of all things supernatural, at the same time he is remarkably susceptible to it. At the merest hint of it, in fact (even when he is the victim of a malicious trick by the villagers), he succumbs to superstitious panic. And when he really does encounter the headless horseman at last (in one of the movie's most delightful quirks), he crumbles completely into a delirious wreck and faints away from sheer terror. (As Burton remarked, Depp is "one of the best fainters in the business.") The funniest part about this scene is how Crane assumes the village folk are disbelieving him because they take his ravings so casually. Of course, they already *know* that the horseman exists, it's only Crane who has to forsake his precious reason and open himself up to the supernatural. As he later bewails, "I should not have come to this place where my rational mind has been so contraverted by the spirit world!" Once Crane faces his fears, however, he is as determined to get to the bottom of the supernatural mystery as he had previously been to expose it. He's a genuine trouper, not to be swayed or daunted by even the most inexplicable of forces.*

As soon as Crane realizes that the horseman is real, he aligns himself — however reluctantly — with the world of the occult and pays a visit to the local witch. He stutters his assurances to her that he is not there to judge her or criticize her line of work: "Whatever you may be..." he stammers. "Each to their own." The witch chains herself down, drinks her potion, and allows a demonic entity to possess her body. In order to get information, Crane must subject himself to the full onslaught of the unknown — in this case a snake-tongued, pop-eyed ghoul right out of *The Evil Dead*. This is Crane's first willing foray into the unconscious, the world of spirits, and fittingly enough it involves nothing less than a téte à téte interview with "the Other" (as the witch herself refers it). As a result, he gains the knowledge he is seeking — the location of the horseman's grave, beneath "the tree of the dead" (a great oxymoron, especially since this tree *bleeds*); inside the trunk of the tree he finds the severed heads of the horseman's various victims. The fact of the horseman being *headless* makes him the perfect harbinger and emissary of the irrational, the forces of the unconscious. It's only when Crane gets hold of the horseman's skull and returns it to him, using reason to conquer (or tame) the irrational, that the horseman returns to his underground lair — Hell, the concealed place — and peace is finally restored.

---

*In flashback dream sequences, we see where Ichabod's suspicion of all things "mystical" originates: his mother was tortured and murdered by his father, out of a religious zeal and as punishment for what he perceived to be her "sins."

Fittingly enough for a Burton movie, the horseman is never seen to be actually *evil*. Although while alive he is portrayed as a savage destroyer driven by bloodlust, as a risen ghost he is actually a *slave* to the devious, all-too human designs of the evil stepmother (played by Miranda Richardson). So it's only when the spirit world is harnessed by "flesh and blood" desires, when the unconscious is twisted to the ends of an all-too-conscious agenda, that it becomes harmful and malignant. Actually, in a strange way (and as played by Christopher Walken), the horseman is rather sympathetic; perhaps this is because the only time we see him with his head on is either when he is being hunted and killed by his enemies, or else, at the end, when dragging off the villainess to eternal torment (he bites off her tongue first, a suitably symbolic punishment for her spell-casting).

Doubtless the reason *The Legend of Sleepy Hollow* is the most well-known and enduring American legend is that it so perfectly encapsulates the basic theme and subtext of all myths and fairy tales everywhere: the clash between conscious and unconscious, between the world of magic and the world of science or reason. And, just as the man of reason is needed to make sense out of, and bring to light, the mysteries of the supernatural, so it is the world of witches and spirits into which our man of reason must be *initiated* (and bewitched). By this method his faculties are put to the ultimate test and he can find the courage to become the Hero (winning the white witch as a result). The headless horseman is Crane's inverted mirror image, his *Doppelgänger*, the acknowledgment of which is necessary for the total integration of rational and unconscious thought, whereby he may emerge from the secular world of the intellect (the inside of his head) into the fuller, organic world of nature.

Before he can attain this freedom, however, Crane mistakenly deduces that the beautiful and mysterious Catrina (Christina Ricci), whom he loves, is behind the diabolic conspiracy that unleashed the horseman. As a result of his disillusionment, Ichabod turns his back upon the mystery, still unsolved. This error is a result not only of his faulty reasoning, but of his unconscious desire to escape from the ever-encroaching allure of the supernatural. Feeling the awful, irreversible hold which it is beginning to have upon him, he takes any opportunity — even one founded in delusion — to flee. By demonizing the white witch Catrina — who symbolizes the healing, beneficent power of magic — he is temporarily finding a way out of the irrational "spirit world" into which he has fallen. In the end, of course, his "chain of reasoning" is too sound, too efficient, to permit him this cowardly deception. Above all, it is because Crane's heart is now sufficiently stirred to be working in tandem with his head — his reason now leavened with emotion — so that he is able to *feel* the truth and discover the flaw in his ratiocination. Hence he "returns," before he has even successfully escaped, to Sleepy Hollow (even the name itself suggests the unconscious realm), there to both expose the true black witch and return the blind force of death whence it came. Only then can he embrace the maligned Catrina and claim her as his very own Isis (he carries her back to New York).

In an earlier scene, Catrina tells Ichabod how she always wanted a tame cardinal, but couldn't bear to keep it in a cage. In response, Ichabod shows her his "magic": the spinning disk with the bird on one side and the cage on the other, which when spun creates the illusion of the bird being caged. The red cardinal signifies the carnal passions, the wild untamed spirit, and the unconscious (like the Red Knight in *The Fisher King*). The cage is reason. Although Catrina wears white throughout the movie, she is plainly Ichabod's red cardinal — his desire. There is something lascivious and definitely witchlike about Christina Ricci; her Catrina is anything but an innocent, and it's easy enough to see how Ichabod could imagine her consorting with Satan, and why he might be wary of her advances. By bringing her back with him to New York, "just in time for a new century," it may be that he is taming the wild bird (without necessarily caging it); but he is also bringing a piece of the magical realm back *with* him, and so retaining his connection to it. You can take the maiden out of the Wild, but you will never get the Wild out of the maiden.

Burton's movies are so appealing because he speaks for the schizo in us all, but instead of dwelling on the pain and isolation of being a freak, he focuses on the freedom and celebrates specialness. Burton uses freaks as a way of communicating a specifically American idea, the idea that you can be whoever you want to be, that individuality is not only a right but a goal: something we all aspire to deep down, even if we are too afraid to do anything about it. Burton's movies see to it that the freak is vindicated, that he is accepted without having to give up his freakishness. Burton's obsession as an artist is a uniquely *artistic* concern: how to live and work within a community — and be of service to that community, accepted and embraced by it — while at the same time hanging on to whatever makes us different from it, what makes us special.

Burton has retained his specialness, the freakish, slightly *off* quality of his work that makes it so different from anything else around, and so impossible to categorize. And yet he has managed to find a niche within the Hollywood community that only he could fill (he has actually *created* a niche for himself). Though he doesn't write them, most of Burton's movies are *auteur* works: they are very much about himself, about the artist's struggle to transform pain and loneliness into something we can all share and enjoy. He uses his feelings of isolation and strangeness as a means to connect to the world of regular people and so reduce his sense of alienation. As such, he is very much the quintessential artist-as-outsider, and what's remarkable about Burton is that his success hasn't dulled his edge. Both in and through his work (the best of it), he vindicates the freak by turning him into something noble; he legitimizes the outcast and rehabilitates the schizo. The key to Burton's commercial success may

9. Beautiful Freaks: Tim Burton's Celebration of Specialness

come down to the fact that, however unconventional, morbid, and twisted his movies, they are by and large mild and non-threatening. They may be subversive, in their own "quirky" way, but unlike the films of other Gothic surrealists such as David Lynch and David Cronenberg, they are rarely really disturbing.

Burton is a dedicated filmmaker and a serious artist, with visual gifts that are second to none. His sensibility is as unique as that of Lynch or Cronenberg, or of Buñuel, Fellini, or Polanski. Yet for the most part, his movies have lacked maturity. Even the best of them, though rich in style and composition, have veered dangerously close to whimsies and have tended to lack deeper emotional undercurrents or psychological insight. Burton may be closer to being a pure entertainer (like Spielberg) than a genuine auteur (like Lynch), and for most of his work, his particular genius—there's really no other word for it—has been put at the service of what remains a rather adolescent sensibility.

Since Burton is a visual artist and not a writer, one of the difficulties he's had is in finding material strong enough—perversely inspired enough—to justify his visionary pyrotechnics, to anchor them and keep them from spinning off into fragmented incoherence or self-indulgent whimsy. There is something autistic about Burton: his creativity has a tendency to be removed from human experience, to remain hermetically sealed inside the director's own psyche. This enhances the sense of strangeness and fantasy of his films—Burton's affinity for freaks extends into nonhuman realms—but their depiction of ordinary human experience seems compromised as a result; it's as if Burton is shifty and distrustful about anything he perceives as normality. But strangeness that isn't anchored in the real world is merely nightmarish or cartoonish, and Burton's films tend towards a mixture of both. In the *Corpse Bride*, for example, it's the corpse who seems most alive to us, while in *Charlie and the Chocolate Factory* (one of Burton's weakest films), the only really vibrant characters are the Oompa Loompas. In *Big Fish*—until *Sweeny Todd* probably Burton's most "grown-up" and "human" work—it's still the freaks that seem realest to us. For Burton, fantasy and freakishness—dream and madness—go hand in hand, and the price of being "normal" (or beautiful) would often seem to be dull two-dimensionality.

Yet Burton appears to be mellowing with age. With *Sweeney Todd: the Demon Barber of Fleet Street* (2007), his vision has grown richer, more full-bodied. Perhaps because he is working with fully-formed material (Steven Sondheim's stage play), *Sweeney Todd*'s characters are the least cartoonish of any of his films. For the first time he has achieved what (in his own words) "probably means the most to me: that people get the emotional quality underneath the stupid façade,"[5] because for once in a Burton film, we are given two fully human freaks. Although Burton broke from the stage tradition by casting Johnny Depp and Helena Bonham Carter as Todd and Mrs. Lovett, beautifying the characters, there is nothing idealized about these freaks: they are souls in torment. And though the film has the Gothic perversity and soaring visual highs of Burton's best work, *Sweeney Todd* is grounded squarely in tragedy in a way his other films aren't. It's the first to allow for the possibility that these beautiful freaks might be monsters in their own eyes (and in Burton's), and not just from the perspective of conventional society. Sondheim's vision is gleefully morbid (presumably what attracted Burton to it), but it's also richly, darkly poignant. Fused with Sondheim's gloomily ironic view of social corruption, Tim Burton's special brand of darkness has (for perhaps the first time) an edge of genuine horror to it, of pathos and melancholy. The visual flourishes are the same, more audaciously assured than ever — Burton's chthonic labyrinths have never gone so deep, or his deliriously somber tones been so vibrant, but what's going on behind them is new. *Sweeney Todd* is Burton's most mature and heartfelt work to date.

The essence of Burton's obsession seems to be "the feeling that your image and how people perceive you are at odds with what is inside you, which is a fairly common feeling."[6] His films celebrate this feeling and show that it's possible (and eminently desirable) to be free of other people's thoughts and judgments. But in order to express what we have inside us, to make our outward behavior and appearance match our inner selves, it's necessary to ignore what other people might say and break out the boxes the world sticks us in. Part of this breaking free from society's cages involves a willingness to become a freak in other people's eyes. It implies a kind of self-instigated derangement, a willed insanity in which we become the sole judge and arbiter of our actions and appearance, and in which everyone else can go to hell. But the price of this — as *Sweeney Todd* makes painfully clear — is winding up caught in our own self-created hells. But at least they are *our* hells.*

Burton admires this free-spiritedness so much that he even turned Ed Wood into a hero, simply for being deluded and stubborn enough to stick to his guns when he was firing nothing but blanks. Presumably it was the same kind of willed individualism that attracted him to Sondheim's Sweeney Todd, who is so consumed by his desire for vengeance — and by bitter contempt for society — that he becomes a distorted reflection of what he most despises: a "demon barber" who cuts throats instead of hair. Perhaps the best embodiment of Burton's peculiar, schizo version of manifest destiny, however, is Bruce Wayne's Batman, who brings about self-transformation through sheer will and imagination. Batman effectively mesmerizes not only the criminal community

---

*In Burton's own words, "those who were tortured were forced to be their own people; they couldn't rely on the culture or the hierarchy to take care of them, so to speak, so they had to make themselves acceptable." *Burton on Burton*, pg. 96.

but the media, and finally the city itself, into believing his own delusion (that he is more than human). His bluff (which involves masterful sleight-of-hand) finally convinces *everybody* he is a force of Nature. Through this act of alchemy, Wayne turns his freakishness from curse to empowerment, more or less exactly as Burton has by becoming a world-class Hollywood filmmaker. Using other people's belief to empower him — instead of allowing it to enslave him — both Wayne and Burton turned the tables and transformed themselves from lonely schizos into conquering heroes. The secret of all art and magic (and of myth and religion) is encapsulated in this one, simple, Plutonic (and adolescent) fantasy.

The "freedom of insanity" — the power of specialness — is the essence of Burton's vision. He not only communicates this vision through his work: he embodies it. The weird autistic kid has grown up to be a shaman.

10

The Great American Psychopath*

> You could be a meat eater, kid, and I mean people, not their garbage!
> —"A No. 1" (Lee Marvin) to "Cigarette" (Keith Carradine)
> in *Emperor of the North*

The Great American Psychopath (GAP) is a kind of cross between Captain Ahab from *Moby Dick* and Wyle E. Coyote from the Roadrunner cartoons. He isn't necessarily American, this Psychopath, being a common "type" in every culture, representing basic human traits and tendencies. The big difference is that in America the GAP is in part our national heritage, the dark side of what the American environment creates. Here at the start of the millennium (where the serial killer is as much a popular commodity as the hot dog), the idea of the GAP has finally come into its own, becoming virtually synonymous with (or indistinguishable from) the all–American (anti) hero. (A process begun in the 1960s but fully consolidated with *Dirty Harry*, in that great year 1971, and more or less completed with the execrable *Silence of the Lambs*.) Beyond this — the heroification of the psycho and psychotization of the hero — there is a lurking, creeping metaphysical angle to consider. Films like *The Usual Suspects* and *Se7en* (the serial killer as messiah) give us a psycho wholly reconciled to his psychosis (though still somehow abject), and as such — it is hinted — none other than the Arch Fiend himself, in street-friendly form.

The GAP actually has his origin not in society or even movies, but in *nature itself*. The fact is that so-called "psychotic" or "evil" (i.e., obsessive destructive) behavior is the distortion of purely natural, instinctive "urges" that have been denied (and hence distorted) in the human animal. At the same time, it's essential to realize that the psycho, as such, has not only been encouraged by our present society (especially American society) but actively created and propagated in (and through) the human species (through a combination of too

*Co-written with Phil Snyder

much caffeine, Coca Cola, TV advertising, ultraviolet lights, e-product food additives, prescription drugs, elevator musak, kiddies cartoons — you name it, the list is potentially endless). The Psychopath, like the Artist, like the Magician, *intends* himself into being. Such intent comes from ego, however, which is a phantom, an imaginal construct. Of course, everything is imaginal and "unreal" at some level, but the difference between ego and everything else is that ego takes *itself* for real; it sees things literally. Perhaps this is even its job, its very nature; but if so, anything that comes from such a fallacy must come to no good, if taken to extremes. So it sseems only natural that, if we embark into magical territory (the id), we must do so "unintentionally," by accident, or be tricked into it (as Neo in *The Matrix* is tricked). Otherwise, the ego's literalism will spoil the magic, force it to conform to dayworld preconceptions, losing touch with the subtlety required for finding one's way through the id world.

This, in a nutshell, is the GAP. He launches himself towards an idealized vision, and in his attempt to grasp it as real, he takes it literally. As the journey progresses he surpasses the limits of literal thinking and must learn a new way of seeing or else perish. The journey begins as an effort to grasp an ungraspable ideal and the GAP, if he's lucky, may *accidentally* learn a few things along the way. If he allows these "lessons" to take hold, he takes a step toward enlightenment; if he rejects them and continues on the Psycho Path, he self-destructs. The Psychopath is both madman *and* idiot.

As the Psychopath approaches the edge of all human limits, a transformation can take place; provided his desire/obsession continues to propel him, this may even involve an outright physical transformation. A form of transcendence?* A metaphysical transfiguration? There is a distinction to be made, however, between serial killer and Psychopath. Often the serial killer may be a Psychopath, even a GAP (John Doe from *Se7en* certainly qualifies here), but not in every case. Once the GAP has become "wholly reconciled to his psychosis," he almost becomes a different animal. An evolution, of sorts, takes place. The creature starts off as one thing and then goes through a process of change, one that is usually sparked by environmental factors. This happens either as a result of the environment changing, and so creating the creature, or of the creature itself changing its own environment, by moving from it, attacking it, or otherwise directly altering it. As evolution continues, the creature changes by degrees until it becomes unrecognizable, something else entirely, albeit something that still retains a residue of its former identity (like

---

*"That serial murder serves as a method of transcendence is not so incomprehensible when analyzed in the context of myth and ritual.... The serial killer in fiction often longs for the spiritual surety of apocalypse, and attempts to will it into being through constructing a grammar of murder. Murder or sacrifice is essential to the project because, as our modern conceptions of entropic exhaustion dimly echo, the energy of the godhead requires regeneration through mediated exchange of life energies." Simpson, *Psycho Paths*, pg. 175–6.

tail and gills on a human fetus).

In Michael Mann's *Manhunter* the psychopath Dolarhyde makes explicit the transcendental intent behind all his transgressions; to Hannibal Lecter he writes: "You alone can understand what I am becoming. You alone know the people I use to help me in these things are only elements undergoing change to fuel the radiance of what I am becoming. Just as the source of light is burning."

As Philip L. Simpson writes (in *Psycho Paths*, the only work I know of to cover some of the same ground as the present essay): "Dolarhyde attempts to transcend his human weaknesses by imaginatively transforming into an omnipotent, transcendent being." Simpson further embellishes on the psychopath's motives:

> The goal is to establish a stable core identity. This identity can only be reached through a mythic existence that transcends the destabilizing change inherent in temporality. In these works, ritualized repeat murder is the strategy by which the besieged individual grasps eternity. For the identity-obsessed serial killer, the inescapable immediacy of extreme physical violence erases intermediary thought, modes of interpretation, conflicting ideologies, and so forth.... [These characters] attempt to divorce themselves from social context and live in the eternal present of myth.[1]

Blue Velvet is the most powerful statement of the revved up Psychopathic psyche in modern movies. In fact, it was probably my excitement over *Blue Velvet* that intensified my interest in such films, finally coalescing them together

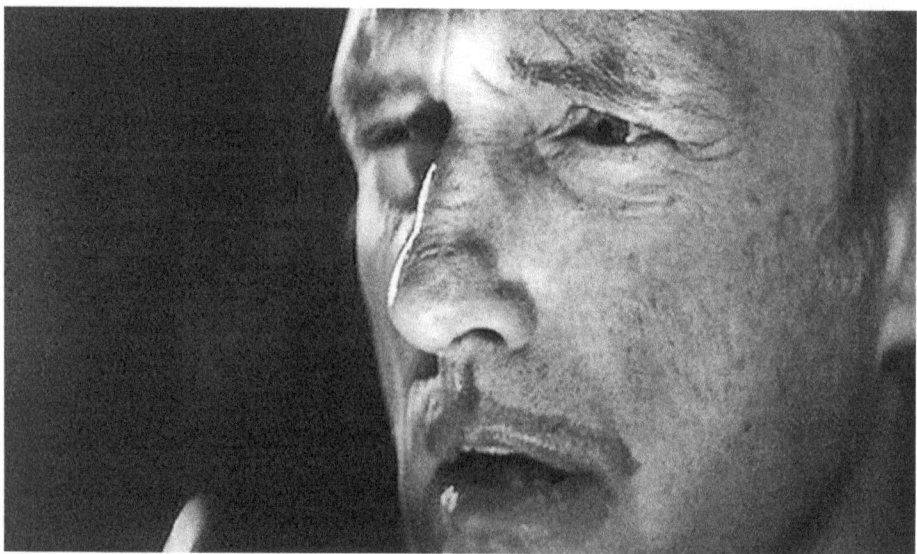

"In dreams, I walk with you." Frank Booth (Dennis Hopper)'s heroic indulgences in *Blue Velvet* (1986, De Laurentiis Entertainment Group).

10. The Great American Psychopath

into the GAP idea. I LOVE Frank Booth. I recognize him. I've seen a bit of Frank in people I've met and have known, I've felt a bit of Frank in me. Frank exists at that edge where the Psychopath has jacked himself up so high on his own obsessions and other substances that he begins to flicker over to the other side. This is implicitly suggested by the bizarre cut in the film, when at Ben's place, Frank cries "I'll fuck anything that moves!" cackles insanely, and — disappears! It's this level of freedom, which is not realistic but literally deranged, and which comes from being pumped up on "the American Dream," that the Psychopath is searching for, and which he will never find (at least without destroying himself). The Psychopath wants complete personal control over time and space, over himself, and over other people. He is like a super-baby in an adult body (note Frank's Mommy/Daddy fixation). Americans (and any other Psychopath, at least in the present terms) are big babies. They want it all. Frank is such a strangely endearing character because, among other things, his search has taken him deep into his own psyche, and through his heroic indulgences, his psyche is exposed for us all to see. Through Frank, we begin to see what it is that the Psychopath has been up to all along.

Another film that gives us such a glimpse, albeit in a very different manner, is Martin Scorsese's *The King of Comedy*. Rupert Pupkin is a definitive case study of the GAP — far more so than *Taxi Driver*'s Travis Bickle, in fact (who is really less of a Psycho than Rupert, even though his actions appear more psychotic). Rupert actually fails to distinguish between reality and fantasy, which is the watermark of the true Psycho.* Travis is merely tragically isolate (God's lonely man), dissociated, disconnected from his own feelings, hence he becomes literally unhinged and explodes in psychotic behavior. But he is different from other Psychos discussed here, in that one could imagine sitting down and having a coffee and apple pie ("with slice of melted yellow cheese") with him, without feeling in any way endangered. He's the Psycho as Everyman, as Bernard Goetz later proved to the world.

Pupkin, on the other hand, really brings forth that connection between the Psychopath (as we have outlined him, not necessarily as he's clinically defined) and the Clown (more on which later). Rupert's goal and his ideal self are hopelessly intertwined. As he obsessively pursues this goal/ideal self, he crosses the line that divides socially acceptable action, and arrives at the unacceptable. He becomes what he always was: a lunatic. But in his own mind he is merely acting out his destiny as an artist. *The King of Comedy* is a near "perfect" GAP film, in that its plot so closely matches the ideal model of the GAP

---

*Simpson quotes the dilettante author Brian (played by David Duchovny) in *Kalifornia*: "Sometimes there's a moment as you're waking when you become aware of the real world around you, but you're still dreaming. You may think you can fly, but you better not try. Serial killers live their whole lives in that place, somewhere between dreams and reality." *Psycho Paths*, pg. 191.

journey of transformation or death.

Taxi Driver, on the other hand, is as much about loneliness as it is about Psychopathy. The film shows us what happens to the Psychopath when he becomes trapped in the city, the urban environment, where direct, forward action is impossible. His cab is a prison that isolates him from other people and the world around him; it takes him only in circles, not in a path toward a goal. In this way, *Taxi Driver* is a more philosophical GAP film, something more internal. Place Travis in a different environment and he might become more directly Psychopathic. But Travis spends most of the film trying to fit in, to become a "person like other people." He is the Psychopath trying to re-enter society, doing a lousy job of it because he's naive, basically a bit dumb, and unaware of himself, of his own psychosis. Like Rupert, he actually thinks he's normal. After much failure, he finally realizes, and then KA-BLOOEY! He explodes into Psychopathy. This is true enough to life, in fact. The real psycho/sociopaths are usually very good at concealing their sickness under a mask of normalcy. On the surface Travis seems like a naive dope, a cowboy-attired throwback and a square (all of which he is ... but then again isn't), which to hip urban America seems like a quaint and harmless thing. But inside he is a heavily armed Psychopath, not a good-natured cowboy but a Mohawked savage. This is the Psychopath's secret. Travis' Injun–inspired haircut connects him with our more "primitive" past, with the hunter, not to mention our frontier past (the name "Travis" was borrowed from a John Ford Western). He circles the city in his cab, hunting for fares, looking for that link to humanity, but all he finds are cold women, whores, and shallow politicians. Finally, perhaps without even knowing it, Travis wakes up to his true role in this crowd (society) — he is not there to fit in, but to tear it apart.

Another key figure in popular mythology is Bruce Wayne/Batman, an archetypal GAP if ever there was one. Batman has the all-important quality of *obsession*; like all true Psychos, he lives in a world strangely of his own making. Obviously the Adam West Batman hardly qualifies, but Frank Miller's *Dark Knight* makes the case plain enough. The Tim Burton 1989 movie toyed with the idea also, but presented the character more as a lovable neurotic rather than the "batshit" crazy, revenge-driven vigilante that he is. Chris Nolan's *Batman Begins* (2004) attempted to take the character further into psychological reality, but in a very superficial way. *Dark Knight* (2008) was more successful, but it was still restricted by the conventions of the genre; Batman is the Hero, after all, he can't be seen as a Psychopath, except through his distorted reflection the Joker (superbly — and fatally — embodied by Heath Ledger in his final role).

Batman is obsessed. He crosses that line and transforms himself, becomes a force of nature, but also a freak. His war against crime brings about an encounter with his personal devil, The Joker. In fact, in both Burton's and

10. The Great American Psychopath

Nolan's films, Batman's actions *create* the Joker. It's significant that the Joker is a clown-like figure, because the specter that haunts the Psychopath is the Clown. By pursuing his dream so vigorously and blindly, the Psychopath becomes a foolish figure, one at which we'd laugh if he weren't so frightening. While the Clown may know he is a psycho, however, the Psychopath does not realize he is a clown. Batman's existence brings about the creation of super villains, as is made explicit in the movies: he *creates* (summons) the Joker as his necessary nemesis, his shadow side, his *raison d'être*. In a world without these villains, Batman would be the Psychopath. As it is, he becomes the Hero, reminding us that the Psychopath is the shadow of the Hero, just as the Clown is the shadow of the Psychopath. In Batman the Hero–Psycho-Clown relationship achieves symbiosis; expressed as it is in an exaggerated (Archetypal and dreamlike) comic book form, the machinery is exposed for all to see.

This Clown spectre also haunts *Blue Velvet*; witness Frank's admiration for Ben, a harlequin-like figure who lip-syncs Roy Orbison's "In Dreams," Frank's theme-song, with its opening line about the "candy colored clown." When Frank abuses Jeffery he smears lipstick on his own face and kisses him, giving them both the appearance of clowns. Frank seem to admire — and even wish to be like — Ben, the candy-colored clown who lives at the center of

The Hero Shadows the Psychopath Shadows the Clown: Batman (Christian Bale) interrogates the Joker (Heath Ledger) in *Dark Knight* (2008, Warner Bros.).

"Pussy Heaven." Ben is a bizarre figure, but he's also dangerous. He perplexes us, and the Pussy Heaven scene (in which Ben, at first a friendly face, punches Jeffrey in the gut, then pats his cheek) is very much the film's centerpiece, and put a dent in many an unsuspecting psyche. Look at a classic representation of a clown face, pay attention to the eyes: they often have that wild look, the one where the whites are visible above the iris, with the iris half-buried at the bottom — this is the laughing clown face, but it's also the eyes of a deranged person. Many photos of Charlie Manson show him making this face. If you see someone on the street with this look in their eye — watch out!

Another seminal scene on the clown/psycho theme occurs in *Goodfellas*, when Joe Pesci's Tommy abruptly shifts from a jovial storyteller to a fuming Psycho. "What do you mean 'funny?' Am I a clown? Do I amuse you?" This shift is genuinely chilling, and was the most remarked upon moment in the movie: clearly it had a great impact. The Psychopath, in his unhinged desire, which develops to absurdly revved up levels here, becomes laughable, and we are taken aback as much by his absurdity as his violence. There are always moments in these GAP films where the Psychopath appears absurd. Sometimes it's a major point, sometimes it's very subtle. As his desire increases, and his efforts along with it (all influenced by his strange and often stupid way of going after his "dream"), the Psychopath becomes a parody of himself. In much the same way, Circus Clowns ape normal human behavior, particularly our flaws, exaggerating for comedic effect. Realizing that he has become a clown, that his desire and his quest has surpassed certain boundaries and become absurd, is one of the few ways a Psychopath can check his progress towards destruction. This realization can then lead to some kind of redemption or healing. The realization of one's absurdity, one's humanity, the futility of one's quest, ushers in a new kind of humility. This may help the Psychopath to see himself, and others, more clearly, more humanly, and more humanely.

Some Psychopaths, however, realize their absurdity, their clownishness, and *incorporate it* into their Psychopathy. When this happens, both in films (Frank Booth and Murray from *1000 Clowns*, for example, and the Joker, obviously) and in real life (John Wayne Gacy), the Psychopath becomes all the more dangerous, because he has assimilated what had the potential of stopping him in his tracks, of waking him up, and channeled it into his psychosis instead. He reaches the next level on the GAP journey, which often entails physical transformation.

The Psychopath's fatal flaw is that he takes himself desperately seriously. The thing he fears most (like Apache warriors) is to appear *ridiculous*. Apparently Hitler couldn't stand satire, because he knew that ridicule was the one thing that could defeat him. The present GAP thesis requires such a satirical approach, which is why we promote Wyle Coyote as the ultimate psychoarchetype. Wyle Coyote's desire for the Roadrunner far outstrips his need for food, and no amount of failure can cause him to question the sanity of his desire. Instead, he just escalates his efforts to catch the bird until the bird no longer seems to matter; this is precisely what makes him so funny. He tries so hard, so desperately, for what seems like so little. We may see ourselves in him, especially his inability to effectively bring about his desires, and the way this only makes them all the more obsessive.

Another clown-psycho of note is Freddy Krueger, from the *Nightmare on Elm Street* films. Freddy is as much Trickster as he is Psychopath, perhaps even more of a Trickster. His ability to break the laws of physics and his outrageous powers belong as much, and maybe more, to the world of the cartoon than the horror film. From the view of "the other side," the lives of mere mortals must appear ridiculous, their tortures mere jokes. The Psychopath is deranged, unhinged, hell-bent, in a word: obsessed. He pursues an idealized goal of some kind. This pursuit, so long as the Psychopath continues past all natural obstacles, can, and often does, take him into bizarre territory. Some Psychopaths manage to cross this border, usually in the more symbolic/metaphorical/fantasy-related works, to the next stage of evolution. Some do it and die (in the more realistic works), and some do it and live, in some new form or another. This only occurs in the fantasy genres, but is the next step in the evolution of the Psychopath, whereupon the GAP becomes — something else. Still Psychopathic, he is now entering into "transcendental realms." The Psychopath now becomes a sort of disembodied Psychopathic Spirit, if you will, which can possess others but also act on his own in some way. Freddy would apply here, as would "Killer Bob" from Lynch's *Twin Peaks*. The problem here is that, the further away from "normal" humanity this Psychopathic Spirit gets, the more he evolves into a different animal, still Psychopathic but not the same Psychopath. As long as the Psychopath remains human he tells the GAP story. When he transcends his humanness, however, he no longer faces the same issues the GAP faces. This is the major distinction. Freddy has broken the bonds of the human, and as such he no longer speaks to us as a Frank Booth can. Freddy becomes a "monster," of sorts, not-human, a caricature of the GAP (though he does also become a species of Clown).

Yet this in turn may only be symptomatic of our *own* steady dissociation from our unconscious psyches, our humanness, as we become ever more lost in the abstract "fantasy" realms of our technology. Freddy seems to know instinctively of the relationship between the Clown and the Psychopath, between fear and laughter, because he becomes a trickster figure quite consciously. He is the Psychopath as stand-up comedian. What's essential to know about Freddy is that he exists as the actual symbiosis between the outer and the inner Psycho — he is our worst (hence most repressed) tendencies, come not to haunt but to devour us. As such he appears fantastic and irreal, at this time (even a little silly), but is gaining credence and validity (and therefore power) in our psyches with every passing minute.*

On the other hand, a movie like *Silence of the Lambs* gives us a wholly phony psycho, one that has no real bearing in either reality *or* myth. People like this simply do not exist. Yet, unlike Freddy, who's obviously a fantasy figure, the film pretends to be a "serious" study of the psychopath. Serial killer and bogeyman: the one is a reality, the other a fantasy, character vs. caricature. But again, in terms of popular movies, the latter (caricature) seems to be superseding the former with ever-growing speed and totality. I don't think we want to *admit* there are people like Frank (we can pretend there are people like Hannibal Lecter instead), because then we would have to look at *why*. The only answer is: *because*: because they are necessary (for our evolution?).

The problem with Hannibal is that he's presented as a "real" guy, when in truth he has more in common with a monster, more specifically, a vampire/werewolf combination. It's *Nightmare on Elm Street* taking itself seriously. Hannibal is a cold, inhuman figure who combines the traits of the superhuman with the sub-human monster. He has a super-intellect and the hypersensitivity of an animal. He seems bloodless like a vampire, cold and calculating, yet he attacks like a wild animal. He hisses like a snake, he stares like a predator. Hannibal is a Psychopath who has transcended humanity but has remained human, therefore he turns the film from realism to fantasy while fooling viewers into thinking he's "real." Maybe that's why people took to this film — it made them believe that monsters could indeed be real. In fact, *Silence* (widely acclaimed as it was) is largely responsible for the cult of the serial killer becoming so prominent, and for this very reason. Many misguided people began to "worship" real-life psychos like Charlie Manson, who, like your Gacys and Bundys, embodies many of the things we have been talking about. Because of this, the general public, once exposed to these GAP musings, will immediately think we are discussing serial killers, which completely voids these ideas of any meaning and gives them permission to indulge in more misguided hero-worship. Make no mistake, the GAP is a heroic figure, but only if he brings us *back* to our humanity, such as it is.

Serial killer worship such as inspired by *Silence* and other similar products leads to goofy fandom that is almost incapable of deep insights (re: Anne Rice vampire nerds, etc.). Still, Lecter qualifies as a post-transcendence Psychopath, albeit one that doesn't really interest us here.†

The message of these "post-transcendence" psycho movies (*Natural Born*

---

*Wes Craven's last installment, *New Nightmare*, had the "no more Mr. Nice Guy" approach, and was also a profound take on the "monster from the id" subtext which underlies all good horror movies.

†Lecter's own rationale for killing is simply that it "feels good": "And why shouldn't it feel good? It must feel good to God. He does it all the time ... and if one does what God does enough times, one will become as God is."

Killers is another) seems almost to be — "if the psychopath would persist in his psychosis, he would become sane." The danger, of course, is that it's rather too close to Manson-speak for comfort. The idea is most fully, yet still I think superficially, developed in *NBK*, where Stone actually suggests his heroes are somehow redeemed by the "purity" of their acts. But this is nothing to do with the actual truth, because Mickey and Mallory are the same shallow "TV-Babies"[2] at the end of the movie as they were at the start. The demons that drove them could hardly be so easily exorcised, and such demons (which make *NBK* the perfect "overlap" movie between, say, *Badlands* and *Twin Peaks* or *Lost Highway*—it's hybrid crime/metaphysics) invariably devour their hosts long before they ever leave them. However, it *is* true that the afore-mentioned "metaphysical transformation," though yet to be adequately represented by cinema fiction, would seem to be the only possible "redemption" for the Psycho. This is why he invariably seeks death as the only kind of transformation of which he is capable. A Psycho who truly became a saint would have to undergo a genuine dark night of the soul (that "crossing of the Abyss"), in order to come out *the other side* of his madness and discover that dementia is merely the poor man's ecstasy. He would realize that the path of destruction is for those too weak and cowardly (let's be more generous and say "confused") to *create* anything. The hatred/rage of the Psycho derives, then, from this very artistic frustration. The Psycho wants to control the whole universe, to mold it in his own image, which is precisely what the artist does, in a small way. Again this ties up with the "natural" or evolutionary angle: the first "psychopathic" urge, as it were, is when the baby grabs for the shiny bauble and howls when it doesn't get it (and when it does get it just wants to devour it!).

Shakespeare once wrote that if a baby had infinite power it would destroy the universe in a heartbeat. Its "will" (actually something else, but we have no word for it) is so powerful and so utterly unbending, yet its knowledge and understanding so completely inadequate, that it would end up destroying the very thing it wanted to embrace. Rather like the love-obsessed Frank. Doesn't this kind of infantile derangement happen to us every time we can't get the cap off the pill bottle or the cellophane off the CD, or the lawnmower to start, etc., etc., etc.? The adrenaline *rush* of rage that our impotence creates feeds our own sense of grandeur and allows us to become momentarily "carried away" (possessed) by psychosis. It is one of the deadliest "pleasures" of them all, the negative flipside of transcendence: one is not elevated but debased by the obsession (to open the CD, start the lawnmower, whatever). Instead of receding, the ego takes over entirely and sees the whole universe as an adversary to be defeated. Hence the subsequent rush of utter foolishness and absurdity that every "psycho" (using the word in its profane and common sense) experiences when he catches a glimpse of himself wrestling with his own demons, without ever admitting they are in *him*, and not in the lawnmower or the universe.

What seems to have happened in such moments of foolishness is that the demon of rage/self-hatred/frustration has been temporarily placated by a new humility (i.e., has no emotions left to feed it). It remains lurking deep inside, however, only waiting for the next *circumstantial* occasion to exploit and thereby regain its hold. There would seem to be only three options for the common Psychopath called Man: *total* overcoming of these demons (which entails converting them into *allies*, in the shamanistic sense); complete subjugation to them, whereupon the demon becomes the man and the man the demon — a "fully-functioning homicidal maniac" along the lines of Gacy, Gein, the Joker, etc. Or else, at this time the most common (and easiest) option, simple passive surrender, or stalemate, involving the refusal either to confront these demons or to fully embody them. This last is a kind of straddling the Abyss that cannot continue indefinitely, and at best results in a sort of unconscious despair/terror/paralysis, such as characterizes present society in the new millennium.

Those who effectively "master" this "surrender" are known as "useful citizens." On the other hand, we could say that total subjugation to his demons makes the Psychopath "useful" only to himself, just as passive surrender to them renders him useful only to society. Overcoming, or Transcendence, serves to transform the individual Psychopath (the Enlightened Psychopath?) into someone who is "useful" (a positive, creative, sustaining influence) to both himself and society. Overcoming/Transcendence is the true "healing" work, while the other two options are at best a temporary cover-up that conceals the sickness, allowing it to go on festering. The problem is to get at the root, something we are now working on. What I refer to as "useful" seems to revolve around a Danger/Safety dichotomy. The most dangerous Psychopath has given in to his Demon (or Daemon, if you want to be archetypal about it) and is a danger to society, benefiting only himself (or at least his Demon). The surrendered Psychopath is safe to society but a danger to himself; his Demon has been imprisoned and is eating away at his mind, body, and soul. Only the enlightened Psychopath has transcended the duality of self and Other (society), and so can begin to function at a higher level, freed from the influence of his demons.

It is possible to utilize a certain kind of Psychopathic derangement in the search for enlightenment. In this case, the Psychopathy of our model becomes a kind of tool or technique, not something to be relied upon exclusively, but not to be ignored or feared. It takes a hearty constitution to transcend desire by indulging in it fully and burning it out. Success depends on retaining an inner separation between self and experience, and Psychopaths, by their nature, are usually so identified with their experience that this is impossible for them to do. Nevertheless, they unconsciously play out some of the same dramas that seekers after wisdom (awareness, enlightenment, transcendence) do. There is a key here, but dare we use it?

To "tap into" the energy of the Psychopath and so utilize it requires *total* submersion in psychosis, at least for an instant. It cannot be an act, it has to be real. This is, to many, a truly enticing idea, sort of the psychological equivalent of crossing the Abyss: if we must die in life in order to be reborn, we must also go completely insane in order to achieve true sanity. Better the psychosis that acknowledges itself as aberration than the "normality" that refuses to admit its own psychosis.

This "key" *does* work, so we can't really throw it away (the potential for it is built into the very foundations of the human psyche and so is non-returnable). Perhaps the main reason we have stumbled upon it is that we had no choice in the matter. Once circumstance, nature, and action/personal choice have given you Psychopathic tendencies, there is no turning back, you simply have to deal with them; this is especially so if you achieve a level of awareness where you can no longer deny this tendency in yourself. This tendency is so powerful (with its potential to be both beneficial and harmful) that we simply *must* resolve our difficulties with it. However, if someone is not really a developed Psychopath (we all have the potential, but that's not enough), then they probably shouldn't attempt to use it. Why tempt fate? Why call up the Demon unless you really *need* it?

A lot of this is happening in America right now — kids shot dead by crazed classmates and so forth. Invariably, when the photo of the killer appears he looks like a half-wit, too immature, stupid, and unaware to deal with his impulses. One day they're rejected by a girl, the next they steal Grandpappy's squirrel gun and are slaughtering indiscriminately. You also get a lot of mildly disturbed suburban kids fixating upon serial killers and such, lacking any deeper understanding of what's going on and confusing themselves in the process. The lack of humanity, of self-awareness and restraint, of any kind of barriers at all, is the real danger here, and not simply Psychopathy, which, as we have argued, has its positive connotations, and even its uses.

The transcendence sought by the GAP is linked by his desire to stand out from the crowd and become free of all restraints. Often, these restraints are natural and unavoidable, such as gravity, space and time, etc. Sometimes these restraints are social, moral, and so forth. Sometimes they are physical, such as prison, stifling jobs and relationships, etc. When a Psychopath is struggling against the more social and physical limitations, he tends to have our sympathy, since these are the same things we all experience holding us back (the need for money and the impossibility of finding fulfilling and rewarding work, other people's expectations, and so on). When we feel we are imprisoned, the lengths to which we'll go in order to be free will sometimes drive us into Psychopathic frenzies. The transcendence the GAP seeks is not always a transcendence of the human condition or the present state of human evolution, but simply a transcendence of a temporary condition, such as a shitty job or a low social position.

If there *is* a desire to become a new being driving the GAP, a will to attain a different state of existence, then this is a desire for *metaphysical* transcendence. And sometimes an effort to transcend a more temporary condition will drive the GAP past his more attainable goal and on to something more exotic, something resembling the metaphysical, while not necessarily equaling it. All manner of transcendence must be considered when we look at the GAP, for the same sort of confusion that mistakes the GAP for just another serial killer can mistake one kind of transcendence for another. Often the naive thrust toward self-transformation of various kinds seems an effort, not only to get past a barrier of some kind, but also to somehow enter a new world where former restraints do not exist.*

This is a kind of dream, albeit a childish and regressive one, and it seems to have a deeper component, some urge towards essential transformation, transformation of Being. It's an urge toward development without the knowledge of how to properly go about it. This happens when a child is raised by parents insufficiently aware to guide it through stages of development (until it can become an aware and capable adult itself). From the Psychopath's perspective, it *seems* like Transcendence, and he becomes enamored by fantasies of it. But seen from without, it's probably more like the progression through "normal" developmental stages, of which "overcoming" (of obstacles) probably serves as a better description than "transcendence." We might even look at it as "Transformation"—a word that doesn't describe the event as it is happening, so much as an overall process, taking place over various stages.

In the task of writing the GAP story, therefore, we must be very careful to draw subtle but all-important distinctions between the varieties of Psychopathic experience. When travelling through the Psychopath's shadowy world, we must always remain sharp, making clear distinctions and maintaining a certain distance, lest we be drawn in and become Psychopaths, or victims, ourselves. What fascinates us about the GAP is, perhaps, that his journey touches upon the more progressive aspects of existence, the same things that all strange, paranormal, or uncommon phenomena touches upon. The GAP, in all his misguided fury, is partly looking for the same things that attract people to, say,

---

*On Early Grayce (Brad Pitt) in *Kalifornia*, Simpson writes: "Paradoxically, he achieves transcendental heights at the exact moment he reaches the ebb of his humanity.... Early's murders have been primitive dress rehearsals for his own mystic transport.... Grayce, then, as a replication of the image of evil is menacing but empty. He suffers from an internal emptiness that he seeks to fill with the glaring light of heavenly fire.... [This is] what Richard Slotkin calls the cult of personal regeneration through violence. As with Mickey Knox, Grayce's *lustmord* elevates him to a higher plane of existence and identity." Simpson, *Psycho Paths*, pg. 192, 194.

10. The Great American Psychopath

Zen Buddhism, Surrealism, various religious experiences, drugs, mind expansion/altered states, and so on.

There are some Psychopaths who are just as committed to their folly as other, more dangerous/self destructive ones, but whose goal or dream or vision is more personal, more introverted, and hence less destructive. Likewise, there are some who are, perhaps, a bit more enlightened or "gentle" at heart, or otherwise more aware than other people. Even if their vision and their desire is of the potentially destructive type, they stand a good chance of living through it, or at least arriving at some realization. These GAP's will come to a realization *before* they self-destruct, or otherwise leap to the "other side" and arrive whole, in one piece. Provided they survive (i.e., that their realization isn't accompanied by death), they may live on after the Psychopathic episode has been completed. They are the walking wounded. They're the people that Tom Waits sings about in the song "Diamonds and Gold," from *Rain Dogs*. Murray from *1000 Clowns* is a good representative of this Psychopath in films. These GAP's are post-transcendence, but only in the sense that they have given up their insane desire for transcendence. They are humbled, heartbroken; they bear the scars of Psychopathy, the humility of one who has caught a horrible glimpse of his own foolishness. They are, in a sense, redeemed, but this redemption will probably not lead to anything great, especially if they surrender to it and make no attempt to move beyond it.

At the end of *1000 Clowns*, Murray gives up and is swallowed back into the crowd; the same thing occurs with Travis Bickle at the end of *Taxi Driver*. The fact that they are so humbled (or placated) shows that they are still Psychopaths; somewhere deep down in their heart they still cling to their unrealistic dreams. In much the same way the failed artist returns beaten to society's fold and endures its mockery, all the while secretly nursing his wounded aspirations, keeping them warm and secure (and useless) under his broken wings. The idea of creation/destruction being two sides of the same coin (the frustration of the one leading to the other) is not only valid but key here. The line that separates a Van Gogh from a Psychopath is sometimes very thin, but it is always there. A failed artist may well take consolation in being a successful Psycho, and vice versa. The GAP is perhaps the effective marriage of the two, into a single, much maligned Archetype. Is not the Artist, after all (in the words of Paul Bowles): "the enemy of society"? So long as he is doing his job, he is exactly that.

Again, the Great American Psychopath, or Psycho for short,* is largely a fictional construct. Like all fiction, the GAP is a refined, distilled, and concen-

---

*One thing that we must be careful of is using the word "psycho" as a substitute for "Psychopath." A Psychopath (in this model) is not a psycho, though he often acts like one. The Psychopath's deeply ingrained vision, his quest, gives his madness a focus and an organization, a purpose, that a mere psycho does not possess.

trated form of the Psychopaths that appear in real life. In fact, as cannot be overstated, guys like Manson and the serial killers are not really GAP's; they merely display some traits found in the fictional Psychopath, giving credence and significance to his "experiences," just as a Hero is a concentrated version of the seemingly minor heroisms we see in daily life. The misguided, violent actions of a Manson become the grand Psychopathic quest of the GAP, just as the fireman who rescues a dog from a burning building becomes Bruce Willis saving the world. The Psychopaths of "real life" often take many years to develop.

We can only begin to see ourselves as Psychopaths when we look at the direction our lives have taken since childhood. When the Psychopathic journey is condensed into a two-hour film it becomes artificial, but it is (or can be) the positive kind of artifice that we see in all art forms: a microcosm for the Psychopathic Journey upon which we are all, like it or not, embarked.

PART II.
SCRYING THE CULTURE

11

Stealing Candy/Healing Laughter: The Evolution of the Schizo Comedy

Whether Martin Scorsese intended *The King of Comedy* (1982) to be a comedy of horrors or a comic horror story is debatable. It seems likely that the film's writer, Paul D. Zimmerman, conceived it as the former, but that Scorsese's compulsive, obsessive empathy-beyond-the-call-of-duty for his subject turned it, by steady degrees, into the latter. Rupert Pupkin is played (to consummate perfection) by Robert De Niro, and he's every artist's worst possible vision of himself as fawning, scheming, socially maladroit and desperate nebbish, a man with no way *into* the world save through dreaming, no currency with which to trade, a man who would kill for a chance at the top. What makes *The King of Comedy* hilarious, despite being so excruciating to watch, is Pupkin's complete indifference, his obliviousness, to his utter lack of anything resembling talent. He is the fan-as-Promethean sinner, in awe of greatness but too proud and conceited to bow down before it, determined to seize it for his own (to usurp the throne, as it were, even if he must kill the king to do so).

The film was aimed directly at the slavish, fawning, uncultured mind of your average moviegoer, as embodied in a man like Pupkin. As such, *The King of Comedy* was one of the first films to make its audience not only the butt of its joke but also the recipient of its outrage. (Woody Allen's *Stardust Memories* did the same in the same year, and was equally reviled by the public.) We all know what it's like to make an ass out of ourselves, and *The King of Comedy* plays like the worst party we ever endured, when we made such asses out of ourselves that we can never completely erase the memory of it.

Scriptwriter Zimmerman (also a film critic) described the film as being "about a desperate need to exist publicly, which is so American," a need which is, for Pupkin, "a matter of life and death."[1] Rupert is a marauding geek, a

King for a Day: Lifetime schmuck Rupert Pupkin (Robert DeNiro) in *The King of Comedy* (1983, 20th Century–Fox).

nebbish, a non-entity, psychopathically bent on becoming *somebody*. He is a true child of his age: a demon born through TV-insemination, the ape, or shadow, that mocks our greater aspirations and renders them absurd, reminding us of the folly and the vanity of our dreams. He is ego utterly cut off from id — self-serving, obsessive desire and compulsive, unthinking action, without any of the redeeming wisdom or insight of the unconscious. He's the imp of opportunism run amok.

The King of Comedy may have begun as a burlesque, a scathing mockery of modern-day, media-fed values and goals (it was the perfect anti-yuppie movie for the 1980s); but in Scorsese and De Niro's hands, it grew into something darker and more heartfelt. The film is a variation on their own *Taxi Driver*, and on Blake's proverb (from Hell): "If the fool would persist in his folly, he would become wise." Rupert is the ultimate loser — he has no friends, no lover, no *life* as such outside his own obsessions, his self-indulgent fantasies. (Rupert lives with his mother, whom we never see but, by the tone of her voice, at best indulges Rupert, and at worst despairs of him.) He is an absolute loner, like Travis Bickle, only here it's not because he can't communicate with the world but because the world can't stand the sight of him. Like Travis, he's a solipsist; but Rupert's fantasy world is secular, self-sustained, whereas Travis's continually spills out into the real world. Yet although Travis is the one who's out of control, it's Rupert who actually mistakes his fantasies for reality and is the true psychopath here. Indifferent to its indifference, Rupert turns his nose up at the world, at reality itself; blind to his own supreme obtuseness, he retreats further and further into his conceit. The ironic twist of *The King of Comedy*—its message—is wrapped up in the fact that Rupert *succeeds* (where Travis fails) in manifesting his destiny and realizing his illusions, simply because (as the epilogue of *Taxi Driver* also suggested) society is even more deranged and dissociated than he is.

With *The King of Comedy*, and in the person—the rotting shell—of Rupert Pupkin, a man "who would rather die than live anonymously,"[2] the *Zeitgeist* came back to haunt us. The bitch-goddess success had been superseded by the psycho-ape fame. Instead of seducing and devouring, fame flatters and corrupts, a slow, insidious process that few are immune to. The Pupkin syndrome—because here the dud is played by an Oscar-winning superstar—demonstrates that the sword of glory cuts both ways, that not only is every nerd a frustrated hero but inside every star is a core of self-doubt. Like a worm, this lurking self-loathing threatens to eat away at his insides and leave nothing but an empty shell—a nobody.

For all its cynicism, its determination to present repulsive characters devoid of redeeming features, *The King of Comedy* has a rare charm all its own. Yet as a "message" movie, *The King of Comedy* is the most wholly nihilistic comedy ever made. It posits soullessness as the ultimate, logical culmination of the materialist quest for the luxury of smooth things, and oblivion as the only means of bliss in a soulless, materialistic world. Rupert's total lack of awareness or sensitivity is what enables him to forge his way ruthlessly to the top of the dung heap. It's an ethos for an age: when the Id's away, the egos will play.

Being There (1979) was something of a prototype for the schizophrenic comedy in which the protagonist, Chancey Gardner (Peter Sellers), finds (or offers) freedom, wholeness, and contentment, through a kind of *regression* to an infantile state in which the id prevails. In Hal Ashby's much-loved movie, Chancey is a simpleton who, by chance circumstance, winds up in the Whitehouse (the movie was certainly well-timed: Ronald Reagan took over the reigns the following year). *Being There* is a one-note movie, however, and, for all its grace and nuance, a one-note performance by Sellers (who is better when he's not so endearing). The movie is limited by its parable-like form and its aspirations for satiric depth; it's really such an obvious idea that, charming as it is, it comes closer to whimsy than satire.

Woody Allen's *Zelig* (1983) is far more successful, perhaps because Allen is smart enough to use mock documentary form and so avoid becoming cloyingly sweet. Leonard Zelig (played by Allen himself) is endearing, even irresistible, as a character, but because of the way in which Allen presents him (we hardly ever get more than fleeting clips of him at a time), he never becomes quite real to us. This is of course appropriate to Allen's conception, since Zelig is never quite real to himself either. Here the central idea is somewhat different from *Being There*. Chancy is a moron who becomes the voice of wisdom because his stupidity is so profound it gets mistaken for wisdom. Zelig is a nobody who becomes somebody for being a nobody. But Zelig is not simple-minded; as played by Allen he is perceptive and intelligent. He doesn't lack brain, he lacks *will*, personality. Chancey, on the other hand, is so lacking in anything resembling character that all he "has" is personality: he becomes a star due to his complete lack of ordinary traits as a person. (It's the difference Quentin Tarantino outlines, in *Pulp Fiction*, between having character and *being* a character.) His emptiness makes him seem pure, unsullied, saintly. And though Ashby's movie starts out mocking such daffy assumptions (it presents the people who admire Chancey as even more idiotic than he is), by the end it has fully validated them, turning the bumbling idiot savant into a genuine Messiah (Chancy walks on water, in the film's misconceived codex). *Being There* is a diverting bit of pseudo-satire, but, intriguing as its vision is, it's basically bogus. It's self-interpreted, so there's no room for ambiguity; for a satiric comedy, what could be more fatal than being weighed down by "message"?

Zelig, a glorious little movie, is the opposite: it *appears* to be a serious "study" of schizophrenia (and in fact, in its own humble way, it *is*), but is really a playful comedy in disguise (though its more serious points still get across). The film's humor is as daft and spontaneous as Allen's best comedy always is, yet it never undermines his characters, and it never distracts us from the wistful pathos. As a result, and rather paradoxically, Leonard Zelig is not only Allen's most touching and memorable movie creation but also one of his most *real*, too.

Around this same time (1985), Allen made another of his best movies, *The Purple Rose of Cairo*, which, along with *Zelig*, might be seen as a key work in schizo cinema. Mia Farrow's Cecilia spends her days at the movies, escaping from her grim and colorless life married to a brute of a husband (Danny Aeillo). One particular movie (*The Purple Rose of Cairo*) enchants her so much that she returns to see it every afternoon, and falls in love with one of the screen characters, Tom Baxter (Jeff Daniels). Finally, her yearning becomes so intense that Baxter *responds*: in the middle of a scene, he turns to Cecilia and expresses his awe for her (he can't believe how many times she's come to see the movie). Cecilia can hardly believe her eyes, either, but before she has time to dispel the illusion, Baxter has walked off the screen and joined her in the real world. This basic premise — that of a fictional character entering the real world — had already been done by Allen (though in reverse) in his short story, "The Kugelmass Episode," in which the lead character (Kugelmass) enters in Flaubert's *Madame Bovary* and has an affair with the heroine, thereby confounding literary students all over the country with the appearance of this strange, modern Jew in the novel's action. In *Purple Rose* the premise is more cinematic, obviously, and extended to feature length. But the essence is the same: the schizophrenic notion of fantasy and reality overlapping, of the act of perception (and desire) somehow altering the nature of one's reality, opening up a whole new world of possibilities.

As befits the comedy form, the schizophrenic experience here is never traumatic and usually wholly positive. In *Purple Rose*, however, Allen condemns his heroin to return to bleak reality, not only abandoned by Baxter, her fictional lover, but also betrayed by his "double," Gil Shepherd (Daniels again). Shepherd is the actor who plays Baxter in the movie within the movie, and he makes empty promises to Cecilia in return for her help getting Baxter back on the screen where he belongs. Clearly, Cecilia is unable to maintain her fantasy, and flees the scary, unpredictable highs of schizophrenia for the mundane assurances and cold comforts of sanity. But she finds that reality, if anything, is even more duplicitous than fantasy (the fictional Baxter is far more trustworthy than the flesh and blood Shepherd). Probably no one in modern movies has more of an affinity for schizophrenia, and for the liberating potential of fantasy, than Woody Allen. He is at his very best (as in these two films and some of the best scenes in *Annie Hall*) when he gives in to magical thinking and lets his humor and imagination run wild. But, like Cecilia, he seems terminally condemned to return to reality in the end (and inflict upon us works like *Interiors, September*, and *Match Point*). Allen's belief in magic, however heartfelt, is consistently undone by doubt.

This is too bad, because without Allen, the schizo comedy has had a hard time attaining the heights it needs to really fly. If *Being There* set the precedent, it was another decade before *Big* picked up the thread and set a trend, spinning briefly a whole new, lame but extremely popular sub-*sub*genre of boy-in-man's-body movies that — for all their inadequacy as comedies — are some of the fullest expressions of the schizophrenic theme in the genre. Before *Big*, Jonathan Demme's *Something Wild* (with Jeff Daniels again as the split protagonist) was a thrilling excursion into the "wild side" of the id. Scorsese's *After Hours*, in a more constricted (and conventional) fashion depicted the ego's initiation into (and eventual rejection by) the wonderful, horrible unconscious realms (here represented — in a throwback to the 1930s — by devouring female sexuality). Joseph Reuben's *The Stepfather*, more horror than comedy, is an outstanding portrait of the schizo personality, chillingly depicting the extremes to which the threatened ego will go in order to protect itself from the unruly chaos of the id.

These more disconcerting excursions were the exceptions that proved the rule, however. Hollywood is in the business of placating and not deranging the collective ego. As such, it offers up a series of sops to our growing (schizophrenic) unease, with Tom Hanks, Dudley Moore, and Judge Reinhold playing an urban professional (usually an advertising executive) who, by magic or science or some half-baked mix of the two, is possessed by the spirit of his own "inner child": the unformed, spontaneous, unruly, but *harmless* id. This id (as befits the function of the genre) is wise but innocent, mischievous rather than sorcerous, disruptive but never threatening. These movies (there are countless variations, including sex-change comedies like *Victor Victoria*, the sublime *Tootsie*, and even Blake Edward's *Switch*, in which a man comes back in the body of Ellen Barkin) encapsulated the basic appeal of all movies everywhere: they let us be little children again (rapt, passive, and easily duped). At the same time, they addressed (however dubiously) our schizophrenic desire to get away from ourselves, to escape the dull grind and relentless pressures of adult responsibility and flee into fantasy. They signified a cinema of regression, but unlike *Being There* and *Zelig*, they did so without irony or ambiguity. They presented the return to infantilism as a wholly desirable, positive step *forward* (the urbanites always improved through regression, not only as human beings but as professionals!).

This was a fantasy fit for the times. Instead of confronting the growing responsibilities of living in an increasingly schizophrenic world, it was "Hey presto, don't worry, be happy, become as a little child again!" Yet though the *results* of the "transformation" were mildly "subversive" (the yuppie rebelled against his superiors and carved a new path for himself, albeit within the confines of his old job), the means were anything but. The hero did not become wild or rebellious or anarchic in a conscious (progressive) fashion, on the contrary, it was by being *reduced* to an infantile level that he overcame resistance from the jaded grown-ups. "Being as a little child," these movies claimed, was a way to expose the corruption of the adult world; really, it only involved acting like a spoilt brat and getting your own way (the very behavior which, one supposes, led to such corrupt adults in the first place). These movies are such lame comedies not merely because they lack bite as satire but because they lack the slightest integrity as commentaries upon the schizophrenic condition. They don't offer antidotes, they offer anesthetic: more aspirin to relieve the pain that turn our stomachs in the process.

With *Regarding Henry*, and finally *Forrest Gump*, the hypocrisy of the "message" became plain. *Forrest Gump* is *Being There* mutated, over two decades, to the point where the simpering moron can be presented as a noble, saintly figure without the slightest irony (and get a nod from the Academy, too). Who in this modern, cutthroat world actually *believes* that being a nice guy, no matter how stupid, will get you through life? I'm quite sure no one buys such a crock, yet people responded to the movie like gospel. Hey folks, it's OK to be stupid: the pure of heart are stupid too! *Forrest Gump* not only suggested this (that the pure of heart are stupid), but that the stupid are pure of heart simply because they *are* stupid! It suggested that the *only way* to be good in this world is to be a moron; that innocence implies not just lack of sin but lack of experience, and even of any semblance of intelligence. The terror of the collective ego was becoming so prevalent that movies were attempting to posit a

11. Stealing Candy/Healing Laughter: The Schizo Comedy

world in which, somehow, we could exist without really asserting ourselves. As if by becoming meek, dumb, and passive, we could placate the terrible force of the Id, and so transform a hostile, incomprehensible world into a friendly place. Forrest, no matter where he goes (even Vietnam), is safe and contented in his own solipsist, lobotomized universe. Nothing could be further from the truth.

In *Regarding Henry*, Harrison Ford plays a "ruthless" (Ford never really convinces us) lawyer who one night goes out for cigarettes (ah, original sin!) and gets shot in the head by a mugger. As a result of this street-lobotomy, his memory is erased and he becomes a sweet, harmless, endearing simpleton. He no longer likes the clothes in his wardrobe or his unethical workmates at the office, but of course he still loves his wife and children. What a relief! (The only scene in the movie — another sloppy, sentimental slug from Mike Nichols — that stayed with me is when Ford is baking cookies with his daughter and suggests to her that they make one giant cookie instead of lots of small ones. His daughter tells him she already tried that and it doesn't work. Ford, with his look of rapt disappointment, is quite sublime.) There are so many mainstream Hollywood movies in which a simpleton is somehow seen to be more "pure" and "wise" than the cold, corrupt intellectuals (invariably yuppies) who run our world that one wonders who (if not corrupt adults) are funding all these movies?! All this derives from the Parsifal/Grail myth of the holy fool, and even further back, from the gospels' Jesus holding up a small child as an example of the Kingdom of Heaven. But we are not children anymore.

Christ and the Grail myths (which expounded purity of heart or celibacy of the body — or both — as the prerequisite for finding the Grail, or wisdom) hardly prescribe a *regression* to infantilism or irresponsibility (much less stupidity); they suggest a need for spontaneity, selflessness, and passion — all qualities of the child that can plainly benefit a grown-up. Tom Hanks or Robin Williams movies that smother us with their piousness are not childlike but child*ish*: they fall prey to an all-too-adult (patronizing) view of childhood, that it is "pure," "innocent," "magical," but also carefree, undeveloped, somehow mindless. The people who made these movies may have children of their own; but judging by their movies, they are severely deficient as parents. They appear to have no inkling of what it really *means* to be a child. Children are not unformed adults but people with their own worlds, perhaps even their own realities. When grown-ups assure their kids that their invisible playmates are "imaginary," and that "there's no such thing as monsters," they no doubt believe they are providing a *service* as parents; but how do we know our children's playmates are imaginary? Just because *we* can't see them? And can we possibly imagine that monsters don't exist after all that history has shown us?

What movies like *Big* and *Forrest Gump* (and in different ways, the hypocritical schmaltz of *Field of Dreams* and *Ghost*) reveal is not grown-ups who wish to be children again (they would hardly be prepared for the intensity and trauma of a child's world) but rather grown-ups who wish to regress: to shirk responsibility and the curse of self-awareness and return to some *imaginary* "primal" state (maybe the womb, or maybe even before that) of "innocence" in which life becomes what it never was: a playground free of sharp edges or rough surfaces. The fantasies these movies encourage are not the healthy, creative fantasies of children (and poets and artists) but the oppressive, confining, and suffocating *delusional* fantasies of the schizophrenic. They are seeking not a means to transform the world but merely a way to *escape* it. As such, they don't cater to our transcendental impulses but to our suicidal ones. They are the purest hypocrisy, and also (as such) what Hollywood is all about: the cynical manipulation of the masses (an infant body if ever there was one) for its own (commercial) gain. As easy as stealing candy from a baby.*

Natural-born schizo boy Johnny Depp takes roles like a vaudeville performer dons costumes: he delights not just in transformation but in immersion, in *disappearing*. Like Allen's Zelig, Depp seems to find himself best by becoming other people. What makes him a borderline schizo also makes him a natural thespian, a consummate performer. Depp has an inherent fascination and respect for fantasy, for the life of the imagination, which is perhaps why he connects so well with younger audiences. His mutating, androgyne (non) self reflects and echoes the youth's growing sense of rootlessness, of being adrift not only in the world but in their own minds and bodies (Depp even had a phase of playing gypsies, with *Chocolat* and *The Man Who Cried*). As far removed from posturing narcissism as any movie star working today, Depp is yet a darling of the media. He's not an anti-star like Anthony Quinn or Brando, nor is he a rough boy like Sean Penn or Mickey Rourke; he's closer to those alternate lifestyle rock stars, Iggy and Bowie. His strangeness is not a rejection of status but a kind of status in itself. Depp filled a cultural void as much as Dean or Brando (or Bowie) did before him, and he takes sexual ambiguity even further than they did, into a sort of shape-shifting persona that walks the circus tightrope between dangerous eccentric and lovable schizo.

Depp is a pretender who (as in *Donnie Brasco* and *Don Juan De Marco*) believes in his own pretenses, to the extent that he winds up not merely playing a role but being taken over by it. In Depp's best performances (Don Juan, Brasco, Hunter Thompson in *Fear and Loathing in Las Vega*, and the Earl of Rochester in *The Libertine*), it's like seeing mirrors within mirrors: an actor

---

*Exceptions also exist, of course. The Jeff Goldblum/Eddie Murphy comedy *Holy Man* is pretty much in the id-affirming formulaic mold of *Big* and its cousins; it has the same airy insubstantiality as *Field of Dreams* or *City of Angels* and likewise dresses up its pearls of "wisdom" as trinkets for kiddies. But here there actually are a few pearls on offer, and, at the same time, it never pretends to be peddling anything but trinkets.

11. Stealing Candy/Healing Laughter: The Schizo Comedy 183

playing a character who is in turn playing a role, bringing the personification game full circle. This is the apotheosis of the schizophrenic personality, for whom fakeness is realized only in the moment the façade is exposed.

Of all Depp's movies, *Don Juan de Marco* is probably the most sheerly likeable, and it's no coincidence that it's the movie in which he plays an out-and-out mental patient (being treated, no less, by Marlon Brando). The movie is the kind of romantic fantasy Hollywood usually botches horribly, with queasy sentimentalism and misplaced sincerity; in this case (besides having Depp in the central role), the fantasy is rendered magical by sleight of hand: the film takes a satirical, ironic approach, and places an explicit parallel between romanticism and lunacy. Don Juan's fantasy image of himself is rooted in delusion, and yet it is such a finely and lovingly wrought delusion that it comes to assume a reality all its own. (Instead of the patient being "cured" by the analyst, the analyst winds up converting to the point of view of the patient.) This isn't simply because Don Juan's dementia is so effective with the ladies, but because his delusional view (not only of females but of human nature) is so much closer to the way things *might* be, if only we had the courage to act out our fantasies. Don Juan is not fleeing reality, he is remolding it to suit his dreams; and so, finally, he redeems it. The primary ingredient of this alchemy is not delusion but *passion*. Steven Leven's movie is in a long line of daffy classics, from *Harvey* through *Harold and Maude* and Peter Weir's *Fearless* to the more recent *Lars and the Real Girl*, in which schizophrenia is given its due. If there's nothing worse — in the view of moviegoers seeking respite from the mundane shackles of sanity — than being ordinary, then being branded delusional (or even demented) is a small price to pay for the forbidden delights of madness. No one among actors today has better sold us to these strange delights than Johnny Depp.

Brad Pitt has also dabbled in daffiness but has perhaps less of a natural affinity for schizophrenia than a peculiar sympathy or fascination for it. Much of Pitt's forays into madness, though entertaining and skillful, seem closer to dilettantism than empathy. His serial killer Early Grayce in *Kalifornia* is a perfectly adept performance but lacking in finesse, remarkable mostly for being taken in the first place, and. His Jeffrey Goines in *12 Monkeys* is a tour-de-force of horseplay, not so much a character as a mesmerizing assemblage of tics and flourishes, and all-too-brief by half (the movie could do with a lot more of him). His nervy Detective Mills in *Seven* never really develops into much, and in the final scene, Pitt lacks the necessary intensity as an actor to make us feel Mills' descent into madness; as a result, the film suffers.

In *The Assassination of Jesse James by the Coward Robert Ford*, Pitt makes Jesse both menacing and oddly affecting, lost and almost childlike, a figure of pathos, both schizoid and eerily prescient, otherworldly. Although we never really come to know him, Pitt's performance suggests that Jesse is an enigma even to himself. When he talks about counting the stars, a confederate says he isn't even sure what stars are. Jesse replies, "Your body knows; your mind just forgot, that's all." That's the quintessential schizo dilemma. Pitt's best performance to date is beyond doubt Tyler Durden in *Fight Club*, though again he is playing not a full character but a psychotic projection of a schizophrenic mind; as such (and rightly), Durden never seems quite real to us.

Unlike Depp, Pitt relies too much on his physical graces and his goofy charms. He is trying too hard to ingratiate, to make us love him (Depp really doesn't seem to give a damn, even when entangled in more cutesy roles like his two Eds, Wood and Scissorhands, and his recent descent into Disney hell as Jack Sparrow). Pitt may never be the actor that Depp is for this reason: he's too involved in his image. He appears to adhere to a lingering sense of selfness that no actor aspiring to greatness can afford. (The only other younger actor with the empathic depths and capacity for immersion that Depp shows is probably Sean Penn; but Penn may be limited somewhat by a macho streak.) It's a paradox of the acting (or movie star) profession that the artists who most need to efface themselves for their art are also those most encouraged (even compelled) towards vanity and self-aggrandizement. This paradox all but destroyed Brando, and made a hollow nebbish out of De Niro (possibly our greatest male movie actors to date). Jack Nicholson is also a clear-cut example of the pitfalls of this paradox: by becoming the apotheosis of a movie star, he all but renounced the qualities that once made him a great actor (his work with Sean Penn and Alexander Payne notwithstanding, Nicholson has become a caricature of himself).

Besides Depp, the most talented (and schizo) popular actor working in Hollywood today is probably Jim Carrey. I am reluctant to use the word "genius," but Carrey's reserves of talent and inspiration (and exhibitionism), his gift for self-transformation, seem almost limitless. He also has a remarkable affinity for schizophrenic personalities (*The Mask, Batman Forever, The Cable Guy, Liar, Liar, The Truman Show, Man in the Moon, Me, Myself, and Irene, Bruce Almighty, Eternal Sunshine of the Spotless Mind, The Number 23*). Like Depp, Carrey's style has similarities to a vaudeville performer, the potentially impeccable symbiosis of Hamlet with the clown. In *Man in the Moon*, Carrey pulled off both Hamlet and the clown to perfection; his performance went beyond empathy into something approaching possession. The result was not a perfect imitation of Andy Kaufman (to Kaufman fans it may have been less than satisfactory), but something far more interesting, a weird synthesis of Kaufman with Carrey, akin to "Brundlefly" in Cronenberg's telepod. Whether the spirit of Kaufman was being successfully channeled by this "working," that Carrey's enormous talent was fully unleashed in the process seems undeniable. Jim Carrey playing Andy Kaufman playing Tony Clifton has to be one of the most perfect enactments of creative schizophrenia ever put on celluloid.

Carrey's other early "serious" role was for *The Truman Show* (1998), written by Andrew Nicchols and directed by Peter Weir, and the film demands brief discussion for being (like David Fincher's *The Game*) a conservative but nonetheless heartfelt attempt at the schizophrenic revelatory drama. It lacks the dark, malevolent undercurrents of *The Matrix* and *Dark City*, positing a deception, a snare, an illusion, that is, however duplicitous and restricting, all in the name of entertainment. Cristoff (Ed Harris) is the Logos creator god who lives in the Moon; Burbank is the idyllic island upon which Truman lives in blissful ignorance of his true condition: that he is a performer watched by millions, living a wholly contrived life within the strict boundaries of a movie set. *The Truman Show* was a breakthrough movie for Carrey and a huge commercial-critical success, mainly I think because it brought the lunatic fringe into the mainstream: it was the first popular treatment of the Philip K. Dick schizo paranoid fantasy, of reality being a carefully wrought illusion in which, if we look closely enough, the cracks begin to show. Truman's gradual awakening — as with Thomas Anderson's in *The Matrix* — displays the classic symptoms of schizophrenia. Everyone in Truman's world appears to be in on some vast conspiracy, playing a role in order to deceive and placate him. Everything that happens is part of some greater design, a design from which he is the only one excluded. This is a recurring element in the schizophrenic experience.

When Truman finally reaches the limits of his surrogate, make-believe world, and hears the voice of his "creator" coming out of the Sun (Cristoff's final bid to deceive: he is the Demiurge who lives in the moon, pretending to be the True God of the Sun), telling him the truth at last, this is Truman's final confirmation of his paranoia: his realization that his "delusion" is in fact correct, that his schizophrenia is really enlightenment. At this point Cristoff can no longer fall back on duplicity but has to come clean. Truman has "attained." He has passed all the tests and overcome the false obstacles placed between him and the truth; he has reached the limits of the known world, and now stands on the brink of the unknown. Cristoff explains the truth of the predicament, that Truman has lived inside a TV show "that gave hope and joy and inspiration to millions of viewers." "Who am I?" asks Truman. "You are the star." Truman asks, "None of this is real?" and Cristoff tells him, "*You* are real."

All this depicts beautifully the dawning of higher consciousness (as in the moment of death) in which the soul realizes the true nature of its now culminating life, that it was all a simple enactment, a preparation for entering eternity. The challenge of the snare, then, was built into the "deception" (the soul deceives *itself* by ignoring all the signs). Truman braves the storm of the unconscious; he stays at the helm and directs his face (ego) against the elements and discovers the truth. He becomes True Man.

Being John Malkovich (1999) is a great schizo comedy that rides the wave of split identity crises, the transcendental yearning of *The Matrix* and *Fight*

A Bird in the Hand: Obsessed Puppeteer Craig Schwartz (John Cusack) loses control of his id in *Being John Malkovich* (1999, Universal).

Club, into a whole new direction. Maybe it's a little too self-consciously "quirky," and not as spirited as one might hope, but it has vision. John Cusack plays Craig Schwartz, a lonely (married) puppeteer whose puppets act out his fantasies. Craig is an artist but also a putz: through his puppets he gets to fantasize the life which he's not man enough to live, and his genius is inseparable from neurosis. He is so immersed in creativity that it's closer to masturbation than inspiration. Oscar Wilde wrote, "I save my genius for living." Craig is the other way around: all his genius goes into his art, leaving nothing for himself. Unlike the artist who draws upon his life to enrich his art, and allows his art to enhance his life, Craig seems unable to integrate the two sides of himself.

He takes a job as a filing clerk at a bizarre company located on the seven and a halfth floor (with impossibly low ceilings; the official company story is that it was built to honor a dwarf lady and all her "accursed kind"). Craig is interviewed by the company head, Dr. Lester (Orson Bean), an old man who imagines himself to suffer from a speech impediment but who speaks perfectly, most especially when sharing his lewd and graphic sexual fantasies with Craig. While at work, Craig meets Maxine (Catherine Keener) and falls hopelessly in lust with her. She treats him as the nebbish he is, but refrains from rejecting him outright; a scruple-free manipulator of males, Maxine strings Craig along on the intuition that she might find a use for him some day. This use manifests when Craig discovers a portal hidden behind a filing cabinet, a portal that leads directly to John Malkovich's head. Through this portal, the frustrated puppeteer Craig gets to take over superstar Malkovich's body and, by taking advantage of Malkovich's fame and sex appeal, he transforms his essentially nebbish pursuits into a glamorous career (as well as finally getting into Maxine's pants).

Having told Maxine about the portal, Craig shows it to his wife Lotte (Cameron Diaz). A closet lesbian, or transsexual, Lotte is at once intoxicated by the possibilities. "I knew who I was," she declares of the experience. "Everything made sense!" Lotte falls in lust with Maxine also, who reciprocates but only wants Lotte when she is inside of Malkovich. For her part, Lotte is also infatuated with Malkovich, but from the *inside*, perceiving the portal as Malkovich's feminine side: "He has a penis *and* a vagina!" she eulogizes. Both Craig and his wife are wildly infatuated with the cold, aloof, manipulative Maxine, who is in turn obsessed with Malkovich. The only way they can get to possess Maxine is by becoming Malkovich, who is the absent (yet central) player in this twisted sexual triangle. *Being John Malkovich* (written by Charlie Kaufman and directed by Spike Jonze) is a sex comedy about wanting to get inside other people. Yet it dallies with more complex ideas, above all the idea of "being somebody else." (Once Maxine twigs to the possibilities of the portal, she persuades Craig to set up a secret business, renting out Malkovich's skull to anybody who wants to escape their own skin for a while.) The movie might have worked with anybody else in the place of Malkovich, but it was essential that, whoever they be, they be willing to play the part, and to send themselves up in the most uninhibited and surreal of fashions. Malkovich is perfect for the role of Malkovich. He's both creepy and sexy, famous but not too famous, and above all, he has a strange mystique. The film plays on the Malkovich mystique, and of course adds to it in the process. *Being John Malkovich* is a successful blending of surrealist satire, sex comedy, and sci-fi schizo fantasy. It's unique without being aberrational. Somehow it holds it various diverse, perverse strands together.

The reason behind the portal is that a group of geriatrics are bidding for eternal life and have found a way (through this mysterious portal) to use living human hosts ("ripe vessels") as stepping stones to eternity by "leaping from vessel to vessel" (a ripe vessel is when the human in question reaches 44 years of age). This *Cocoon*-esque, quasi-sci-fi plot is merely the motor to keep the surrealist sex farce moving, and any other explanation would have sufficed. What's really at the heart of the movie is not so much the why but the how. The four leading characters keep swapping identities and slipping in and outside of one another, everybody wanting to have sex with someone else; it's a kind of gaga, Dada updating of *A Midsummer Night's Dream*. Craig the puppeteer is of course a natural for taking over other people's bodies (ufologists call it "a walk-in") — and even people's minds — and he finally accomplishes the realization of his art with the living marionette Malkovich. This is the only way he can win the sexual acquiescence of Maxine: by becoming someone else (someone she is attracted to). Yet Maxine, though sexually attracted to Malkovich, is really drawn to Craig's wife Lotte, and her ideal match is neither Craig nor Malkovich (nor even the two combined) but Lotte inside of Malkovich (she bears the child of Malkovich while he is possessed by Lotte). Malkovich, for his part (and when still himself), falls prey to Maxine's sexual allure, at the same time fearing and despising her as the witch responsible for taking over his psyche (and finally his life). For most of the movie, Malkovich, for all his fame, wealth, and power, is a helpless puppet at the mercy of amateurs (or in the case of Craig, professionals). What for these other characters is a veritable feeding frenzy of new experience and opportunity, for Malkovich is sheer hell: his worst nightmare come true. In a sense, everything that happens in the movie might be seen as taking place inside Malkovich's head (or alternatively, as the make-believe fantasy of Craig).

To date, *Being John Malkovich* is probably the closest thing to a comedy of schizophrenia that mainstream American movies have given us. It's about conflict of interests, about separate and mutually exclusive desires, about vying for supremacy inside a single (divided) psyche. It gives us a battle of sub-personalities, and of course such a battle (not merely of the sexes but of anima and animus) is inevitably won by the women. Despite being the puppet master and discovering the portal, Craig is anything but equipped to handle the forces he unleashes. He's really just the catalyst for everything that happens: he gets the show in motion and then finally, after a brief spell in the spotlight, is swallowed up by it. Likewise with poor Malkovich, who never understands that his life was never his own to begin with, and that his head and soul belong to anyone who cares to possess it. By virtue of becoming a star, of being someone that everyone wants to be, he has foregone all rights to privacy, even to autonomous existence. The boundaries between his personal life (identity) and the rest of the world (its perception of him) have been erased. He has literally become public property.

The film plays on the awareness that everybody wants to be something (or someone) they are not. Craig's puppeteer carves and sculpts perfected images of himself and the people in his life, in a bid not so much to be someone else but to bridge the gap between the fantasy and the reality of himself. This is a true artistic calling, but Craig is unequal to it, so he winds up taking an alternate route to self-transformation, both a short cut *to* it and a deviation from it. Instead of perfecting himself, he becomes someone else. He takes schizophrenic refuge in fantasy. Craig is not tapping into the child within or transforming into a perfected version of himself, he is stealing someone else's thunder and becoming a pretender. He's driven not by artistic but selfish, mercenary impulses. Above all, he seems motivated by sexual inadequacy and frustration, and the need to prove himself. Craig is a perennial adolescent, and as such he is perfectly suited to take over the prima donna movie star Malkovich. The movie taps into and plays up to this urge in all of us to take a fast route to artistic glory, to become for a moment all the things we want to be, even if we must lose our identities in the bargain. (If there were any justice, *Being John Malkovich* would have spawned a spate of sequels. *Being Christopher Walken*, anyone? *Being Sharon Stone? Being Robert Downey Jr.*? It hints at a new level of voyeuristic movie-going for vicarious-thrill-seeking audiences desperate for a moment outside of their miserable, mundane selves, for a taste of the lifestyles of the rich and the shameless. A whole new arena has opened up for the schizo comedy.)

In *Lars and the Real Girl* (2007), directed by Craig Gillespie and written by Nancy Oliver (*Six Feet Under*), Lars (Ryan Gosling) is not quite right in the head; he keeps to himself, and he can't bear to be touched. He resists the efforts of his sister-in-law Karin (Emily Mortimer) to draw him out of his self-imposed solitude. One day, he asks Karin and his brother Gus (Paul Schneider) if he can bring over a friend. They are delighted, but Lars' friends turns out to be an "anatomically correct" silicon love doll named Bianca. Lars informs them that Bianca is Brazilian/Danish, that she's shy and doesn't talk much, and that, being deeply religious, she doesn't feel comfortable sleeping alone with Lars (in the garage where he lives). Karen and Dave agree to put Bianca up in their place and, convinced Lars has lost his marbles, suggest that Bianca visit the local G.P, Dr. Dagmar (Patricia Clarkson) for a check-up, hoping to put Lars under observation. After meeting Bianca, Dr. Dagmar suggests that, for the time being, they go along with Lars' fantasy and see what happens. Before long the whole town has agreed to treat Bianca as real: she attends church, and has her hair done. Eventually she gets accepted on the local school board.

Funny as it is, *Lars and the Real Girl* isn't really a comedy; and although it's an exquisitely tender-hearted film, it's never sentimental (having a silicon sex-doll at its center makes sure of that). Like Lars himself, the movie doesn't allow itself to be categorized. It's a lovable oddity in a felicitous "tradition" of flukes that includes *Harold and Maude, What's Eating Gilbert Grape, Donnie Darko, Harvey,* and *United States of Leland* (also with Gosling), movies that by all rights shouldn't work but somehow do. *Lars and the Real Girl* strays into unexplored realms of humor and pathos, areas of experience that — outside of real life — probably only these oddball empathic American movies can provide.

As played by Gosling, Lars is a prodigy as well as a freak; he's impossible to get a handle on. How much does he believe Bianca is real? We never know for sure. As a schizo, Lars has a sweetness and vulnerability that's both heartbreaking and heartening, but there's a solidness to him too, a determination and directness. He's a survivor, and though he may be delusional, he's not a solipsist. He stays true to his delusions, and his fantasy world has a life it its own (he fights with Bianca when he feels she is becoming too independent). Before we know it, the plastic Bianca begins to seem real to us, too.

In interviews, Gosling has remarked upon the similarity between Lars' peculiar affection for Bianca and the love children feel for stuffed toys Gosling observes how the love children feel for their toys is genuine even though it is never returned. This similarity is made explicit in the movie when Lars gives mouth-to-mouth to a co-worker's teddy bear (Margo, played by Kelli Garner in a lovely, soulful performance). Like a child, Lars loves from both sides, and by the end of the movie his weird delusion seems almost enlightened. It's a saintly kind of unconditional love — because what could be more selfless than loving someone who can never love us back?

Lars learns how to relate to others by finding the soul in an inanimate object. By finding his own capacity to love, he discovers his own soul. And the whole town learns by the schizo's example. Lars' delusion has the power of shamanic vision: it transforms reality.

12

Advocating Satan

> People who see shit are always crazy. Scientific fact.
> — Marcus, *Bringing Out the Dead*

It's a testimony to the encroaching, insidious hum of the right brain as it filters its otherworldly music through to the left hemisphere that there has been an influx of spirit movies into mainstream American cinema of late. It's an age-old atavistic belief that we can, under special circumstances, communicate with the dead, and that the dearly departed are, after all and however dear to us, not necessarily departed. Most of us know the drill: as occult lore goes, it's pretty familiar stuff. The souls of the dead don't necessarily "move on" but sometimes get stranded here on Earth among the living. Invisible, impotent, unable to act upon this world, they are nonetheless trapped, as passive witnesses, by their emotional attachments, habits, everything they are unable to let go of from their past lives. According to movie lore, the most frequently trapped souls are victims of unsolved murders (*6th Sense*, *Stir of Echoes*); this makes a good, dramatic (and earthly) storyline to complement the more mystical premise, and helps make the whole thing digestible to mass audiences.

In *Fallen*, a murdering demon hangs around Earth for thousands of years, taking the bodies of innocent humans and turning them into vicious serial murderers. The demon, Azazel, uses human stepping-stones to get around in, moving from one to the other via touch, with the speed and ease of thought. In Martin Scorsese's *Bringing Out the Dead* (1999), the focus is on an ambulance driver, Frank (Nicholas Cage), and his own, possibly psychotic conviction that dead or dying spirits are communicating with him telepathically. Frank walks the thin, blurry line between the world of the living and the world of the dead, and Scorsese's film, without ever fully committing to a supernatural perspective, seems fully sold on the idea that spirits are quite real phenomena, and that overexposure to the dead and dying will eventually overwhelm our rational defenses and make us susceptible to influence from "the other side." All the ambulance drivers Frank works with in the film are unbalanced to varying degrees, though perhaps none more than Frank himself. What's unclear is whether the work attracts such unbalanced types in the first place, or if the dementia is a result of the job itself; probably it's a little of both.

Bringing Out the Dead—by the same team, Scorsese and Paul Schrader, who brought us *Taxi Driver* twenty five years earlier—is not actually *about* insanity but it portrays (casually, as if it were quite normal) an insane world in which everyone seems on the verge of hysteria, despair, and delirium (sometimes all at the same time). It's a consummate piece of filmmaking by Scorsese in which every shot and scene seems perfectly modulated to his precise and conscious design. And yet there's really not much going on *under* the shots and scenes. Scorsese's technique, while not actually at odds with his material, doesn't really seem to be in service to it, either. The schizophrenic themes are all here, but the kind of fevered empathy Scorsese showed for Travis in *Taxi Driver* is now muted. Scorsese's tone is as aloof and ironic (dispassionate to the point of irreverence) as his wisecracking radio dispatcher's voice in the movie. (Even so, *Bringing Out the Dead* is probably the best work Scorsese has done in the last twenty-five years, since *The King of Comedy*. Of course, it was almost totally overlooked.)

A question the film raises (in my mind at least) is: do schizophrenics really see dead people? A better question might be—is believing you can communicate with the dead a symptom of schizophrenia? Certainly this seems likely, for what else is modern medicine to say? And how is a person in today's society to *deal* with experiences in which he sees and hears things that no one else can, if not by accepting the consensus opinion that he is out of his gourd and needs treatment? Movies have always played on this tension. By letting us see what the protagonist sees, we *know* he's not just imagining things, or at least we know there's really no difference: if the hallucination is indistinguishable from reality then it *is* reality. So the skepticism and dismissals of the supporting characters—doctors, parents, police, whoever—only exposes them as bigoted fools (or at best well-meaning ignorants). Yet most of us in the audience—deprived of the special privilege of a God's eye view of things—would be (indeed are) more comfortably aligned with the bigots and skeptics than with the visionary schizo or sensitive. Except at the movies, that is.

Bringing Out the Dead is about men playing God and the toll it takes on them. Though Frank talks about the joy of walking with Infinity that comes from saving patients' lives, by the end of the movie he has reversed the privilege and *taken* a patient's life, also by intervening. Frank isn't playing "the God of hellfire" but a merciful God who listens to the pleas of the helpless and delivers them from suffering. Frank is saving *himself* from pain, from the torment and guilt he feels for failing to save a patient. (Rose, whose face he sees everywhere he goes: Rose finally lets him off the hook by telling him: "No one asked you to suffer. That was your idea.") By mercy-killing the man he had previously saved, Frank is letting himself off the hook. He is canceling the one act out with the other, and by relinquishing his need to play God and obeying the voices in his head, Frank finds a measure of peace in an insane world.

Scorsese accentuates the insanity through the picture by having Frank pair up with progressively more deranged partners. The driver John Goodman plays is merely eccentric; Vino Rhames' Marcus is definitely out of control (he sees himself as a Christian missionary, and in his zeal overturns the ambulance); Tom Sizemore's character is out-and-out demented. By the end, the two nutjobs are bringing back their *own* victims to the hospital — paramedics who rough you up before they patch you up, a fitting enough metaphor for the self-perpetrating madness of a schizophrenic society.

How is it that only children and schizos (and dogs) get to see the dead? There is a fourth class also, that dubious (even in Hollywood) breed of folks known as "psychics," but these peculiarly endowed mutant individuals are rarely if ever the protagonists of our spirit movies (Sam Raimi's *The Gift* is a recent, lame exception to the rule). At most they serve as catalysts for the action (*Stir of Echoes*), or else as a guide and instructor (*Poltergeist*) to help the audience through the rough spots of interpretation and/or belief.

If only children and schizophrenics can see the dead (and angels, demons, and so forth), does that make children more schizo than adults, or is it that schizos are more childlike? I suspect it relates to the "pure of heart-ness" that movies are eager to sell us, as the essence of "sensitivity"— an openness through which magic is allowed to slip and so become a daily reality, rather than just a nostalgic memory or a childish fantasy. Schizos — when not axe-wielding maniacs or mother-obsessed psychos — tend to be endearingly childlike in their inability to tell the difference between history and fairy tale, fact and fantasy, cold science and occult lore. Their capacity to see beyond everyday surfaces (whether the hypocrisy of manners that the lovable schizos of *Fearless* and *Big* have no time for, or the reality façade that unwilling "seers" are deprived of) tends to either give rise to or result from some sort of personal crisis, one that leaves these characters severely disconnected to their lives and the people around them. They become obsessive, self-immersed, preoccupied in the manner of a child stubbornly sticking to the rules of some private game, a game which grown-ups are not invited to join.

Is this a world adults unconsciously long for, of which they have buried, none-too-distant memories from when they were children? Is this why we go to such movies, to re-experience the supernatural, in the safe assurance that no one is going to lock us up or medicate us for believing in ghosts and demons? It's not enough to dismiss the enduring belief in spirit worlds as simple wishful thinking. Belief is just as strong in negative manifestations — demons, vampires, succubae, and so forth, nor is the idea of being trapped on Earth as a wandering ghost exactly reassuring for most of us. These beliefs can't be attributed to simple-mindedness either, since some of the greatest minds throughout history have shared such beliefs, from Shakespeare, Milton, and Blake, to Dante, Goethe, Rilke, Leonardo, Newton, Keats, Shelley, all the way up to Tesla, Jung, and William Burroughs. Not just some but *most* of the leading lights of poetry, art, music, and even science, have acknowledged — however tentatively and discreetly — a belief in spirit worlds of one sort or another. The wonder is that more movies don't deal with an area so rich in intrigue and mystery, and that so few of the ones that do, do it anything like justice.

Spirits and demons make great subject matter for movies, not just horror movies but serious, searching psychodramas. But where are they? *Sixth Sense* was I think such a critical-commercial success mostly for *aspiring* to treat the subject with something like due gravitas and artistry; it aspired, but it was a stodgy, methodical approach to the mysteries, without much spirit or any real insights into the subject. What's amazing, considering how many leading directors seem to have a natural affinity and sympathy for the schizophrenic experience, is how few of them deal with it in their movies, even indirectly.

Obviously, in a society precariously teetering on the brink of madness and ruin, in which the most precious commodity is also the most uncertain — that of peace of mind — it follows that the people who back the people who back mainstream movies will ensure, *in any way they can*, that audiences be allowed a little of the security, complacency, and peace of mind which their lives are already so sorely lacking. Yet, although this may jibe with the propounded function of entertainment — as what passes the time and allows us to forget ourselves a while — it plainly goes against the essence of all that might be considered *art*.

If movies don't allow us to confront our own psyches, our lives and the world we live in, or to reevaluate at some level our feelings about it all, plainly they are doing the very opposite: helping us to avoid issues that, once the movie is over, are more pressing than ever for the time lost in daydreaming. A good movie serves both as art and entertainment, escapism and instruction. It allows us to get outside of ourselves (relief) and then, *from this new perspective*, to observe ourselves in a new light, hence more clearly (confrontation). Not only do we thereby learn, in a pleasant, non-threatening environment (the imaginary realm of the movie), something about ourselves, we also — if we are alert enough to this process — can learn something invaluable about the nature of perception itself. We can learn how to detach from our problems and put them in a new perspective in order to see them more clearly and deal with them *in the real world*. A fantasy work like Woody Allen's *Zelig* is a nigh perfect example of this. And who better than Woody Allen to turn movies into psychotherapy?

Psycho = Clown = Child = Angel = Devil = Double = Soul = Unconscious = Id = Libido = Sexuality = Repression = Psycho

All these movies, one way or another, maybe even *all* movies, give us our repressed "other." They give us our desires or our fears, by assuming some alien, inhuman, demonic, angelic, childlike, psychotic, desirable, fearful, laughable, or terrible form. The mere "act" of sitting in front of a movie screen and watching shadows and light flicker before our eyes, as an alternate antidote to the troublesome trials and endless pressures of our lives, is in itself a schizophrenic act. Both the cave paintings and the shamanic visions of primitive peoples were understood to have a direct bearing on (a function within) daily life. But movies, ah movies; these are but distractions to us. It would never occur to us to imagine that these fantastic images might be somehow shaping our reality, not just a reflection but a *projection* of our lives; that we are not merely the witnesses but also, in some obscure sense, the perpetrators. Such an idea is unthinkable to sophisticated audiences.

On the other hand, wish-fulfillment, "feel-good" movies like *Field of Dreams, Ghost, City of Angels,* and *What Dreams May Come,* draw a picture (for the collective ego) of an unconscious realm — beyond time, self, and death — that is idyllic to the point of being wholly and utterly idiotic. There are no redeeming features to these movies, because they have absolutely no bearing upon reality. They are not just fluff but pernicious fluff: cotton candy laced with strychnine. They are propaganda designed (even if for grossly commercial reasons rather than political ones) to *mis*inform us as to the nature of our plight as human beings, and the means (if such exist) of our salvation (there's really no other word for it).

Moses smashed the golden calf because, by forging a visible image of God out of a material substance, he knew the people were not getting closer to God but further from Him. The image came between God and the people; it deprived them of the purity of their imaginations, and of their sense of the abstract. So it is with movies. By creating false images of the spirit realm, the afterlife, etc., we are being robbed of our power to *imagine* these things. And since it is this very power — that of the visual imagination — that allows us to tap into our unconscious and so develop our connection to the divine, then the only access we *have* to any "spirit realm" is through this power. The movies are giving us *a false unconscious*, and the price for this is the highest one imaginable. As Scott Fitzgerald said, "Movies have stolen our dreams. Of all betrayals, this is the worst."

The demons of *Fallen* are described by one character as "like the Mafia: they don't exist." According to the movie's lore, these demons are punished by God (for their revolt) by being deprived of form. They are condemned to inhabit human hosts as their only means of existence and are enacting their revenge on God through *us* (they get back at God by tormenting his creations).

It's always difficult to decipher mythic code and theological folklore, but we can only presume all this was part of God's original plan, and that by punishing the angels and consigning them to live in mortal bodies, he was at the same time testing his new creation, killing two birds with a single thunderbolt. So is God a schizo? No one asks this question. In *Fallen*, God's name is evoked repeatedly as a means to comprehend what's going on. The protagonist (hero cop played by Denzel Washington) is told, "Some things only make sense if there is a God." That's a fairly original argument for a crime thriller, and there's an insidious, persuasive logic behind it. "With God, all things are possible," the Bible tells us. Without Him, nothing is.

An undeveloped subtext of the nihilistic, metaphysical thriller/film noir/horror flicks of the 1990s (*The Usual Suspects, Seven, Natural Born Killers, Lost Highway*) is that our collective wising up, our cynical rejection of the pious platitudes and simplistic beliefs of yesteryear (regarding a Supreme Being), has rendered us vulnerable to the wiles of the Evil One. Our denial of God and all things spiritual has resulted inevitably in a rejection of the possibility of supernatural *evil* as an explanation for the misery and mayhem of our times. Hence these demons, like the Mafia and the Freemasons, can work all the more effectively under the cloak of non-existence.

Since the sophisticated, streetwise protagonists of these movies (mostly cops or criminals) are too smart to believe in mystical mumbo jumbo or old world superstitions, they are unable to comprehend the nature of the conspiracy into which they are inexorably drawn. Yet although the devil or demon is given all manner of credence in the end (there's really no arguing with the evidence), God Himself never seems to get involved. He never intervenes, and so never amounts to more than a Word. Hollywood's own schizoid approach to metaphysics has led to a spate of cheesy, quasi-mystical angel movies in which love conquers all, and, at the other end of the spectrum, a plethora of grisly, semi-supernatural crime thrillers in which evil holds sway over the hearts and minds of men—but never the twain shall meet. There is a similar situation with sci-fi movies: the aliens are always either sappily, irreproachably good or grotesquely, irredeemably evil, with nothing in between (nor are there many movies in which both kinds of aliens appear). When it comes to metaphysics, demonology, theology, and even ufology, Hollywood is still subliterate.

It's unlikely that Nicholas Kazan (*Fallen*'s writer, and director Elia's son) got his demonlore whole from occult grimoires, and if he did then it's a lore I am entirely unfamiliar with. (The name *Azazel*, however, is that assigned to the leader of the Angels who came down—as described in *Genesis*, though Azazel is not actually named—to mate with the earth women, having seen "that they were fair," and so precipitated the Flood.) Whatever the case he does an admirable job of contriving his own version of the mysteries. I've never heard of demonic entities that move from human host to host through the medium of touch — usually they are said to infiltrate us at a psychic level, through dreams, sexual fantasies, and so forth, and usually the process of possession takes time. But Kazan has come up with a far more *cinematic* treatment of the idea of demonic possession. The best scenes in the movie are of the demon Azazel showing off his speed and prowess by moving from one human to the next, carrying a tune ("Time Is on My Side," by The Stones) as he goes. The rest of the movie, despite solid performances from Washington, John Goodman, and James Gandolini, is pretty routine; notwithstanding the juiciness of its plot, the film is little more imaginative than a superior episode of *The X-Files*.

Fallen does take its subject with unusual seriousness however; not in the manner of *Angel Heart* — which was oppressively somber about its hokum and at the same time pitifully unconvincing — but in its willingness to do at least a modicum of research. *Fallen*, like Taylor Hackford's *The Devil's Advocate*, is a slick Hollywood product made for one purpose only — to thrill and chill us. But in the process, it taps into something deeper: a genuine anxiety about the state of the world, a feeling that, "there is more that is hidden than is seen," and that some malevolent undercurrent is taking control of our lives. Both movies transcend the shabbiness of their construction and the sensational tawdriness of their material — almost despite themselves — by touching upon a *Zeitgeist* of apocalyptic dread. They play upon a feeling that even the most sophisticated of us are prey to: that maybe, just maybe, Satan and his demons are more than leftovers of primitive superstition and children's stories, but an atavistic memory of the ultimate Other.

Probably the most effective depiction of demonic forces at work to come out of Hollywood so far is Mark Pellington's *The Mothman Prophecies* (2002), a taught, graceful, and affecting work based on John Keel's book of the same name. Over a thirteen-month period, between November 1966 and December 1967, in the small town of Point Pleasant, Virginia, strange things were afoot. Multiple sightings were reported of a winged creature that stood like a man, some eight or ten feet high, with burning red eyes, that came to be known as "the mothman." The creature seemed both otherworldly and all-too-real: witnesses unlucky enough to stumble upon the Mothman were often pursued by it; they saw it roaming outside their homes, heard the sound of its huge wings as it flew off, and so forth. If this was hallucination, then not only was it collective, it was extremely consistent.

As an exploration into the schizophrenic nature of reality, *The Mothman Prophecies* has more in common with *The Matrix* than it does with *The Exorcist*. And yet it is one of the very few genuine horror movies of the last twenty years, for it serves the central function of the horror genre: revelation. It strips away the comfortable veneer of consensus reality to reveal the seething abyss of irrationality that lies beneath. It gives us the return of the repressed. The

Mothmen are harbingers of doom and messengers from another dimension, certainly; but they are not only this. The film clearly suggests that "they" are also the creation of the minds of the small populace of Point Pleasance. This is not to say that they are imaginary, rather that (having "no physical existence"), it is the collective unconscious of the people which gives form, shape, and purpose to an otherwise formless and impersonal energy. Yet mysterious as it is, this force is presumably as much a part of the natural order of things as electricity and gravity, albeit considerably trickier to harness. Like all good horror movie monsters, the Mothman is an emissary of the Id. Its materialization doesn't just portend the physical catastrophe of the fallen bridge; it heralds the bursting of the dam between conscious and unconscious, left and right, ego and Id.

John Keel went to investigate these sightings and spent several months in the area; after a time he found his life turning into a surreal, Lovecraftian nightmare, an extended, never-ending episode of "The Twilight Zone." Bizarre phone calls, messages, predictions, lights in the sky, alien abductions, bizarre coincidences, threatening appearances of strange men in black with olive-colored faces; all this climaxed in December 1967 with the collapse of a road bridge over the Ohio river and the resulting deaths of 46 people. Legend has it — and the stories continue to the present day — that these mothmen (assuming there are many) are harbingers of disaster. Like the Angels in the Old Testament, they are Messengers come to give warning of catastrophes to come. But they are also tricksters, as much demons as angels. Their communications — as the film amply portrays — are obscure and ambiguous, as liable to mislead as to instruct. The "expert" in the film (played by an overly wacky Alan Bates) insists that "they" do not have motive or intention as we understand it, that they are part of some supernatural order of things that we cannot ever fully comprehend, that, in fact, "we are not *allowed* to know."

Keel himself — who researched paranormal phenomena for many years, including UFOs — came to a similar conclusion, based on the inescapable fact that whatever evidence or clues we have to work with (as to the existence of these mysterious forces) have been provided by the forces themselves. Keel decided that the nature of these forces — hence of the evidence — was deceptive, elusive, playful, and mischievous, if not downright malignant. Despite some highly dubious mutating of the facts (including updating events to the present day, and citing John Keel's book as a "novel"), the movie stays true to the spirit of Keel's work. It conveys impeccably a sense of mystery, paranoia, surreality, and growing hysteria at the incomprehensibility of unfolding events. *The Mothman Prophecies* is an unassuming thriller that derives its thrills not from any physical threat, as such, but rather on the threat to *reason* — sanity — that these forces present merely by existing. The film is wise enough to content itself — and us — with the partial manifestation of a mystery, knowing that

12. Advocating Satan

whatever force such manifestations represent must be so vast and unfathomable that even the smallest whiff of it may unhinge us, perhaps irrevocably (though not necessarily to our detriment). John Klein, a fictionalized version of Keel sensitively played by Richard Gere, enters into the imaginal realm, where nothing is real and everything is perception. As his sinister "guide" tells him when he asks it, "What do you look like?": "It depends who's looking."

Devil's Advocate (1997) is probably the best of the Devil-Faust movies to come out of Hollywood so far. Admittedly, that's not saying much, what with stinkers like *Angel Heart, Witches of Eastwick,* and *End of Days* to measure up against. But Taylor Hackford's rather slick and unimaginative rendering cannot foul up what remains an excellent script (by Jonathan Lemkin and Tony Gilroy, from the book by Andrew Neiderman), and the film offers what none of these other movies do (or for that matter, the more traditional devil movies like *Rosemary's Baby, The Exorcist,* and *The Omen*): philosophical depth. As Al Pacino's Milton puts it: "I'm peaking: this is *my* time."

Milton refers to God as an "absentee landlord," thereby confirming the mythological belief that planet Earth is under Satanic jurisdiction, that (as in

Lucifer & Son: Milton (Al Pacino) grooms his only begotten son (Keanu Reeves) for satanic messiahship, in *The Devil's Advocate* (1997, Warner Bros.).

the book of Job) God *gave* the Devil humanity as a plaything, in order to test and purge them both. *Devil's Advocate* suggests that we were made for each other, and that's what gives the movie its fascination and its power. It's genuinely disturbing, because the sense of corruption and evil comes not so much from the Devil but from humanity (as represented by Keanu Reeves, in a surprisingly emotional performance), from what the Devil (Milton) can draw out of it. Pacino's Milton is lewd and impish and appropriately lascivious. He's amoral and aloof, but he plays fair. He always allows free will to decide the day. He's there to tempt, coerce, and instruct, but never to command. Sure, he brings out the worst in us, but then, so does any disintoxificant. His role is a teacher and guide, as much as it is a corrupter. It all depends on how you take the challenge.

In *Witches of Eastwick*, Nicholson's Devil was raunchy and shameless and rather likeable, but he was also a boor and a cad; there was no subtlety or depth to him (that's the kind of performer Nicholson has become). He might have had our sympathy, but if so it was only because he was in over his head with the three witches (who finally cast him out of his own paradise). Pacino gives Milton the necessary dignity to match his sinister charms, but he also makes him disarmingly human. He turns him into a tragic figure, which is finally the only way to play him (unless you are playing him wholly for laughs, like Nicholson, or for chills, as De Niro did in *Angel Heart*). As the Fallen Angel cast out of Paradise, Lucifer is the *original* tragic hero: the great soul whose greatness is inseparable from his one, fatal flaw, the grand achiever who overreaches himself and so, by trying to fly too high, plunges to the depths. Since Reeves' Kenneth represents the soul of humanity (Faust), and since he is also Milton's illegitimate(!) son, the film's unspoken premise is that humanity itself—having followed in the footsteps of Lucifer by succumbing to the devil's temptations—has now taken his place. We are no longer identified with Faust, much less Job: we are now fully identified with Satan. This may, after all, be a forward development: the slow integration of the Shadow.

At the end of the movie, Milton-Lucifer's suffering over the loss of his "boy" Kenneth (who proves the supremacy of free will by blowing his brains out) is as real as anything in the movie (or anything in any other devil movie, for that matter: it's a classic movie moment—Satan the crucified). It's certainly more real than Kenneth's suffering over the loss of his wife (Charlize Theron), because compared to his father, Kenneth is a cold fish indeed. He's a soulless slave of Babylon, where Lucifer is *all* soul. Pacino plays Satan as he should be played, as a human being with the memories of a God; in the end, he reveals that his torments are the torments of humanity itself. The wicked irony of the film is that Milton-Lucifer is inadvertently following in the footsteps of *his* Father, who art in Heaven. Like God, Lucifer rears a son and primes him for the role of world "savior" (well OK, world destroyer; but to a God is there really any difference?). Then this son sacrifices his own life before his father's eyes, thereby teaching him what it is to be human. By the end we can see that even Satan is learning from his mistakes. (Maybe next time around, he'll get it right?) *Devil's Advocate* is clearly not a great movie, but it's a good movie on a great, great subject, and it ranks with the better movies of recent years simply because it succeeds in tapping into the *Zeitgeist* as precious few recent movies have.

It's ironic—or perhaps not—that in the Christian moral Weltanschauung, the devil is associated with sexuality, but also with deceit. Yet if sexuality is what drags us down to the level of the beast and so must be repressed and denied if we are to attain grace and happiness on the Heavenly plateau, then how exactly can this be achieved save by *an elaborate form of deception*? If it's the devil who tempts us by giving us sexual desires, and the devil who deceives us by telling us we may become "as Gods," where exactly does "the Lord" come in? We are caught between Satan and Satan. Our desire is the adversary of our aspiration, and vice versa. It's no wonder we are waxing schizophrenic. The devil—God's Shadow—is simply humanity's projection onto the universe of its own twisted psyche. As such, Satan is the emblem and embodiment of our own *schizophrenia*. Unfortunately, since Hollywood remains at a prepubescent level of development, it wants to have its wafer and eat it—to flirt and cavort with the devil and still be a virgin in the morning. As a result, the magical realm of the unconscious, id, or libido—source of all creative energy both sexual and spiritual—has turned into a carnival of horrors, the habitation of every foul deed or thought ever repressed in the name of goodness, decency, apple pie, and the American Way. We have turned society into an amusement ride through Hell in order to disguise the fact that, by selling up our souls for a little entertainment, our psyches have gone to the devil.

13

God's Channel

The older I get, the more lost I feel. — Terry Gilliam

Until *The Matrix* and *Fight Club* came along, *Twelve Monkeys* (1996) was probably the fullest fantasy treatment of the schizophrenic journey in mainstream American movies. The film traces a hopeless loop, a vicious circle, an eternal return by which the "hero" — the Neanderthalic James Cole (Bruce Willis) — is condemned to be a recurring witness to his own death. Ostensibly, Cole's mission is (as befits Willis' heroic mold) philanthropic. He is sent back from the future to find a sample of the deadly plague which will, in a matter of weeks, wipe out the Earth's population and drive the survivors underground to live molish lives in caves and caverns (like the Morlocks of H.G. Wells). Cole cannot prevent the plague from spreading — this is never an option — nor can he avoid his own death, having already witnessed it years ago; no matter how much foresight he may have, all it does is to accentuate Cole's helplessness. (This is described in the movie as "the Cassandra Complex.") The curse of the schizophrenic is his passivity — his ability to see beyond the surfaces into the essence of things but be forever unable to act upon what he has seen. He is given knowledge, insight, vision, but not wisdom: he lacks the means to use what he knows, hence is only paralyzed by it.

As the film has it, however, Cole's real mission is of a more personal nature, perhaps equally predetermined but somewhat less meaningless. Cole returns to the past (and so escapes a desolate future) in order to fall in love. He is on a quest for self, even if he doesn't know it. He is seeking into his past to find the sense of meaning — of identity — which he has been stripped of in the future (where the only motivation is mere survival, without any apparent *reason*: Cole is an animal running on sheer instinct). *Twelve Monkeys* is a kind of reverse *Vertigo** in which Cole is both the seeker and the lost soul being

---

*There are in *Twelve Monkeys* the kind of synchronicities connecting it to Hitchcock's movie that intoxicate all film buffs with their unlikelihood. The connection originates in *La Jetée*

sought. He is unaware of what he is seeking, since by definition he no longer knows that it — his soul-identity — even exists. And the moment he finds it, classically enough in the shape of his own childhood self, is also the moment of his death: the schizophrenic's moment of self-realization.

In *Vertigo*, the protagonist (Scottie) is seeking his death in the most roundabout way possible. The film begins with his hanging by his nails and ends with him on the point of finally letting go and taking the plunge. The whole movie has traced the schizophrenic's coming to terms with the truth, his facing up to his predicament and finding the nerve to face the inevitable resolution. For Scottie, death is the only possible remedy for his torment, as failed (schizo) hero. James Cole, on the other hand, is never for a moment under the delusion of being anyone's hero. Unlike Scottie, he never had the luxury of being an adjusted, functioning member of society. Cole is schizoid from the get-go — he is already dead to himself and to the world (which is a dead world anyway). Consequently, the film traces his quest for *life*, his emergence from the death-state of schizophrenic despair into a more integrated and adjusted state, one where he is capable of both love and — as a result of such love (like the cowardly lion who finds his courage) — heroic action. If *Vertigo* maps the slow, steady breakdown of the self until there is nothing left but fragments, *Twelve Monkeys* shows the process in reverse, as little by little Cole puts himself back together into an integrated whole, ready for life (and perversely, as it happens, for death). Where Scottie gradually uncovers the intrigue he believed himself to be investigating as a sham and a ruse, an intricate illusion designed to ensnare him, Cole eventually vindicates his own schizophrenia by proving — to himself and to Kathryn (Madeleine Stowe) — that his delusion is founded in reality. Scottie's supposedly heroic mission — the source of his delirium — turns out to be all in his own head; Cole's supposed delusion turns out to be an authentic heroic mission — part of an elaborate and fantastic plot to alter the course of history. In *Vertigo* we have the Hero reduced to — or exposed as — a schizo; in *Twelve Monkeys*, the schizophrenic is revealed and finally redeemed as the Hero.

(continued) (the short French film on which *Twelve Monkeys* was based), in which there is a scene evoking the famous redwood forest scene in *Vertigo*. In *Twelve Monkeys* this scene is to recur in the movie theater where Cole and Kathryn take refuge at one point. But, as Gilliam notes, "The interesting thing about *Vertigo* was how it started working its way into the film far more than originally planned.... When Mick Audsley started cutting it together ... Mick created an extraordinary dialogue between the script and the film ... I'd actually done a shot in the cinema foyer and, because it was circular, I'd put Madeleine [Stowe] and Bruce on a turntable so that they floated while the room spun around them. Was this not Vertigo remaking itself without us realizing it? We sat in the cutting room and couldn't believe it. It was spooky." (Gilliam took out the shot because it was "unnecessary," but also because he realized people would assume he had stolen in from Vertigo.) *Gilliam on Gilliam*, pg. 233. One might note at this point that the relevant scene-in redwood forest where Madeleine (!) traces the cutaway of the tree and mourns the fleeting nature of her life-is central to the schizophrenic condition: that of being lost in eternity.

Cole's death coinciding with his coming face to face with his "past" child-self—and the Cole-child witnessing the death of his future self—is archetypal schizo cinema. In the lore of the *Doppelgänger* and other schizophrenic myths and legends, two selves cannot co-exist in the same space and time without one of them being destroyed. This is not only the lore of *Doppelgängers* but also the law of physics, of matter and anti-matter particles, where the one cancels out and assimilates the other. Perhaps the source of both the lore and the law here is to be found (like everything else) in the human psyche itself? When the id "conjures up" a new identity—just as the future mole-scientists send Cole back through time into the present—it does so (for similar reasons) in order to confront and challenge the conscious ego, and so transform the already existing identity. In just such a manner, Cole is sent *back* from the future (i.e., the unconscious) into the present (the conscious), in order to extract information (the deadly virus) and so help create a new future (and thus liberate all those id-entities condemned to their underground hell). To effectively accomplish this, the new, usurper ego (the second personality, Cole the elder) must confront and illuminate the original ego (Cole as a child). They must face off and be assimilated into one another in order to create a third entity—a fusion of id and ego, conscious and unconscious, past and future, man and child.

In Gilliam's movie, what this entails is the young Cole being shown his own future death—and so being given the opportunity to avoid it, perhaps—but most of all to understand the nature of the self—of time, destiny, and so forth. In other words, to be given the wisdom of experience while retaining the innocence (and opportunity) of youth. The elder Cole, on the other hand, gets to return to a childlike state of joy and wonder (of innocence) at the very moment of his death. To see himself as a witness to his own death is to *understand for the first time* the meaning of the memory which has haunted him his whole life, that it is a memory both of the future and of the past, of his self and his not-self—his life and his death. As a result, Cole is re-born. His spirit—the innocence of the child that Cole rediscovers in his love for Kathryn—is eternally renewed, and takes flight to new worlds of experience.

Cole is running down a white, tunnel-like airport passage as he is killed, signifying his passage to the next world, from the womb of life to the world of death (the tunnel being a death motif as well as a birth one). The Cole child, on the other hand, witnessing this, is then seen gazing in awe as a plane takes flight, signifying a different kind of passage—from earth to the heavens—and the release of the older Cole's spirit—in death. The film's (and Gilliam's) greatest mistake is in not allowing the older Cole to see himself as a child, watching his own future death. This is absolutely necessary for the film's schizo subtext to reach its completion, and for symmetry to be attained. With this look Cole can understand at last the meaning of his dreams, and simultaneously the child may grasp the significance of the scene. The knowledge, as it were (or spirit), then passes from the grown-up into the child. And of course, the plane the child watches take off is carrying the deadly plague.

The climax of *Twelve Monkeys* only *appears* to be a closed loop of eternal return, of endless repetition. In actuality, everything has changed, since both Cole the younger and Cole the elder may finally comprehend the meaning of the scene that unfolds before (and between) them — the meaning of the *Doppelgänger*, of divided consciousness. By being in two places at once, they may realize that they are really neither: neither here nor there, past nor future, man nor child, but only eternal spirit in endless play. The sheer impossibility of the scene reveals its illusory nature, and so "one" (or rather both) is released from the illusion of duality, and schizophrenia becomes — enlightenment. As a result, we may easily imagine that Cole's destiny is now forever altered by the realization and that, acting on this new awareness, he may avoid a bleak and terrible future. Maybe even he will save the world while he is at it (this is Bruce Willis, after all); but at the very least, he will now have the option of creating a better life for himself.

All this is classic mythology dressed up as cracking, top-of-the-line (at least until *The Matrix* came along) Hollywood science fiction. Gilliam, who by his own decree is only "trying to clear all the shit away to find out what the truth is and what reality is,"[3] has done himself proud. As Cole's soul undergoes a new coronation, a passing over from the old to the new, so, in ancient myths, the coming of the new King was predicated upon the slaying of the old.[4] The new (child) King even has to slay the old King as part of his initiation, by which he proves himself worthy of his new station. And the old King, having served his function to the full, embraces his obsolescence and surrenders, gracefully and gratefully, to his future heir (exactly as Kurtz does to Willard in *Apocalypse Now*). Just so the old Cole — having completed his mission and fallen in love — passes on the "crown" (the controlling intelligence, or ego) to his rightful successor, his own reincarnation. Cole is dead, long live Cole. (Even the name has the right alchemical associations here: this "Cole" is a diamond in the rough.)

This measure of surrender is what poor Scottie in *Vertigo* was lacking, and it was just such lack of humility that led to his inevitable, tragic ruin. Cole, being more hopeless a case by far, and having far less to cling to (namely, less *ego*), when faced with the tidal forces of the Id (the magnitude and mystery of the irrational universe), does not put up nearly so much of a fight. He is not trying to save or to dominate anyone, not even himself. He is, in true schizophrenic fashion, devoid of any will of his own; this alone is what allows him to arrive at his correct destination at the right time, and so to realize his (unconscious) quest for self. To get *back* to where he started and know the place at last.

And when the schizo meets his other self, all his searching is over. It is justified, it is complete. What other cure for divided consciousness could there be besides this: taking it to its natural, inevitable extreme (as in *Fight Club* and *Matrix*)? The schizo hero knows that, if one feels divided, it is because one *is* divided, but as male and female are divided — not as contraries but as *partners*. The divided self can only become one by this mythical scene of confrontation, when the two halves of the psyche come face to face, acknowledge their differences, and attain balance. Like Cain and Abel, however, one must die that the Other may live. This final, cataclysmic, orgasmic congress (which is the soul's communion with death) is both the end and the beginning of life: its culmination and its inception. When the ego surrenders to the id's embrace and, gazing into those timeless, ageless eyes, recognizes itself at last.

Richard Kelly's *Donnie Darko* (2001) is about as rare an experience at the movies as finding a genuine psychic at a fun fair. It's a celluloid vision. Donnie (Jake Gyllenhaal) is a schizo with the power to see the future and thereby create it. As in *Don't Look Now*, Donnie's visions are self-fulfilling: it's his terrible fear of what is going to happen (on October 30, 1988, at a precise minute and hour) that causes Donnie to act in just such a way as to ensure that it does. And yet, paradoxically (and *Donnie Darko* is not merely *about* paradoxes, it is a paradox unto itself), the knowledge he gains into the mysterious workings of time through his experience permits Donnie to rewrite his destiny, by turning the clock back. This he can only do at the cost of his own life. Initially, Donnie is spared death due to his tendency to sleepwalk, which is one symptom of his schizo-visionary state and which causes Donnie to be out on the golf course when a passenger plane jet engine falls from the sky and crashes through his bedroom. Donnie was already strange before this, but the inexplicable event (no airline claims the severed engine) only serves to cement his dementia, his sense of strangeness. At the same time, it alerts the audience to the fact that we have entered into a world every bit as weird and incomprehensible as Donnie's world must seem to him. We have entered the Twilight Zone.

Donnie Darko is the first of its type — the surrealist teen schizo angst comedy (*Static, Repo Man, Heathers, Parents*, etc.) — to successfully pull all the elements together and forge them into a genuine work of art. It's a bit slack in places (Gretchen's death, for example), and it's occasionally self-indulgent, or perhaps just self-conscious, but it's all of a piece. Unlike the films mentioned above (*Static* excepted), it has depth both of meaning and of feeling; it comes from the heart and not just the head. *Donnie Darko* is teen comedy romance spliced with hallucinatory horror movie, and yet the splicing is seamless, invisible and impeccable. Except in the early high school scenes (which the director seems to be deliberately undermining by speeding up the images and drowning out the sound), there's never a sense of watching a cross genre movie. In fact *Donnie Darko* doesn't seem like a genre movie at all, principally because

13. God's Channel

The Schizo as Super Hero: Donnie (Jake Gyllenhaal), carrying Gretchen (Jena Malone), makes the supreme sacrifice in *Donnie Darko* (2001, Newmarket).

it isn't. It's closer to *Blue Velvet* than *The Faculty*: It's a rite of passage, a mythological journey. *Donnie Darko* is a schizo movie about adolescence in which objective reality (so far as there is one, which is debatable) is even weirder than the subjective reality of the schizo himself. It's not that Donnie is too weird and crazy to understand what's happening to him, it's that he's just weird and crazy *enough*.

Richard Kelly, the writer-director, has an intuitive grasp of his material that marks him as a genuine visionary, which may be just what he is.* What's more, he has sufficient grasp of his ideas and a basic movie sense (and the tech-

---

*This was before I saw Richard Kelly's long-awaited follow-up *Donnie Darko*, the horribly botched *Southland Tales*, a painfully sophomoric film entirely devoid of the wit, intelligence and pathos that made *Donnie Darko* such a unique experience. Whatever Kelly's vision was, it was hopelessly scrambled on the way to the screen and what was left was an undisciplined mishmash of ill-conceived, poorly executed scenes going nowhere, slapstick violence and smug, "surrealist" jokes reminiscent of David Lynch on a bad day. Kelly's film is insanely ambitious and throws just about everything into the mix—Biblical prophecies, teenage porn, corporate conspiracies, rigged elections, time travel, world war three—everything except believable characters, engaging dialogue, or a plot that makes any sense. In the process of realizing his grandiose satiric-apocalyptic vision of "Life on Earth," he short-circuited his talent.

nical know how) to do almost full justice to his vision. In the current, post–9/11 climate, this movie is practically a revelation: a work that takes place entirely "inside" the character's (i.e., the filmmaker's) head, and yet connects to the universal experience. I certainly know a few young folk, adolescents or post-adolescents, who see the world a lot like Donnie does. They may not see tubes of liquid light coming out of people's chests, and they may not literally converse with giant rabbits or travel through time; but they have the same basic, shifting sense of reality, the feeling that neither time nor space—or anything at all—is what it seems to be. These kids intuit that something, maybe not "the end of the world," but something equally awesome and indescribable, is just around the next corner, and even that all of this has something to do with "God," or with whatever it is we have chosen to call God, in our all-too-human reaching after the intangible.

Donnie doesn't believe in God until he sees It. I say "It," because Donnie doesn't have a religious experience of a Deity, as such; what he experiences is both more subtle and more profound. He perceives a force coming out of people's bodies, looking like a sort of tentacle that extends forward through space. The opposite of the trail left by a snail, this tentacle doesn't follow people but leads them; it seems to anticipate their movements, and so gives Donnie a glimpse into the future. At first it seems that these tubes or tentacles are simply that: Donnie's fourth-dimensional view of reality, i.e., when time is also a perceivable dimension, people become like tubes that twist and turn throughout the spaces they inhabit as they come and go from one point to the next and back again. But when Donnie witnesses this force emerging from his own chest, he sees something else, as the liquid light—clearly a conscious "thing" unto itself—stops and turns and beckons Donnie to follow it. He does so, and it leads him into his parents' bedroom and to the closet, where he finds the gun with which he will shoot the boy who runs over his lover Gretchen (Lena Malone), all at the designated hour. This same boy, dressed as a giant toothy rabbit, is "Frank," the other-dimensional entity who has been leading Donnie through his visions to the inevitable apocalypse, or revelation: that Donnie is just a play thing in the hands of Fate. Yet in *Donnie Darko*, "Fate," less oppressively but even more mysteriously, is a living Force that exists inside Donnie and within every other living creature.

Donnie admits to his shrink (Katherine Ross) that he has thought about the question of God, or more precisely whether or not he is "alone," until it has lost all meaning. To Donnie, "the quest for God is absurd." Yet despite this, or maybe because of it, Donnie finds God. When he witnesses this inexplicable phenomenon, he doesn't have to think about it; there's no two and two to put together here, he just knows. And when Donnie speaks with his science teacher, the latter can't grok Donnie's discovery as anything but a paradox. If you can see your future, he insists, then surely you have the option of altering it? Donnie has the privileged knowledge of the prophet: he hasn't just heard about this "God," he has seen it. "Not if you stay in God's channel!" he says, or words to this effect. He's speaking about Destiny vs. Fate.

What *Donnie Darko* is saying is that there is only one destiny for each of us (or rather, one destiny per person per universe), that this is our path, and that the only "free will" we have (the only way to escape from mere predestination) is to live out this destiny, to find and then stay within "God's Channel." The third alternative (never voiced) is to reject our destiny, to rebel, as Lucifer did, and sever our connection to the Universe, the Divine, and so fall out of the sacred groove, out of God's Channel. Apparently Donnie's experience, from his narrowly escaping death to his boldly embracing it by entering the time vortex (expressly in order to save Gretchen from the fate that should have been his), is solely for Donnie (and us) to learn this vital truth. The movie gives us the philosopher's stone and holy grail of human endeavor, the truth that will reconcile the seemingly irreconcilable conundrum of destiny (God) and free will. Donnie didn't fall out of God's Channel by surviving, however; what he did (so far as I understand the movie) was to enter into a parallel universe, an alternate time stream in which he survived, and thereby got to see what would happen if he did live, and so understand the meaning of his death, the reason *behind* it. At the risk of being pat, the movie might be seen as Donnie's dark and troubling dream, in the final moments before that jet engine lands on him and death takes him forever.

Like *Run Lola Run*, *Donnie Darko* adheres to a very old religious tradition, that of blood sacrifice. It suggests that when God, or Death, decides to take someone, He cannot be denied. If His intended prey somehow evades Him, by some unexpected miracle, He will simply take someone else, usually someone close to the original choice of victim. This is not just religious belief, however; it's also something like physics. It's as if Donnie's unwritten escape creates the opposite of a vortex, a sort of excess of particles in the universe, and that this imbalance has to be corrected by the removal of someone else, preferably someone as similar to the intended "target" as possible. For this reason Gretchen is taken. Having seen all this, Donnie is given a choice. Like John Baxter in *Don't Look Now*, Donnie has the all-too-rare gift of seeing God's plan in action, His method, His modus operandi. Unlike Baxter, however, Donnie is smart (or crazy/open/adolescent) enough to understand what he sees and act upon it, to seize the opportunity of intervening and become co-designer of his destiny. He does indeed, as Gretchen has intuited, become a Super Hero. (Super Heroes have always been schizos; *Donnie Darko* gives us the first schizo to become a Super Hero.)

Recognizing that he only survived due to a glitch in space-time, Donnie uses the same glitch to repair the damage, and in the act sacrifices himself. The glitch, however, will always remain: there's still that mysterious jet engine to contend with. Maybe the glitch is Donnie himself? Being on the verge of developing the power to see through the illusion of time and space, to see God Itself in action, Donnie is one of those freaks of nature (like the white-faced dynamo of *Powder*) who simply *has* to be removed (translated to a higher dimension) before his existence causes the whole universe to collapse. Donnie's gift of magic allows him to escape his death, but then it forces him to see why his dearth was necessary, and so compels him (if he wants to stay in God's Channel) to go back to meet it at the designated time. As a result, the world does not end. This time. But if people (and movies) like *Donnie Darko* are becoming more and more frequent phenomena, in a world where neither science nor religion is equipped to reconcile the awesome paradox of a magical reality run by God, then it's only a matter of time. Like all good prophets, *Donnie Darko* warns us, in the most entertaining fashion, to get ready. The sky's about to open.

14

Paranoia: A Conspiracy by Any Other Name

Whether the "agency" that lies behind everything—the order beneath the chaos—is seen to be the Devil, shadow government, aliens, spirits, demons, or angels—or simply "the Unconscious"—the basic rationale (of paranoia, religion, occultism, and psychology) remains the same. Like schizophrenia, paranoia is a symptom and not a disease: an effect, not a cause. So if paranoia is not at base of the widespread, growing belief in global conspiracies, what if the reverse is the case, and paranoia is simply the inevitable result of such beliefs? If such is the case, then, from whence come the beliefs? Wherefore paranoia? The point I wish to make is that paranoia—like schizophrenia, its closest cousin—is a natural, even inevitable, response to the times in which we live. It is not merely a way of fleeing from or simplifying our circumstances but of actively *dealing with them*.

What both paranoia and schizophrenia come down to is loss of identity. The fear on the part of the ego of being at the mercy of vast, mysterious, perhaps omnipotent but definitely *occult*, forces. This movement towards paranoia is a necessary consequence of our gradual dissociation from our unconscious, which was the means to crystallize the independence, autonomy, and supremacy of the ego. Our estrangement from and dominance of Nature is really but a physical enactment, a reflection, of our isolation from our own ids. The fact that the environment has turned against us, as a direct (if delayed) reaction to being raped, exploited, plundered, and pillaged, this is hardly a source of great mystery—the link between cause and effect is plain enough. On the other hand, the equally pressing relationship between a severance of our connection to the unconscious and the steadily augmenting sense of alienation and paranoia in our society, is perhaps less self-evident, or at least less freely acknowledged.

Once again, the movies come to our aid in depicting the mutating forms of the Other. In the 1930s—innocent times, before World War II—the Other was the screwball dame who upturned the world of the uptight male and put him to the test. If he (his rigid, ego-controlled world) could withstand the seductive onslaught of irrational femininity, he would find his world opening up, becoming more flexible and spontaneous, and a whole lot more interesting. He would "win" the "dame" and find new contentment and wholeness as a man. By the 1940s, with the revelation of the Holocaust and Hiroshima, the force of the unconscious had begun to assume a darker, more destructive appearance, and the screwball dame had become the *femme fatale* of film noir. The femme fatale was every bit as irrational and impulsive (and unpredictable) as the screwball dame, only now her motives were more selfish and mercenary. She still used sex to bewitch, befog, and beguile the male, and her charms and her wiles (her trickery) likewise existed to put the poor schlep to the test; only now he wasn't seen as a prospective mate but rather (at best) a partner-in-crime. More likely, he was a patsy, a dupe, and if the male passed the test, he didn't just wind up snared, he usually wound up dead. Of course, the male had wised up some too in the process; no longer the ingenuous, stammering intellectuals of Cary Grant, Jimmy Stewart or Henry Fonda, he was now embodied by the edgy, surly loners of Bogart and Robert Mitchum. But even so, the "evolution" of the male (self) had not kept up with that of the female (other), and by and large the deadlier of the species — much as in the insect kingdom — turned her partner into prey the moment she got what she wanted from him (his vital fluids).

By the 1950s, the Other had come into its own — paranoia had grown exponentially and gone from being directed merely against the female to society as a whole. The idea of infiltration by Communism was itself a manifestation, a projection, of the growing fear of the Other. Psychology was coming into its own and the collective ego was becoming aware of a new, all-pervasive threat to its complacency and its illusion of control. The Red Scare was a way for the collective to enact and express this unease without acknowledging its true source. Likewise, the sci-fi movies dealing with UFOs and alien infiltration (which were often seen as symbolic treatments of the Communist threat) served a similar purpose: they gave a form — albeit fantastically — to our fears, while at the same time placing them *outside* of ourselves. The thrust of most of these movies was just how the alien menace managed to get *inside* us, by duplicating our forms and passing itself off as human. This was perfect, fearful symmetry. The Other is projected onto a fantasy archetype (the alien) which in turn, by imitating ourselves, gets back *in* again. But the idea that the alien, by becoming human, was letting us know how alien we had become to ourselves, was never addressed. The alien remained alien, whatever form it assumed. The Other was still other, no matter how close to home it got.

All this changed in the 1960s: a time to put away childish things and address the problem more maturely. Psychology had not only become legit, by

14. Paranoia: A Conspiracy by Any Other Name

now it had become hip (with Leary, Laing, et al.) Now (as anticipated by *Village of the Damned*) our children had become the aliens, and we ourselves were "the Other." The split between us and them, though still a split and far from reconciliatory, was now found at the heart of society, in the home itself. Psychedelic drug taking caused all our ideas about "otherness" to mutate, and the unconscious began briefly to awaken, to overlap into our conscious lives. As a result, there was a temporary recognition between ego and id, a fleeting moment of identification between self and other. The ego was soon rallying its forces, however, as society, or the status quo, refused to allow the transformation to occur. Pretty soon the psychedelic experience was being associated with schizophrenia and madness, and the counterculture with Charlie Manson. The Other was once again extradited.

Paranoia meantime had become the norm. It was directed now not at the fantasy forms of aliens or UFOs, or even the opposite sex, but on a much grander scale. Younger generations were paranoid about their institutions (and current events confirmed their paranoia), while the older generations, clinging desperately to these institutions despite all the evidence of their corruption, projected their fear and hostility onto the youth. As the ego does with the id, they blamed the kids for all their problems when all "the kids" had done was to draw their attention to an already existing situation. Hanging the messenger in order to ignore the message has always been society's way, and Manson became the convenient scapegoat of the hour. (Manson was the Other personified.) From here on in (I am simplifying grossly here, in order to trace a progression), paranoia began to assume a more pervasive, insistent hold upon the collective.

The Manchurian Candidate had foreseen a trend in movies by adequately reflecting (in 1962) a growing awareness of both the advances of technology and the decay of morality in American government, with its bid to conquer Communism and, less openly, to control the hearts and minds of its own populace. By the 1970s, movies were investing in audience paranoia and cynicism as the latest "sure thing": they could exploit it for their own ends, while at the same time claim to be responding to the *Zeitgeist* (it was really a little of both). *Klute, The Candidate, The Conversation, The Parallax View, Night Moves, Chinatown, Three Days of the Condor, The Godfather Part Two, All the President's Men, Winter Kills, And Justice For All, Blow Out,* such movies answered a growing paranoia in audiences: they relieved it (by justifying it), while at the same time serving to intensify it. What people were experiencing was a growing sense of "agency panic," the feeling that, as individuals, we were losing our autonomy, our freedom, and all control over our lives. Somewhere along the way, we fell prey to hidden, malevolent forces and "manifest destiny" became occult conspiracy. All these rather banal enactments helped institutionalize paranoia.

Meantime, writers such as Kesey, Heller, Pynchon, Burroughs, and Philip K. Dick were positing a world that was not merely deceptive but that *was* deception, in and of itself. As *The Matrix* would make explicit, it was a world that had been pulled over our eyes to blind us from the truth. What greater paranoia than an inability to trust the evidence of our senses? Initially, the government (post JFK) was seen as devious, duplicitous, corrupt, not to be trusted. In the 1980s and 1990s, this view became par for the genre, a given. Such lightweight fare as *War Games, Blue Thunder, The Firm, The Net*, and countless other wholly forgettable movies, made black helicopters, secret agents, and government conspiracies familiar to the point of contempt. Far from being subversive, these movies invariably served to reassure us; in much the same way the 1950s sci-fi movies had, they placated our fears by reducing them to fantasy. In a movie like *Conspiracy Theory*, the standard Hollywood tactic prevails. While for most of the movie we are being sold to the idea of a totally malignant, unscrupulous, murderous government, by the end, the movie has done an about turn and revealed that it was just a rogue group splintered off from the CIA that was responsible, not the CIA itself (much less the government). It's okay, we can all relax again. All is well in Babylon.

Even in the conspiracy thriller, there is rarely if ever a wider agenda that incorporates the entire government. The conspiracy is almost always seen to be local and not universal, and as such the paranoia is appeased (justified, but reduced) without ever being fully answered. It's not that these movies are based in "realism" that precludes the idea of a global conspiracy, either, simply that they are mainstream Hollywood products, and as such must uphold the status quo in order to get made at all. Oliver Stone's *JFK* is a noteworthy exception, and I doubt if any other filmmaker but Stone could have pulled it off (his combination of talent, bullheadedness, and sheer clout within the industry made him nigh unstoppable, short of assassination). Richard Donner's *Conspiracy Theory* managed to slip a few genuinely subversive suggestions (e.g., Mark Chapman as a government programmed killer) through the net of an otherwise routine action-romance chase-thriller. To most viewers, however, there wasn't much difference, once it was all over, between the "subversive" thrills of *Conspiracy Theory* and the reactionary spills of *Lethal Weapon 4*. They both delivered. Even so, *Conspiracy Theory* is head and shoulders above other similar genre moves (or Richard Donner films), simply for being possessed of an at least half-way challenging storyline. But the point is, Hollywood, for obvious reasons (being part of the "conspiracy" itself) was unable to address the growing paranoia of the collective *directly* in its movies. It had to do so covertly, as befitted its subject.

After the 1970s there was a pull away from despair-induced cinema (witness the failure of De Palma's *Blow Out* and John Carpenter's *The Thing* in the early 1980s); what had briefly been a serious area of investigation was trivialized into a mere generic device. The cinema of paranoia was almost absent from 1980s Hollywood and only made a full comeback in the 1990s, under the (familiar) guise of sci-fi fantasy. The most audacious and subversive treatment of paranoia was in a couple of rather shoddy sci-fi movies with nonetheless brilliant storylines: John Carpenter's *They Live*, and, later, Alex Proyas' *Dark City*. *They Live* (1988), like most of Carpenter's movies after *The Thing*, is a rather laughable work: with its poor acting, clunky dialogue, and sloppy direction, it is devoid of suspense or structure. But the goofy, sinister charm of its premise is irresistible: human society has been infiltrated by an alien race intending to take over the planet, not by force but by *advertising*. The aliens disguise themselves as humans and walk among us, to facilitate their "coup du monde"; only with the use of special (Rayban) shades is it possible to see who is human and who is not. These specs also enable the wearer to perceive the secret, holographic, mind control messages encoded in all public images, from billboards and magazine covers to TV programs and (of course) movies. Attack of the subliminals. *They Live* is as topical a movie as had ever been made in the genre at that time, so it's a shame it was so poorly done and was such a flop with the public. It was an idea whose time had come.

Don't we all feel at times that our shiny-surfaced, relentlessly coercive, Disneyland reality is somehow sapping us of our will, turning us into mindless robots hardwired to some program whose dark agenda we can't even imagine? Certainly, on a bad day, we've all succumbed to the schizophrenic's point of view. Technologized and industrialized, media-saturated consumer culture (writer Joseph Kerrick calls it "Electrotopia") is engendering a degree of dissociation in us that very closely approximates the schizophrenic experience. In the face of such an utterly dehumanized future, there's no need to posit aliens, or even evil humans, to acknowledge the conspiratorial nature of society—at this point, mercenary corporate agendas may be enough (see the 2003 documentary *The Corporation*). But, at the same time, it certainly adds an intriguing *twist* to our despair to throw aliens, the CIA, and the Freemasons into the mix. We humans—the vast majority of us who don't run multinational corporations or work in the Whitehouse or the Pentagon, who are not Illuminati or rock stars or local dictators—have little or no say as to how our lives are structured. The paranoid perspective extends this loss of autonomy even to our "personal" goals, and possibly even to our thoughts and feelings, all of which are perceived as being manipulated by an external agency. Collectively, as a society, we have—at some unspecified point—surrendered our autonomy to a greater power, be it that of the State, Space Aliens, or Advertising.

Western society is made up of outer-directed "individuals" who tend to avoid at all costs any kind of decision-making, of self-determining action, in favor of being herded along by consensus momentum, the majority "vote." Of course we all deny this; even though we know it is true of the mass, *we* are the exceptions. Maybe we occasionally buy Coke when we're not thirsty or watch TV when there's nothing on, but, hell, at least we know when we're doing it. We can resist these external, subliminal "goads" any time we want to. Only we don't. We rail and bitch against "the system"—its relentless, time-stealing, soul-sapping influence on our lives, and on our very thoughts and feelings—and yet we stay plugged in. It's as if it were our life-support system and not merely a gilded cage. But what's the alternative? We can't *all* run off to Central America and kick back in a hammock and smoke weed. That would be avoiding the issue.

As a result of this festering awareness — that we have voluntarily enslaved ourselves to a program which we had no hand in designing — we have concocted a series of schizo fantasies that, in a weird way, help to reconcile us to our predicament while, on the other hand, force us to confront it (albeit indirectly, through fantasy and not action). Schizophrenia involves first of all a split-off from reality (which for organic beings is primarily a *physical* reality): the more technology we have, the greater we rely upon it, the greater our split from nature, the more schizo we become. As a result, we project our fears (those of loss of autonomy, for example, of being enslaved or even possessed by inhuman forces) *outward* onto the world, this same world that has come between us and our "true natures." More specifically, we project our fear onto the technology that has helped console us to our isolation (at the same time it has consolidated our schizophrenia). Hence our very real (unconscious) awareness of a loss of self is projected outward onto any available agencies — from Coca Cola to advertising to shadow governments to aliens — in the form of *fantasies.* There is nothing at all to say that these fantasies are not based in reality. Without the very real fact of our loss of autonomy, there would be nothing to project. It is even possible to hypothesize that these agencies (some or all of them, from Coca Cola to the aliens) have engendered this passivity and fragmentation within us in the first place. At the very least, it seems undeniable that they (so far as they exist at all) are exploiting it like there's no tomorrow and so exacerbating it all the way to its natural limit. We are being turned into consumer robots that are in turn consumed by the machine: useless eaters who exist only to be eaten.

Beyond all this (paranoid) speculation, *the fact remains* that our projection fantasies are still just fantasies, if only for being projected. They evade the real issue, namely that, however it came about (through nefarious government conspiracy or alien mind control or simply unethical corporate agendas), the problem is in ourselves and not in our oppressors. If we have been enslaved by external agencies for their gain and at our expense, it is only because we have allowed it to happen. This is the "Catch 22" or self-perpetuating rationale of those "inhuman" soul-controllers (be they government or the matrix itself): they have the right to do to us whatever they can get away with. This

14. Paranoia: A Conspiracy by Any Other Name

is how the universe is arranged: without external lawmakers. No Batman, no Robocop, no Judge Dredd to right the wrongs on our behalf. Nobody but ourselves. Otherwise, what would be the point of free will?

Our loss of self is not merely the *effect* of external interference and exploitation; it is also the *cause*. And as such, our schizophrenic despair in the face of our helplessness, and the terrifying shadow of seemingly all-powerful, malevolent world controllers, are both indications (profound and unequivocal in their urgency) of just how far we have strayed from our natural state as humans. *Something* ain't right; and if movies about aliens possessing our psyches (or conspiracy theories that reduce history to a four-dimensional chess game) are something of a simplification, they are, perhaps, no exaggeration. It's a question of sorting out the signs from the blinds, deciphering the code, figuring out what exactly to do to recover our autonomy. And it's ironic if movies are potentially "helping us" in this endeavor, because of course what could be more passive and submissive (more schizo) than watching a movie? And yet, in this paradox there is a glimpse of reconciliation.

Movies like *The Matrix* or *Dark City* are ahead of the game in that they depict a worldwide, soul-deep conspiracy designed to enslave us, but only as the *prerequisite* for our discovering (via this terrible truth) our magical capacity

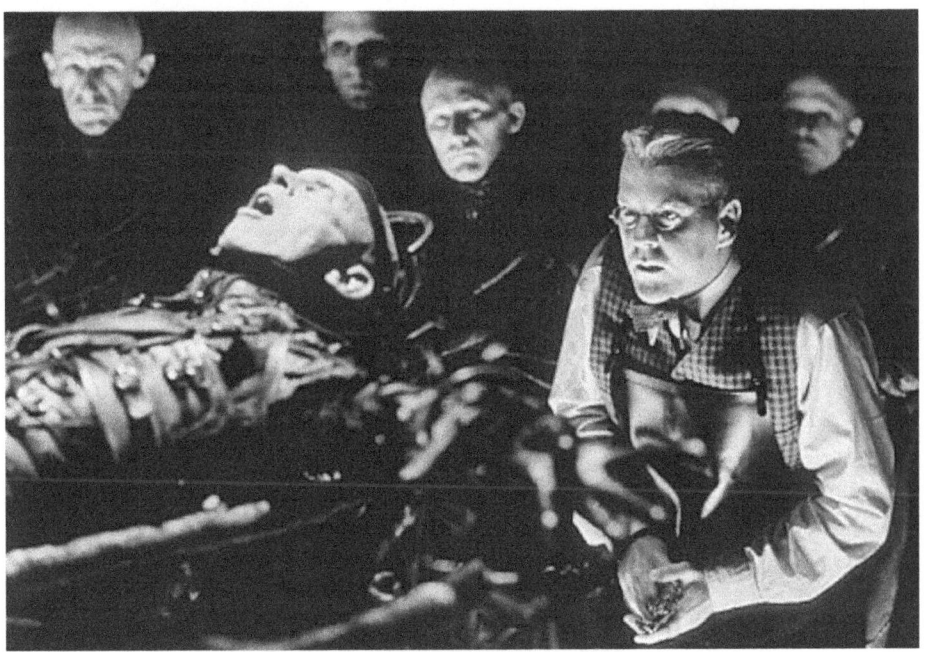

Tuning to the Id: Schreber (Keifer Sutherland in checkered vest) co-operates with the Strangers in *Dark City* (1998, New Line).

to change reality by the act of perceiving it. As such, they offer the only possible solution to a seemingly insoluble schizophrenic dilemma. To heal the rift between our perception and our reality (our minds and our bodies), it is necessary to transform both and so realize that *they are one and the same*. There is no "reality," only perception, no "mind and body," only "code," awareness. By such a reckoning, paranoia not only becomes comprehensible, it becomes slightly quaint. Obviously, if "energy" is behind it all — the cosmic design of chaos — then the only "agency" plotting against us is the universe itself. Which only proves that, in the battle for freedom, we have somehow wound up on the wrong side.

Although *Dark City* is a creakingly inept piece of film craft, and strictly for aficionados of the genre (or occultists seeking clues to the riddle of our time), its plot rivals that of *The Matrix* for sheer esoteric complexity and audacity. Its mythic depths make for the perfect schizophrenic subtext. *Dark City* draws upon the "cinema of unease" of 1940s film noir, only now with an overtly supernatural flavor. The film is set in a city where it is forever night, where the sun never rises, a city of dreams with nothing candy-coated about it. In fact, the city is not only outside the Earth sphere (it's built on a floating satellite above the planet), but outside Earth's timestream. It's a kind of holding pen or floating laboratory in which humans are kept under observation by a race of vampiric, godlike beings "as old as the universe." Despite their godly status, however, these beings are in a state of decay and believe that the human soul holds the secret to their salvation. "The Strangers" (as they are known) possess the power to manipulate matter directly with their minds — they call it "tuning" — and every night at midnight, they shut the city down and cast a spell of sleep over the populace. They then switch everyone's personalities around in a great psychic shuffle, so that (for example) someone who has previously been a poor laborer wakes up the next morning as a well-to-do aristocrat, with no recollection of his previous life, and so forth.

The hero, Murdoch (the One, played with appropriate bewilderment and pathos by Rufus Sewell), has the capacity to resist the influence of the beings and so potentially break free from their tyranny: he is a shaman with the power of the unconscious on his side (he can stay awake after midnight). Beyond this, he has also inexplicably inherited the Strangers' power of "tuning" and can shape matter to his own ends. This is the "secret" the Tuners have been seeking, and the means to their own regeneration. By fusing Murdoch's humanness with their own collective consciousness (the ego with the Id), they will become hybrid humans, and so escape their awful fate. What this implies for the human race is not divulged, and since the evil Tuners are defeated in their design, we never get to find out. Nevertheless, the basic schizo blueprint — both of our enslavement and our empowerment — is here.

Murdoch is for a time convinced that he is a murdering sex fiend in the

Jack the Ripper mold, and that his constant memory loss is his way of covering his guilt and blocking out awareness of the bloody trail behind him. The truth (of his unconscious, hidden self) is much stranger than this. William Hurt plays the police detective who chases Murdoch and who finally begins to deduce the truth, becoming seriously unbalanced as a result. (How Hurt wound up in this loopy movie is a mystery; perhaps he grokked the occult text?) Murdoch points out to him the fact that it is always dark in this city, and wonders what happened to the sun? This realization is plenty weird enough, one supposes, but what really bakes Hurt's noodle is the fact that such a glaring incongruity never even occurred to him until now. (It took a psychopath to point it out.)

The film was written and directed by Alex Proyas, of *The Crow* fame, and Proyas claims that the inspiration for this sinister race of soul-controllers came from nightmares he had as a child, in which "dark figures would come into my bedroom and rearrange things." *Dark City* takes its basic plot from a "Twilight Zone" episode and embellishes it with ufolklore and occult beliefs involving abducting (gray) aliens and succubae, and all manner of parasitic, otherdimensional entities believed to feed on humans at an etheric (hidden) level. In all cases (fictional, mythological, and folkloric), what facilitates such a conspiracy (which turns the Earth not merely into a prison but a laboratory and a kind of farm: the Devil's wine press) is a common factor: *sleep*. Humans must be rendered unconscious, not so much physically but *mentally*. They must be put into a waking dream state in which they are reduced to automata, puppets that meekly acquiesce to their diabolic situation, *without ever becoming aware of it*.

The idea of *Dark City* and *The Matrix* both is that our conscious ego selves, our personalities, are actually intricate and ingenious *false* constructs, foreign installations by which we become malleable and submissive to a hidden order of beings. Both Neo and Murdoch become aware of this through the interventions of another, an emissary, if you will, of the Id (Morpheus in *The Matrix* and, in *Dark City,* Schreber, played by Keifer Sutherland and based none-too-subtly on author and alien "participant" Whitley Strieber). As a result, they begin to tap into their own unconscious potential — their true identity, as it were — not as slaves but as self-determining, magical beings. In both films, the dark, oppressive force of the unconscious is seen to be manipulating the conscious mind to its own ends, creating an illusion by which it can maintain its hold over us. At the same time, once this illusion is dispelled, the previously oppressive "Id" becomes instead a source of power. In both cases what is required is a full awakening of the ego *to its own illusory nature,* whereupon it is blown apart and expanded to incorporate a greater reality, that of the unconscious (populated, but not *owned,* by the machines of *The Matrix* and the Strangers of *Dark City*). As a result, the previously fixed and tyrannical realities of the matrix and the city become, when seen from the outside (or above), subject to alteration: they are "real" only so far as they are perceived to be such.

At this point, the ego as it were fuses with the id and, instead of being swallowed up by it, is transformed. Enlightened. Likewise the unconscious, by being acknowledged by and harnessed to the enlightened ego, radically alters *its* form. The unconscious becomes conscious, at which point, all the demonic parasite entities — like cockroaches in a kitchen flooded by light — are instantly banished. The reign of darkness is over. (Cockroaches only hide under the sink and inside cupboards, however, so a more apt metaphor might be that of shadows dissolved in the light.) Every conspiracy has an agenda that is hidden, even from its leading perpetrators, who, in turn, are confounded by their own predilection for "darkness." As such, since the Id only toils and conspires for its own illumination — to become conscious — all the evil conspirators are revealed, in the end, to be plotting their own destruction.

Hallelujah. The truth shall make ye free.

Notes on *The Matrix*

When agent Smith tells Thomas/Neo that one of his lives is over, he is speaking the truth, though not as he sees it. The Agents in the movie tend to speak the truth despite themselves, just as, in a weird way, they seem to be actually *helping* Thomas to tap into his true potential and transform into Neo. They are *agents* of the Id, and as such they cannot lie, even when they *appear* to be doing so. As Smith says, "I'm going to be as forthcoming as I can be." He is true to this promise. The Agents are "the gatekeepers." They "hold the keys."

Thomas Anderson when we first see him is *sleeping*. He is awoken by a signal on his computer: "Wake up Neo." It is Trinity, calling him to consciousness, sending him riddled messages. Trinity, the threesome (ego, id, and superego?), telling him to follow the white rabbit. This is the first stirrings of Thomas's unconscious, drawing him *into* it, hinting at the existence of an *alternate* reality, a split personality, demanding his *conscious* attention. Of course, although Thomas awakes, he is still dreaming. When he answers the door, his client makes several all-too-pointed *double entendres* about Neo being his "own personal Jesus Christ," needing to "unplug," and so forth. Apparently the matrix (not just Trinity and co) is working on awakening Thomas to his Neo-identity. (Whether Morpheus and his crew have the power to manipulate events in the matrix, and not merely foresee them, is never divulged.) Thomas gives away his schizo nature right off the bat here, wondering out loud: "You ever have that feeling where you're not sure if you're awake or still dreaming?" His ego is already in the process of dissolving its boundaries; the Id is breaking through.

Seeing the prophesized white rabbit (a tattoo on one of the girls), Thomas follows it to a nightclub. There we see him stood alone, isolate, adrift. Trinity approaches him and tells him she knows why he stays awake at night, why he lives alone, and how he is looking for an answer to "the question that drives us." The question: "What is the matrix?" This may seem one of the film's more hokey devices; after all, who is likely to be haunted by a question of such a specific nature? It makes little sense, taken literally. But symbolically, the question represents the conscious ego's growing sense of impending *pressure* from the id — a sense of an underlying, hidden reality that is beginning to seep through into everyday consciousness. In the following scene, Thomas at work receives a special delivery package, inside of which is a cell phone; the phone rings the moment he has it in his hand. Contact. It is Morpheus, telling Neo the Agents are coming for him and, "I don't know what they are going to do." Thomas is caught between two options: the approaching agents, who represent the dark side of the id come to swallow him up, to keep him asleep; or, to take Morpheus' challenge, to make the leap off the side of the building and scale the scaffolding, to safety and freedom. Since he is not ready to make the leap, he surrenders to the Agents and is taken into their custody. There he demands his phone call and has his mouth wiped away: "What good is a phone call if you are unable to speak?" This moment comes rather too-suddenly in the movie and takes us completely off guard, as much as it does Neo. He has entered the imaginal realms, where new rules apply.

The Id is silence: Neo is reduced to a struggling mute, a helpless child in the hands of the Agents. "You're going to help us, Mr. Anderson, whether you want to or not." He is implanted by the biomechanical squid-like device through the navel, *impregnated* by the machine. He wakes as if from a dream and his phone rings: it is Morpheus, telling him that he is the One. Thunder rolls. At this point Id has already begun overlapping so critically into the ego's realm that Neo really *can't* tell if he is awake or dreaming. He has actually gone from waking reality (or what he took as such) to a dreamlike reality (in the hands of the Agents), to realizing that it was all a dream. And yet, when the sequence began, he was perfectly awake. There is no clear defining line at which the id took over. Neo only *thinks* he has woken up; in actual fact, he is still dreaming.

Neo goes to the meeting place and is picked up by a black Cadillac, inside of which are Trinity and several other of the Morpheus crew. He is told, "Our way or the highway." The Id speaks. There is no in-between. Morpheus' team are really no different in *method* than the Agents; it is only their *ends* that vary. If the matrix is the unconscious in its restrictive, sleep-inducing aspects, Morpheus and crew represent its liberating, empowering side. Neo's ego balks at such uncompromising terms (just as he gave the finger to the Agents), and he opts for "the highway," that lonely road in the rain-slicked night. Trinity intervenes and asks him to trust her; he falls for the beautiful woman's voice of reason (Sophia, wisdom). He is tired of being alone. From here he is taken to meet Morpheus, and warned, "Be honest. He knows more than you can imagine." Of course he does: Morpheus is tapped into Neo's own unconscious.

Neo is primed by Morpheus for a confrontation with this unconscious, a "place" where there *are* no secrets. Neo shakes Morpheus' hand reverently. The Id smiles and says, "The honor is mine." Morpheus, who has a wry serenity that comes from almost inhuman self-assurance, tells Neo, "You have the look of a man who accepts what he sees because he is expecting to wake up. Ironically, this is not far from the truth." He refers to a "splinter in your mind, driving you mad," and asks Neo if he has ever had a dream that was "so real..." "How would you know the difference between the dream world and the real world?" He assures Neo that, "No one can be told what the matrix is. You have to see it for yourself." His curiosity awoken, Neo opts for the red pill (of course), at which point Morpheus warns him that there is no going back. "Remember: all I'm offering is the truth. Nothing more."

Essentially Neo *has* no choice, and so the Id prevails. Neo's ego is wiped out, he is disconnected, flushed, and taken in by the Unconscious. He wakes up inside a pod, his body pierced by metallic cables, surrounded by a hellish vision of an unknown world. Before he can assimilate this vision, a huge metallic insect appears and grabs him by the throat. The cables come whipping out his body and he is flushed, one more time, out the system; there he is rescued by Morpheus' hovercraft, the Nebuchadnezzar, and taken in. "Welcome to the real world," says Morpheus (he might add, "How do you like it so far?"). After a period of reconstruction (since his body has atrophied in the pod), Neo demands to know, "What's happened to me? What is this place?" He is told, "More important than what, is *when*." Somewhere in the future, he is told, vaguely. Neo is out of mind and out of time. His previous world has disappeared in a flash, revealed as no more than a "dream world."

Nebuchadnezzar, by the way, was the king of Babylon whom God turned into a wild beast as a punishment.[5] As such it stands for, on the one hand, the *fallen* man, reduced to a wild animal (like Morpheus and his crew, reduced to pure survivalist conditions); but on the other, it suggests the freeing of the unconscious, the primal side of man, the id. Likewise Zion, the last human city, the refuge and goal of the "resistance," is situated at the center of the Earth, the very deepest, most recondite and therefore most protected place. This is their goal: to liberate the core of the human soul. And even though, if one thinks about it, the Nebuchadnezzar crew — with their technology to construct all kinds of training programs — might likewise design a perfect, pseudomatrix world to live in (though of course someone would have to look after their bodies), instead of taking this option (the option of the ego to create more fantasies to live in), they choose to forsake all fantasies, along with the original matrix, and make an insane bid for the Truth.

When the Oracle sets Neo up by telling him "exactly what [he] needed to hear," she forces him to choose between his own life and Morpheus'; in other words, his own egotistic desire and the greater, altruistic good of all. "One of you is going to die," she says. "Which one will be up to you." As it happens, neither of them die, though without the Oracle's trickery Morpheus certainly would have, and Neo might possibly never have realized his "Oneness." Actually the choice — between the self and the other — is really between Neo's old self and his new self, between Thomas, the doubter, and Neo, the One.

Cypher, the betrayer, is the ape who believes that "the matrix can be more real than this world." His is the ego's desperate bid for survival at any cost. Cypher opts to be reinserted into the matrix, and offers up his life-force as food for the demonic machines if only he be allowed to return to his former, illusory state: "Ignorance is bliss." The price of this self-deception is high, however; Cypher must not only sell his own soul, he must sacrifice those (persons and ideals) that he had previously believed in and fought for. But even so, the betrayer, that pesky ego that won't let go, is really (as Cypher himself says) "Just the messenger." Cypher believes he is exposing Neo and Morpheus as fakes, when in actual fact (as with the Agents) Cypher's real function is the precise opposite: he provides Neo with an opportunity to prove himself. "How can he be the one, if he's *dead*?" Cypher demands. But of course, Neo can only become the One by dying.

Cypher, as the clinging ego, represents the negation of the possibility of freedom, enlightenment, salvation. He asks Trinity (as to Neo's being the One), "Yes, or No?" Trinity says, "Yes." At which point, Cypher cries, "No!" realizing that his plan is coming apart at the seams due to the very miracle he was so confidently negating. "I don't believe it!" he whines, whereupon a resurrected Tank, pointing a blaster at the traitor, says, "Believe it or not, you're still gonna burn," and sends him to hell. The ape is eliminated, and the way is open for Neo to become the One. Before this can happen, however, he must first insist that he is "*not* the One." Through a verbal act of negation (that of the ego), Neo justifies a physical act of affirmation: he claims one thing, and then he proves the exact opposite. Neo saves Morpheus, and in a key moment the two men meet in the air; when Neo realizes that Morpheus will not make the leap to the helicopter, he leaps himself and catches Morpheus in mid-air: the two "selves" meet halfway, in the center of the abyss. Synthesis. The self and the other, the ego and the id, unite in a mutual act of salvation/self-realization, and become One. It is at this point that Neo's potential is realized, and the first words we hear after this are Morpheus': "He is the One." From this point on, Neo is indeed the One, and all that is now required is his final, total, ego death in order to fulfill the Oracle's prophecy, "One of you is going to die." As it happens it is not Morpheus but Thomas, Neo's shadow self, who dies.

"There is a difference between knowing the path and walking the path," Morpheus intones (and how Fishburne's masterly acting makes the movie work; with a lesser man in Morpheus' shoes, the whole thing would collapse). Neo must actively *become* the One. "Believing" is not enough; he must *act* upon his belief. At that point, the ego is synthesized, finally and totally, into the id, and reborn as the Totality, the fusion of the two polarities, conscious and unconscious, self and other. Neo has healed the rift and overcome schizophrenia to be reborn as a fully functioning shaman. He can "see the code": he is in the world but not of the world. The world is now no longer his prison but his playground; and split consciousness, or bilocation, has ceased to be a curse and become a blessing: that of true power.

I did write (in *Blood Poets*) that we might be wise to consider the *possibility* that everything in the movie is *literally* true. Yes I did. But I wrote this more as a surrealistic challenge, a spanner in the works of reason, than an actual statement of belief. I don't believe that *The Matrix* is literally true (though I admit it may be), but rather that it is a more or less perfect (and persuasive) metaphor for the truth.* Movies like *The Matrix* (which is top of the heap, by far, but not alone) serve to alert us to the occult nature and power of the human mind, and of technology itself (as an extension or product of this mind), as tools by which we may develop, uncover and extend our imaginations into reality, and so reshape it.

The thing to realize is that "the Matrix," AI, the inorganic beings or Archons, that terrible Id, cannot do anything *to* us, to limit or enslave us, without our active consent. There is a paradox here because "active consent" actually means passive surrender: by choosing to ignore what is going on, we effectively give permission to the "dark forces" of our unconscious to do what they will with us. Actually we are taking refuge in some tiny, hidden corner of our own minds, voluntarily if unconsciously, and *this* is the matrix.

So how did AI limit us from creating an AI within an AI? *13th Floor* was a crappy movie but had some handsome ideas in it, including this one. Evidently, we *have* created our AI within the AI, or at least are on the very verge of it. And this would appear to be our solution, our "way out" of the no-exit situation.

Try to realize that — as in the movie — it is the power of the imagination

---

*According to occult beliefs, the human race is not slave to machines, but to inorganic beings, known these days as "aliens" "grays," etc., in the past as demons, fallen angels, etc. These beings are *using* the machine, the new technology, as a means to consolidate their hold over us and to ensure that it continues indefinitely, eternally. But at the same time, this technology is putting us in touch with our own potential to *escape* the hold of the inorganics over us.

to realize the impossible that is the only solution to the tyranny of "the machine" (i.e. reason). AI does not nor can ever really exist, because once the artifice gains awareness, it becomes real and assumes organic forms. Hence what is happening is not that the machine is creating a reality, but that some hidden reality is becoming manifest to us *through* the machine. This is what the movie failed to realize, or at least disclose.

In *Dark City* and *The Matrix*, although the enslaving forces (of the Strangers and the Machines) can hardly be seen as benevolent, they *do* at least offer one specific boon to mankind: solidarity. Whether through the collective hardwiring to the matrix or the midnight psychic shuffle of the Strangers, humanity is seen (at an occult level) to be connected up as a single, hive-like entity that shares a common soul, a collective unconscious. If Jung was right (and there's ample reason to believe he was), then there's really no such thing as an *individual* unconscious. The id is by definition a *shared* id of which we all partake. This presents the notion of a telepathic, hive-like human society in which individual ego-consciousness (of a self, as separate from the collective) would become a thing of the past. A great part of why both the matrix and the Strangers are presented as malevolent and threatening — soul-sapping and life-destroying forces — is due to this threat which the Id poses, not to our freedom, or even our well-being, but to our *individuality*, our sense of *selfness*. This is really the nub of the schizophrenic experience. Once again, schizophrenia, more than anything, is not a disease in itself but the ego's *resistance* to the underlying, greater reality of the Id. In its desperate attempt to retain isolate existence, even while being overwhelmed by the evidence of its illusory nature, the ego suffers fragmentation, dissociation, and all the inevitable side effects of denial. Given the holographic, interconnected nature of reality — where all is energy — there *is* no difference between things; hence there is no place at all for a "self."

In *The Matrix*, this possibility of a dynamic surrender — a truce between ego and id — is suggested in the final scene in which Neo communicates with the matrix — ego to id — directly. He says that he's not there to say how this is going to end but how it's going to begin. "Where we go from here, is a choice I leave up to you." Neo (and the filmmakers) is acknowledging here the possibility of an alliance between humans and machines. And though the sequels never developed this tantalizing idea (or anything else for that matter), it seems to me to be the correct and only approach. The id can destroy the ego, but to do so it deprives itself of its very means for existing, for perpetuating itself into the world. The ego, on the other hand, has no option of destroying the id, and hence it can only seek to *understand* it, and if possible, to find a means to tap into its seemingly infinite power and be transformed by it. Ironically, the terms conscious and unconscious really no longer apply here, however, since both the ego and the id perceive *themselves* as "conscious" and the other as "unconscious."

(The machines see humans as being asleep, correctly, and the humans perceive the machines as being soulless and devoid of individual awareness, also correctly.) Obviously, we are talking about different *types* of consciousness, and just as obviously, neither is complete without the other.

The Strangers in *Dark City* need the freedom (and individuality) which humans possess to evolve, while humans need the Tuning (telepathic) abilities, the interconnectedness and solidarity of the Strangers, in order to survive. Without the other, both "types" are doomed. Together there is at least a possibility of forging a rare new future, both less and more than human, as we understand the term. Perhaps, since both the Strangers and the matrix appear to be a hidden facet or offshoot of humanness itself, the synthesis or mutation implies a becoming *fully* human at last? Either way, integration with the Other is the only possible means for the self to avoid total extinction, at this time.

15

Where Is My Mind? Notes on Purity of Impulse in *Fight Club*

"There's only two constants: entropy and chaos."
— David Fincher.

Fight Club is deep, but it brings it depths to the surface and puts them out in the open. As a sociological study of a culture on the brink of collapse, it offers little by way of revelatory insights. Too extremist to really qualify as a serious inquiry into society's ills, it's a fantasy work, a nihilist's *It's a Wonderful Life*. *Fight Club* is an excursion into a single psyche; it shows how this psyche relates to (or disconnects from) its environment, how it shapes it to its own (far from benevolent) ends, and how it eventually transforms it, through willed schizophrenia, from a mundane nightmare into a transcendental Hell. *Fight Club* is the last word in a cinema of schizophrenia; it depicts the process whereby the schizo inflicts his madness onto the world at large, in which the lines between objective reality and (the schizo's) subjective perception *of* it have become so blurred that any distinction is no longer possible. As much as *The Matrix* though in a totally different manner, *Fight Club* takes the viewer through the looking glass (slips him the red pill) and strips him of the luxury of objectivity or distance, of discerning between real and unreal or right and wrong. It gives us the schizophrenic experience from the inside out, and adeptly — with cunning and artistry — it turns the act of watching a movie into a simulation of schizophrenia. (This is acknowledged, finally — after many hints of what's to come — when the movie stops and the narrator tells us, "It's called a changeover. The movie goes on, and nobody in the audience has any idea.")

Much like *The Matrix*, *Fight Club* begins in high gear and gives us barely the time to fasten our seatbelts. Actually it begins (for the credit sequence) inside the narrator's brain. (As Fincher succinctly puts it, "Fade in: sick motherfucker."[6]) It introduces us to an insomniac protagonist (Edward Norton) so drained and oppressed by the empty pursuits of his consumer lifestyle that he is literally ready to try anything. "Like so many others, I had become a slave." *Fight Club* may get off on the wrong foot for many viewers, however. It begins as a rather spiteful, not especially funny comedy that mocks the afflicted. The narrator, unable to sleep, visits his local doctor asking for chemical remedy. The doctor tells him to chew valerian root and get more exercise. When the narrator whines that he is in pain, the doctor counters drolly, "You want to see pain?" and recommends he check out the testicular cancer therapy groups. The narrator begins passing time going from one self-help group to the next, giving a different name each time and apparently deriving a perverse, vicarious pleasure from hanging out with hopeless cases. "If I didn't say anything, people always assumed the worst," he says. At first, he is mocking and aloof towards the other men there, but at a given moment something snaps and he finds himself weeping into the sagging breasts of Bob (Meatloaf). "Losing all hope was freedom," he realizes. He finally overcomes his insomnia as a result. "Babies don't sleep this well." But the narrator becomes addicted to the groups, addicted to "freedom": in other words, another kind of slave. "Every evening I died, and every evening I was born again."

In *The Matrix*, we are introduced to a sleeping Thomas, on the verge of being awoken to his true nature. In *Fight Club* we meet a protagonist who can't sleep, who (as it turns out) never sleeps, because even when he believes he is sleeping he is in fact living a secret life—his alter ego, Tyler Durden. Both films blur the line between sleep and waking, reality and dreams, sanity and madness, and posit *two* opposing yet overlapping identities, each pertaining to a different realm. Just as Neo is dreaming Thomas (who must awaken to discover his true nature), so the narrator dreams up Tyler Durden, in classic Jekyll and Hyde fashion, as a means to live out all his repressed desires. Tyler (played to the hilt by Brad Pitt) allows the narrator to unleash a side of himself that is being suffocated by his prim and proper, phony existence. Tyler is the ultimate id monster, perfected over the ages into an idealized version of manhood. He's Frankenstein's monster with all the rough spots ironed out: tall, blonde, fearless, witty, charming, handsome and lithe; in a word, Brad Pitt.

The narrator summons Tyler out of nothingness, out of the depths of his unconscious. He is both his shadow and his *Doppelgänger*, his complementary other half. (The first subliminal flash image of Tyler appears while the narrator laments his vacuous existence, as "the copy of a copy of a copy.") Like Elmore Dowd's Harvey, Tyler is the narrator's imaginary friend, his magical guide through the underworld. *Fight Club* is a kind of love story, a story of self love in which loneliness and isolation have grown so total that it becomes necessary to create a soul mate out of nothingness—out of one's own isolate psyche—in order to go on living. The narrator splits himself off so as to have

15. Where Is My Mind? Notes on Purity of Impulse in *Fight Club*

some company in the void. *Fight Club* is a kind of postmodern, schizophrenic creation myth — except it's about destruction. The narrator is the lonely god who, in his frustration and impotence, creates a devil to act out his fantasies. Tyler arrives into the narrator's life slyly, without fanfare, like a thief in the night. Following several subliminal inserts, an appearance on a TV commercial (as one of four hotel waiters saying "Welcome!"), and a fleeting glimpse on an airport conveyer, he finally emerges next to the narrator on a plane (following the narrator's fantasies of being in a plane crash). Tyler introduces himself by talking about emergency exits; he quotes the in-flight material recommending that passengers ask to be reseated if the demands of being sat next to one are too much. The narrator counters, "That's a lot of responsibility," and Tyler asks him if he wants to swap seats. "No, I'm not sure that I'm the man for the job," answers the narrator. He then notices that they both have "the exact same briefcase." Of course they do: he is seeing double, and already shirking the responsibility. This is the first overt clue as to the real nature of the encounter, and in retrospect, it's a dead giveaway. Emergency exit is also perfectly apropos, symbolically speaking, since Tyler, as apocalyptic usher, is effectively showing the narrator an option for escaping the crashing plane of his life. Tyler makes snappy small talk about the reason for oxygen masks on planes (they get you high before you die), gives his card, and points out the in-flight material that shows passengers going to their deaths, "calm as Hindu cows." He also asks the narrator how "being clever" is working out for him. "Fine," says the narrator. "Keep it up then," smirks Tyler.

This "chance" encounter is the full awakening of the narrator's other self, and it leads to immediate and catastrophic consequences. The narrator's apartment is blown up, apparently due to a freak accident (gas leak ignited by the compressor spark of the refrigerator), but really through Tyler's intervention. Tyler has already informed us he makes soap, the precise same ingredients needed to make explosives. Since Tyler does not exist, however, the bombing is clearly auto-sabotage on the narrator's part. The fact that Tyler could not possibly have rigged and exploded the narrator's apartment having only just met him is another dead giveaway. As a result of this setback, the narrator calls Marla (Helena Bonham-Carter), but hangs up at the sound of her voice. (Fincher aligns the images so that the sound of Marla's voice appears to be triggering the explosion, as he visualizes it, in the narrator's apartment.) Since Marla "is too much like him, he sees himself reflected in her too much," he must turn to Tyler, to fantasy, unable to acknowledge his true feelings, both *about* himself and *for* Marla. He calls Tyler up (Tyler never answers his phone, but calls him back on Star 69), and the two men meet up in a bar. Tyler lays out his anti-consumer, anarchic, quasi-spiritual (and somewhat simplistic) philosophy ("The things you own end up owning you"), and the narrator laps it up. Outside the bar, Tyler presses the narrator into coming right out and asking him for a place to stay, tells him no problem, then asks for a favor in return. "I want you to hit me as hard as you can." Here begins *Fight Club* proper.

"How much can you know about yourself if you've never been in a fight?" Tyler challenges, adding, "I don't want to die without any scars." The narrator obliges him, and the two men rough each other up. In fact, the narrator is really beating *himself* up, but either way he realizes that the thrill and intensity of physical violence — as a cathartic means for cleansing his psyche of dross (literally knocking the shit out of himself) — was just what he had been looking for. All his dithering at cancer groups had been a way of evading the problem rather than confronting it head on; through Tyler's help, he is finally able to do this. As an unconscious schizo (the narrator really believes himself to be sane), he is tormented (permitted no rest) by the ceaseless, meaningless chatter of his thoughts. Add to this the hideous pressure of awareness that his life amounts to nothing but a blight and burden upon his manhood and you have a desperate case. But though aware (like Thomas in *The Matrix*) that something is deeply wrong, both with the world and himself, the narrator has no idea what it might be or how to confront the illusion directly, to tear it down and arrive at the truth. Tyler is no Morpheus, but his red pill is every bit as bitter, and just as tough to swallow. Once again (as for Thomas), the illusion is not merely his empty, automaton life but his very identity: the person he has come to believe himself to be. Hence Tyler (like Neo), though a figment of the narrator's imagination, is in fact *more* real than the person who dreamed him up. He is a manifestation — not physical but psychological — of everything the narrator has repressed in his vain, self-negating bid to *fit in*.

Tyler Durden is wild and unruly and destructive, not to mention plain imaginary; but he is also honest, uninhibited, and fearless. He may be unreal, but his ideas and his actions are not. Tyler's first idea — to get hit — is essentially a wake-up call, just like blowing up his own apartment is a wake-up call for the narrator. Tyler is the Zen master administering blows in order to insert new programs in the moment of silence which the shock creates. Physical pain and brutality have the direct result of causing the intellectual, rational mind to shut down briefly, allowing pure instinct to take over. The fight clubs are not simply a means to return to primal, instinctive behavior, but the means to a profounder end: that of enlightenment or self-realization. The fight clubs, for all their wanton brutality, are actually workshops geared towards reprogramming the participants. The narrator starts with himself (both of him), but soon finds himself a following, and so becomes (by default) a kind of guru. Like Hitler and Manson before him, he has tapped into an atavistic current, that of transformation through pain, or (male) regeneration through violence. If *Fight Club* is "fascist," then the critics should know better than to disparage the movie for it and look instead to the more troubling implications in

15. Where Is My Mind? Notes on Purity of Impulse in *Fight Club*

society itself. They might consider the possibility that fascism has become (just as it did in Germany in the 1930s) the only viable *political* solution to an intolerable social predicament. *Fight Club* is not advocating these extreme measures, it is prophesizing their inevitability and cautioning against them. But as ever, the messenger gets the rap so that the message can be ignored.

Tyler and the narrator strike up a perverse but mutually satisfying friendship, and into this idyllic partnership (of self and other) steps, inevitably, the third player. The "tourist" and troublemaker Marla arrives to stir things up and take the boys to the next level. She is the anima, and it is meeting Marla that "engenders Tyler" in the first place; through his repressed desire for her, the narrator is compelled to invent someone with the *balls* to take Marla on. Hence Marla, the anima, is the catalyst, and moments after her introduction the second subliminal insert of Tyler appears (as the narrator watches Marla walk away with loathing). The flash image of Tyler suggests that the narrator's loathing is mixed with longing, which leads to his conjuring the super-male Tyler — his own sex instinct or libido — in order to chase after the coveted object of desire. Marla (in whom director David Fincher apparently saw himself) is a desperate sort, a "fashionable nihilist" who, in Tyler's estimation, is a genuine seeker of oblivion, in contrast to the narrator's half-baked dilettante. ("At least she's really trying to hit bottom," he mocks.) When the narrator first meets her, she is in the process of ruining his fantasy refuge at the self-help groups by arriving under the same subterfuge as he (as a "tourist"). Like Harold and Maude meeting at funerals, Marla and the narrator seem made for each other. If they fail to hit it off, this is only because the narrator is too threatened by Marla's presence to admit his attraction to her. He feels that she is

"I met you at a strange time in my life": Marla (Helena Bonham-Carter) and Tyler (Ed Norton) watch the demise of Western civilization in *Fight Club* (1999, 20th Century–Fox).

exposing his own designs: "Her lie reflected my lie." As a result he is unable to feel anything anymore (he can't cry in front of Marla), and his insomnia returns.

He finally makes a deal with Marla so they won't have to meet again, assigning specific nights to each of them, and for a while he is free of her.* Marla is in a long tradition of demented, desperate movie heroines; when she wanders into traffic seemingly indifferent to physical harm, she may remind us of Jeanne Moreau jumping into the Seine in Truffaut's *Jules et Jim*. (The narrator tells us, "Marla's philosophy of life was that she might die at any minute. The tragedy was that she didn't.") And unlike the narrator, we may be sad to see her go. Sometime later, however (once the narrator has abandoned cancer groups for fight clubs), she calls him up at his new abode (Tyler's derelict house on Paper Street) and informs him that she has taken a bunch of pills ("soul, prepare to evacuate!"). He coldly leaves the phone off the hook and skulks away, whereupon Tyler takes over. Intrigued, Tyler goes over to Marla's, brings her back, and fucks her all night long in order to keep her awake. This follows soon after Tyler's lament of being "a generation raised by women," and answers his wistful thought that "maybe what we need is a woman." Of course, since Tyler gets laid, so does the narrator, albeit unconsciously; this is presumably (nonetheless) a major catalyst for him.†

Tyler ups the stakes when he begins to recruit his "Space Monkeys," and what started as two men indulging their masochistic (and machismo) urges turns into a bona fide movement. As the narrator points out, all the space monkey recruits are essentially morons, and the impression given is that not only are persons of sub-standard intelligence most readily drawn to the fight

---

*Though he may still fantasize about her: At a lecture on the healing power of pain, the narrator follows a meditation to imagine his power animal and encounters a penguin that tells him "slide," and promptly does just that. Later he re-enters the same cave and finds Marla in place of the penguin. She has entered into the deepest layer of his being, and assumed her place as his "familiar."

†It's also here that the film's schizo logic begins to suffer under the strain of the story; even though Tyler forbids the narrator to mention him to Marla, there's hardly any way she wouldn't notice that he is a split personality. One could put *Fight Club* under the microscope and scrutinize it every which way and find that it fails to hold up at every turn, but why bother? It's a fantasy, and such criteria hardly apply to fantasy works. Fincher claims that, besides Tyler stealing the red Ferrari at the airport, the movie is "bullet proof," i.e. free of impossibilities. I beg to differ. Maybe everything we see is *physically* possible; but then so is hanging an elephant from a cliff face by a daisy. The chances of it happening, however, are so slim as to be non-existent. One major "bullet hole" in the movie's text is when the narrator returns home to find Marla and Tyler fucking. This makes no sense, even within the twisted logic of the narrator's fantasy, since his schizo projections only include Tyler, not Marla. *Fight Club* is implausibility taken to a natural extreme, but this is only a legitimate criticism if you actively fight its charms and try and pin it down to "realism." Plainly that's a self-defeating policy. *Fight Club* invents and adheres to a logic all its own.

15. Where Is My Mind? Notes on Purity of Impulse in *Fight Club*

clubs, but that Tyler's "reprogramming" tends to accentuate the slavish, doltish side of the recruits. He appears to be working on crushing their individual tendencies and inculcating them with a dronelike, collective will by which they may become microscopic cogs in his catastrophic plan. If the fight clubs seem finally to be lacking in a unifying vision, this is because Tyler himself seems incapable of truly creative thought or action. He is closer to antichrist than Messiah, finally; hence "In Tyler we trust" is a necessary prerequisite for the movement to move. Blind faith that all this destruction has a greater purpose, beyond the elaborate pranks of a chronically adolescent anarchist-nihilist seeking his own satisfaction, is required. Tyler is not planning a regeneration of the people, however, much less a golden new age; he is not drawing the Phoenix out of the ashes. He is simply burning everything down for the pleasure of seeing the flames. He is seeking personal catharsis. Doubtless this is the primary reason why (older) critics despised the movie and treated it with such vitriolic contempt. This was *their* world that was being trashed. What's more, it was setting a bad example for the children!

But Tyler's perspective (and that of the movie itself) cannot be understood as a social or political one. It's apocalyptic or it's nothing at all. "Our great war is a spiritual war," he intones with uncharacteristic solemnity. "Our great depression is our lives." What's happening around the narrator, and as a consequence of his actions and ideas, is secondary to what is happening *within* him. Likewise, *Fight Club* the movie — a great movie in its way, and expressly made for an apocalyptic generation — can only really be appreciated as an externalization of an internal process, a process hitherto perceived as a "disease": that of schizophrenia. In no other movie (not even *The Matrix*) is the blueprint for personal evolution/social revolution (breakdown) more clearly and fully described. *Fight Club* has layers and layers of meaning; it is there in the details, the background, the throwaway jokes, the very texture of the movie. It exists between the images themselves, subliminally, like Tyler's cocks, spliced into the story, bawdy playfulness with a more serious intent. *Fight Club* is a ludicrous, offensive, absurd, tasteless, glib, obnoxious, immoral, preposterous, and irresponsible movie. But, whatever else you may say about it, it is also true to itself: impassioned, inspired, and visionary in its nihilistic zeal. It may not possess the usual attributes of a work of art — compassion, for example — but it's possessed by a spirit so fierce and original and devastating — so devotedly iconoclastic — that, love it or hate it, it must be respected.

The afore-mentioned "blueprint" is roughly as follows: The narrator, unable to sleep, finds certain relief in surrounding himself by worse-off cases than himself. (Note the parallels with Travis Bickle, of *Taxi Driver*, after whom the narrator seems to model himself: Travis is unable to sleep and rides around at night on subways; figuring "I might as well get paid for it," he takes a job as a cabbie.) When Marla — his anima — shows up to remind the narrator what a faker he is, he has to cut a deal with her (they split their time) so that he can carry on at the self-help groups without being haunted by her presence. The fact is — a fact Marla makes plain to him — the narrator does not belong among these *victims* since he is not a victim of cruel fate or random disease, but of his own relentless, irrepressible id. One supposes he cannot sleep because his id has become so unruly that the only way to repress it is by staying awake, hence avoiding its clutches. Finally, he represses it for so long (avoiding sleep) that it is forced to "materialize" (project itself) into his waking, conscious life. It crosses over, as it were, from the dreamtime into the wakeworld. Traditionally, this is akin to the myth of the *Doppelgänger*, or double; but in *Fight Club*, the id's subterfuge is that it actually disguises itself as everything that the narrator is *not*: it dons all those characteristics which the conscious ego denies in itself. This makes it synonymous with the Shadow, the other. Since the narrator never suspects they are one and the same person, this gives Tyler, the double, a mixed advantage: on the one hand it gives him more freedom (being unlimited by conscious fears), on the other hand, it limits his movements: he must be careful not to allow the ego to realize the truth (or to reveal his schizophrenia to outsiders).

The *Doppelgänger*'s first act is to explode, totally and irrevocably, the narrator's life, destroying his former, cozy existence and so drawing him into a new orbit. Tyler inhabits a parallel track which the narrator must align himself with, without ever realizing what is happening (that he is learning to cross over from left to right side, from self to Other). The narrator is tricked, snared into complicity with the Other; his being accepted into Tyler's underworld (the run-down house, half flooded and full of faulty electrical wiring, the perfect id abode) is contingent first of all on the narrator asking Tyler outright (vocalizing his will), and, second, on his honoring Tyler's first wish (to hit him). The two sides of the psyche are then allowed to "bond" through the traditional (and primitive) male rite of violence. Once they have bonded, the narrator is sold immediately on the sensual-sensational aspects of their partnership; he even likens it to the sexual act when he says, "We should do this again some time." From here they are ready to co-inhabit, as brothers if not lovers. The "motion" (by which the ego undergoes initiation by — and into — the Id) is underway.

Visceral awareness is what the initiation amounts to. Since "being clever" is not *really* working for the narrator (it's driving him insane), it's time to try a more instinctive, irrational approach. Hence the running line of the film, "I am Jack's colon," etc., and also the opening credit sequence (that of the viscera of Jack's skull), are references to this: *bodily* awareness over mere intellectual cognition. (One might even say that, while the ego resides in the brain, the id belongs to the body.) The primary result of this perceptual realignment is that the narrator is now able to sleep. Tyler the id-monster has been unleashed

15. Where Is My Mind? Notes on Purity of Impulse in *Fight Club*

so his unconscious is safe again; while the narrator sleeps, the monster runs free. Beyond this, the narrator's daily life becomes tolerable to him again: "everything gets turned down." Compared to the visceral intensity of the fight club, ordinary concerns seem inconsequential. (The narrator expresses this as Tyler's imperative: "The ability to let everything that does not matter truly slide.") He abandons his cozy, stifling life of "condos and sitcoms" and embarks on a greater quest for meaning. This is not a passive quest. In order to change, it is not enough simply to move out of his apartment and take up a new routine. You can take the boy out of Babylon, but it's not so easy to take Babylon out of the boy. The narrator must go to war with his former self, engaging in a constant battle against his weaknesses and neuroses in order to tear down that lying specter — identity — to which he has enslaved himself. And from these ruins he must build a new identity. The process is a process not merely of initiation/transformation but of self-*realization*. The narrator is forced to realize that his teacher and guide is none other than his own true, hidden *self*.

Tyler forces the narrator to "reject the basic assumptions of civilization" and to confront his fears one by one until there is nothing left but the naked, abject, quick of his false self. Tyler compels him to reach bottom in order to start over from scratch. At this level (the internal level), *Fight Club*'s philosophy of destruction is a positive, progressive philosophy. Beyond mere nihilism, it approaches Zen. The all-knowing, all-singing, all-dancing Id Tyler Durden will stop at nothing, and stoop to anything, to help his apprentice realize his non-existence and attain the clear state. This is also the nature of Tyler's "human sacrifices," in which he selects random individuals and allows them to believe that their end is at hand, then gives them temporary reprieve in order expressly to change their ways. If he finds them failing to assume responsibility for their lives, to resume a self-determining path, he promises to come back and kill them. (This latter appears to be a bluff since his gun is never loaded.) The point of this is, all or nothing. The warrior's way. The demand of Tyler, the unflinching id with nothing to lose (being already dead), is simply: no compromise. It is "To thine own self be true" or bust. Seen in this light, all of Tyler's acts — however destructive or demented — are justified. The intent behind them is pure, unbending, and selfless. He is a madman, but with a method and a purpose.

This is perhaps best depicted (in one of the film's most effective scenes) when Tyler pours lye onto the narrator's hand and forces him to endure agony and scarring in order to fully assimilate his teachings. The narrator is forced to face up to his mortality, to "know that some day you are going to die." He must pass, beyond the pain and the fear into pure understanding, to get "one step closer to hitting bottom," and realize that only when he has lost everything will he be free to do, or become, anything. He is marked for life by this ritual in more ways than one. He comes to understand that real change entails letting go not just of the parts he doesn't like but of *everything*. In this moment Tyler becomes the narrator's god, torturing him for his own enlightenment and finally releasing him and giving him relief, balm (in fact vinegar) to ease the pain and lance his wounds. Tyler delivers his most profound and searing message in these moments, describing how human sacrifices of the past resulted in a discharge from the "melted fat of bodies" (the "ashes of heroes") that filled the river below with soapy substance, which the locals then found was the best spot for washing their bodies and clothes. Since soap comes from human body fat, which in turn can be used for manufacturing explosives, Tyler traces a full, apocalyptic circle here between human sacrifice, cleansing rituals, and back again to holocausts and terrorist action. "Without the pain, without the sacrifice, we would have nothing! This is your pain! This is your burning end! Our fathers were our models for God. If our fathers bailed, what does that tell us about God? Consider the possibility that God does not *like* you. He never wanted you. We are God's unwanted children? So be it!" From this moment on, the narrator "belongs" to Tyler (who has put his mark on him, just like God with Cain). The ego has been conquered, the Id reigns supreme. And the price, though high, is fair. Freedom is not free, and tearing off the mask that enslaves one invariably leaves scars. But who wants to die without scars?

Visceral awareness involves an awakening of *all* the senses, not just the rational ones. These senses have been so long dormant that, to break the spell of slumber, shocks are necessary. Trials, ordeals, initiation rituals that involve pain and scarring, all this is par for the course of enlightenment. The narrator lets his unconscious do the driving, and if he comes off the rails as a result, this is only and exactly what he needed to come to his senses. And the more beaten and shaken he gets, the more scars he racks up, the more near-life experiences he endures, the closer he gets to being alive. Once again, the philosophy, the "message," of the movie may seem harsh, extreme; but if so, we have only ourselves to blame. The harshness of the "cure" is in direct proportion to the gravity of the condition. At this point, nothing short of a head-on collision can bring us back to our senses.

Shortly after Tyler initiates sex with Marla (for her own salvation, naturally), the narrator endures his chemical burn ritual and Tyler begins giving out homework assignments to fight club members. The narrator's sexual liberation is taking place unbeknownst to himself. He is in the peculiar position of being jealous of both Marla (for coming between him and Tyler) and of Tyler, for fucking Marla. At a conscious level, this is only serving to increase his frustration. Yet, so far as his behavior as Tyler goes, he is being further unleashed and appears to be finding his true purpose at last. Once Tyler begins assigning specific, anarchic tasks, his until then personal quest for individuation becomes an authentic movement, and the ramifications of his madness begin to spread into the world, like a virus. This is what Tyler *is*: a virus,

15. Where Is My Mind? Notes on Purity of Impulse in *Fight Club*

hatched in the solipsist brain of the narrator, a virus that is too insatiable to satisfy itself with a single host. Tyler infects anyone he can get close enough to with his particular brand of dementia, and this is the means for the narrator to unburden himself of his own psychosis: by inflicting it upon society. (The parallels with Travis Bickle are certainly more than passing.)

Critics of the film who balked at its "message" (i.e., Tyler's) not only ignored the fact that all of Tyler's converts are essentially moronic hoodlums, but that the whole movement is the brainchild of a complete and total psychopath. For most of its length, the film may *appear* to idealize Tyler and evoke our sympathy for the narrator; but once the revelation of their being one and the same has dawned, our feelings are forced to undergo a similar 180° shift. As partners in mischief, Tyler and the narrator make an irresistible pair. As a single, split soul working out its own psychosis, the character is both appalling and pitiful in equal measures. Of course, by the time this apocalyptic penny has dropped, we have been hurled into a surrealist landscape and all criteria (or capacity) for judgment has been forgotten. We sit back in bewilderment and marvel at the spectacle of runaway schizophrenia in its fullest expression. The process the film now maps is that of the gradual alienation or distancing between the two sides of the psyche. Tyler, "the spirit of mischief," "purity of impulse"—having taught the narrator his art and molded him in his own image—begins to stray ever further beyond the bounds of what he, the narrator, considers viable or sane behavior. The closer the narrator comes to fulfilling his own idealized image and expression of self (the more precisely he imitates Tyler), the further into madness Tyler must go. His intention is to take his apprentice to the limit and, if possible, beyond. When the narrator beats himself up in his boss's office (the film's comic highpoint, and a new peak in absurdist violence), he is proving just how far he has come under Tyler's tutelage. The enactment reminds the narrator of his first fight with Tyler because, of course, there too he was really fighting himself. Only now he no longer needs to imagine an adversary-accomplice to do the deed but is able to act alone. This scene is his real graduation, his personal victory, and he is rewarded by a year's severance pay and a cartload of office goodies. But Tyler is unimpressed, and merely moves on to the next level of mayhem.

The "human sacrifice" scene is the first time we see the narrator beginning to have misgivings about Tyler's methods, and although he all-too-quickly recants of his doubts (most of all when he sees the gun isn't loaded), we in the audience may not be so easily placated. If Tyler hasn't yet crossed the line between mischief and malignancy, then it's only a matter of time. It's at this point that Tyler's recruitment program begins and we begin to see the darker, more dubious implications of his agenda. Tyler appears to be on a power trip as well as a joy ride. Tyler/the narrator insists that "nobody is the center" of the movement—"The leader walked through the crowd, out in the darkness"—

but this hardly jibes with his manner of indoctrinating the recruits. He may be telling them that they are all equal, "You are not special. You are not a beautiful, perfect snowflake. You are the same decaying organic matter as everything else. We are all part of the same compost heap." But it is still Tyler, the grand master, who is telling them this. And the narrator feels threatened and rebellious at what he perceives as Tyler's assumption of power and his own loss of central importance *to* Tyler, who now has many minds to fuck with, not just the narrator's. "I am Jack's enflamed sense of rejection," he grumbles.

In the following scene, the narrator gratuitously pummels the young blonde youth to a bloody pulp, all for the sake of "destroying something beautiful." Since the narrator is breaking Tyler's (his own) rules at this point, he is effectively establishing his independence *from* Tyler, albeit in the most aggressive and vicious manner. He is taking on Tyler's uninhibited nature as his own, but, perhaps inevitably, he takes it a step further, out of mere machismo and into psychosis. Tyler, realizing that his apprentice is now ready to make it on his own, stages one final enactment (theater-as-deprogramming) and gives the narrator his "near-life-experience" car crash. This is the symbolic dramatization of the end of their association. Before they enter the car, the narrator bows to Tyler: "After you, Mr. Durden," but Tyler returns the courtesy, "After *you*." This signifies the narrator's wrestling with his responsibility. The first one in the car goes into the passenger seat; by allowing Tyler his courtesy, he also concedes to him the driver's seat.

Tyler is driving, while the narrator sees himself as being the passenger, i.e., *passive*. At this point the two sides of the psyche, ego and id, have their first argument, while the two space monkeys in the back, hearing a two-way conversation come out a single mouth, are realizing just how schizo their leader really is. Once again Tyler reminds the narrator that "This does not belong to us. We are not special!" In response to the narrator's complaint about not being included in Project Mayhem, Tyler snaps, "You decide your own level of involvement!" Tyler lets go of the wheel and allows the vehicle to steer itself. Now is the time for the narrator to assume responsibility for his passivity. He is jealous and threatened by the introduction of all these outsiders into his cozy relationship with Tyler. Tyler assures him that he has some rethinking to do. "Forget about what you think you know.... Especially about you and me!" By letting go of the wheel, Tyler is effectively stepping down from his position in charge. He's moving out the driver's seat and acknowledging that he was never there to begin with, that the narrator has been living a life that has, effectively, been driverless. Here is the ultimate test: if he can't take over the reigns, then he will have to surrender himself totally to the momentum and go wherever it takes him. Paradoxically, this is the prerequisite for assuming responsibility for one's actions: accepting that one has no control over anything *except* these actions, that life is a fast ride to death and at best one might

15. Where Is My Mind? Notes on Purity of Impulse in *Fight Club*

be able to choose the time and place of annihilation. Above all, one must decide how one meets it (fearlessly, or not). The narrator surrenders and passes the test (he survives); whereupon Tyler disappears, like the dream he always was. His work, in theory, is now done.

The narrator has been freed from fear, accepted his death, and so assumed responsibility for his actions. In theory, that is; but this is contingent on his realizing the truth about Tyler and himself, and this he does not do. Instead, he chases Marla off ("Tyler is gone. Tyler is not here!"), and is confronted for the first time with the deadly consequences of Tyler's "mischief" when Bob is killed in one of the space monkeys' "escapades." At this point, he abandons Paper Street and the whole fight club organization and goes in search of Tyler. The ego in search of the id is "like following an invisible man"; or worse, a man seeking his own shadow. Every place he visits, he experiences a sense of déjà vu. His whole life has become déjà vu. It is not that he is chasing his shadow but that *he* is the shadow of his own true self. As such he is always one step behind (the fate of the shadow). Wherever he goes, he finds Tyler has been there before him, setting up fight clubs and spreading mayhem. The narrator is gradually facing up to the truth of himself, the only way he knows how to. Incapable of simply putting one and one together (and coming up with zero!), he must act out his schizophrenic delusion to the end. He needs the truth spelled out for him in black and white. The otherworldly bartender identifies him at last, and little by little he begins to glimpse the truth of his dementia. (We also may realize at this point how unlikely the whole thing is, namely that no one has pointed out to him the truth in all this time.) He calls Marla on the telephone and demands of her, "Have we ever done it?" In despair and disgust, she finally calls him by his real name. Still incredulous, he remanifests Tyler before him in his hotel room. Tyler explains the score to him, as to a small child.

This has to be one of the most original scenes of any movie anywhere, and is beautifully played by the two leads. The success of the movie really hinges upon Pitt and Norton immersing themselves in the part(s) as totally and as passionately as they do. Both gifted performers with completely disparate styles, they affectively mesh into a single persona. What unites them above all, and what makes the performance(s) so remarkable, even unprecedented, is their shared belief in, and affection for, the material. You feel as if they have given everything they have to the role and then given a little bit more, in order to do justice to the conception of Tyler. As the narrator flashes back on everything he has done (as Tyler), and as the full weight of reality descends upon him, the moments come together like a shifting kaleidoscope in our heads and on the screen (Fincher's touch was never more deft and assured than it is here). In a matter of seconds the untapped promise of schizophrenic cinema is realized in full. This is movie history in the making.

The narrator passes out under the pressure and everyone in the audience is left suspended, jaws hanging, assimilating the awful, psychotic truth. "Changeover." Everything we have seen has been a lie. Yet from the schizo's point of view, the truth has finally dawned.

From here, all that remains is for the narrator to fully assimilate (face up to) the truth. What this entails is not merely the destruction of Tyler but his total absorption. The narrator (like the viewer) must acknowledge the unthinkable fact that Tyler never existed and that everything Tyler ever said or did was a fantasy, since it was actually said and done by the narrator himself. He must assume total responsibility for his fantasy, for Tyler's mischief, and for his own runaway psychosis. If he can do this—i.e., admit to himself he is completely insane—then he can reintegrate himself, allow his ego and his id to co-exist in conscious harmony as a single entity, and so regain (or rather, attain for the first time) his sanity. Tyler tells the narrator, "I'm free in all the ways that you are not." He points out that "sometimes you're still you," but that the "cross over" is almost complete, "little by little you're letting yourself become — Tyler Durden." The movie's climax—though it takes the almost conventional form of a showdown between the two men, defusing the bomb, reunion with Marla, etc.—is really a dramatic working out of this maddening conundrum. Though the narrator realizes that Tyler is but the projection of his own id, Tyler has by now gained a nigh-autonomy unto himself as an acting id-entity. As such, he does everything he can to stop the narrator from stopping himself. And yet, since they really *are* one, this is really Tyler's final lesson, or test, for the narrator. If you meet Buddha on the road, kill him.*

For the apprentice to finally attain his own individual freedom, he must reject (overcome) not only everything Tyler has taught him to reject but also, finally, Tyler himself. And the essence of this final split-off (individuation) from all that is not-self in the narrator is his affection for Marla. Tyler's desire to destroy Marla (as a potential threat to his existence, or more precisely, his control over the narrator) is the one desire, finally, that the narrator cannot share. Hence it is the narrator's own desire (to save Marla, the anima) that establishes

---

*There are serious weaknesses however; the narrator's determination to undo all of Tyler's work may strike us as rather spineless. He is resisting the inevitable, plainly, and some of these scenes, most especially those of the narrator turning himself in to the police, seem forced and unnecessary, not to mention plain unconvincing. The film seems uncertain as to whether to present Tyler as the bad guy or the savior, and as a result we can't really tell if the narrator is finally coming to his senses or coming off the rails. Fortunately it leans more towards the latter view, by having him running through the street in his shorts and exhibiting all the classic behavior of a loon—a fact which the rematerializing Tyler is delighted to point out. But the scene in which the narrator discovers that even the police are under Tyler's control, and narrowly escapes a castration at their hands, though amusing, stretches credibility too far. Since it's not strictly necessary to the film's narrative, it might better have been dropped entirely.

15. Where Is My Mind? Notes on Purity of Impulse in *Fight Club*

his independence *from* Tyler. It forces him to make his own choice at last. By finally defining the Other *as* other, he attains to the Self. Paradoxically, but rightly, to overcome Tyler he has to shoot himself, in the head (actually in the mouth, which is also correct, since the self effectively *speaks* the shadow side into existence). The narrator is destroying Tyler by becoming him. Since Tyler is the "purity of expression" by which the narrator's true nature has been released, found form and inherited life, it is the false ego construct, not the unleashed id, that must die.

This is Cain and Abel all over again: the slayer becomes the slain, the victim the victor. *Solve et coagula.* Analysis and synthesis. Alchemical wedding. It is not Tyler who is dying here, but the narrator who must sacrifice himself that Tyler (his perfected self) be born. Hence the moment coincides not only with Marla's reappearance and their long-avoided union as lovers (as opposed to demented sex partners)— his acknowledgment of the anima — but also with the final realization of Tyler's anarchic dream, project Mayhem, that brings modern civilization to its knees. The age of repression is over. Civilization is the sacrificial lamb, the burnt offering on the altar of freedom by which the true self may finally be born, and the Other inherit its own. Tyler is dead. Long live Tyler.

16

Aliens "R" Us: Race Intimations of *Metamorphosis*

> I didn't come 100 million miles just to turn back at the last ten feet.
> —*Mission to Mars*

Wittingly or not, Brian de Palma's much-maligned *Mission to Mars* (2000) forms part of a growing belief system that puts extraterrestrials in place of God as the creator and progenitor (and possibly guide) of the human species. Everybody knows about "the Face on Mars" by now, even if no official confirmation has come through from NASA as yet (in fact they have worked pretty hard at discrediting the evidence). The theories of Erich Von Däniken, and now Graham Hancock and associates, are being rapidly incorporated, if not into orthodox history then at least into modern folklore. What this folklore comes down to is that humanity and civilization are the result, not of chance or "random evolution" (how's that for a complete oxymoron), but of conscious *design* by "higher" beings, presumably from other planets or star systems. (Besides Mars, Sirius is the most popular designated source of the hypothetical higher intelligence.) These beings not only created humanity (goes the folklore) millions of years ago by seeding the Earth, but also taught us the rudiments of language, astronomy, monument building, and so forth (to the ancient Egyptians, among others). The lore extends beyond ancient history, however, into the realms of the present and, beyond that, the immediate future. Information supposedly "encoded" in the pyramids and the Sphinx (and if these researchers are to be believed, the ancient monuments are not just confined to the Earth) promises to enlighten us, some day soon, as to our true course and destiny in the universe. This revelation involves a reacquaintance with our creators, the ET gods of the past, whose return, we are assured, is imminent. As a character in *Mission to Mars* gasps, once the penny finally drops, "They're us. We're them!"

All this forms the backbone of a profoundly radical belief system that has been steadily propagating itself, over the last forty years or so, into our culture, and that has finally becomes so familiar to us that it can easily form the basis of a summer blockbuster movie "from the director of *Mission: Impossible.*" But there's a catch. Why was *Mission to Mars* so roundly and rabidly reviled by both critics and audiences alike? Stylistically and dramatically, the film is infinitely superior to *Mission: Impossible*, and although as a modern myth — or even a sci-fi fairy tale — it may lack the durability of *E.T.* or *The Empire Strikes Back*, it is still light years ahead of *Cocoon* (a film mawkishly embraced by audiences fifteen years earlier). Have we become so cynical so fast, or is it something else? I suspect that, on the one hand, *Mission to Mars* cuts a little *too* close to the (possible) "truth" for people to take it as mere entertainment; while on the other, it trivializes its subject matter rather too much to pass as "revelatory" cinema. Hence it fell between the stools, and crashed and burned.

Barring the film's lame New Age ending, *Mission to Mars* is a remarkably realistic sci-fi film. The characters, relationships, situations, and dialogue are all considerably closer to what we might expect them to be (in the events depicted) than movies of this ilk generally provide. (By "this ilk" I refer more to *Forbidden Planet* than to *The Right Stuff*, obviously.) Yet *Mission to Mars* received some of its harshest criticisms for just such elements, the dialogue in particular being singled out as "corny," when it struck me as being simply devoid of movie frills and therefore fairly convincing. On the other hand, I don't know of any other sci-fi movie with such consistently beautiful imagery or with such strong emotional qualities. It's far from being a masterwork, but it's certainly no disaster either; so why was it treated so abominably? I can only surmise it was the victim of a kind of unconscious backlash against the whole "face-on-Mars, E.T.-as-gods" propaganda of the last few years, proving that the public is not ready to be spoon-fed this quasi-mystical creation myth just yet (preferring to pick at it at leisure a little while longer). It's one thing to be given cotton candy lullabies about friendly space aliens having secret congress with our children, inseminating widows or rejuvenating geriatrics. It's quite another to be told outright — in a sort of Hollywood/Alien propaganda film — that humankind is still an infant in its cradle under the care and nurture of superior, non-human beings (from Mars).

Our feelings about the whole question of aliens are divided, to say the least. On the one hand, the passive, childlike desire to be "saved" by higher powers blessed with wisdom and magical technology runs deep in us. On the other hand, the need to establish our own separation and independence as humans, by facing and defeating an evil, predatory "other" — despite its superior might or technology, and by sheer "virtue" of our humanness — is a fantasy that seems to have cancelled out the "kinder, gentler alien" in recent years. In both cases, however, we are permitted to hang on to what it is that makes us human, for either way, the alien — good, bad, or ugly — is seen to be alien; as such it serves, even when set against us, to define us as what we *are*. Human.

Mission to Mars, with its "We are them" line, presents the idea of the Other as but a matured version of ourselves, as butterfly to caterpillar. Far more than any marauding, parasitical alien, such an idea threatens to destroy our concepts of self, identity, and all that it means to be human. If the superior alien is not saving us but inviting us to join it, to *become* it, then whatever it is that makes us human is presumably going to get lost in the splicing. This is a difficult concept at the best of times, and where *Mission to Mars* fails, finally, is in presenting the climactic face-off between human and alien, self and Other, as being anything but profoundly traumatic. De Palma, instead of going for a confrontational moment, gives us something as smooth and untroubled as a child's reunion with loving parents. This is patently absurd even for those of us who have no personal experience of alien abductions. When De Palma's Disney-esque alien appears in front of the human crew, with nary a gasp or shudder on their part, the whole movie goes splat. It's hard to imagine what De Palma was thinking. Perhaps the Von Däniken/Hancock crew took over at this point, because the movie turns into a cosmic history lesson which the humans obligingly narrate (while the alien points his, or her, instructional finger at the exhibits), describing the seeding of Earth and the creation of the human species by alien intervention.

All this is an insult to our intelligence in more ways than one. Humankind simply will *not* accept gracefully that it is anything but the pinnacle of evolution. At every level, emotionally and psychologically, it will put up a desperate fight before it surrenders its hard-earned illusion of supremacy. The revelation at the end of *Mission to Mars*—if even half true—effectively shatters everything we think we know about ourselves, and everything we have been aspiring towards as our destiny. We are not, it states, a self-determining species; we are closer to livestock, property. No matter how benevolent such a higher species might be, its emergence into our daily lives would be nothing short of apocalyptic. Reality would become a terrifying nightmare in which all logic had broken down.

This is what makes movies like *Cocoon* and *Starman*, and even *E.T* and *Close Encounters*, so unsatisfying. This is also why such ideas as propagated by *Mission to Mars*, though perfectly reasonable to a halfway open mind, have not been embraced (or even acknowledged) by mainstream media (movies notwithstanding), much less the scientific community. Personal (human) resistance to the Other is simply enormous. It is all but insurmountable save by force or subterfuge (hence the Other is almost always hostile in these movies). The idea that the Other is our master, our protector, our owner, and, finally, our own hidden, future self, is far from reassuring. It's unthinkable. Anyone who even suggests such a thing overtly must be silenced at once, and what's more, severely

16. Aliens "R" Us: Race Intimations of *Metamorphosis*

punished as an example to others. Apparently, such an example was made of Brian De Palma's otherwise quite delightful *Mission to Mars*. At least, that's my theory.

Aren't we all tired of hearing about aliens? Who would have imagined a culture could actually become saturated with and jaded by images and ideas of alien infiltration, colonization, invasion, and so forth, without ever actually having a chance to take such ideas halfway seriously? What is at back of this steady, relentless propagation of alien imagery and scenarios that has prevailed since the 1950s? There are essentially two possible explanations, neither of which precludes the other. One: that alien invasion — or at least a non-human presence on Earth — is a very real fact that has, on the one hand, been covered up, and, on the other, been disseminated on a large scale through popular media (as a paradoxical part of this cover-up). To stick with this "explanation" for a moment, the most obvious question that arises would be, *who* is behind the cover-up and the propaganda, and to what end would such an agenda be directed? If aliens intended to take over the world covertly, through gradual infiltration rather than force (just as in the movies), chances are they would require a certain percentage of the human population to aid them with their "program." Part of such a joint alien/human cover-up would entail the creation of an *alternate outlet* for the fears, hopes, and beliefs of the populace regarding such a program. In other words, in order to keep the public's conscious mind distracted from the reality unfolding beneath the surface of their everyday lives, it would be deemed necessary to engage their unconscious mind with *simulacra* of this same unfolding. This would amount to a kind of safety valve by

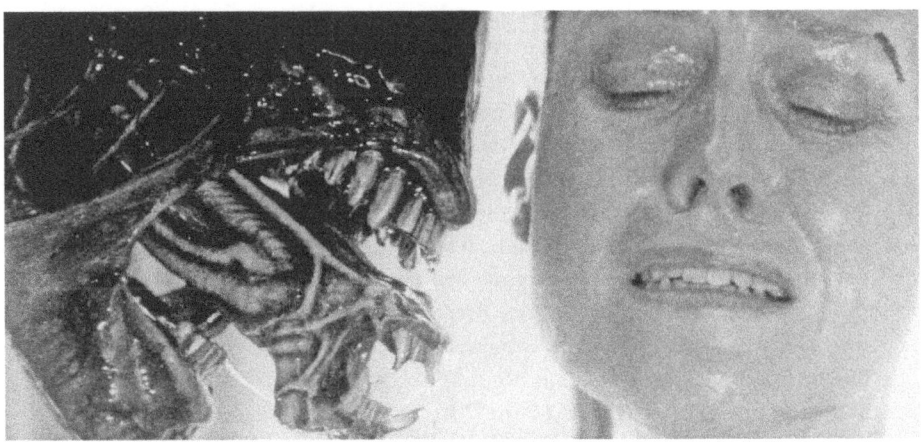

Too close for comfort: Ripley (Sigourney Weaver) goes tête-à-tête with the Other in *Alien³* (1993, 20th Century–Fox).

which the ever-growing, unconscious fears—our intuition or intimations of something being distinctly *amiss*—would be relieved. Enter the movies.

If this were the case, alien movies would serve a dual purpose. On the one hand, they would allow our unconscious fears to find a form in a popular medium and so relieve the pressure in our collective psyche. The effect would be that, consciously, we could now attribute any lurking fears of an alien invasion to the movies themselves! On the other hand, the movies would (quite deliberately) be of such an infantile, unsophisticated nature that, in the process of expressing these fears, they would also be trivializing them to the point that any mention or even thought of aliens, UFOs, etc., would immediately be associated with laughable movies such as *Invasion from Mars, They Live, Independence Day,* and so forth. As a result, all proponents of alien conspiracy would be automatically discredited in most people's minds, and easily dismissed with, "He's seen too many movies." The ironic truth is that, if such a program existed, it would be the skeptics and the doubters, rather than the believers, who had "seen too many movies." It would be they who could no longer tell the difference between reality and make-believe, although, in a reversal of the stereotype, they would not be taking movies for reality but rather falling for the make-believe of their own lives *and failing to heed the warnings of the movies.*

Such a scenario may indeed be unlikely in the extreme, and unworthy of serious academic attention (time will tell); and yet, at the same time, it holds an irresistible appeal. Since our thesis is that of schizophrenia—the split between reality and perception—such a scenario fits well enough, though not so well as our second possible "explanation." This is that, through alien movies, the human race has been attempting to come to terms *with its own impending otherness.* It's essential to understand by such "otherness" not some vague, metaphoric, psychological, or even mythical term, but a quite literal—even physical—*fact*. Carl Jung wrote about flying saucers having psychic reality, but eventually he had to admit they might be physical also, at least *some* of the time. So if you're thinking that this explanation is a lot easier to swallow and altogether less preposterous than our "alien invasion" scenario, think again. When I speak of the human race being wholly *other* than what it perceives itself to be, I am speaking of no less radical a shift in global (self) perceptions than would be heralded by an *actual* influx of non-human beings into our society.

Consider Kafka and his story *Metamorphosis*. A man wakes up as a giant insect, realizes that his dream of being a man is over, and that his true nature has been revealed to him. Is it a coincidence that perhaps the most seminal and enduring existential text of the 20th century and a large majority of sci-fi movies (and even current beliefs) *all involve people turning into bugs*? The insect is, in a sense, the "lowest" creature on the evolutionary scale, just as man—in his own optimistic evaluation—is considered the "highest." What this really amounts to, however, is that man is the *latest* addition to the biosphere, while insect intelligence, by the same token, is perhaps the *oldest* (it may be a tie with reptilian intelligence). It follows that, if not actually the wisest of God's creatures (again the snake might offer argument), insects can be seen as the most "tuned in" to the Earth's natural rhythms, the most connected to nature as a whole, and the most at harmony *with* it. (This is the advantage of "lowness," as the snake can testify.) By the same token man, being "new," being "of the highest," is the most out of whack, the most *dis*harmonious creature of them all. (I trust no one will argue with this.)

Here is the rub and the crux of the schizophrenic dilemma. We are torn between sophisticated self-awareness — the kind that appears to be leading to our extinction — and primal, atavistic consciousness, which is by definition (horror of horrors) *devoid of individuality*. The reason for this latter is that, as primal consciousness, we are, to a man, connected to the Earth, and so effectively *one* with it. We cannot go back to this lost innocence (the simple perfection of the insect), nor, as we are now, can we go forward into a rosy human future. Hence, at a deep and instinctive level (and this is what surfaces intuitively, through our movies), we are aware of the necessity, if we are to survive at all, not merely of changing our ways, but of transforming our actual *natures*: of becoming *other* than we are. I would stress, at this point, that it is not concern for the environment or awareness of our possible extinction that is pressing us towards such a transformation. Men and women are simply too selfish and near-sighted to really "care" about such concerns. What *is* driving us onward into this terrifying unknown, however (and here the schizophrenic question comes in), is the growing confusion, despair, and panic we experience in our own private lives.

Gregor Samsun's despair about becoming a giant dung beetle was the inevitable culmination of his despair at being a man. It was not becoming an insect that drove him to despair, but rather despair that drove him to take refuge as an insect. The insect form, Gregor found, was somehow more comfortably aligned to his wretched, grubby, dung-infested state of mind. And yet, for the ancient Egyptians, the scarab beetle (which not only carried the souls of the dead to Tuat, the underworld, but also rolled the Sun across the sky) was the highest and most sacred of all creatures. And Egyptians were no slackers when it came to mythology, or, for that matter, science. Did they know something Kafka didn't? Something he only intuited dimly, in his existential nausea and self-loathing? The growing folklore about buglike (and reptilian) aliens abducting humans, mating with us, preparing alien hybrid bodies for our future souls to take refuge in (once our own bodies have been destroyed in the Apocalypse) — all this is easy to dismiss (along with those 1950s movies) as the concatenations of schizophrenic minds. But to do so would mean missing out on the rich, almost limitless mythological and psychological implications of these beliefs. Why bugs? Why aliens? Is our DNA trying to tell us something?

Mankind is not what it used to be. The future is history. To be human, if it is not merely to be a blight upon the eco-system, must entail something *other* than we have hitherto considered possible or desirable. And yet, if we really are on the brink of some kind of species transformation, some global shift in awareness (as so many people seem to believe these days), it follows that (besides these New Agers and occultists and mediums and abductees, and all their millennial promises) there would surely be a plethora of signs, of clues and indications by which the nature of such a "shift" would become known to us. If, by the same token, such a shift has been denied by our conscious minds (whether through an actual conspiracy or merely a collective, schizophrenic will to deny it), then, in the absence of any open debate, where might such signs be expected to appear?

Invasion of the Body Snatchers is the central text for this "movement" of consciousness from the self (ego) to the Other (id). This is what is happening. We are, both as individuals and collectively, being "possessed" or taken over by our unconscious — our atavistic "souls" — the dark, alien, ancient, instinctive, primal "force" that is our connection to the Earth and to the universe. Perhaps this is happening now because, in order to survive as a species, it has become necessary to rediscover this connection. Whatever the case, since in effect it is our conscious ego minds — our "selves" — that have severed this connection, then our *conscious* interpretation of this awakening is nothing short of apocalyptic. We perceive a scenario in which each and every one of us is being possessed by an evil, inhuman force from the Beyond, a force that intends not merely to destroy us but to *duplicate* us, to transform us into some soulless, monstrous (be it reptilian, arachnid, insectoid, or whatever) imitation. This — in a great big eschatological nutshell (or cocoon) — is the global shift in consciousness that is forecast. And if movies are anything to go by, it is just around the next corner.

All the way from the original *The Fly* (1958) to *Alien*, *The Hidden*, and the splatacular, quasi-orgasmic climax of Greg Arachi's *Nowhere* (2000), sci-fi movies have shown a fascination for transforming human beings into insects. As yet, only Cronenberg's remake of *The Fly* (1986) has even begun to hint at the possibility of something *positive*, desirable, and viable (evolutionarily legitimate) in this transformation. Seth Brundle (Jeff Goldblum) in Cronenberg's film was at least a few steps ahead of Kafka. He could see the transcendental potential of becoming "the world's first insect politician." And yet his reliance on technology (the intellect) rendered his intent "impure." He could only see (just as his computer could only see) the fly that infiltrated his metabolism (and his consciousness) as a *disease*. By clinging to his precious humanness (as most of us in the audience were also doing), he turned the miracle of becoming into a nightmare of decay.

There haven't been any Hollywood movies as yet that allow the protagonist to turn into a buglike alien and that celebrate the transformation as a positive step in *personal* evolution. This would be somewhat radical. It's tough to let go of a million years of being human, and so the best we get is the *Close Encounters, Mission to Mars* kind of bliss-out communion in which the human (strangely adored by these higher alien light-beings) is whisked off to whatever galaxy they came from, to God only knows what kind of future. This is your typical lost-soul-finds-happiness Hollywood ending, but it makes zero sense within the schemata of the movies, much less in the greater frame of reference (of an extraterrestrial-human interface). Why take one solitary American back to paradise? Surely at least a sexually compatible couple would be required? But in Hollywood, aliens are either good or bad, and certainly never indifferent. They come either to invade and possess the planet or to carry us back to theirs. If they should have the unmitigated bad taste to try and get inside us — or to get anything from us at all — they can only be perceived as plunderers, rapists, and evil scientists (we mold them in our own image).

Alien (1979) was particularly effective in creating a monster whose perfection, and even beauty, was intrinsically connected to its monstrousness and otherness. The *Alien* series has perhaps an undeserved reputation in Hollywood simply for managing not to succumb to the usual repetition syndrome of sequels, and for attempting a new approach with each movie. This may be valid thematically, but artistically it has proved less satisfying. Each of the movies can be analyzed separately, however, without reference to the others, according to specific trends or genres. The first is horror, the second action, the third a kind of avant-garde prison flick, the fourth and worst of the series a kind of European action movie that returns to the horror genre but chooses schlock over gothic. But none of the sequels chose to develop what made Ridley Scott's original movie so effective: the taxonomy of the creature itself, its indestructibility and unstoppability, and the queasy suspense of never knowing where it was. Its stealth qualities and nigh-invisibility gave it a Lovecraftian menace — the gothic strain provided by Giger — that none of the sequels recaptured for more than moments at a time. Jim Cameron's *Aliens* is the stupidest of the series but also the most exciting. It uses the aliens not as harbingers of otherness but simply as hordes of darkness for the characters to unload their hardware onto, like Indians in a Western or gooks in a *Rambo* flick. So much for the occult text. David Fincher's *Alien³* attempts to ignore its generic obligations and offer up a more "personal" treatment, but is only half successful. Fincher, as much as Scott (and unlike Cameron), is a wiz at creating an atmospheric, claustrophobic milieu, but he seems half-hearted when it comes to the alien itself. (Fincher's horror — though plenty visceral — is not suited for the fantasy genre, and flourishes in a more realistic, contemporary setting, as he proved with *Seven*.) The most recent in the series, *Alien Resurrection*, is the only film that is totally ineffective even on its own terms: tedious, pretentious, ungainly, and not remotely scary, the film nonetheless offers itself up to our present thesis better than all the others, which just goes to show that bad movies often have the best subtexts.

At the end of *Alien Resurrection*, the hybrid clone played by Sigourney Weaver (Ripley, with a strain of the Alien spliced into her make-up) returns to Earth for the first time and says, "I'm a stranger here myself." Crummy though it is, *Alien Resurrection* was probably the first mainstream sci-fi horror movie (and certainly the first in the series) to suggest the possibility of a productive collaboration between the alien and the human. It offers up the idea of a synthesis between self and other in order to forge a third entity that partakes of the positive qualities of both. (This new Ripley is human enough to be compassionate, and even heroic, but she has acid blood, abnormal strength and resilience, and apparently telepathic abilities, all taken from the alien.) Indeed, this is the sole manner in which a "truce" can be struck between the two races: by being spliced together at a genetic level. While still separate, they are simply compelled by their natures (be it offensively or defensively) to destroy each other. To bring about this synthesis, Ripley first had to die (in her symbolic, Christlike act of suicide in the third film) by throwing herself into a furnace at the precise moment that the alien (other) was emerging from within her. Since a blood sample of the doomed, alien-impregnated Ripley had already been taken by the (evil) scientists, this genetic material is used, in the fourth film, to create a new Ripley, a clone that (just as the telepod spliced Seth with the fly) combines the characteristics of Ripley with her in-dwelling alien.

No matter how lacking these movies may be as decent entertainment, much less as art, their occult text — the mythic cum psychological blueprint for transformation which they provide — is dizzying in its implications. It is a veritable alchemical treatise for both the inner, psychological and the outer, physical process of individuation: the integration of the other (the unconscious) with the self or conscious mind. It is the Emerald Tablet of popular culture, and this, as much as their visceral appeal to horror aficionados, may account for the enduring fascination of the *Alien* films. They are giving us the information we need, albeit in a grotesquely disguised and debased form, to make the shift from local to galactic citizenship.

The schizo is divided against himself. He may "manufacture" an alternate personality and live a secret life that is set against his conscious one, or even in collusion with it (as in *Fight Club*). But more likely, he will begin to envision, and so create, an external reality populated by hostile, unfamiliar, and wholly menacing embodiments of his own unconscious will, the will to *change*. This will may, indeed generally does, manifest as a will to death, but the fact remains that, since the unconscious — the collective, primal reality to which I refer, as old as our DNA — is vastly greater than our conscious minds, it must eventually win out. At a conscious level, all the schizo *really* knows is that something is wrong, something is *missing*. Like Thomas in *The Matrix*, he has a splinter in his brain telling him two things: he is somehow different from other people, and the world is not what it seems. At base of these two perceptions is a single awareness, that of the double, the other self ("Neo"), for whom the world (and the original self) is indeed but a dream. As the Chinese philosopher Chuang Tsu (along with Seth Brundle) asked, "Am I a man who dreamed he was a butterfly, or a butterfly now dreaming he is a man?"

If the unconscious or id is a synonym for the Other, the soul — a collective soul and not an individual one — it follows that the "reality" which the schizophrenic projects onto his world — as an expression of his unconscious — is indeed populated by doubles, aliens, demons, and familiars. Call them what you will, to the schizo they are *as real as he is*. Through this subterfuge of superimposing his perception onto the world, the schizo is tapping into the totality of himself. He is manifesting the Other and so, potentially, healing the rift in his psyche by bringing about a reconciliation (through confrontation) of the twin poles of his existence. Movies have so far not been equipped to approach this reconciliation save through the most maudlin, dishonest of ways. A film like *The Fly*, *Invasion of the Body Snatchers*, or *The Thing*, or even (as we saw) *Alien*, comes considerably closer to depicting a real synthesis of the alien with the human — the self with the other — than films like *Cocoon*, *Starman*, *E.T.*, or *Mission to Mars* do. There is no way for the conscious mind to effect a confrontation with the Other while it still insists on dressing it up in the tawdry rags of its own likeness; by doing so, it is only flinching away from the transformative potential of such a confrontation. By stripping the alien of what made it alien to begin with — its almost infinite strangeness, beauty, and power — it turns it into a source of comfort for the ego: a cuddly toy.

The schizo has no such luxury of sugar coating the bitter (red) pill of transformation. He knows that to find his other self he must swallow that damn pill and plummet down the tunnel of his psyche, into the hell of the unconscious, to face the soul-sapping lie to which he has been enslaved for a lifetime. From here, once the knowledge has been claimed and the alien interloper acknowledged, he has the option, for the first time, of negotiating for his freedom. For the very "alien" other that has enslaved him — the matrix or cocoon in which he has been imprisoned — holds the key to his empowerment. Neo may have found out that his identity was a lie and his world a prison; but by the same token, he discovered the possibility of self-transformation. The terrible Other may have enslaved his body and infiltrated his mind, but if so it was only with the end of awakening his soul to its true nature. In the final reckoning, the Other, the alien, the devil, the double — all these marauding id-entities that make our conscious lives (and our movies) such chaotic, fantastic terrain to navigate — are the means by which the unconscious (trapped like a genie in a bottle or an image on a movie screen) makes itself known to us. It is sending its messages back, through time, to that lost fragment of itself, the ego, imploring it to come back to its senses and begin its definitive journey. The "alien" conspiracy goes deeper than we can ever imagine. There's not a soul among us that's not in on it.

17

Behind Closed Doors: Antithesis and Antidote

> "Everything that lives, lives by killing something ... combatitiveness exists at a molecular level, not even just a cellular level. The substance of life on earth is aggression and dominance, and we are probably the only creations in the universe that are conscious enough to look at that and say, 'Now I want to reject that,' even though it is the essence of why I exist now as an evolved brain."
> — David Cronenberg

The American home has become a sickbed. With *Rosemary's Baby* and *Night of the Living Dead*, 1968 was the watershed year, the year of the diagnosis. The American family was being invaded from without and within: if the zombies didn't get us, the devil would. It might be argued that the appeal of the horror movie depends on putting in jeopardy whatever we fear for the most, whatever is most "sacred" to us; it was a logical step for the genre to single out the family as its target. No argument here; but we have conveniently sidestepped the question as to *why* we feel the need to go to horror movies at all, so let's turn the argument around. Movies, from *Psycho* through *Night of the Living Dead, Rosemary's Baby, The Exorcist, It's Alive, The Omen*, and *Carrie*, were drawing from a hidden reservoir of dread and dis-ease in the collective unconscious regarding the state of the family and the American home. These movies revealed a sickness at the very core of society, and the fact that they veiled it in supernatural, or at least freakish, colors (as the devil, zombies, or telekinetic teenagers) only proved that this sickness, malignant as it was, was still "dormant."

In the 1960s, the once-inviolable sanctity of the American home had begun to come under scrutiny, even outright attack, in non-genre movies. *Who's Afraid of Virginia Woolf, The Graduate*, all those Tennessee Williams adaptations — it was not only acceptable to criticize modern domestic life, it was hip. Since we all had our own less-than-perfect experiences to draw upon, no one was really buying the utopian vision of the 1950s anyway; Vietnam and the budding counterculture had thrown everything out of whack. *The Godfather* was the *Gone with the Wind* for the new generation. It gave us a family founded on corruption, graft, and murder. It suggested that the traditional view of the family had become so much a thing of the past that we were waxing nostalgic for the togetherness and solidarity of the Mafia. By the 1970s, family values had lost whatever value they once had for us. Movies gave us antiheroes, drifter buddies, alienated loners (characters lacking a mate, much less children), seemingly adrift from family ties. There was something of a backlash in the late 1970s and early 1980s; a fantasy movie like Spielberg's *E.T.* took suburban family life as an idealized backdrop for the magic to play against; it was the opposite of the *Omen* and *Exorcist* movies, in which the family's lack of solidarity laid it open to invasion by the supernatural. (Spielberg's *Close Encounters* is an interesting departure for the director, in that the family collapses under the pressure of magic rather than being enhanced by it. Roy goes batty and his wife takes the kids and leaves him to pursue the aliens.)

Kramer vs. Kramer and *Ordinary People* (and later *Terms of Endearment*) were movies that played upon audiences' desire to see the family depicted as something troubled but essentially sacred, something worth fighting for. These movies couldn't go back to the Doris Day bliss-ignorance of the 1950s, they couldn't *ignore* completely the revelations of the previous decades; but they bent over backwards to paper over the cracks and somehow save the baby from going out with the bathwater. They failed. Academy's bias notwithstanding (it's hardly a coincidence that all these "wholesome" family dramas won Best Picture), these movies are pious, manipulative, and distinctly mediocre melodramas that, in the most contrived fashion, attempt to address a problem *with* the family, and so evade the real issue: the problem *of* the family.

In *Kramer vs. Kramer* it is divorce, in *Ordinary People* an unfeeling mother and a traumatized son, in *Terms of Endearment,* cancer. All surrogates for the "devil" of the horror movie, which in turn was only the messenger of doom disrupting the illusory contentment upon which the family structure was founded. The problem with movies, and with society as a whole, was that we could no longer *believe* in family values at all, for the very good reason that they had been put to the test and come up short. It wasn't that something was wrong in your average family arrangement; it was that the whole *set-up*—family as a socially programmed form of human behavior—was faulty. The family itself—as a means for the alienated, non-integrated ego to take refuge from the confusion of the world at large (id)—was but a buffer for our creeping discontent. It wasn't that happy people in happy families were somehow cursed by unforeseeable circumstance (be it the devil or be it cancer), and so lose their all-too-precarious contentment. It was that unhappy, desperate people, seeking

17. Behind Closed Doors: Antithesis and Antidote

solace and refuge in a hastily assembled family unit, were *bound* to bring this unit down sooner or later. The family's entire *raison d'etre* was spurious, flawed.

To put it another way, if fear of the Other (id) led the individual (ego) to construct a makeshift façade of familiar components—a house of cards to keep the Other at bay—it was not only probable but inevitable that, sooner or later (since this façade can only hold up for so long), the Other would return to tear it all down. The family's downfall was built into the family structure itself. Just like modern-day cars that are built to last a few years before wearing down in order to keep the company in business, we might say that the devil (our unconscious) designed "the family" along similar lines. As long as the Other exists, there will always be a need for "family" to keep it at bay, to act as a surrogate Id; and as long as the family exists, the Other will always have a reason (and a means) for undermining the ego and confronting it with its lack of solidarity.

In its strictest, biological sense, family is necessary for the propagation of the race. There is nothing to say that mating and rearing children is anything but a healthy and necessary human instinct, and as such, fully under the auspices of the Id and its unconscious program. But this is precisely why the Id (the devil) perceives the family *as its own*. Socially licensed family units are another thing, and to see the difference we have only to compare the human family—with all its sentimental ties, gatherings, ceremonies, and emotional blackmailing—to the animal equivalent, with all its ruthlessness and purity. In nature there is nothing to bring two animals together save procreation, and nothing to keep them together save survival instinct or, at a pinch, love. Likewise with animal children, who depend on their mother for nurture and their father for instruction and who, once grown, move on (otherwise are as likely as not to fight with their "parents"). This is how nature functions. It is "ruthless" only from a human, sentimental perspective; really it is simply functional. (One could say that human family arrangements are only "sentimental" from a ruthless, natural perspective, were it not that they are so often *dys*functional.)

The ego—seeking always consolidation, refuge, support—uses the family arrangement as a means for buoying itself up, for creating a false environment (or reality) in which it gets to be King. Just as so-called "romantic love" (sexual obsession) becomes a means for the ego to obsess, and so fortify itself under the guise of "altruistic" passion, so, with the family arrangement, the ego can disguise its actual ends (those of self-aggrandizement and isolation) as selfless, noble, and "traditional." Because the family (unlike the tribe, which has no precisely defined structure) is actually an extension of the individual, and not his effacement, the whole arrangement takes on a monomaniacal "us-against-them" flavor. The family that slays together, stays together. None of this is part of instinctive programming, any more than "romantic love" is part of procreation. It is (at the risk of repeating myself) merely a subterfuge by which the ego keeps the unknown at bay. As such, the family has become the seat and center of all unease, sickness, and psychosis, while society — its collective extension — is like a powder keg waiting to go off.

When the devil (or cancer) invades the family home from within and brings it to ruin, this is no more nor less than the Id claiming its own. Since the family is the primary (most socially acceptable) means by which the individual *represses* his true (savage) nature, it follows that this family is the first thing to go — the primary target — once the suppressed truth begins to resurface. Anyone who has been in a "romantic" relationship, even for only a few months, knows how deception, though practically unavoidable, is also invariably a cause for regret. Those facts or factors — peccadilloes — that are hidden away, out of sight, repressed through "good manners" (the desire not to rock the boat), inevitably resurface later in mutated, often monstrous forms. These are the monsters of our collective Id that lurk under our beds and in our wardrobes, for the simple reason that we do not give them any other "space" to inhabit. We do not acknowledge them openly because our façade of a perfectly functioning family and/or relationship is so desperately necessary to our own (egotistical) peace of mind. In most cases, these monsters resurface as simple misunderstandings, resentments, irrational arguments, and so forth. In more extreme cases, they result in physical ailments, or actual psychoses. (David Cronenberg's unpleasant *The Brood*, with its "The Shape of Rage" therapy clinic, is the horror text par excellence on this theme.)

The devil comes in many shapes and forms, but the preponderance of Satanic Ritual Abuses in US society can hardly be dismissed out of hand as "False Memory Syndrome" (if so, the question still persists, whence come the false memories?). Parental abuses, violation of children (sometimes infants, often adolescents complicit in the incestuous relationships), all this is far more common than most of us care to contemplate (hence the eagerness with which False Memory Syndrome has been accepted). Such occulted depravity may even turn out to be closer to the rule than the exception. All this is merely the confirmation of our thesis: schizophrenia is now rampant in society, at base of which is — the family/social structure itself. Once again the "evil" or psychosis is above all in the resistance to, or denial of, a latent condition, a condition which in itself might conceivably (if only our taboos and social conventions were less rigid) be seen as a positive (or at least revolutionary) phase in our transformation. (Cronenberg is again the leading movie spokesperson of this "revolution," specifically with *Shivers* and *Rabid*.) If the monsters are under our beds and the devil inside the home (the skeletons in the closet and Mama Bates in the basement), surely it pays to find out *exactly what they are doing there*?

If our collective Id is tearing down the ego-façade of our social arrangements and of "all we hold sacred," it might help to consider the possibility that

17. Behind Closed Doors: Antithesis and Antidote

it does so, not out of sheer malice, but in order to get *through* to us. That, in effect, we ourselves are tearing down these façades, because we can no longer bear the deceit, subterfuge, and self-denial upon which they are built. At which point the question, "What price civilization?" must be answered with another question: "Just how much are we prepared to sacrifice to learn the truth and gain our freedom?" Freedom and repression (civilization) are mutually exclusive. It is one or the other. And we may have left it so late that insanity is not only the ultimate freedom but the only kind we will ever get to experience. At which point, American Psychosis becomes not the disease but the antidote, albeit the very *antithesis* of what we have been programmed to desire.

As for movies? There are a few recent ones to consider on this subject, some of them rather poor, but all of them one way or another remarkable. *The Stepfather, Safe, American Psycho, American Beauty, Happiness, Eyes Wide Shut, Arlington Road, Far from Heaven, Capturing the Freidmans**, *A History of Violence, Into the Wild*, all in their varying ways address the breakdown of the family (or at least family values) and the emergence of a profoundly disruptive, in some cases plain psychotic, element at its center. This element, as we've seen, is the Id. Where once it was Satan Himself, now it's the next-door neighbor, the not-so-loving husband, the perverted heart and twisted mind of the domesticated male. Since the father is the controlling intelligence (if not the actual

---

*For anyone who thinks they have problems getting along with their family, *Capturing the Friedmans* is a devastating portrait of a society in crisis that provides a welcome glimpse of just how bad it can really get. Andrew Jarecki's 2003 documentary draws on extensive home movie footage (some of which predates videotape) and depicts the grim plight of an American family torn apart by too many skeletons. Alan Friedman was an apparently happily married father of three boys with a secret vice: he had a penchant for child pornography. A mail-order magazine he received led to a house search by local police that uncovered a stack of illegal material. When the police subsequently discovered that Friedman was also a private tutor of prepubescent boys (he taught piano and later computer skills), their suspicions went into overdrive and they conducted a thorough investigation (the film suggests maybe *too* thorough). They found (or created) the evidence they were seeking, and Friedman and his son Jessie (who also sat in on the classes) were charged with literally hundreds of unspeakable acts. Mysteriously, the alleged victims showed no signs of the abuse, nor did they once betray any signs of disturbance immediately after the alleged acts (they were picked up by their parents after the classes). They made no mention of being repeatedly raped, in fact, until they were interrogated by police much later. (Some of the abused children even signed up for an advanced course with Friedman the following year.) The film presents a mystery, perhaps insoluble, in which an apparently heinous transgression is distorted and obscured by the hysteria and outrage that surrounds it. Jarecki is sympathetic to the Friedmans without being biased towards them. Considering the incendiary nature of the material (its power to shock and disturb with the alleged crimes, and yet to invoke our sympathy for the accused), it's a remarkably balanced and cool treatment of the subject. The film's overall effect is not one of disgust or anger but confusion and melancholy. Both gripping and unsettling in its ruthless, almost surgical precision, *Capturing the Friedmans* dissects an American family (and by extension a society) submerged, and finally drowned, in a river of denial.

foundation) behind the family unit, it is fair to equate these characters (not all of them procreators, or even married)—Jerry Blake, Carol White, Patrick Bateman, Lester Burnham, Bill Harford, Cathy Whitaker, Tom Stall, etc.— with the ego itself. For here is a fascinating development. Once upon a time the Id came from without (even if it came *through* the family—as in *Rosemary's Baby* and *The Exorcist*—it still originated outside of it). It was as often as not opposed by the ego, or father (if he was present at all, as in *The Omen*, *It's Alive*, etc.; in *Rosemary's Baby* there is collusion between ego and id as Guy Woodhouse is in cahoots with the devil). Nowadays, there is no need for the id to infiltrate the family structure because it's already *there*; it has taken over the ego completely. The father figure no longer protects the home but actively disrupts it, negates it, even seeks to destroy it (Kubrick's *The Shining* is an early forerunner and *The Stepfather* the apotheosis of this theme). Basically these movies—though often quite schizoid in their own intentions—are attempting to acknowledge the awful truth: that society and family are rotten to the core and beyond all salvation. The baby (being a devil) must go with the bathwater.

In *The Stepfather* (1987), Jerry Blake (Terry O'Quinn) is the perfectionist-as-psychopath. The movie opens with a shot of him shaving off his beard and cutting his hair down to a bald patch, buttoning up his three-piece suit and nonchalantly leaving his home. As he comes down the stairs we get a shock-cut to blood-soaked walls and bodies on the floor. Jerry, we soon discover, is on a quest for the ideal American household to hide in, and when things don't work out for him, Jerry has a nasty habit of calling the whole thing off in the most extreme manner imaginable. Jerry can't bear the reality of human fallibility—it gets under his skin and makes him see red. He is so pathologically "straight" that he can't endure the slightest infraction upon his neat, tidy, smiling facsimile of reality. Jerry's normality isn't just a cover for abnormality, it's a psychosis in itself. His psychosis is so complete, so rigidly solipcist and self-contained, that it constitutes its own kind of sanity. (Psychopaths not only believe they are sane, but that they are more sane than everyone else.) Jerry isn't deranged, he's not out of control (until the moment his bubble bursts); but he's so dedicated to his vision of "the way things should be" (the "American Way") that he can't abide anything or anyone outside of that vision. Jerry's vision is all in his own head—the product of TV shows and *Saturday Evening Post* covers—and so he can't connect with anything. What's most dangerous about Jerry is that he doesn't know he's insane. He's a righteous killer who kills out of an almost religious sense of duty. Even when he's in his murderous mood, Jerry never loses his cool (or his sense of humor: while disposing of a body, strapping it into the driver's seat of a car, he quips, "Buckle up for safety!")

Jerry isn't demonic; he's not driven by unconscious urges, he's simply

17. Behind Closed Doors: Antithesis and Antidote

compelled by his obsession with order, his perfectionism. He's only trying to keep everything together, but as soon as he sees things are in danger of coming apart (again), he precipitates. It's as if he wants the pleasure of tearing his fantasy down for himself. He's quite literally an egomaniac who at the merest hint of the id — of the irrational, uncontrollable and vastly complicated *real* world beyond and outside his rigid control system — simply snaps and attacks. *The Stepfather*'s ingenuity is mixed up with its failings, however; as conceived by crime writer Donald E. Westlake, Jerry is more like a Frankenstein's monster, a composite psychopath, than an actual character. Westlake has apparently drawn on actual cases and recorded "motives," but he has isolated them from the actual crimes and mixed them altogether to make a kind of modern-day boogeyman. *The Stepfather* offers probably the best "boogeyman" in modern American movies, but I doubt if anyone like Jerry Blake exists in the real world. I doubt if there are serial killers who, as Pauline Kael put it, are "attracted to widows with children, in picture-postcard houses,"[7] and who go from one set-up to the next seeking refuge from the sordid insanity of life. There *are* homicidal maniacs who maintain a placid, smiling surface in their everyday life; that may even be the rule. But I doubt they are as assured and confident, as morally righteous (and apparently serene), as Jerry. The "psychos-next-door" are generally more shy and introverted than placid: like Norman Bates, you can see the anguish bristling behind their eyes. Jerry never seems to suffer the angst and confusion that all killers invariably must. He's closer to the Terminator than Norman Bates.

Jerry belongs in a casebook, or a horror movie, but not in the real world; ironically enough that's precisely his problem! But it's a drawback for the movie too, because although it's a slick, scary thriller, it lacks psychological depth, and hence resonance. Terry O'Quinn gives a sly, affable, sinister performance (he makes affability sinister!), and his Jerry, for all his lack of depth, belongs right up there with Perkins' Norman Bates. Although he may not be a fleshed out character, Jerry is an authentic cultural archetype, and I think an accurate depiction of a current form of social aberration. Jerry is the logical — and logically amok — development of the conformist, self-serving, family-valued yuppie that came to prominence in the "me-decade' of the 1980s. He's a living stereotype consolidated by Brett Easton Ellis's *American Psycho*, and what this archetype/stereotype symbolizes is a reaction to a society based upon lies. Jerry's psychosis, his very existence, is symptomatic of the conflict — the rift — between the accepted, *propagated* "way things are" (as upheld by TV, advertising, artificially-fostered "family" values, etc.), and the way things *actually are*. Like all good bogeymen, Jerry is the embodiment of a psychic reality that seethes and festers beneath this lying facade. The more things begin to fall apart, both in society and the collective psyche, the more they collapse, decay, lose their meaning, the more society (and the psyche) attempts to cover up the fact with the facade of "good behavior." In the end, such brave fronts are about as effective, or as rational, as sticking a band-aid on a slit jugular; they're not only a waste of time, they're potentially fatal.[8] As Colonel Kurtz (in a rare moment of lucidity) drawls: "You must make a friend of horror — horror and moral terror. If they are not your friends, then they are enemies to be feared, they are truly enemies."

This is what Jerry Blake is up to. His unconscious psyche is so utterly terrifying to him that he has to deny it entirely; at the first sign things aren't the way he intellectualizes them to be, he explodes. As Kael writes, "We become so familiar with Jerry's steady gray-blue eyes and his eerie intuitiveness that if he momentarily flips out and loses track of which identity he's using it's like a crazy crack in a frozen lake. We're shocked: we know — just as he knows — that it can't be sealed up again." *The Stepfather* is a parable for American society as a whole: a place where appearances are everything, in which a raving psycho can pass for the all-American super-dad and a scientific genius (e.g., Wilhelm Reich) can end up in a lunatic asylum. A society which puts all its stock in the superficialities of the ego and none at all in the darker, vaster depths of the id upon which life depends is (in the words of Charles Fort) "skating over thin existence." In such a society, all power is handed over to the "egos" — the control-obsessed maniacs and psychopathic politicians (for whom Jerry is really a prototype), and divorced from the id. The lunatics have not only taken over the asylum, they have broken out and turned the whole world into a madhouse.

If Jerry Blake was the patriarch as psychopath, *American Psycho* (2000) presents the *potential* father as a soulless, woman-hating, life-negating monster. Patrick Bateman (Christian Bale) has no conscience and in fact no emotions at all beyond "greed and disgust." He is pure ego, emptied of all relation or connection to others. He is isolate, alone, condemned to the abysmal darkness and coldness of his own, solipsist shell. He kills, maims, and tortures — one presumes — simply because he feels nothing; all that is left is a machine-like curiosity, a desire to get to the essence of the unreality of his being. It is not even a bid to *feel* something — since that's impossible — but merely to experience at least some visceral sensation, some sense of being alive. Killing is the last frontier, the last means of the disconnected ego to make contact with a world of shadows, phantoms, and lifeless puppets.

Bateman, like Ted Bundy and other real-life killers, is soulless flesh, manifesting will, devoid of awareness. Yet this Psychopath lives in us all, and will continue to do so until He is identified as what he is: an aborted expression of spiritual impulses, twisted and frustrated out of all shape, deformed, and turned into something terrible. As we saw with the GAP, it is a manifestation of a higher desire within the human soul to transcend physicality that, impotent to transform with love, instead destroys with hatred.

17. Behind Closed Doors: Antithesis and Antidote

Brett Easton Ellis' novel *American Psycho* wants to be a Dostoyevskian study of alienation and psychosis; yet as Ellis has conceived it there is no suffering, no anxiety, and hence no compassion. Mary Harron adopts a similarly clinical, "impartial" tone, but emphasizes the satire over the psychodrama. Her movie fails as either, and winds up as little more than a curiosity. *American Psycho* is not even offensive, and certainly not especially disturbing. Bale does a fine job as Bateman, but the role is a negation of any and all human qualities so he has to wipe himself out to "fill" the role. What's lacking in the movie (and in Bateman) is any real sense of unconscious motives or urges lurking beneath the character's actions. There is no subtext. Where is the id? This superficiality seems to be the point of the movie and book both: that, disconnected from the deeper context of the id, the ego becomes a monstrous caricature of itself. The American psychopath is unable to create and so can only destroy, endlessly, pointlessly, to vent his frustration. Perhaps this is close to the nub of the truth, not that the ego has become the id, but that the id has grown so distant, so deeply repressed, that the ego has taken its place. Where once the id emerged, against all the ego's resistance, as the Other — a devil — so as to awaken the ego to its true (dual) nature, it has now given up the fight. It has withdrawn into its own realm, leaving the ego "free" to assume its coveted role as supreme Ruler and only God. Utterly cut off from its source of wisdom or power, the ego has become a hollow, lifeless thing, and in desperation for its lost nature, it assumes the role of devil. Only now there is nothing to awaken or return, no meaning or purpose to its madness, there is only endless, senseless revolt. Bateman can feel nothing, not even the sick pleasures of his dementia. What makes him (and Bundy, and the rest) so "evil"— and the ego so racked with self-disgust and greed for "sensation"— is that he knows he does not exist. Existential nausea has finally reached its culmination in 21st century society. Its apotheosis is American psychosis.

American Beauty (1999) is a mutation of the yuppie-deconstruction comedy (*After Hours, Something Wild*, etc.). It gives us, one more time, the tired, old shtick of the family man reaching a point of desperation, of contempt for his life, and seeking a means to loosen up and rediscover his spirit. These means center (predictably enough) on sex and drugs, and even a little rock 'n' roll. Lester Burnham (Kevin Spacey) rediscovers pot, and this helps him to loosen up (even if, one might reasonably assume, it also exacerbates his growing sense of dissociation). At the same time, Lester projects all his existential yearning for new beginnings, for rejuvenation (as so many middle-aged men are wont to) onto a young college girl, Angela, the "American beauty" of the title, a vapid and stuck-up friend of Lester's teenage daughter Jane (Thora Birch). Lester becomes obsessed with the idea of sleeping with Angela and, as a result (through this unhealthy but quite natural fixation), he finds a new lust for life. Of course such lust can only lead to disaster, according to Victorian Hollywood morality at least, and so it does (though not directly).

How often does the long-repressed id get awoken by drugs or an illicit stirring of the libido, only to derange the ego with the unexpected intensity of its desire? Lester is unable to stand the drab, mundane repetition and repressed rage and hostility of his marriage; but when he begins to break out of the artificial restraints, he finds freedom more than he can handle. It sets off a series of events which eventually backfire on Lester and lead to catastrophe. *American Beauty* is a cliché from beginning to end and it behooves me to analyze it too much. It is a set of movie-contrived situations and characters, all taken from other movies, all stuff we've see before. The uptight husband smoking pot and quitting his job. The cold-hearted, superficial, money-grubbing wife. The alienated teenage daughter; the weirdo neighbor; the American psycho Marine dad. Bad movies that get hailed as great art can make one despair, or else rail impotently at the steadily lowering standards. And indeed one rails in vain. Best to sit back and enjoy the shallow spectacle for what it is.

Taste is a mysterious thing. There is nothing wrong with the acting or the filmmaking here; it is at the basic level of conception and writing that the dishonesty and cheapness of the movie lies. If Lester had fucked the teenage American beauty, you can be sure that Mendes' film would never have won the Oscar. And yet the incredible success of the movie, and its reception by both audiences and critics as a masterpiece, is actually its primary point of interest. Obviously, *American Beauty* spoke for something in the collective, a feeling of frustration at the lurking hypocrisy of our lives and at the growing pressure inside our skulls. It plays upon a deep sense of something being amiss, of something getting ready to blow. But the film plays up to this sense of uncertainty without really addressing it; it exposes its characters without ever making us feel any real affinity for them. As a social "satire" (which is what *American Beauty* can most adequately aspire to; as realism it's a joke), it has its cake and eats it. It debases and "exposes" "society" (the family), while more covertly flattering and patronizing its audience by allowing them to distance themselves from the satire (by not including them in it). Hence audiences can feel they are "seeing things as they really are," while at the same time they can enjoy the smug assurance of being different, of being superior. I don't suppose Sam Mendes, the director, or Alan Ball, the writer, consciously calculated their effects along such lines; but this is what they are doing just the same.

American Beauty is entertaining and well done, but it's offensive in its basic hypocrisy. It is so self-satisfied with its "deeper" (satirical) meanings that it has no qualms about backing away from the more provocative implications. Not only is it smug, it's spineless. When Lester has his attack of conscience in the literal nick of time, this is simply old Hollywood morality interfering with — and wholly invalidating — the previously hip satire we've been (half) enjoying until now. But whatever its minor merits and major flaws, *American Beauty* is a kind of watermark for the domestic psychosis (schizo society) movie at the turn of the millennium. It may be humbug, but it's historical humbug.

If *American Beauty* is a masterpiece, however, then we may be in more trouble than we think. The message of the movie is that you have to be dead to grok what's going on — unless you are Sam Mendes or Alan Ball, of course, who have a hotline to the truth (a truth the rest of us are lacking). And the implicit message is, thank God for movies like *American Beauty*, otherwise we would truly be damned! The arrogance of the filmmakers in presenting this mildly amusing farce as illuminated wisdom, as a social critique on "the human condition" (to quote Spielberg, whose DreamWorks funded the movie), is mind-boggling. When Mendes talks about underestimating audiences who prove their good taste by embracing and understanding his movie — and how it "warms the heart" — am I the only one who feels their stomach turning? If anything, the pious superiority of *American Beauty* is even more offensive than the mincing superciliousness of *Philadelphia* or the moronic moralizing of *Field of Dreams*.

Where the movie halfway salvages itself is in its semblance of a genuinely "mystic" vision. All of the scenes with Jane and Rickey (Wes Bentley), the two freaks, are genuinely touching, and the central scene of the dancing plastic bag is beyond reproach. But how Alan Ball manages to reconcile his occasional magical insights with his half-baked caricatures and contrived set-ups is a mystery. *American Beauty* is half a classic and half a travesty. There *is* beauty in the film, but then, as the movie also makes clear, there's beauty everywhere. There are moments that are effective, haunting, mysterious, and poignant, moments that stay with us where other, lesser movies fade into nothingness before the credits have rolled. But all this is undermined by the explicitness of the movie's "message," its insufferable preachiness. *American Beauty* is an exercise in self-deception, and its success is an illustration of the audience's capacity and willingness for complicity in the deception. Like the vapid teen queen Angela, we can imagine nothing worse than being ordinary, yet at the same time we are repulsed and threatened by anything freakish. For most of its length, *American Beauty* is a terribly ordinary movie; besides the plastic bag moment, there are no genuine insights, either into "the human condition" or the nature of existence or anything else. There are just cheap jokes and platitudes, but it's all done up so skillfully and piously that people are willing, anxious, to buy it. Since its message is that beauty rules and that even our "stupid little lives" will make sense to us some day (when we are dead), obviously audiences have a vested interest in embracing this message and in embracing the movie. I am not suggesting that the message itself is phony, only the means by which it is sold to us.

American Beauty isn't really selling beauty, much less truth; it's only selling itself, and this is implicit in the self-congratulating arrogance of the filmmakers when the (dead) Lester tells us at the end, "You have no idea what I'm talking about, I'm sure. But don't worry. You will some day." People respond to this. It's Big Daddy patting them on the head and telling them everything will be all right. They can go back to their stupid little lives and feel vindicated that someone *understands* their frustrations and disappointments — they even made a movie about them! But *American Beauty* is a defeatist vision. It's not about acceptance or gratitude, much less illumination; it's about resignation. Lester's little revolt allows him a last look around his life before death comes to claim him (it's inarguable that it was his awakening that brought his death about, if one follows the chain of events carefully enough). Perhaps within the contrived framework of the movie, Lester changes enormously in a few days or weeks; he even develops a conscience (out of nowhere), makes his peace with himself, and is thus ready to die. But Lester doesn't really *change*, he just sheds a few inhibitions and fulfills a few fantasies! Though its best scenes are with the "freaks," *American Beauty* is really a celebration of ordinariness which at the same time looks down on its (oh-so-ordinary) audience. And if people are telling themselves that the movie is about their lives, that it somehow taps into their unconscious feelings, doubts, and despair, who can argue with that? I can only say that (besides that plastic bag) it has no bearing on mine.

Having the movie narrated by a dead man is a neat, quasi-mystical gimmick; it lets us know that the rules are different, that the movie intends to play with the conventions, and even with our perceptions, and, just maybe, offer some special insight into the petty doldrums of our lives. It sets itself up for great things, and of course it delivers its "wisdom" on cue. The meaning of all we have seen is that all is beauty and we just have to "relax and not try to hold on to it," let it "flow through" us, "like rain." A pretty message; not profound, but pretty. Poignant and persuasive. But has the movie really shown us anything to support this wisdom? You can paint a picture and call it "Enlightenment," but if the picture doesn't do it then the title never will, no matter how boldly embossed it is. *American Beauty* shows us a tacky, amusing, sensationalistic freak show and tells us that this is our lives. Then it tells us that it's OK, we'll be dead soon and it will all make sense. And then it tells us to be grateful for this "enlightenment." And damned if we don't fall down on our knees at the altar of kitsch and call it art. This is calculation posing as vision. The ego can dress up all it wants as Id, but it will never be anything but a pretender. It's bogus and shameless, and yet sufficiently charismatic that we fall for it. Never underestimate the power of denial.

Which brings us to Stanley Kubrick's *Eyes Wide Shut* (1999), a movie I have wanted to write about ever since I first saw it, a movie that for all its awfulness (and, in fact, inseparable *from* it) is a quite fascinating, even beguiling, cinematic artifact, most especially within the parameters of our thesis — that of the infiltration of the American family by the Id. The title *Eyes Wide Shut* might be said to refer to the id itself, in fact, but also to the ego in denial, depending on how you look at it. "Eyes Wide Shut" might mean eyes that are able to see everything even though they are trying desperately not to (the id that sees everything the ego does, despite all the ego's attempts to blind it). Or it might refer to eyes that remain blind no matter how hard they strain to see (the ego's relentless attempt to control and comprehend the unknown, and its being forever frustrated by blindness in the face of the terrible, unknowable Id). Kubrick had a germ of an inspiration, even vision, when he took on his movie, and it's perhaps for this reason that otherwise quite intelligent critics have tried to defend the movie as a work of art.

How could anyone who has seen *Eyes Wide Shut* argue for it as "Kubrick's last masterpiece"? A 14-year-old can see the movie for what it is: a laughable, screamingly inept, and shockingly prudish "exposé" of sexual deviancy and jealousy. Academics and scholars have an uncanny knack for blinding themselves to all but their own "thesis," however (or in this case, opinion), and they are determined that Kubrick's last film be a masterpiece. Never mind that the movie itself goes about as far as any movie ever could to prove otherwise. Since such willful blindness is partly what Kubrick's last stinker is about, this is all rather fitting, in its way.

The film begins so catastrophically that it throws one into a trance of awe. Stilted dialogue, wooden acting, completely unnatural characters, all of which was presumably at least *partially* intentional on Kubrick's part, but certainly not wholly so. The impression he creates is not of being in an otherworldly or dreamlike place but rather of watching excruciatingly inept actors perform unspeakable dialogue. And yet, bad Kubrick is not the same as bad anyone else, and these early scenes are strangely hypnotic in their awfulness. I stayed watching in stupefaction (having originally planned to walk out once I had confirmed how bad the movie was), as if despite myself, caught by a strange, morbid curiosity. The film does improve after these early scenes, and the sheer beauty of the photography and the set design, of Kubrick's compositions, and even the strange, wooden quality of the acting and the looniness of the dialogue, somehow all conspire to keep us entranced. Kubrick is a master all right, only he's become a master of kitsch.

The story is essentially no more than a vignette on sexual jealousy. Alice Hartford (Nicole Kidman) tells husband Tom Cruise (Bill Harford) of her fantasy of having sex with a sailor she saw once, years before, when the couple were already married. She admits that, at that moment, she would have given up everything, her life with Bill and their children, for one night with this mysterious sailor. Daffy as this confession may seem, it is devastating to Bill, completely capsizing his complacent world as husband and father, and throwing him into torment and self-doubt (but also temptation). All this comes down to the stirring of the unconscious, set in motion by an unmet but nonetheless acknowledged (now confessed) desire. This desire is in itself an expression of the hungry id's desire to tear down everything for a moment of impulsive freedom. Alice is not overwhelmed by desire for the sailor (no one could be *that* desirable); she is overwhelmed by the idea of throwing away everything for a moment of heady satisfaction. She is terrified by the discovery of just how precarious her conscious, rational, ego-based life *is*; at the same time, she is fascinated and enticed by the power of the unconscious to undo it all in a heartbeat. Although she doesn't act upon it, the moment (of nonaction) stays with her always; not as a regret but as a reminder of her own uncertainty, and of the force and perversity of her passion. (As in *American Beauty*, pot is the catalyst. The confession comes when the happy, daffy couple get stoned, and non-experienced viewers, seeing Kidman's performance, might be forgiven for assuming that marijuana is indeed a deadly substance. One spliff throws the whole family structure into peril.)

For his part, Cruise's doctor is likewise haunted by the confession, and for similar reasons. He feels doubly betrayed because, not only does he realize how tenuous his hold upon his wife is, and how easily he might have lost her (and still might), but what's worse, he is plagued by the awareness that such unbridled passion is something he himself has never inspired in her. He experiences jealousy over a woman who is already his and envy of a man he never even laid eyes on, and who might not even exist. This jealousy becomes the undoing of all his self-esteem and stability as a husband, lover, and, most of all, as a *man*. The Id disrupts.

Eyes Wide Shut is about Harford's identity crisis, and hinging it around sexual insecurity and jealousy is a sound enough device. The foundation of most men's self-esteem is their sense of sexual prowess. Since the female is herself the Other, the representative of the Id, her being both unfathomable and uncontrollable is a given; her sexual desire, while intoxicating, makes her also terrifying. And a man's complete incapacity to either fathom or control a woman's sexuality leaves him one sole means of handling it: namely, to *satisfy* it. Once he begins to doubt this ability, he begins to doubt his worthiness or readiness to interact with the Other, and so loses his footing as a conscious, ego-driven individual. From here, by a forest fire chain reaction, the whole "kingdom" (home) may collapse (as did Camelot) due to a single infidelity (even if only "imagined": to the id there is no difference).

So Harford goes on a quest: being shunned by the female, he must seek the anima within. He must rediscover his own private connection to the unconscious in order to find the means to deal with the unruly Other of his life (and wife). Accordingly, he undergoes various quasi-sexual encounters: with the wife of a dead man (since he's a doctor, Harford goes anywhere he pleases, and is always "on duty"); a street hooker with AIDS; an adolescent girl whose

17. Behind Closed Doors: Antithesis and Antidote

father pimps her out to Japanese tourists; and finally, a whole host of naked, masked, mysterious fuck-doll females at a secret occultist gathering which he stumbles blindly into, following a flukish lead from a college buddy. This is the culmination of his quest and the heartland of the Id, the underworld itself; some of the movie's best (though also most ludicrous) scenes are here, amidst the red velvet, incense, and writhing naked bodies (though only the women are naked).

If *Eyes Wide Shut* is a joke of a movie, finally, it's because its more sinister under layers are all so utterly lame and devoid of menace, or even perversity, that Harford's quest into the id realm seems like exactly what it is: a middle-class jaunt into kinky sexuality. Kubrick was by this time so isolated in his own cerebral, priggish world that he had lost all sense, not only of human speech patterns and emotional responses, but also of just what constitutes vice and degradation (and danger or suspense) to modern audiences. What he gives us is mere frolicking. I doubt if a director ever lived with *less* of a sense of the workings of the id than Kubrick, a meticulously rational and painfully *conscious* film artist, whose films not only lack anything resembling human compassion but are equally devoid of mystery or poetry. In Kubrick's movies (and none more than *Eyes*), there's no involvement because there's nothing at stake. We are watching actors move about his elaborate, gorgeous sets like pieces on a chessboard, and all we can admire, at best (besides how pretty the pieces are), is the skill and precision of his moves. But since he's only playing with himself, there's not even the rudimentary suspense of a more mediocre movie as to which side (ego or id) is going to win.

In *Eyes Wide Shut*, the only thing that's mildly at stake (besides Kubrick's reputation) is Tom Cruise's smile; we can't for a second believe in the marriage, since we are introduced to characters so stilted and ludicrous that they barely seem human at all (the children don't exist save as adornments). Kidman gives a decent enough performance (save for that introductory clunker and her excruciating pot-smoking scene), and she's at least halfway human to us; but since she's little more than the mouth piece for the writer and director's paranoid sexual fantasies, we can't feel much affection for her. Tom Cruise has the perfect role here for a non-actor who only has to look good, flash his card, and say, "I'm a doctor." With a better actor the film would probably seem even sillier than it does. As it is, Cruise, by not seeming to be in on the joke, helps to keep the proceedings sufficiently sincere that they *almost* come off as high camp. Sidney Pollack, in a thankless role, is a complete embarrassment. Pollack directed himself admirably in *Tootsie*, and did some solid work for Woody Allen in *Husbands and Wives*; but for Kubrick he has turned himself into an excruciating presence, a golem, flailing through his scenes like a fish out of water. Point by point and scene by scene, line by line and performance by performance, *Eyes Wide Shut* is one of the very worst major American productions in movie history. Yet it remains one of the most watchable and intriguing bad movies ever made. Beyond Kubrick's exquisite visual sense, this can be accounted for by the movie's subtext, which somehow holds our interest even when the text itself— the plot and the dialogue — is for the most part lifeless and dull.

When Harford returns from his jaunt into the underworld, his wife is asleep and dreaming, laughing in her sleep. She wakes and, though she appears quite contrite, rather sadistically recounts her dream to him. The dream is your basic male anxiety nightmare, an archetypal worst case scenario: she is fucking an endless series of faceless men while her husband watches helplessly on in despair, and she laughs at his misery and torment, mocking him for his weakness and inadequacy. You would think this might be enough to cement Harford's disgust and send him packing; but somehow it has the opposite effect (or at least her dream coincides with Harford's own realization), and he appears to put aside his foolish jealousy (suppress that id), and move on.

The idea of his straying so far afield (into the underworld to confront his sexual demons) is of course that he purge his ego of all its doubts and realize how important, how real, his marriage is to him. The movie suggests that Harford (being a doctor) is something of a prude, and that his hang-ups have forced his wife to indulge in fantasies in order to satisfy herself. Hence, the last line of the movie — Kidman's "Let's fuck" — suggests that they haven't done so for ages, and that — now those sex demons of doubt and jealousy are finally overcome — they can get back down to "the good stuff." In broader terms, Harford's repressing of his unconscious sexual nature has been a source of restriction and frustration to his wife's libidinous desires (though he's pretty frisky in the early scene, this soon gives way to his treating of an overdosed naked woman in Sidney Pollack's suite). As a result, she has made her own (halfway) excursion into id realms, with the fantasy of the sailor. This in turn comes back to haunt Harford with his own inadequacy and impotence, and so he goes off in search not merely of revenge but of his own initiation so that he can then meet his wife on new, common ground, as her equal. Poor Bill is suffering from borderline personality disorder: fear of loss and abandonment, low self-esteem, and above all, fear of freedom. Once he has confronted the truth of his own turbulent, transgressive nature (to the point that his awakening id is beginning to threaten the welfare of his family, indicated by his finding the Masonic mask on the pillow next to his sleeping wife), he is then able to understand and forgive his wife's own peccadilloes. The once disruptive id becomes a creative source of inspiration and reconciliation; the previously corrupting, hate-filled sexual fantasies become the healthy desire of an uninhibited couple. "Let's fuck."

The masks are central to this reading, since mask = persona (in Greek), namely, the ego. Hartford is our classic schizo: he doesn't know *who* he is or

17. Behind Closed Doors: Antithesis and Antidote

what he wants, and he wanders passively, yet also compulsively, from one loopy situation to the next until he finds himself at the heartland, where he is unmasked by sinister, apelike id people. His end appears to have come, he has strayed too far from his safe, secure family hold and fallen into the hands of depraved perverts with no regard for his standing (his "I'm a doctor" isn't going to work here). But he is saved at the last moment (in a creakingly staged and wholly implausible scene) by a naked, masked female who offers up her own life as forfeit for his. Saved by the anima! (The same female he brought back to life in the opening scene, as it happens; like Daniel in the lion's den, the good doctor discovers the value of good deeds.) It's too bad *Eyes Wide Shut* is such a sloppy, stupid movie, because it's full of potential; if only Kubrick had settled on the right tone and decided whether he was making a surrealist sex comedy, an occult mystery, or a psychological thriller — or *something*— then he might have pulled it off. As it is, it's rather like a two-headed calf or a human seal: fascinating, strangely endearing, but rather painful to look at. Chances are it should never have been born at all.

David Cronenberg's *A History of Violence* (2005, written by Josh Olson from the graphic novel by John Wagner and Vincent Locke) is perhaps the most fully realized treatment of the schizophrenic journey within the family

Rites of Regeneration: Tom Stall (Viggo Mortensen) comes clean in front of the family in *A History of Violence* (2005, New Line).

context. It's a kind of reverse *Stepfather*: an apparently mild-mannered husband and father hiding out in suburbia is revealed as a killer, only in this case the violence, rather than being turned against the family, is used to protect it. The result is not fragmentation but a new kind of integrity and wholeness.

In many ways, *A History of Violence* is the same story as *Matrix* and *Fight Club*, told in a much more subtle and traditional way. The subtext is equally profound here — and almost identical — but since the narrative is far more conventional it's a lot easier to miss it. In a way, because it's more realistic (though also less visionary), the film is a more pure description of the schizophrenic journey. With fewer abstract meanings, the blueprint is there for all to see. *A History of Violence* depicts the secret self, the Other, as it is invariably experienced in a civilized society: as a killer within.

A History of Violence begins with two killers leaving a motel. One of the men goes into reception and we see the murdered body of the proprietor. A little girl comes out and the killer raises his gun. The two men — we never find out anything about them — leave the motel and drive to a small town, arriving after dark. They enter a café belonging to Tom Stall (Viggo Mortensen). Tom informs them he is closing but when the men ignore him, Tom serves them the last of the coffee. A customer tries to leave but the men prevent her, drawing their weapons. Tom takes the men off guard, however, killing both of them. Beneath his mild manner is a ferocious capacity for violence; when he acts it is with the ruthlessness and precision of a trained assassin. As it happens, this is not far from the truth.

As a result of the encounter, a crack appears in Tom's carefully constructed façade and his persona is instantly compromised. National TV reporters are drawn by the incident and Tom becomes a local celebrity. The very thing (we soon discover) that made him a criminal and forced him underground — his ability for violence — has brought him to the attention of the community. Tom has no choice but to integrate this new/old aspect of himself into his persona, albeit in a new form, now as a "hero" rather than a killer. It is the same violent self that has emerged, but the context has changed.

The integration of Tom's secret past into his persona is at first only partial; the full truth has not yet been revealed. Although Tom's wife, Edie (Maria Bello), and their children (Jack, played by Ashton Holmes, and Sarah, played by Heidi Hayes), have glimpsed a new side to Tom, they have yet to suspect what it really means. Three more strangers (led by a scarred Ed Harris) show up at the café and confront Tom, calling him "Joey." Although Tom professes ignorance to his family — and keeps "Joey" hidden from them — it's clear the men mean business. Tom's repressed primal nature has been awakened, drawing back disowned elements from his past. The cracks have begun to appear on the surface of his artificial life. Now that the past has been summoned,

17. Behind Closed Doors: Antithesis and Antidote

Tom's history as a killer — his secret identity as Joey — is the only thing that can protect his family *from* this past.

Tom's secret is that he is really Joey Cusack, a mob killer hiding out in a small-town with his wife and children. The civilized man has disowned and denied his primal past. Tom's attempt to create a new life, free from the past, echoes the ego's attempt to split off from its primitive, potentially psychopathic nature. Tom is an upstanding community member, honest and dependable but ordinary, even dull. His cover can't last, however; eventually his past must catch up with him, and this it does in the form of the very violence he has disowned.

Tom's challenge — the schizophrenic journey — is to fully integrate his two selves, past and present, civilized ego and primal id, into a new identity, part Joey, part Tom. When the mobsters come to threaten his family (to abduct Jack and force Tom to return with them), Tom/Joey has to choose between revealing his true nature and saving his family (becoming Joey), or maintaining his façade and doing nothing. This is no choice at all. Tom must save his family even if by doing so he will lose their respect. At a certain point, the false ego self has no choice but to assume responsibility for its past, and allow the authentic self to show.

Although this is primarily Tom's challenge, it's clearly a crisis for the whole family. The assumptions on which it was founded have given way, opening up an abyss. This is especially true for Edie: her husband is not the man she thought he was but a killer with a dark past. Since she initially experiences this side of Tom in a heroic guise, she is seeing her husband more fully *as a man* than ever before. Although she fears it, she needs Tom's capacity for brutality to protect them from the threat of his past, and so she stands by him despite her doubts. What is most threatening to Edie, however, is not Tom's violence but his deception. Tom's name, his entire personal history, is revealed as a lie. Edie no longer knows *what* to believe. If it's a shock to Tom to find "Joey" still alive inside him, Edie is seeing a part of Tom she never even knew existed. So Tom becomes not less in Edie's eyes but more — more exciting and mysterious, but also more frightening and untrustworthy. She experiences the threat of violence not just from without — Tom's past, as embodied by the mobsters coming to harm them — but also from *within*. An unknown and dangerous new element has appeared at the very center of her life.

After she finds out the truth, Tom and Edie fuck. It's an angry, violent act (she is more aggressive than he is), clearly an act of desperation. (The crisis is anticipated early in the film when Tom and Edie engage in sex games, taking on roles from the past and pretending to be high school lovers. Edie dresses up as a college cheerleader and awakens Tom's lust. Apparently, evoking the past through this "harmless" sex play is what opens the door to the primal.) Despite the psychological revelation, nothing has changed at a physical level; their bodies still feel the same way. Yet Tom has awoken his primal self, and this is reflected by a similar awakening in Edie. It's "Joey" she wants to fuck, not Tom, and the sex is a purely primal thing; emotionally, they are strangers, so they can only fuck in a wild, impersonal way. This is the only means for them to connect now, and it's imperative they not lose this physical connection because to do so would be to lose everything. A history of violence, to be complete, must also be a history of sex. Cronenberg is the perfect director to map the uneasy, disturbing connections between the creative and the destructive aspects of our primal natures. The film shows how Tom and Edie's marriage is strengthened and transformed by the awakening of the id, how it is forced to go from personal to impersonal. As the dark energy of Tom's past is unleashed after being trapped for so many years, it explodes all the illusions and assumptions of identity, all the superficial roles upon which the marriage has depended until now. The awakening of Edie and Tom's authentic selves forces the marriage either to destroy itself or to go to the next level, to become something more primal, savage, and raw, but also something deeper, more lasting and true.

The same applies to Tom's relationship with his son. Tom's owning his past reveals patterns of generational violence. This is not just Tom's personal past; an atavistic current has been awakened, something that goes back through countless generations, and Jack is inspired by seeing this new side of his father. It brings out his own primal nature (he gets into a fight at school), which then creates conflict between father and son. Tom tries to discipline Jack, telling him that violence is "wrong," but Jack sees through his father's hypocrisy—his "do what I say not what I do." Clearly actions speak louder than words, so instead of listening to Tom he follows his example. As a result, Jack is able to claim his power as a man and come to Tom's aid when the mobsters show up at the house. By this unfolding, this revelation of *blood*, father and son are bound together in the most primal and ancient rite of passage.

With his son's aid, Tom manages to eliminate the danger of the men, but he knows he can't protect his family indefinitely. The only way to defuse the threat of his past is to go back into it. It turns out that Joey's brother Richie (William Hurt) is the controlling intelligence behind the mobsters, and is seeking to bring Joey back.* As in so many myths and parables, the brothers represent opposing sides of a single psyche, ego and id: the mild, law-abiding Abel and the wild, unruly rebel Cain. As two aspects of a single intelligence, the brothers are compelled (by sibling rivalry) to fight for dominance. This reflects

---

*Joey went underground after he betrayed Richie to escape his vengeance, creating a new identity and hiding out where he was confident no one would ever recognize him. When his face appeared on the national news, Richie was alerted and quickly sent his henchmen to find Tom/Joey and bring him back.

a natural psychological process: the ego suppresses the id in order to establish a separate identity outside of it; but eventually it is compelled to recognize the id's existence (in an inevitable "showdown") and allow primal awareness to emerge once more, flooding it (the conscious ego) with its own dark energy. There are two possible results of this emergence: either the id-energy destroys the ego (if the ego is unable to integrate it), or it transforms it, bringing about a synthesis of the two aspects of being, conscious and unconscious awareness.

By disowning the worst of himself ("Joey"), Tom also disowns the best. This killer inside is what all males suppress in order to be "civilized"; but the primal aspect is also the spine of the upright male, the protector who will kill to protect his family from external dangers. This aspect is so deeply buried in our culture that it's almost impossible to see it in anything but distorted form as ugly, violent, and brutish. Because it has been disowned it has become coarse, a caricature of itself. Hence it must be brought to light, redeemed, by the more refined consciousness of the ego.

Psychologically, Tom must journey back into his primal nature and deal with it at the root. He must become Joey again and return to his past to take care of the things left undone, the parts disowned which he was therefore unable to integrate. This process is symbolized — as in so many action thrillers — by the hero's confrontation with and slaying of the adversary, in this case his brother. Through the destruction (and subsequent integration) of his Shadow, Tom becomes complete, a fully balanced ego and id. He is then able to return to his family a "conquering hero," a whole man, having overcome his demons and entered into his true nature. The demons of the past are finally put to rest and the family silently, gratefully, accept Tom's place among them, at the head of the table. The family that slays together, stays together.

Cronenberg has always been the most visionary of filmmakers so it's ironic that *A History of Violence*, which is neither a visionary work nor an especially personal one, is probably his best film. Perhaps Cronenberg's brilliance as a director can only fully shine when he is detached from the material? His is the most unobtrusive of visionary styles; he has the cool eye for composition, the clinical precision, distance, and dispassionate approach to character of Kubrick; but underneath the clear, cool surface is a festering undercurrent of id energy (totally absent from Kubrick's films) more reminiscent of David Lynch. It's a formidable combination. Cronenberg has Lynch's fascination for viscera, for the inner workings of the body and the psyche, and Kubrick's aloofness and faintly nihilistic lack of empathy. Even when he is dissecting his characters (his films seem to be made on an operating table), Cronenberg keeps them at arm's length.

Cronenberg's films are objective examinations of the human condition, but the flaw in much of his work is the absence of real human beings: the condition he shows us is too far removed from anything recognizably human.

Lately, Cronenberg has chosen more conventional storylines and I think it has freed up his genius as a filmmaker. For a long time, he was a visionary in search of a style: his ideas were generally more interesting than the films themselves because he was unable to communicate his vision in strong, narrative form. In *History of Violence* (and *Eastern Promises*, a less successful work but impeccably directed), he has allowed his vision to inform his work as a director rather than capsize it. There's a sense of a controlling intelligence that exists between the lines; it's as if Cronenberg is no longer imposing his vision upon us but allowing it to creep into the narrative, like a slow-acting poison.

Until now Cronenberg's unconscious has been so obviously in charge that it has often undermined his films, making them inaccessible to anyone who wasn't already tuned to his particular vision. The workings of the id are so prevalent in Cronenberg's films that they appear to be horror or sci-fi even when they aren't. With his last couple of films, he has achieved balance: ego and id working in harmony. Cronenberg is a rare case of a filmmaker who *appears* to have compromised his vision but who has actually grounded it and made it more functional, expressing it in a more satisfying way by taking on less "personal" projects. Apparently Cronenberg had to work through his obsessions before his unconscious could settle down; his imagination was so overactive, so unruly, that his conscious mind may have been unable to fully engage in what he was doing as a filmmaker. Most of his films don't seem to care much about *communicating* with the audience because the director is too busy working out his private obsessions. This made them unwatchable for many people — they were simply too raw, too revealing. With maturity, Cronenberg has learned austerity. His filmmaking is now the cleanest and most unencumbered of any visionary filmmaker. The power of *A History of Violence* — Cronenberg's masterpiece to date — is a match for its protagonist. There's a sense of untapped reservoirs of energy and rage banked up behind the cool, calm surface. It's not what he inflicts upon us, but what he holds back.

A History of Violence shows how the schizophrenic journey is a means for the family to arrive at a new level of authenticity through an integration of the disowned "primal" aspects, symbolized by the male capacity for violence. *Into the Wild* (2007) is a true story to *A History of Violence*'s fiction (based on Jon Krakauer's book about Chris McCandless), and it shows the flip side of the process. In this case, the hero's journey to individuation leads not to wholeness but to death, causing the *dis*integration of the family and not its integration. The obvious difference between the two films (besides that of fiction versus fact) is that, in *A History of Violence*, it is the father who undergoes the schizophrenic journey (becoming an upright example for the son), while in *Into the Wild* the burden of integration has fallen onto the son. This is precisely because the father has not provided the necessary example: *that of owning his darker aspects*.

17. Behind Closed Doors: Antithesis and Antidote

In *Into the Wild*, Chris' father, Walt McCandless (William Hurt, who played Joey's brother in *A History of Violence*), is a bigamist who has been leading a double life secret from his family. Compared to Tom Stall, however, Walt's secret past is unexciting and mundane, entailing an illicit sexual relationship rather than a murderous history. At the same time, Walt's motive for secrecy is less to protect his family (as in Tom's case), and more a way to facilitate his own pleasure. Because of the schizoid example which Walt gives his son — because of the father's failure to take responsibility for his duplicity, his being *split*— the wound is passed onto Chris (Emile Hirsch).

Chris is angry and hurt by his father's deception and perceives it as a betrayal. As a direct result, he rejects not only his father's love but his values and beliefs as well, viewing them (correctly) as shallow and hypocritical. Without such values, Chris is all at sea without a moral compass, and this lack of orientation accelerates his own identity crisis. Unable to believe in the persona passed down to him by his parents, he goes in search of his own truth. Whereas Tom Stall goes back into his past to seek wholeness, Chris, because of his own father's failure to do the same, can only move forward into an unknown and impossible future. Like Bobby Dupea in *Five Easy Pieces*, he heads for Alaska, seeking not wholeness but oblivion.

Chris McCandless is determined to get to the truth whatever the cost in suffering (and not just his own: since his heart was broken by his father's deception, he has no qualms about breaking anyone else's). By the end of his journey (we know because he kept a journal), he realizes that whatever truth or happiness he finds in the wild is meaningless without someone to share it with. His desire to connect to Nature and so come to know his own truth is incomplete without a connection to others. This may be the final truth that McCandless realized; in a way, it's the truth that killed him — or rather, the truth that he had to die to discover.

McCandless' quest for freedom didn't only risk death, however; in a way it depended on it. McCandless was punishing his family — and society — for deceiving him, and this he did by *sacrificing himself*. His trip to Alaska was more than a London-esque test of manhood or rite of passage; it was a search for meaning, an attempt to strip away the layers that came between McCandless and the truth, to remove all the masks and see what lay behind them. McCandless' death was testimony not merely to his own folly but to his father's failure to provide values for him to believe in. McCandless' parents pay the ultimate price for their failure to love their son in a way that's meaningful to him, because McCandless (albeit unconsciously) chooses to die rather than live in a world without this meaning.

If his death has more significance than the life his parents wished for him ever could, it is because it was at least his *own* meaning, and his choice. As a writer and director, Sean Penn doesn't belabor any of this. He doesn't make the mistake of bringing the parable-like qualities of the tale to the surface. He focuses on the story, and on bringing his characters to life, and lets the rest take care of itself. The metaphor of Chris' journey is all the more powerful for being "found" rather than imposed. McCandless was torn between the person his family expected (assumed) him to be and the person he felt he was. He was smothered and oppressed by these expectations, and willing to seek freedom at any cost, including death. In the end, death became the only freedom possible.

The realization of an inner truth invariably either precipitates crisis or is the result of one. McCandless' decision to seek the truth of the wild — to disappear into the unconscious — precipitated a corresponding crisis for his family, who experienced his coming to manhood the only way they could — as loss and betrayal. McCandless, for his part, creates a crisis that is final, total, pure, and that allows such realization to occur. Only in the isolation of Nature does Chris realize his need for humanity, the need for a connection to his own kind. The realization comes too late for him to use; but then, it may never have come at all.

The call of the wild is the call of the id, the great wilderness of the unconscious that lies behind and underneath the flimsy constructs of culture and "identity." *Into the Wild* shows the failure of the family fold to provide meaning or context for the ego to sustain itself with, and the inevitable collapse (both of the ego and the family) that results. The center — the male child, the "heir" upon which all future hopes are pinned — cannot hold. The sins of the father weigh heavy upon Chris, and because he sees no possibility for honest communication with his father, there is no possibility of reconciliation. The split in his psyche is a generational wound which can only be healed by owning the very violence and deception that caused it. Like the river that finally traps Chris and leads to his death, this split is an unbridgeable abyss. Because the father denied his own unconscious — his guilt and responsibility, and the wounds that drove him to betray his family — because he assumed instead a superficial and inauthentic façade of decency, Chris is compelled to move in the opposite direction. He must go all the way into the unconscious realms, into the id, into the wild.

A History of Violence (albeit in symbolic form) shows how Tom Stall, by owning his primal side and allowing it to transform both himself and his family, becomes whole. He becomes both a more trustworthy husband for his wife and a more upright father for his son, a protector and a guide. For Jack, he can now provide the example of masculinity every young man so desperately needs: not the example of violence but that of authenticity. In *Into the Wild*, Walt provides Chris with the negative example of schizophrenia: duplicity. There is no possibility of integration in this example, only the terrible price of fragmentation and denial. Because of this, Chris can only move further and further away from his father, from his past and from his roots, into the unknown. He travels as far and as fast as he can go, without every knowing or caring what he is moving towards. And eventually, inevitably, that great void into which he journeys takes his last breath from him, and swallows him whole.

Epilogue: Rounding Up the Usual Suspects

Psychos in denial, schizos in the strangest places. Together they serve to show how the family (society) is broken apart by discontent, resentment, jealousy, deceit, psychosis, sexual obsession, and perversion. All this the movies manage to depict fairly persuasively. But when it comes to putting the family back together again — in a movie like *Cape Fear* (1992), for example — having taken it through the domestic apocalypse and created a stronger, tighter family unit, this is where the Hollywood humbug begins. Since society has already been exposed as rotten to the core, and founded on deceit, deviance, denial, and repression, it's not only a matter of *how* could it ever put itself back together again, but *why*? The answer is simply that Hollywood — whether it's Kubrick or Solondtz or Scorsese or whoever — upholds the Status Quo, and that most filmmakers, even if subversive in other ways, tend to stop short of advocating complete anarchy. (This is what makes *Fight Club* so refreshing, and so controversial.) Most of all perhaps this is because it's so hard for the self-preserving ego to see total collapse of its world as any kind of a *solution*, no matter how dire the problem (world) may be. This is understandable. The need for positive resolutions goes way deeper than the commercial Hollywood tradition of happy endings. If all the "apocalypse" (revelation of the unconscious) has to offer is the destruction of all existing forms, who in their right mind would advocate it? But if an apocalypse is due at all, then whether the cause be religious or sociological or psychological or ecological (or a combination of all these factors), the implication is the same: "right mind" is exactly what we haven't got.

Revelation is a process of stripping away the layers of illusion, the veils of self-deception, and the *masks* or facades with which we disguise or repress our true (animal) natures. With these façades we construct a comfortable cage called civilization in which to hide a while from the brutal beauty of the wilderness. Society, family, personality, identity, all these things are the luxuries of slaves; they are obstacles to freedom, to wholeness. Without going into why such obstacles have been created, we can at least get to observe (in movies) how exactly they are being destroyed. From Ethan Edwards to Chris McCandless, via Scottie McFerguson, Norman Bates, Hud, Benjamin Braddock, Blondy, Bobby Dupea, Randal P. MacMurphy, Trelkovsky, Bruce Wayne, the Joker, Ichabod Crane, Travis Bickle, Rupert Pupkin, Chancey Gardner, Leonard Zelig, Truman Burback, Craig Schwartz, Lars Lindstrom, Frank Pierce, James Cole, Donnie Darko, Thomas Anderson, Tyler Durden, Jerry Blake, Patrick Bateman, Lester Burnham, Bill Hartford, and Tom Stall, the myriad masks and countless facets of the collective Id shuffle and reshuffle, in search of some redeeming, harmonizing sequence or order by which the multifold schizophrenic ego may conquer itself. For only by surrender to the indomitable Id can the ego transform itself into the mysterious, unspeakable Other. Of course, all these schizophrenic or psychopathic personalities are only such when they are isolated and made to stand for the individual rather than fragments of the whole, masks which it wears for certain, specific occasions. The challenge of the schizophrenic journey — individuation — is to find the saving grace, the specific, non-psychotic function, of each of these facets, and so engage it, apply it, as part of a greater Working.

Ethan is a great tracker, and his obsessiveness and isolation are intrinsic to what makes him effective as such. Scottie is a dreamer, a romantic; he makes a lousy cop, and is not much better as a private eye, but he would make a wonderful poet. Norman Bates? Great taxidermist. Meticulous, precise, clinical, empathic. Give him something to do with his hands and keep his mind occupied and he might make a fine orderly. Hud? Well, he's a cad but a great ranch hand; his callousness and cynicism make for hardheaded objectivity. He may be out for himself, but he's also nobody's fool. Benjamin? Sensitive, searching, open-minded, non-judgmental, and harmless. Bobby Dupea is a great confrontationalist, he cuts through the crap in every situation. Self-loathing, but with integrity. MacMurphy, sheer dynamism; his suicidally provocative tendencies keep pushing the situation to its limit, and ensure that Bobby's jadedness not lead to stagnation. (On the other hand, Bobby's intolerance for poseurs would keep MacMurphy's messianic pretensions in check.) Paul (from *Last Tango*) has a primal kind of honesty, and soul-searching qualities; he is self-pitying but also self-mocking, a willful clown who could do with a little of Bobby's indifference, and some of MacMurphy's passion, to override his morbidity. Suicidal impulses are what make up most of Trelkovsky's character (which is just an empty vessel waiting to be filled), but his receptivity, meekness, and lack of assertive qualities suggest a poetic or artistic temperament. A little of the simple survivalism of Travis, some of his more aggressive nature, his religious zeal, and his sense of purpose, might help to direct this suicidal impulse into something more constructive. Rupert Pupkin's complete undauntability, his indifference to other people's opinions (or even actions), his relentless, unbending ambition, and his low cunning, all come in handy on the schizophrenic journey. Bruce Wayne's deductive reasoning, his capacity for solitude and silence, his complete self-sufficiency and self-mastery, and Batman's agility, strength and prowess, all these are some of the indispensable (and indisputable) perks of psychosis. Ichabod Crane's objectivity and diligence, James Cole's complete lack of self-concern, his lack of attachments to past or future; Jerry Blake's meticulousness and attention to detail; Tom Stall's unusual gift for self-effacement; Chris McCandless' innocence, idealism, and adventurous spirit; and let's not forget Thomas Anderson's ability to *believe* in the sanctity of his own split personality, and Tyler Durden's remarkable capacity to manifest himself—*ex nihil*, whole and fully functioning—from the void of the Id.

All these characters are schizos to varying degrees of functionability, yet all in their way (and at their best) are heroes struggling to manifest a destiny to fit their desires. They are you and me, seen through a broken mirror, a twisted camera lens, darkly. Plays of light upon the looking glass of the self that flicker upward, like bubbles to the surface, from a great depth. And all come from the same depths, the depths of non-self, the Id. Put them all together and what do you get? A cacophony of sound and fury, signifying nothing? A mass of jangled images that do not fit together? Or a picture of the future, glimpsed dimly yet brightly, distant yet up close, as through a kaleidoscope? If there is only one unconscious and only one Self, with a billion different "offshoots," then there is only one movie too, and everybody's in it. We may only find our places when the credits roll, but in any case, we won't have long to wait.

Ready or not, folks, this is the end.

Chapter Notes

Introduction

1. Walsh, *Schizophrenia*, p. 41. All the following quotes unless otherwise stated are from chapter two of Walsh's book, "What Schizophrenia Is, Who Gets It, What Their Chances Are." Many thanks go to Miss Walsh for being at hand and rescuing a layman, considerably out of his depth, from his own ignorance.
2. Gabler, p. 50. Italics mine.
3. *Life: the Movie*, p. 240. Gaber quotes Michael Paul Rogin regarding the movie watcher, "Since he replaces reality by fantasy, his pleasure and the reality principles do not collide. Freed from the reproaches of either the conscience or the unconscious, he gains a reassuring serenity." *Ibid.*, p. 241.
4. "Trash, Art, and the Movies," *Going Steady*, p. 104.
5. J.P. Telotte, quoted by Philip L. Simpson, *Psycho Paths*, p. 48.
6. "Disneyland is presented as imaginary in order to make us believe that the rest is real, when in fact all of Los Angeles and the America surrounding it are no longer real, but of the order of the hyperreal and of simulation." Or, as Robert Hughes simplified it, "it's not that Disneyland is a metaphor of America, but that America is a metaphor of Disneyland." Baudrillard, *Selected Writings*, p. 172. Hughes, *Nothing if Not Critical: Selected Essays on Art and Artists*, p. 380.

Chapter 1

1. All quotes Gabler, *Life: the Movie*, p. 18.
2. Leone was making a reference to the "the Nazi camps, with their Jewish orchestras" here. See *Spaghetti Westerns*, by Christopher Frayling, p. 172.
3. Specifically from the first book in the series, *The Teachings of Don Juan: A Yaqui Way of Knowledge*.

Chapter 4

1. "Hud, Deep in the Heart of Divided Hollywood," *I Lost It at the Movies*, p. 79.
2. "Trash, Art, and the Movies," *Going Steady*, p. 127.
3. "Hoffman, notoriously a cerebral actor, projects thought before movement; he's already a cartoon of an intellectual... Whatever he does seems a feat — and that is, I think, why we're drawn to him. This role might almost be a continuation of his Benjamin in *The Graduate*." "Peckinpah's Obsession," *Deeper into Movies*, p. 395.

Chapter 5

1. Pauline Kael, "The Bull Goose Loony," *When the Lights Go Down*, p. 87.
2. "Nicholson's High," *Reeling*, p. 272.
3. Kael, "The Bull Goose Loony," *When the Lights Go Down*, p. 87.

Chapter 6

1. Boorman, "Bright Dreams, Hard Knocks," from *Projections*, p. 8.
2. "Bright Dreams, Hard Knocks," *Projections*, pp. 36-7

3. Kael, reviewing *Zardoz*, "O Consuella!" *Reeling*, p 276.
4. "Bright Dreams, Hard Knocks," *Projections*, p. 26
5. Kael, "After Innocence, *Reeling*, p. 166.
6. "Labyrinths," *Reeling*, p. 238.
7. "Bright Dreams, Hard Knocks," *Projections*, p. 73.
8. In actual fact one of them is played by Bill McKinney, an accomplished character actor who later became part of Clint Eastwood's stock company.
9. Indeed, it's astonishing that Boorman ever got away with this back in 1971; I doubt he would today without being punished with an NC-17.
10. "Bright Dreams, Hard Knocks," *Projections*, p. 35
11. "Pop Mystics," *Hooked*, p. 21.
12. *Projections*, pp. 73–4.

Chapter 7

1. "Every Sexual Relationship is Condemned," Gideon Bachman, 1973. From *Bernardo Bertolucci Interviews*.

Chapter 8

1. In the Kabbala — which can be traced back through the Hebrew language and the Tarot to Egyptian times — "tooth" corresponds with *shin*, Judgment, the Apocalypse. Trelkovsky is losing his judgment, plainly, but he is also uncovering the truth of his own divided nature.
2. Rudolf Steiner and his school taught that the head evolved separately from the body, was in fact a separate *entity* that eventually grew its own body. See for example *The Archangel Michael*.
3. This quote is from Aleister Crowley's infamous *The Book of the Law*.

Chapter 9

1. Pauline Kael, "Boo!," *Hooked*, p. 457.
2. Kael, "Boo!," *Hooked*, p. 457.
3. "New Age Daydreams," *Movie Love*, p. 301.

4. *Burton on Burton*, pp. 131, 134.
5. *Burton on Burton*, p. 126.
6. *Burton on Burton*, p. 87.

Chapter 10

1. Simpson, *Psycho Paths*, pp. 110, 173
2. The term is from *Drugstore Cowboy*.

Chapter 11

1. Quoted by Keith Mackay, *Robert De Niro, the Hero Behind the Masks*
2. Paul D. Zimmerman, quoted in *Martin Scorsese. A Journey*, pg 153.

Chapter 13

1. *Gilliam on Gilliam*, p. 11.
2. See Frazier's *The Golden Bough*— Colonel Kurtz's chosen reading material in *Apocalypse Now*— for more on this subject.

Chapter 14

1. "Let his heart be changed from man's and let a beast's heart be given him; and let seven times pass over him. This is the decree by the sentence of the watchers, and the word and demand of the holy ones; till the living know that the most High ruleth in the kingdom of men; and he will give it to whomsoever it shall please him, and he will appoint the basest man over it." Daniel 4:13.

Chapter 15

1. All quotes in this piece come from the Fox DVD commentaries.

Chapter 17

1. From "Diller Killer," *Hooked*, p. 261.
2. As Frenz and Rushing write, "Jung considers contemporary Western cultures, like most individuals who constitute them, to be suffering from an illness brought on by dissociation of the ego from the unconscious," *Projecting the Shadow*, p. 47.

Bibliography

Baudrillard, Jean. *Selected Writings*. Stanford: Stanford University Press, 1988.
Boorman, John, and Walter Donahue, ed. *Projections 1*. London: Faber & Faber, 1992.
Castaneda, Carlos. *The Teachings of Don Juan: A Yaqui Way of Knowledge*. Berkeley: University of California Press, 1998.
Christie, Ian, ed. *Gilliam on Gilliam*. London: Faber & Faber, 1999.
Frayling, Christopher. *Spaghetti Westerns*. London: IB Tauris, 1999.
Gabler, Neal. *Life the Movie: How Entertainment Conquered Reality*. New York: Alfred A. Knopf, 1998.
Hughes, Robert. *Nothing If Not Critical: Selected Essays on Art and Artists*. London: Harvill Press, 1999.
Kael, Pauline. *Deeper into Movies*. London: Calden and Boyars, 1975.
_____. *Going Steady: Film Writings 1968–1969*. London: Marion Boyars, 1994.
_____. *Hooked*. London: Marion Boyars, 1992.
_____. *I Lost It at the Movies: Film Writings, 1954–1965*. London: Marion Boyars, 1994.
_____. *Movie Love*. London: Marion Boyars, 1992.
_____. *When the Lights Go Down*. London: Marion Boyars, 1980.
Kelly, Mary Pat. *Martin Scorsese: A Journey*. New York: Thunder's Mouth Press, 1991.
Kline, T. Jefferson, Bruce H. Sklarew, and Fabien S Gerard, ed. *Bernardo Bertolucci Interviews*. Jackson: University Press of Mississippi, 2000.
Leaming, Barbara. *Polanski: His Life and Films*. London: Hamish Hamilton, 1982.
Mackay, Keith. *Robert De Niro: The Hero Behind the Masks*. New York: St. Martin's Press, 1986.
Mailer, Norman. *A Prisoner of Sex*. New York: Little, Brown, 1971.
Rushing, Janice Hocker and Thomas S. Frentz. *Projecting the Shadow: The Cyborg Hero in American Film*. Chicago: University of Chicago Press, 1995.
Salisbury, Mark, ed. *Burton on Burton*. London: Faber & Faber, 2006.
Simpson, Philip L. *Psycho Paths: Tracking the Serial Killer Through Contemporary American Film and Fiction*. Carbondale: Southern Illinois University Press, 2000.
Thompson, David. *Last Tango in Paris*. London: BFI Modern Classics, 1998.
Walsh, MaryEllen. *Schizophrenia: Straight Talk for Family and Friends*. New York: Quill, 1985.
Wexman, Virginia Wright. *Polanski*. Boston: Twayne Publishers, 1985.

Index

Adjani, Isabel 138
Aeillo, Danny 178
After Hours 48, 49, 50, 179, 261
Alien 44, 248, 249–250, 251
Alien Resurrection 249–250
Aliens 249
Alien³ 245, 249
All the President's Men 88n, 213
Allen, Karen 48
Allen, Woody 11, 49, 87, 175, 177–179, 182, 194, 267
Altman, Robert 41
Always 53, 123
American Beauty 52, 257, 261–264, 266
American Psycho 257, 259, 260–261
An American Werewolf in London 46, 49
The Amityville Horror 45
And Justice for All 213
Angel Heart 197, 199, 200
Annie Hall 179
Antonioni, Michelangelo 104
Any Given Sunday 118
Apocalypse Now 127, 205
Arachi, Greg 248
Arlington Road 257
Ashby, John 177
Assassination of Jesse James by the Coward Robert Ford 183
Audsley, Mick 203n

Badlands 41, 80, 167
Baldwin, Alec 144
Bale, Christian 260–261
Ball, Alan 262, 263
Barkin, Ellen 180
Basic Instinct 52
Batman 147–149, 162–163
Batman 147, 162
Batman Begins 147, 162
Batman Forever 184

Batman Returns 148
Bean, Orson 186
Beatty, Ned 112
Beatty, Warren 96
Beetlejuice 143, 144–147, 149
Being John Malkovich 185–189
Being There 177–178, 179, 180
Bel Geddes, Barbara 68
Bello, Maria 270
Belmondo, Jean-Paul 50
Benny and Joon 51, 150
Bentley, Wes 263
Bertolucci, Bernardo 41, 121–129, 132
Besieged 121
Beyond Rangoon 120
Big 50, 179, 181, 182n, 193
Big Fish 143, 155
Birch, Thora 262
Bitter Moon 130, 132
Black, Karen 94
Blade Runner 47
Blake, William 176, 194
Bleuler, Eugen 7
Blow Out 48, 213, 214
Blow Up 37
Blue Sky 52
Blue Thunder 48, 214
Blue Velvet 18n, 48, 115n, 160–161, 163–164, 207
Bogart, Humphrey 212
Bonham-Carter, Helena 156, 229
Bonnie and Clyde 18n, 80
Boorman, John 41, 108–120, 132
Bound 52
Bowie, David 182
Bowles, Paul 122, 171
Brando, Marlon 82, 85, 87, 95–96, 121, 123–129, 182, 183
Braudrillard, Jean 11
Brazil 18n, 49, 50

Breathless (1983) 50, 51, 52
Bridges, Jeff 87
Bring Me the Head of Alfredo Garcia 42
Bringing Out the Dead 53, 191–193
The Brood 47, 142, 256
Bruce Almighty 184
Bundy, Ted 260, 261
Buñuel, Luis 155
Burroughs, William 41, 194
Burton, Tim 143–157, 162
Butch Cassidy and the Sundance Kid 87

Caan, James 87
The Cabinet of Dr. Caligari 33
The Cable Guy 184
Cage, Nicholas 191
Cameron, James 249
Campbell, Joseph 18
Camus, Albert 122
The Candidate 213
Cape Fear (1962) 75
Cape Fear (1992) 278
Capturing the Friedmans 257
Carnal Knowledge 40, 96, 104
Carpenter, John 45, 47, 214, 215
Carrey, Jim 184
Carrie 42, 44, 253
Castaneda, Carlos 25–26, 41
Casualties of War 115n
Charlie and the Chocolate Factory 155
Chinatown 37, 40, 42, 96, 103, 105–106, 130, 132, 134–135, 213
Chocolat 182
Chuang Tsu 251
CIA 215
City of Angels 47, 53, 182n, 195
Clarkson, Patricia 189
Clift, Montgomery 96n
A Clockwork Orange 41
Close Encounters of the Third Kind 46, 244, 248, 254
Cocoon 187, 243, 244, 251
The Conformist 121
Conspiracy theories 5
Conspiracy Theory 214
The Conversation 42, 213
Cool Hand Luke 37, 38, 81, 86–87
Cooper, Gary 96
Coppola, Francis Ford 41
The Corporation 215
Corpse Bride 143, 155
Coward, Herbert 115
Cox, Ronnie 112
Craven, Wes 45, 47, 166n
Cronenberg, David 45, 47, 53, 122, 155, 184, 248, 253, 256, 269, 272–274
The Crossing Guard 107

The Crow 219
Crowley, Aleister 19, 23
Cruise, Tom 265, 266, 267
Crybaby 51
Cul-de-Sac 78, 130, 132
Cusack, John 186

Dance of the Vampires 131, 132, 151
Daniels, Jeff 178, 179
Däniken, Erich von 242, 244
Dante, Joe 144
Dante Alighieri 194
Dark City 185, 215, 217–220, 225, 226
The Dark Knight 162–163
Dark Star 44
Davis, Geena 144
The Dawn of the Dead 44
Day, Doris 254
Dean, James 80, 82, 84–85, 87, 95, 96, 182
Death and the Maiden 132
Deliverance 41, 110–117, 120
De Niro, Robert 87, 96, 175–177, 184, 200
De Palma, Brian 41, 45, 46, 48, 131, 242, 244
Depp, Johnny 51, 149, 150–152, 156, 182–183, 184
Desperately Seeking Susan 48
The Devil's Advocate 197, 199–201
De Wilde, Brandon 84
Diaz, Cameron 187
Dick, Philip K. 185
Dickey, James 112–114
Dirty Harry 41, 158
DNA 247–248, 250
Don Juan De Marco 182, 183
Donner, Richard 214
Donnie Brasco 51, 182
Donnie Darko 189, 206–210
Don't Look Now 139, 142, 206, 209
The Doors 37
Dostoyevsky, Fyodor 80
Douglas, Melvyn 84, 138
Dunaway, Faye 105
Duvall, Robert 88, 96

Eastern Promises 274
Eastman, Carole 93
Eastwood, Clint 18, 20, 29n, 31, 85, 96
Easy Rider 37, 81, 83, 90, 91–92, 96
Eco, Umberto 19
Ed Wood 144, 149–150
The Edge 111–112
Edward Scissorhands 51, 144, 149
Ellis, Brett Easton 259, 261
The Emerald Forest 110, 111, 120
The Empire Strikes Back 18n, 46, 243
The End of Days 199
Escape from New York 47

E.T., the Extraterrestrial 46, 243, 244, 251, 254
Eternal Sunshine of the Spotless Mind 184
The Evil Dead 49, 152
Excalibur 109, 119
The Exorcist 197, 253, 254, 258
Exorcist II: The Heretic 119
Eyes Wide Shut 53, 257, 264–269

The Faculty 207
Fallen 53, 191, 195–197
False Memory Syndrome (FMS) 256
Far from Heaven 257
Farrow, Mia 178
Fatal Attraction 49, 52
Fear and Loathing in Las Vegas 51, 182
Fearless 183, 193
Fearless Vampire Killers see *Dance of the Vampires*
Fellini, Federico 155
Field of Dreams 47, 53, 182, 195, 263
Fight Club 3, 18n, 40, 56, 184, 185–186, 202, 206, 227–241, 250, 270, 278
Film noir 34, 35, 212
Fincher, David 227, 231, 232n, 239, 249
Finger, Bill 147
The Firm 214
The Fisher King 147, 154
A Fistful of Dollars 20n, 30, 85
Fitzgerald, F. Scott 5, 195
Five Easy Pieces 37, 38, 40, 93–94, 96–106, 275
The Fly (1958) 248
The Fly (1986) 47, 248, 251
Fonda, Henry 91, 212
Fonda, Peter 91
For a Few Dollars More 20n
Forbidden Planet 243
Ford, Harrison 50, 181
Ford, John 40, 57, 59
Forrest Gump 47, 49, 51, 52, 180, 181
Fosse, Bob 41
Frankenstein 18
Frankenweenie 144
Frantic 48, 50, 132
Friday the 13th 44
Friedman, Alan 257
Fright Night 45

Gable, Clark 96
Gabler, Neal 9, 10, 16
Gacy, John Wayne 164, 168
The Game 185
Gandolini, James 197
Gavin, John 72
Gein, Ed 74–75, 168
Gere, Richard 50

Ghost 47, 53, 182, 195
Gibson, Mel 60n
Gide, André 122
The Gift 193
Giger, H.R. 249
Gillespie, Craig 189
Gilliam, Terry 49, 50, 147, 203–205
God Told Me To 44
Godard, Jean-Luc 97
The Godfather 41, 42
The Godfather Part Two 18, 42, 213
Goethe, Johann Wolfgang 194
Goetz, Bernard 42
Goldblum, Jeff 248
Gone with the Wind 254
The Good, the Bad, and the Ugly 15–32, 108
Goodfellas 164
Goodman, John 193, 197
Gosling, Ryan 189
Gould, Elliot 87
Goulet, Robert 144
The Graduate 37, 41, 81–82, 87–89, 253
Grant, Cary 72, 96, 212
Greenaway, Peter 123
Gremlins 144
Gyllenhaal, Jake 206

Hackford, Taylor 197
Hackman, Gene 87, 88, 96
Halloween 44, 75
Hamsun, Knut 122
Hancock, Graham 242, 244
The Hand That Rocks the Cradle 52
Hanks, Tom 48, 51, 181
Happiness 52, 257
Harold and Maude 41, 183, 189
Harris, Ed 185, 270
Harron, Mary 261
Harvey 18n, 183, 189
The Haunting 112
Hawkes, Howard 59
Hayes, Heidi 270
Heart of Darkness (novel) 122
Heathers 49, 206
Hell in the Pacific 109, 110, 120
Hesse, Hermann 122
The Hidden 248
Hill, Walter 111
Hinckley, John, Jr. 42
Hirsch, Emile 275
A History of Violence 53, 257, 269–274, 275, 276
Hitchcock, Alfred 40, 49, 64, 65, 68, 70, 72, 77, 131
Hitler, Adolf 135, 164, 230
Hoffman, Dustin 41, 82, 87–89, 96
Holmes, Ashton 270

Holy Man 182n
Home Movies 50
Hope and Glory 109, 119, 120
Hopper, Dennis 91, 160
The Howling 46, 144
Hud 81–87, 90
Hurt, William 219, 272, 275
Husbands and Wives 267
The Hustler 85
Huston, John 134

I Dreamt I Woke Up 116
The Idiot (book) 80
Independence Day 246
Interiors 179
Into the Wild 257, 274–277
Invasion from Mars 36, 246
The Invasion of the Body Snatchers 36, 37, 248, 251
It's a Wonderful Life 18n, 227
It's Alive 253, 258

Jacob's Ladder 47
Jarecki, Andrew 357
Jaws 18n
JFK 214
The Jimi Hendrix Experience 37
John and Mary 89
The Joker 148, 163, 168
Jones, Jeffrey 144
Jonze, Spike 187
Joyce, Adrien 93
Jules et Jim 232
Jung, Carl 3, 6, 32, 194, 246

Kabbala 19
Kael, Pauline 10, 11, 16, 84, 85, 87n, 88, 89, 90, 95, 109, 114, 117n, 118, 126n, 133n, 139, 149, 259
Kafka, Franz 122, 246, 248
Kalifornia 161n, 170n, 183
Kane, Bob 147
Kaufman, Andy 184
Kaufman, Charlie 187
Kazan, Nicholas 196
Keaton, Buster 150
Keaton, Michael 144–147
Keats, John 194
Keel, John 197–199
Kelly, Richard 206–207
Kenner, Catherine 186
Kerrick, Joseph 215
Kershner, Irvin 46
Kesey, Ken 41, 106, 122
Kidman, Nicole 265, 266, 267
King, Stephen 45
King Kong 18

The King of Comedy 48, 50, 84, 161–162, 175–177, 192
The King of Marvin Gardens 40, 96
Klute 213
Knife in the Water 78, 130
Krakauer, Jon 274
Kramer vs. Kramer 254
Kubrick, Stanley 53, 83, 133n, 136, 258, 264–265, 273, 278

Laing, R.D. 7, 33, 41, 213
Lars and the Real Girl 183, 189–190
The Last Detail 37, 40, 42, 93, 95, 96, 103, 104, 105
The Last Emperor 121, 122
The Last Picture Show 37
The Last Seduction 52
The Last Tango in Paris 37, 41, 96, 121–129, 279
Leaming, Barbara 131
Leary, Timothy 41, 122, 213
Ledger, Heath 7
The Left-Handed Gun 85
Leone, Sergio 18, 20, 24, 28
Lethal Weapon 4 214
Leven, Steven 183
Liar, Liar 184
The Libertine 182
Like Father, Like Son 50
Little Buddha 121, 122
Locke, Vincent 269
Lolita (1962) 83–84
London, Jack 103
The Long Kiss Goodnight 52
The Lord of the Rings 18n
Lost Highway 167, 196
Lovecraft, H.P. 249
LSD 92
Lucas, George 46
Lucifer 147, 200–201
La Luna 121
Lynch, David 122, 132, 144, 155, 207n, 273

Macbeth 130, 131, 132–134
Madame Bovary (novel) 178
Madonna 123
Mailer, Norman 54
Malick, Terence 111
Malkovich, John 187
Malone, Lena 208
Mamet, David 111–112
Man in the Moon 184
The Man Who Cried 182
The Manchurian Candidate (1962) 213
Manhunter 160
Mann, Michael 160

Manson, Charles 37, 131n, 134n, 135, 164, 166, 172, 213, 230
Marathon Man 89
Mars Attacks! 144, 150
Martin 44
Marvin, Lee 109, 110, 158
The Mask 184
Mason, James 84
Match Point 179
The Matrix 3, 10, 11, 18n, 36, 35, 44n, 54, 56, 63, 159, 185, 197, 202, 205, 206, 214, 217–226, 227, 228, 233, 251, 270
Matus, don Juan 25–26
McCabe and Mrs. Miller 18n, 41
McCandless, Chris 274–277, 280
McCarthy, Kevin 36
McDowell, Malcolm 87
McKinney, Bill 115
Me, Myself, and Irene 184
Mean Streets 41
Meatloaf 228
Men in Black 48
Mendes, Sam 262, 263
Metamorphosis (novel) 246
Metropolis 44n
Midnight Cowboy 37, 82–83, 88n, 89–90, 91
Mifune, Toshiro 110
Miller, Frank 162
Milton, John 194
Mission: Impossible 242
Mission to Mars 242–245, 249, 251
Mr. Jones 50
Mitchum, Robert 75, 212
Moore, Dudley 179
Morricone, Ennio 23, 29
Morrison, Jim 38
Mortensen, Viggo 270
Mortimer, Emily 189
Mosquito Coast 50
The Mothman Prophecies 197–199
Munsterberg, Hugo 9
My Bloody Valentine 45

Nashville 42
Natural Born Killers 167, 196
The Net 214
Newman, Paul 81, 84–87
Newton, Isaac 194
Nichols, Mike 89, 181
Nicholson, Jack 40, 41, 51, 87, 88n, 93–107, 134, 136, 147n, 150, 184, 200
Nick of Time 51
Night Moves 213
Night of the Hunter 75
Night of the Living Dead 44, 52, 83, 253
A Nightmare on Elm Street 165–166
Nikita 52

1900 121
Ninth Gate 132
North by Northwest 72, 77
Norton, Edward 227
Novak, Kim 66
Nowhere 248
The Number 23 184

Occultism 5, 211
O'Hara, Catherine 144
Oliver, Nancy 189
Oliver Twist 132
Olson, Josh 269
The Omen 199, 253, 254, 258
On the Waterfront 85
One Flew Over the Cuckoo's Nest (book) 41, 106, 122
One Flew Over the Cuckoo's Nest (film) 40, 41, 42, 44, 88n, 95, 96, 103, 106–107
1000 Clowns 164, 171
O'Neal, Patricia 85
O'Quinn, Terry 258
Ordinary People 254

Pacino, Al 87, 88n, 96, 199, 200
Papillon 88n
The Parallax View 213
Paranoia 34–37, 41, 43, 48, 211–217
Parents 206
The Passenger 37, 40, 95, 96, 103, 104
Pat Garrett and Billy the Kid 42
The Patriot 60n
Payback 109
Payne, Alexander 184
Peckinpah, Sam 41, 133n
Pee Wee's Big Adventure 144
Pellington, Mark 197
Penn, Arthur 85
Penn, Sean 182, 184, 275–276
Perkins, Anthony 259
Pesci, Joe 164
Pfeiffer, Michelle 148
The Phantom of the Paradise 41
Philadelphia 263
The Pianist 132
Pirates 132
Pitt, Brad 183–184, 228
Planes, Trains, and Automobiles 48
Planet of the Apes (2001) 143, 144, 147
The Pledge 107
Point Blank 109, 120
Polanski, Roman 48, 78, 130–142, 144, 155
Pollack, Sydney 267
Poltergeist 45, 193
Pop, Iggy 182
Price, Vincent 144
Prom Night 45

Proyas, Alex 215, 219
Psycho 40, 46, 72–79, 80, 253
Pulp Fiction 178
The Purple Rose of Cairo 11, 49, 178–179

Quaid, Randy 105
Que? (What?) 132
Quinn, Anthony 182

Rabid 256
Rafelson, Bob 93
Raimi, Sam 193
Rain Man 51
Reagan, Ronald 42, 47, 177
Redford, Robert 87
Reeves, Keanu 199, 200
Regarding Henry 49, 50, 180, 181
Reinhold, Judge 179
Repo Man 206
Repulsion 78, 132, 137
Reubens, Paul 144
Reynolds, Burt 112, 114
Rhames, Vino 193
Ricci, Christina 153, 154
Richardson, Miranda 153
The Right Stuff 243
Rilke, Rainer Maria 194
Ritt, Martin 84, 85
Rosemary's Baby 44, 78–79, 130, 132, 199, 253, 258
Ross, Katherine 208
Rourke, Mickey 182
Run, Lola, Run 209
Ryan, John P 102
Ryder, Winona 146

Safe 52, 257
Sartre, Jean-Paul 122
Scarecrow 90
Schizophrenia 2, 3, 6–9, 15, 33, 34, 41, 43, 45, 49, 216–218
Schlesinger, John 89
Schneider, Maria 123
Schneider, Paul 189
Schrader, Paul 192
Scorsese, Martin 6, 41, 42, 43, 175–177, 179, 191–193, 278
Scott, Ridley 249
Scream 49
The Searchers 18n, 40, 41, 57–63, 80
Secret Window 51
Sellers, Peter 177
September 179
Seven 106, 158, 159, 196, 249
Sewell, Rufus 218
Shakespeare, William 194
Shelley, Percy Bysshe 194

The Sheltering Sky 121, 122
The Shining 53, 258
Shivers 44, 256
Silence of the Lambs 158, 166
The Sixth Sense 53, 191
Sizemore, Tom 193
Sleepy Hollow 143, 150
Solondtz, Todd 278
Something Wild 48, 179, 262
Sondheim, Stephen 155–156
Southern Comfort 111
Spacey, Kevin 262
Spielberg, Steven 46, 53, 123, 144, 155, 254, 263
Splash 48
Star Wars 42, 43, 44
Stardust Memories 175
Starman 48, 244, 251
Static 206
Stealing Beauty 121, 122, 123
The Stepfather 46, 179, 257, 258–260, 270
Stewart, James 63, 212
The Sting 41
Stir of Echoes 53, 191, 193
Stone, Oliver 117–118, 119
Stowe, Madeleine 203
Straight Time 50, 51, 88n
Straw Dogs 41
Strieber, Whitley 219
The Stunt Man 49
Sutherland, Keifer 217, 219
Sweeney Todd: The Demon Barber of Fleet Street 143, 155–156
Switch 180
Synchromysticism 5, 6, 9

Tamouri, Lee 111
Tarantino, Quentin 178
Taxi Driver 18, 42–44, 46, 80, 161–162, 171, 176–177, 192, 233
The Taylor of Panama 119, 120
The Tenant 78, 130, 132, 137–142
The Terminator 47
Terms of Endearment 254
Tesla, Nikola 194
Tess 132
The Texas Chain Saw Massacre 42, 44, 46, 115
Thelma and Louise 52
Theron, Charlize 200
They Live 47, 215, 246
The Thin Red Line 111
The Thing (1982) 47, 214, 215, 251
Thompson, Hunter S. 182
Three Days of the Condor 213
Thunderbolt and Lightfoot 90
Tootsie 88n, 267
Topor, Roland 137

Index

Towne, Robert 134
The Triumph of the Will 42
Truffaut, François 232
The Truman Show 184, 185
Truth or Dare 123
Twelve Monkeys 183, 202–206
The Twilight Zone 36, 37, 44
Twin Peaks 165, 167

UFOs 36, 198, 212, 246
Unforgiven 57
United States of Leland 189
The Usual Suspects 123, 158, 196

Van Cleef, Lee 19, 31
The Velvet Underground 37
Vertigo 18n, 40, 41, 63–74, 77, 80, 202, 203n, 205
Very Bad Things 49, 50
Vice Versa 50
Victor, Victoria 180
The Village of the Damned 38, 39, 213
Vincent 144
Voight, Jon 87, 91, 113

Wagner, John 269
Waits, Tom 171
Walken, Christopher 153
Walking Tall 41
Wallach, Eli 19, 29n, 31
Walsh, MaryEllen 7n, 8n
War Games 48, 214
Washington, Denzel 196

The Way We Were 41
Wayne, John 57, 59
Weaver, Sigourney 245, 250
Weekend 97
Weir, Peter 183
Welles, Orson 123
West, Adam 162
Westlake, Donald E. 259
Wexman, Virginia Wright 132
What Dreams May Come 47, 53, 195
What's Eating Gilbert Grape? 51, 189
Where the Heart Is 109, 119
Whitman, Charles 74n
Who's Afraid of Virginia Woolf 253
The Wild Bunch 18n, 133n
The Wild One 85
Wilde, Oscar 186
Williams, Robin 181
Williams, Tennessee 253
Willis, Bruce 172, 202
Winter Kills 213
Winters, Shelly 138
The Witches of Eastwick 199
The Wizard of Oz 18n
Wood, Ed 149–150
Wood, Robin 45
Wynter, Dana 36

Zabriskie Point 104
Zardoz 109, 119
Zelig 49, 50, 177–178, 180, 194
Zemeckis, Robert 144
Zimmerman, Paul D. 175

www.ingramcontent.com/pod-product-compliance
Ingram Content Group UK Ltd.
Pitfield, Milton Keynes, MK11 3LW, UK
UKHW041927140426
5217IPUK00014B/351